धर्मे सर्वं प्रतिष्ठितम्

DHARMA FOR STABILITY OF ALL

धर्मे सर्वं प्रतिष्ठितम्

DHARMA FOR STABILITY OF ALL

(A collection of Articles)

of

The Late Vedaśāstrasampanna Paṇḍita

Jagannath Shridhar Padeshastri

Compiled and Edited by

SHRI P.H. JOSHI

(Research Officer, Oriental Institute,

M.S. Uni. of Baroda, Vadodara)

and

PROF. DR. M.L. WADEKAR

(General Editor/Professor,

Critical Editions Wing, Oriental Institute, Vadodara)

BKP

BHARATIYA KALA PRAKASHAN

DELHI INDIA

Published by:
C.P. Gautam
Bharatiya Kala Prakashan
3421-A, IInd Floor,
Narang Colony,
Tri Nagar, Delhi-110035
Ph.7153083

First Published : 2000

ISBN : 81-86050-40-X

Laser Typesetting by:
Ishan Comprint
G 16/14, Qutab Enclave-I, (DLF)
Gurgaon (H.R.), Ph. 91-352412

Printed at:
Santosh Offset Press
Inder Lok, Delhi-110035

कै. जगन्नाथ-श्रीधर-पदेशास्त्री

(जन्म - २९-४-१९१२, स्वर्गवासः - ९-१२-१९८२)

श्रीलक्ष्मीसहितो हिरण्मयवपुर्भद्रं वितन्वन्करै-
रात्मास्थावरजङ्गमस्य मुनिभिर्ध्यातो हृदानेकधा ।
आगोपं प्रथितस्त्रयीमय इति श्रुत्या मुहुर्वर्णितो
भास्वन्मण्डलमध्यगः स भगवान् कुर्यात्सदा मङ्गलम् ।।

वे.शा.सं. (कै.) ज. श्री. पदेशास्त्री

CONTENTS

III APPENDICES

PREFACE

The late *Vedaśāstrasampanna Paṇḍita* Jagannath Shridhar Pade was a versatile and profound indological scholar of great international repute. He wrote an independent treatise in Sanskrit entitled *"Dharme Sarvaṁ Pratiṣṭhitam"* which was serially published in twentynine different articles in the monthly Sanskrit magazine namely, the *"Sūryodaya"* of Varanasi. These articles were warmly received and highly appreciated by the scholarly world. These articles incorporated not only the cream of all the different Vedic and Shastric lores, culminating into the main theme of all-sustaining principle of *Dharma*, but also reflected the attitude of cohesion (*samanvaya*) of them. Though based upon our traditional treatises, it represents a novel contribution to our understanding of the concept of *Dharma* and Vedic culture.

In the present book, we, therefore, wish to present all these Sanskrit articles in the form of a book, which can give a more coherent understanding of his thesis on *Dharma* and which will be more convenient also as one can get all articles at one place. We have also presented the biography of scholar & his contribution and at the end, some useful appendices containing his scholarly articles in different languages are given, which would also be useful and enlightening.

We express our sense of gratitude to the publisher for nicely bringing out this book. We are indebted to the editors of magazines and journals, like *Sūryodaya* & others from where we have reprinted these articles in a collected form in this book. We especially mention Dr. Kapildev Pandey, editor of 'Sūryodaya' for his prompt and cordial co-operation by giving permission to reprint the articles. We are also thankful to Prof. R.I. Nanavati, Dr. S.Y. Wakankar and other colleagues of the Oriental Institute for their constant encouragement and co-operation for this work.

P.H. Joshi
M.L. Wadekar

ABBREVIATIONS

अ. = अध्यायः

अ.सं.सू.स्था. = अष्टाङ्गसंग्रहः, सूत्रस्थानम्

आ.ध. = आपस्तम्बधर्मसूत्रम्

ईश. = ईशोपनिषत्

उ.मी. = उत्तरमीमांसा

उणादिसू. = उणादिसूत्राणि

ऋ. = ऋग्वेदः

कठ. = कठ-उपनिषत्

का.बृ. = काण्वबृहदारण्यकोपनिषत्

का.श्रौ.सू. = कात्यायनश्रौतसूत्रम्

कौषी. = कौषीतकि-उपनिषद्

गी. = भगवद्गीता

गौ.का. = गौडपादकारिका

गौ.ध.सू. = गौतमधर्मसूत्रम्

छा. = छान्दोग्य-उपनिषत्

जाबा. = जाबाल-उपनिषत्

जै.न्या.मा. = जैमिनीयन्यायमाला

जै.सू. = जैमिनिसूत्रम्

तै.आ. = तैत्तिरीय-आरण्यकम्

तै.उ. = तैत्तिरीय-उपनिषत्

तै.ब्रा. = तैत्तिरीय-ब्राह्मण

नारदप. = नारदपाञ्चरात्रम्

न्या.सू. = न्यायसूत्रम्

प.प.उ. = परमहंसपरिव्राजक-उपनिषत्

पार.गृ.सू. = पारस्करगृह्यसूत्रम्

पा.सू. = पाणिनिसूत्रम्

पू.मी. = पूर्वमीमांसासूत्रम्

पृ. = पृष्ठम्

बृ. = बृहदारण्यकोपनिषत्

बृ.भा. = बृहदारण्यकोपनिषद्भाष्यम्

ब्र.सू. = ब्रह्मसूत्रम्

ब्रह्म.शां.भा. = ब्रह्मसूत्रशांकरभाष्यम्

बौ.ध.सू. = बौधयनधर्मसूत्रम्

भावनोप. = भावनोपनिषत्

मनु. = मनुस्मृतिः

म.भा. = महाभारतम्

म.ना. = महानारायणीय-उपनिषत्

महा.भा. = महाभाष्यं पतञ्जलिकृतम्

मा.सं. = माध्यंदिनसंहिता शुक्लयजुर्वेदस्य

मा.बृ. = माध्यंदिन-बृहदारण्यकोपनिषत्

मा.शत. = माध्यंदिनशतपथब्राह्मणम्

मुण्ड. = मुण्डक-उपनिषत्

याज्ञ. = याज्ञवल्क्यस्मृतिः

याज्ञव. = याज्ञवल्क्य-उपनिषत्

यो.भा. = योगसूत्रभाष्यम्

यो.सू. = योगसूत्रम्

वा. = वार्तिकम्

वै.उ. = वैखानस-उपनिषत्

वै.सू. = वैशेषिकसूत्रम्

शत. = शतपथब्राह्मणम्

शाब.भा. = शाबरभाष्यम्

शां.भा. = ब्रह्मसूत्रशांकरभाष्यम्

शां.भ.गी. = भगवद्गीता शांकरभाष्यम्

श्लो. = श्लोकः

श्वे. = श्वेताश्वतर-उपनिषत्

स.द.सं. = सर्वदर्शनसंग्रहः

सां.का. = सांख्यकारिका

सि.कौ. = सिद्धान्तकौमुदी

सु.सू.स्था. = सुश्रुतः, सूत्रस्थानम्

ACKNOWLEDGEMENTS

The articles in this book are reproduced from the following Journals and Magazines. We are grateful to all of them.

1. Sūryodaya, Monthly magazine, Shri Bhāratadharma Mahāmaṇḍala, Lahurabir, Varanasi. Present editor - Dr. Kapildev Pandey, C-27/239-1 (K) Jagatganj, Varanasi-221002.
2. Journal of the Oriental Institute-Oriental Institute, M.S. University of Baroda, Near Palace Gate, Palace Road, Vadodara. Present Editor, Prof. R.I. Nanavati.
3. The Baroda College Magazine, Baroda.
4. The Baroda Homeopathic Bulletin.
5. Prof. P.K. Gode Commemoration Volume.
6. Sheth Todarmal Smarak Grantha.
7. Siddhānta, Monthly, Magazine from Varanasi. (Hindi).

1
BIOGRAPHY OF Pt. JAGANNĀTHA ŚRĪDHARA PADEŚĀSTRĪ

by J.P. Thaker

Pt. Jagannātha-Śāstrī alias Vidyādhara-Śāstrī Pade was popularly known simply as *'Padeśāstrī'* and among the vast circle of intimate persons he was affectionately and respectfully called *'Śāstrījī'*.

Śāstrījī was born at Vaḍodarā (i.e. Baroda) on the 26th April 1912 in a family of well-known traditional scholars. The original native place of this learned family was a small town named Pohe-gaon in Ahamadnagar district of Mahārāṣṭra. His ancestors left this place for reasons best known to them and settled in Nārāyaṇa-gaon near Puṇe. One of his ancestors was the preceptor of Ahallyābāī Holkar, the famous queen of Indore Pt. Tryambaka-Śāstrī Pade, *Śāstrījī's* great grand-father, again, left Nārāyaṇa-gaon and went to Vaḍodarā in the reign of Śrīmanta Sayājī Rāo II and settled there. He was well-versed in *Śruti, Smṛti, Āyurveda* and *Jyotiṣa*.

The original surname of this family was *'Pada-pāṭhaka'* or *'Pade-pāṭhaka'*, since they were known for their traditional study of the Vedic texts by separating each and every word and teaching the same in the same fashion. The term *'Pāṭhaka'* having been dropped in course of time, they came to be known simply as *'Pade'*.

Jagannātha's father, Pt. Śrīdhara Śāstrī Pade, was skilled in such traditional lores as the Vedas, the *Smṛtis, Dharmaśāstra, Āyurveda, Jyotiṣa, Vyākaraṇa* and *Saṅgīta*. The present 'Saṁskṛta Mahāvidyālaya' and 'College of Indian Music, Dance and Dramatics' run by the M.S. University of Baroda were in those days Government Institutions respectively called *'Saṁskṛta Pāṭhaśālā'* and *'Saṅgīta Śālā'*. Pt. Śrīdhara Pade was a teacher in both these institutions. A disciple of such a dexterous scholar as Pt. Rājārāma

Śāstrī Ṭopale, he achieved the traditional degrees of *'Vaiyākaraṇa-kesarī'* (lit. 'a lion among Grammarians') and *'Vaidya-pañcānana'* (lit. 'a lion among traditional Physicians'). He was known for his strictness and love for discipline.

Pt. Śaṅkara Dājī Pade, the famous author of the *'Ārya-bhiṣak'* who had covened an All-India Conference of Scholars of Indian Medicine or *Āyurveda*, also belonged to the same family and was a distant uncle of *Śāstrījī*.

His Mother's name was Kāśībāī and his maternal uncle Rāhurkar also was a reputed practitioner of Indian Medicine.

In this way Jagannātha Śāstrī inherited traditional scholarship from both the paternal side as well as the maternal one. His wife Sumatibāī hailed from Āḷe, a village near Puṇe in Mahārāṣṭra. He had three sisters named Rādhābāī, Sarasvatībāī and Lakṣmībāī. Though himself having no issue, he happily and affectionately took upon him all the responsibilities of breeding and educating the children of two of these sisters. Not-with-standing precarious financial condition of the family the benevolent Āryan soul kept cows in his house and those mute animals also reciprocated his love for them. In this way his was an ideal Āryan family. An interesting and significant speciality of the house was that it was a temple of Lord Rāma. This temple-house was presented to the family during the reign of Mahārājā Kaṇḍerāo Gāekwāḍ and thenceforth they have been residing there. The installation ceremony of the temple having taken place on the 1st May 1882, its first Centenary festival was celebrated in 1982. *Śāstrījī* worshipped Lord Rāma with complete devotion and passed away with simultaneous utterances of the names of the Lord and the Divine Mother. Every year during the first nine days of the bright half of the lunar month of *Caitra* the birth anniversary of the Lord used to be celebrated in the temple in a devout, simple, pompless, unassuming manner.

Brought up in such a holy atmosphere, he started his education in his very childhood under his grand-father Pt. Lakṣmaṇa-Śāstrī alias Balavanta-Śāstrī Pade who taught him in the traditional way such works as the *Śabda-rūpāvali, Dhātu-rūpāvali, Amarakośa, Nitya-pūjā* and the *Laghu-trayī* viz. *Raghuvaṁśa, Kumārasambhava* and *Megha-dūta*. He had told this writer that his mother, while engaged in cooking food, very carefully used to take his recitations especially of the *Amarakośa*. As a consequence of this type of teaching he had many works on the tip of his tongue.

He received his School and College education solely at Vaḍodarā. He took his degree of B.A. of the University of Bombay with Sanskrit as the principal subject in 1937 and M.A. in 1939 with the very tough subject of Sanskrit Grammar as his special *Śāstra*, wherein, having secured the highest number of marks, he won the S.R. Bhandarkar Prize of the University.

Side by side with the western type of education, he also studied from his learned father, purely in the ancient traditional fashion, such important subjects as the *Yajurveda Saṁhitā*, the *Vedāṅgas, Dharmaśāstra, Jotiṣa-śāstra, Āyurveda,* Music, the six systems of philosophy and literature. He had occasions of holding discussions with his father on various scriptures and he read out very perseverantly a number of books on a variety of subjects. He had formed a habit of pondering over whatever he read or studied. Therefore it was real '*abhyāsa*'. His father also carefully saw that he should never be free and should always be engaged in this or that work promoting knowledge. He always valued this home-study far more than the college studies.

Having been brought up in the pure environments of Indian Culture, *Śāstrījī* always respected the desires and commandments of his elders. Consequently, as desired by his revered father, he did not leave Vaḍodarā for better prospects and had to start his career in 1940 as an ordinary clerk in the Gaekwar Baroda State Railways (G.B.S.R.). In 1941 he joined the State Police Department as a Head-clerk. During three years of service there he could obtain certain practical knowledge so useful and essential in life. At the outset of his career there he used to draft well-arranged detailed departmental letters. His superior officer - probably the Commissioner of Police - was one Dalapatarāmabhāī who summoned him and gave a piece of his mind quite tactfully in the following words:

"Well, Mr. Pade. You are a *Paṇḍita* and this is Police Department. Therefore always keep in mind one thing viz. that a teacher is an ass. Such lengthy drafts won't do here. Our papers will go to the Political Department. Every word of our letters, therefore, bears significance. Never write a single word more than required."

Śāstrījī instantly accepted this advice and replied very politely :

"Very well, sir, that was the practice of our ancient *Sūtrakāras*."

This incident had great impact on his writings. Thenceforth succinctness and compactness became the specialities of his style, which, afterwords, not only proved very useful but even became an ornament of his writings.

In those days the Oriental Institute was being run by the Baroda State Government. Till January 1958, when it shifted to the present premises, it was housed on the first floor of the fire- proof building of the State Record Office in the midst of the Government Offices at Koṭhī. The office of the Commissioner of Police was separated from it just by the common wall. It was in 1944 that *Śāstrījī* could cross this curtain and secure a transfer in this prestigious research institute so suited to his nature as well as education. He was appointed there as the Superintendent of the Printed Section. In 1952 he was promoted to the post of the Superintendent of the Manuscripts Section. In 1953 he was recognised by the M.S. University of Baroda as a Post-Graduate Teacher in Sanskrit and in 1957 he was awarded the rare honour of recognition as a guiding teacher for researches *in all the Śāstras*. When the Superintendents were given the designation of Research Officers in April 1958, he became the Senior-most Research Officer of the Institute, which position he adorned till his retirement on the 25th April 1973.

When *Śāstrījī* joined the Institute, Dr. Benoytosh Bhattacharya was its Director. He usually entrusted to the Superientendent of the Printed Section the task of taking essential gists from standard works on various subjects. *Śāstrījī* looked into the books very carefully and provided all essential information. Scholarly replies to the numerous queries received from scholars all around the globe were also prepared by him. Local scholars too could get from him up-to-date information about reference books, papers published in various journals and even manuscripts pertaining to their respective subjects. This habit was a boon to *Śāstrījī* in as much as it offered every opportunity to him to enhance his knowledge in the various fields of Indology. He had full information regarding even Buddhist and Jaina literatures and philosophies. He used to say : "Here is our *prapā* (i.e. water-place) of knowledge and lores; anybody can come here and quench his thirst of knowledge". The variedness, vastness and validity of his knowledge had been lauded even by his superiors.

The present writer has, however, felt sorry about one thing. The Oriental Institute has been publishing books and papers prepared by scholars mostly not on its staff. All the three proofs of these have to be corrected by the Research Officers of the Institute and this work goes on practically throughout the year. The talents of our *Śāstrījī* also were wasted away in this mechanical and mostly unacknowledged task. When he was persuaded to resist, he simply replied: "We cannot go against the wish of the Almighty. That might be His wish. Therefore, whatever work is entrusted to us has to be done and done with full sincerity. *That* is our duty". Such type of work also he used to do very minutely and accurately. The present writer feels confident that had his time and calibre been spared from this tedious and time- consuming task, he would have been able to do more useful and valuable scholarly work that would have definitely been in the interest of Indology.

Śāstrījī completed 50 years of age on 25-4-1962. His friends, disciples and appreciators celebrated his Golden Jubilee in Vaḍodarā on 16.1.1964. A felicitation volume also was presented to him on the occasion, appropriately called *"Homage to Pade Shastree"*. This indifferent personage did not like to be felicitated publicly in that manner. Consequently everything in this connection had to be planned keeping him in the dark. When he came to learn of this "plot against him" he felt ill. He firmly believed that such public felicitation functions would destroy the *Dharma* of the felicitated personage. He said: "*Dharma* is formed out of the support (*Dhāraṇā*) of our actions. Such a *Dharma* should not be spent away for the sake of *artha* and *kāma*. It may be spent only if there is possibility of production of another *Dharma* from it. This is indeed an activity arising from the prominence of *Rajas* and *Tamas*." Thus, being uneasy at the very idea of his public honour, *Śāstrījī* proved himself a true *Brāhmaṇa* as laid down by Manu in the following half-verse :

"सम्मानाद् ब्राह्मणो नित्यम् उद्विजेत विषादिव ।"

Just the next year after retirement an award as a dexterous scholar of Sanskrit was bestowed upon him by the Government of Gujarāta. On that occasion also he did not go to the Capital to accept the same in person.

He did not like to exhibit his knowledge and scholarship through public lectures. All the same when such an occasion occurred, an affectionate speech would stream forth in a very natural way from his mouth. Having made a special study of the *Bhagavatgītā* he had put into practice the instructions imparted by it. The present writer saw in him a *sthita-prajña* of the *Gītā*.

In response to the insistence of several individuals in his contact he started giving lectures in Marāṭhī on the teachings of the *Gītā* at his residence in front of the idol of Lord Rāma. Even college teachers used to go to listen to these lectures that took place every Saturday. He used to analyse the interpretations of the great *Ācāryas* and pointed out, quite indifferently, with illustrations and due arguments, in a simple, clear and profound way, what the Lord really meant. This lecture series continued for about seven years. But this earned him praise and fame and as a consequence he stopped it all of a sudden.

All his writings were characterised by critical acumen; for himself being a truth-seeker, he always valued quality more than quantity. Considering life as a duty entrusted by Providence, he fulfilled all his responsibilities with care and perseverence, may be at home or in the office. He was a rare personality who disregarded worldly fame and was never attracted by 'degrees'. He used to say that a sincere man must try to practise in life the four *Bhāvanās* taught by the *Yoga-darśana* viz. *'maitrī'* or friendship, *'Karuṇā'* or mercy, *'muditā'* or pleasure and *'upekṣā'* or magnanimity and the rest would follow of its own accord.

The present writer was related to *Śāstrījī*, so to say, as was Arjuna to Śrīkṛṣṇa. By this statement he does not intend to compare his humble self to the great hero. Comparison is of the relations. While reading and thinking, studying and teaching, his untrained mind used every now and then to create doubts and queries. *Śāstrījī*, who had affirmedly realised the oneness of the Supreme Soul and the individual soul, could very easily solve all his queries. He considered it the Grace of God that he had been placed in his company since 1952. As a result his services in the Oriental Institute had turned into a laboratory, so to say, for realising the soul in its true airs. He has very humbly to admit, however, that due to his own limitations he could not take full advantage of this very rare and excellent opportunity. All the same he does believe that that *Yogin* had a considerable share in the moulding of his life. In all his affairs-worldy as well as scholarly-he could always get his guidance. Though *Śāstrījī*'s mouth-tongue was Marāṭhī, he could occasionally furnish him with certain Gujarātī words not so prevalent in urban areas but quite common in rural ones, which are so near to the original Sanskrit words.

After retiring from University service *Śāstrījī* led a completely retired life spending his time in reading, thinking and meditating (*vācana, manana* and *nididhyāsana*). When his eyes failed due to cataract, reading could not be continued. At that time, however, his habit of getting everything-even whole books-on the tip of his tongue helped him a lot. Even in such times whenever the writer went to him, hours would be spent in questions and answers-and occasionally even without any query-in serious as well as light and witty dialogues. When a tumour was formed on his throat and he was requested to consult an expert doctor, he replied,

"Here I am sitting near Rāma. There also He is there. Is there any place where he does not exist? He will keep me here in His presence so long as He wishes so and will conduce me there when He wishes to take me there in His presence. Why worry about this particular body or place?"

On seeing Śāstrījī one was many a time reminded of Justice Rāmaśāstrī of the Marāṭhā history. The Upaniṣadic couplet-

क्षुरस्य धारा निशिता दुरत्यया
दुर्गं पथस्तत्कवयो वदन्ति ।

can indeed be applied to his every day life.

But, alas! at the precious occasion of his preceptor's soul's merging with the Supreme Soul after casting off the bonds of the gross body, the disciple, who retained his ignorance despite such an excellent company, felt deceived. Though some queries had accumulated with him, he could not go to him for so many days and all his queries remained unsolved. All the same, as that great soul had proved to him the unity of souls, he is confident and has full faith that, with the gross limitaions cut off, he will be able now to secure the inspiration from that Omnipresent Soul.

The great soul of the *Karmayogin* has left the mundane body and the world for merging into the Supreme Soul and as such it will not have to be embodied again as we usually do. We have just to pray to *the* Supreme Soul:

"Lead Kindly Light"

2
CONTRIBUTION OF PT. J.S. PADE ŚĀSTRĪ

Books :

1. ताम्बूलमञ्जरी, M.S. University Oriental Series, no. 1, Oriental Institute, Baroda, 1957. A model of critical editing of ancient texts.
2. वीणालक्षणम् and वीणाप्रपाठकः, Gaekwad's Oriental Series, no. 131, O.I., Baroda, 1959.
3. भरतमुनिविरचितम् नाट्यशास्त्रम्-अभिनवगुप्तकृत-अभिनवभारती'टीकासहितम्, Vol. IV, G. O. Series, No. 145, O.I., Baroda. 1964.
4. बादरायणविरचिता प्रश्नविद्या उत्पलकृतटीकासहिता, M.S.U.O. Series, No. 10, O.I., Baroda, 1972.

Papers :

[A] In Sanskrit :

1. दण्डकौशलम्, 'Baroda College Magazine', Baroda, Sept. 1931
2. गीर्वाणवाणीवैभवम्, *Ibid.*, September 1932.
3. कुमारपरीक्षा, *Ibid.*, February 1933.
4. रुक्मिणीस्वयंवरम्, *Ibid.*, Sept. 1933 to Mar. 1937. An excellent poem.
5. श्रीमन्तः टोडरमलमहोदयाः श्रेष्ठिवर्याः, 'Todaramal Smārak granthamala, Baroda, 1957.
6. धर्मे सर्वं प्रतिष्ठितम्, 'सूर्योदयः', Varanasi, 1968-1973. A long series of about 30 papers. Incomplete.

[B] In Gujarātī :

1. Śrīgaṇeśapūjārahasya 'Śāradā:, Baroda. Dec. 1950 and Jan. 1951: 'Sayājī Vijaya', Baroda 24-8-1952.
2. Nāmasmaraṇamīmāṁsā 'Jana-kalyāṇa, Ahmedabad, Feb. 1951.
3. Pracīna Kālamā Gujarātamā bolāti Saṁskṛtabhāṣā 'Svādhyāya', 1, Baroda, 1963-64.

[C] In Marāṭhī :

1. 'Period' ला प्रतिशब्द 'पाठ', 'Kesarī', Poona, Feb. 1949.

2. श्रीगणेशपूजा-रहस्य (पूर्वार्ध), 'Jñāneśvara', Poona, Sept. 1950.
3. उत्तरमीमांसेवरील चार प्रसिद्ध आचार्यांच्या सिद्धान्तांचे दिग्दर्शन, *Ibid.*,Dec. 1950.
4. श्रीगणेशपूजा-रहस्य (उत्तरार्ध), *Ibid.*, Mar. 1951.
5. उपाकर्माच्या कालाची मीमांसा—1.*Ibid.*, June 1951.
6. उपाकर्माच्या कालाची मीमांसा—2. *Ibid.*, Nov. 1951.
7. नामस्मरण-मीमांसा, *Ibid.*, Aug. 1951.
8. माध्यन्दिन शाखेंत ज्ञानयोगास प्राधान्य, *Ibid.*, May 1952.
9. प्रजापतिदेवतेचें स्वरूप,*Ibid.*, Nov., 1952.
10. पाणिनीय व्याकरण व माध्यन्दिन शाखेचीं कांही वैशिष्ट्यें, *Ibid.*, Feb. 1953.
11. भगवद्‌गीतेचा अभिप्राय, *Ibid.*, May 1953.
12. महाराष्ट्रातील कथेचा संप्रदाय, *Ibid.*, Dec. 1953.
13. फलज्योतिषाचा प्रामाण्यवाद, *Ibid.*, Nov. 1954; *'Jyotir-bhūṣaṇa'*, Poona, Mar. 1953.
14. चातुर्वर्ण्यम् 'Jñāneśvara', Feb. 1955.
15. विजयादशमीचा शास्त्रार्थ, *Ibid.*, May 1956.
16. गीताशास्त्राचे ऐदम्पर्य. *Ibid.*, 1969 ff. A Series of 6 papers, Incomplete.
17. वैदिक संस्कृति, *'Saṁskṛti-Sugandha'*, Shete Abhinandana Grantha, Poona, 1977, pp. 68-77.

[D] In English :

1. Ayurvedic Uses of Iron, *'Baroda Homeopathic Bulletin'*, II 3, April 1947.
2. Ayurvedic Uses of Silver, *Ibid.*, II. 4, July 1947.
3. Ayurvedic Uses of Gold, *Ibid.*, III, 1, Oct. 1947.
4. Ayurvedic Uses of Copper, *Ibid*, III, 2, Jan. 1948.
5. Ayurvedic Uses of Tin, *Ibid.*, III. 3, April 1948.
6. The Rāmāyaṇa Department, *'JOIB'*, 1.1, Sept. 1951.
7. *Jambeera*, 'Prof. P.K. Gode Commemoration Volume', 1960, pp. 133 ff.
8. Dr. Benoytosh Bhattacharya-A Unique Personality, *'JOIB'*, XIV, pp. 217 ff.
9. Prof. Govindlal H. Bhatt—In Memorium, *'JOIB'*, XV, pp. 233 ff.

[E] In Hindi :

1. फलज्योतिषका प्रामाण्यवाद—*Siddhanta*, Varanasi, *Varṣa* 17, *Aṅka* 12 & *Varṣa* 18, *Aṅka* 1, 1964.

[E] Obituaries in English :

10. Prof. G.H. Bhatt, '*JOIB*', XIV, 469 ff.
11. Prof. D.D. Kosambi, *JOIB*', XVI, 110 ff.
12. Mm. Dr. P.V. Kane, '*JOIB*', XXI, 381 ff.

Over and above these, his reviews in English of several books have been published.

Reviews

		Vol. Nos.* JOIB & Page No.
1.	(The) *Atharvavedic Civilization : Its Place in the Indo-Aryan Culture* by V.W. Karambelkar.	11.185
2.	*Ātmabodhaprakaraṇa* of Śaṅkarācārya ed. by D.C. Bhattacarya	14.215
3.	*Āyurveda Vyākhyānamālā* by B.V. Vaidya	8.208
4.	*Cāṇakya-Nīti-Text-Tradition*, Vol. I, Pt. I ed., by Ludwic Sternbach	15.227
5.	*G.D. College Bulletin Series* No. 2: *Archaeological Record of Begusarai* by Radha Krishna Chaudhry	2. 94
6.	*Gandhi's View of Life* by Chandarshanker Shukla	1.372
7.	*Gaṅgālaharī-A Sanskrit Poem* by K.V.N. Appa Rao	1.372
8.	*Heat in the Rig-Veda and Atharva-Veda* by C.G. Blair	13.87
9.	*Hymns to the Elephant Faced Lord of Success and Wisdom* by T.K. Rajagopalan.	1.98
10.	*India of Vedic Kalpasūtras* by Ram Gopal	14.208
11.	*Mahāyāna-Sūtra-Saṁgraha*, Pt. I ed. by P.L. Vaidya	12.102
12.	(The) *Meghadūta of Kālidāsa* ed. by Sushil Kumar De	12.466

* Journal of the Oriental Institute, M.S. Uni. of

13. *Non-Ṛgvedic Mantras in the Marriage Ceremonies* by P.K. Narayana Pillai 14.206
14. *Paramalaghumañjuṣā*—of Nāgeśa with the Comm. *Jyotsnā* by Kalikaprasad Shukla 12,106
15. *Praṇava Bhāratī-Prathama Vīṇā-Bhāratīya Svaraśāstra* by Omkaranath Thakur 5.447
16. *Progress of Kannada Research in Bombay State* (1947-52) by R.S. Panchamukhi 3.225
17. *Rāmāyaṇakālīna Samāja* by S.N. Vyas 8.97
18. *Rāmāyaṇakālīna Saṁskṛti* by S.N. Vyas 8.97
19. *Saṅgītarāja of Mahārāṇā Kumbha* Vol. I ed. by Premalata Sharma 15.230
20. *Saṅkarṣa Kāṇḍa Sūtras of Jaimini* ed. by R.V. Sharma 13.293
21. *Sanskrit Comic Characters* by J.T. Parikh 2.93
22. *Śāradīyākhya-Nāmamālā of Harṣakīrti* ed. by Madhukar Mangesh Patkar 1.183
23. *Science in the Vedas* by Hans Raj ed. by H.R. Agrawala 5.452
24. *Similies in Manusmṛti* by M.D. Paradkar 10.458
25. *Some Economic Aspects of the Caste System in Ancient India* by Ram Sharan Sharma 3.313
26. *Studies in Ancient Indian Law and Justice* by R.K. Chudhary 5.111
27. *Studies in Indian Cultural History*, Vol. I by P.K. Gode 11.454
28. *Studies in Indian Cultural History*, Vol. II by P.K. Gode 10.459
29. *Talks on Jñānayoga* by Swami Isvarananda 3.225
30. *Travancore University Oriental Mss. Lib., Report for 1950 and 1951* 2.93
31. (Sri) *Tukāramacaritam* with Eng. translation by Pandita Ksama Row 1.98
32. (The) *Vidūṣaka* : Theory and Practice by J.T. Parikh 3.224

3

PRESENT COLLECTION

धर्मे सर्वं प्रतिष्ठितम्

SUMMARY OF CONTENTS

There are several passages from the Vedas, Smṛtis, *Itihāsa* and the Purāṇas, that expound that the *Dharma* is the sustainer of the *Dharmī* i.e. that entity which constitutes the *Dharma*. e.g. *'Dharmo Viśvasya jagataḥ pratiṣṭhā'* .... *'Dhame sarvam pratiṣṭhitam'* (*Tai. Āra.* 10.79) (The *Dharma* is sustainer of the entire world,....Everything is sustained by the *Dharma*). Whenever there is a deterioration of the *Dharma* and the *Adharma* gets a dominating position, the God himself frequently gets incarnated in the form of a precector and sets right the position of the *Dharma* through His grace and blessings on the beings. Similarly, at the turn of each *yuga* (aeon), the God gets himself incarnated in the form of a *Kṣatriya* for forcibly establishing the *Dharma*. This is the import of the *Smṛti* text. For the *Vaidikas*, there is nothing superior to the *Dharma*.

The word *'Dharma'* is derived from the root *'Dhṛ'* in accordance with the *Uṇādi sūtra-Artistusuhusudhṛ* ...... *bhyo man* (1.137). It grammatically means that by which the *Dharmī* is sustained or which sustains the *Dharmī*, is the *Dharma*. The *Dharma* is the entity which is in the form of a permanent existence or which is the constitutent element. The principal characteristic of the *Dharma* is its nature of permanent existence. The *Dharma* and the *Dharmī* have a relation of non-difference, identity or *Samavāya* (constituting), just as heat and the fire have mutual relation of identity, non- difference etc. When the *Dharma* is destroyed, the *Dharmī* is destroyed and *vice versa*. There is a permanent relation between the *Dharma* and the *Dharmī*. Hence the proposition of the *Śruti* that *'Dharme sarvam pratiṣṭhitam'* becomes true in its real sense. The *Vaidikas* (the genuine followers of *Veda*) have incessantly, devoted their entire life to the task of sustaining the *Dharmī* by the establishment of vedic *Dharma*— by protecting the *Dharma* and destroying the *Adharma*.

The knowledge of the *Dharma* can be possible only if one has the understanding of the *Dharmī*. One can not talk of the *Dharmas*, without the knowledge of the *Dharmī*. (Only when we have seen the mango, we can talk of its properties). It is therefore better to have knowledge of the *Dharmī*, before we know about its *Dharmas*. Moreover, when we apprehend the *Dharmī*, we can decide all its *Dharmas*. In fact, *Tattva-jñāna* means the knowledge or comprehension of all the *Dharmas* of the *Dharmī*. When we know the *Dharmī*, we can think of those elements of it which sustain and destroy it. Those elements which sustain it are accepted as sustainers of the *Dharmī* and those elements that destroy it are eliminated as they are being destructive of its very nature. Thus, a particular *Śāstra* or a science is developed by collecting the elements namely entity, quality and action that are to be enjoined or prohibited. The *Śāstra* is that which prescribes, that which preaches us do's and don'ts (prescriptions and restrictions) by collecting certain rules of action and prohibition. In this way, any *Dharmiśāstra* should incorporate in its purview these elements—the *Dharmī*, its characteristic & uncommon constituent elements, all its common and peculiar *Dharmas*, the injunctions, sustaining the *Dharmī* and Prohibitions, destroying the *Dharmī*, and the enumeration of elements like entities, qualities and action that are deliberately enjoined and/or prohibited. Thus the *Śāstras* or sciences of the *Dharmī* are being expounded and will shoot forth in the same line.

All other movable and immovable things in the world, right from the *Brahman* upto the small blade of grass except the *Brahman* are perishable and are entangled in the duel of the *Dharma* and the *Adharma*. Of them, the *Dharma* tries to sustain it, while the *Adharma* tries to destroy it. The

Dharma, when mixed with the *Adharma* becomes the *Adharma* only and hence as all things in the world (except the *Brahman*) being mixed with the *Adharma* become *Adharmī* i.e. perishable only. The *Brahman* alone is without any *Adharma* and is of the nature of the *Dharma* only and is therefore imperishable. Hence the *Brahman* alone is the *Dharmī*. As all other entities except the *Brahman* are *Adharmī*, perishable, impermanent and hence there is no presence, entity or existence of them. *The Bhagavadgītā* (2.16) *'Nāsato Vidyate Bhāvo* etc." as also the *Gauḍapāda Kārikā* (2.6) "*Ādāvante ca yannāsti*" etc. expound the same view that these entities that are not everlasting can not be called the *Dharmī*. Thus, the entire visible world - having the nature of light, action and (temporary) existence, - consisting of the created beings and organs - is not entitled to be called the *Dharmī*. Only the *Brahman* is the *Dharmī*. This is the conclusion.

The other entities in the world have the duel of the *Dharma* and the *Adharma*- i.e. the sustaining and destroying elements. Here the *Dharma* mixed with the *Adharma* also becomes the *Adharma*. As there is a predominance of the *Adharma* over the *Dharma*, the entities get destroyed in course of time, even though we make efforts to establish the *Dharma* and destroy the *Adharma* in that case. Hence these all must be considered to be the *Adharmīs*. The word *Dharmī* is used in a secondary sense in case of these other entities. In their case also, an attempt is made to establish their sustaining elements and to eliminate the destructive ones - and thus towards the establishment of the *Dharma*. This is the *Dharmavāda* which is different from the *Kāmavāda* or *Svabhāvavāda*, which again has given rise to the *Bhogavāda*, *Apavargavāda* and *Puruṣārthavāda* or *Bhogāpavargavāda*. None of these is at all conducive to the sustaining of the world. The *Dharmavāda* alone being based upon self-less action & dedication is conducive to the maintainance of the entire world.

The Vedas and Smṛtis have conclusively proved that

the *Brahman* alone - one without a second-is the only knowable and the *Dharmī*. For determining the *Dharma*, the *Pūrvamiāṁsā- śāstra* was introduced and for deciding the *Dharmī*, the *Brahman*, the *Uttaramīmāṁsā* was introduced with the inquiry into the nature of the *Brahman*.

The *Brahmadarśana* or *Ātmaikattvadarśana* is the *Vaidika darśana*, as the *Brahman* can be comprehended only through the *Veda*... It shines forth in the *Citiśakti*. The *Anātmadarśana* or the perception of this entire objective world is based upon the non-vedic means of knowledge and is mostly supported by *tarka*, the logical argument. It can be known with other means even without the knowledge of the *Veda*.

This *Brahmadarśana* is of Gods; while the comprehension of all this - the objective world i.e. the *dehātmadarśana* is of *asuras*. As the *Brahman* is ever-existing, the *Brahmavādins* are *āstikas*, while *Anātmavādins* are *nāstikas*, the *Brahman* being of the nature of *Dharma*-sustaining - the *Brahmavādins* are *Dhārmikas*, while the *Jaḍavādins* are *Adhārmikas* or *Kāmahata*. All these philosophers - *Avaidika* and *Vedḁbāhya* make unending dispute regarding the cause of the world. But without entering into any controversy with them, the *Vaidikas* propound the theory of *Ajātivāda* (theory of non-birth). There is no place for *Puruṣārthavāda* in the *Brahmadarśana* or *Ātmaikatvavāda*, because this can be possible only when the *artha* and *arthī* both are two different entities. As there is no other entity except the *Brahman*, there is no possibility of *Puruṣārthavāda*. The fourfold division of *Puruṣārtha* into *Dharma*, *Artha*, *Kāma* and *Mokṣa* in fact could be included only in several varieties of *Kāma* and is followed by the *Daityas* who are *Bhogāpavargavādins*. As the *Brahman* is *Dharmī* there is possibility only of the *Dharmavāda*. The *Bhoga* (enjoyment is possible only in duality, when there are two entities like *Bhogya* (the thing to be enjoyed) & *Bhoktā* (the enjoyer). The *Anātmavādins* make various guesses regarding the origin, existence & dissolution of the world.

The *Vaidikas* are followers of the *Dharmavāda* & think of the *Dharma* and the *Dharmī* in all cases. They extend this rule to all entities in the world. The fruit of action is always residing in the action and it does not go to the agent. Only the *Kāmahata* persons make worldly contracts for monetary gains etc. by imposing the fruit of action upon the agent. For destroying the *Kāma*, the *Vaidikas* expound the renunciation of the fruit of action. Action is always the self-less action which amounts to sustaining the *Dharmī*. Action is not meant for the enjoyment of the desired objectives. Just as the bondage is not the *Ātmadharma*, so also *Mokṣa* is also not. Only the *asuras*, indulging in the *avidyā*, have invented the concept of *Mokṣa*. In fact, there is neither *Bandha* nor *Mokṣa*. Even there can be no preaching of *Saṁnyāsa* in the real sense, as the *Dharma* can never be renounced. *Bhoga* (enjoyment) and *Saṁnyāsa* are two opposite entities. *Bhoga* (enjoyment) or *Bhogya* (things of enjoyment) can be renounced. In the *Vaidikadarśana*, however there is an attempt at establishing of the *Dharma* and for this purpose only the great preceptors and God even get incarnated. They do not incarnate for propagating the *Mokṣa* or the *Bhoga* in the form of the *Dharma*, the *Artha* and the *Kāma*.

The *Brahman* is self-luminous and therefore the *Brahmavādins*, daily propitiate the sun-the fire in the sky or the sacrificial fire through the *Agnihotra* sacrifice. But the *Dehātmavādins* resort to the idol-worship, arising out of the *Prakṛtivāda and the Dehātmavāda.*

As per the *Dehātmavāda* or the *Bhogāpavargavāda*, there is no other thing of enjoyment in this world like lady, which can appease all the sense-organs simultaneously. While in the *Dharmavāda*, the wife is the *Dharma* and the husband, the *Dharmī*. There is a relation of oneness or unity between the couple (the *Dampatī*). No religious ceremony like the *Agnihotra* can be possible without the wife. She is in the form of the *Dharma*. The *Bhagavatgītā* calls the *Dehātmavādins* or the *Bhogāpavargavādins* as *duṣkṛtin* (evil-doer), while the *Ātmaikatvavādin* or the *Dharmavādin* as *Sukṛtin* (Good- doer). The sacrifice is the supermost beneficial act (this is the opinion of the *Dharmavādins*), which is not vitiated by *Kāma*. While the *Bhogavādins*, the *daityas* those that are vitiated by the *Kāma* call it 'a lower act'. The *Vaidikas* always practise the five great *Mahāyajñas* from the point of view of the *Sāmyavāda* (treating all creatures as equal) and appease all the beings by distributing food and water in the *Pañcamahāyajña*. There is comprehension of one *Ātman*, residing in all the creatures. From this point of view of the *Ātmavāda*, all the creatures are regarded as equal. From the point of view of their physical body, however they are all different.

For establishing the unity or oneness which is the *Brahmadharma*, the *Mīmāṁsakas* anticipated a ladder of higher steps (*sopānapaṅkti*) in the following manner. e.g. (1) unity in the couple, (2) unity in the *Kuṭumba*, (3) unity in the threefold *Sapiṇḍas*- forming the seven *gotras*-family-ancestors. *Nityatarpaṇa*, *Mahālaya-śrāddha*, *Tīrthaśrāddha* etc. are enjoined for this purpose. The *Kula* is formed by the twentyone *Kinsmen* (7 *Sapiṇḍas*, 7 *Samānodakas*, 7 *Sagotras*). Establishing the unity among these is the establishment of the *Kuladharma*. (4) Then follows unity among castes, but caste is from the point of view of the *dehadharma*. Here there is determination of action in accordance with the *prakṛtidharma*. The *Dharmavādins* have proper arrangement of occupation & subsistence for everybody, but the *Bhogavādins* have disturbed the entire cohesion and created a chaos. In the *Dharmavāda*, the occupation is looked upon as one's *Dharma*, while in the *Bhogavāda*, there is only one's own free desire.

The *Bhogavādins* can never give stability to the entire world. Even the *Apavargavādins*, renouncing or going away from the entire world, can never help for in the stability of the entire world. They, going away from the world, would cause the destruction of the world. In short, the entire doctrine of *Bhogāpavarga* can lead to the destruction of the world and not to its stability. The *Dharmavāda* alone is such that creates stability in the world. Hence the *Mīmāṁsā darśana* alone is the promulgator of the *Dharmadharmivāda*. All other *Darśanas* are intent on the *Bhogavāda* or the *Apavargavāda*. Only the *Vaidikas* have discussed and tried to establish the *Dharma*. And when the *Dharma* is stabilized, the *Dharmī* is also established. The *pīṭhas* of Jagadguru Śaṅkarācārya are therefore the *Dharmapīṭhas* - the centres for the establishment of the *Dharma* and are not for propounding the *Mokṣa*-renunciation of the world.

The *Kalpasūtrakāras* have expounded the practice of 48 kinds of *Saṁskāras*. The self gradually relinquishes the vulgarity (*Vikṛtatva*), arising out of superimposition due to ignorance upon the sixteen *Vikṛtis-manas*, five sense organs, five motor organs and five great elements - and becomes purified. Here he gives up the desire for enjoyment here and hereafter and enters the *Vijñānamayakośa* and becomes *Prākṛta*. With *Śrauta* and *Smārta saṁskāras*, he becomes free from the physical nature, (*Prākṛtatva*), arising due to wrong attachment with seven *Prakṛtis*. By renouncing agentship (*Kartṛtva*) and the (*ahaṅkāra*) egoism, he becomes *Saṁskṛta* (cultured) and enters the *Ānandamayakośa*. There is an awakening of all the *Dharmas* of the *Ātman*. With *Bhaktiyoga*, he becomes one and with the *Jñānayoga*, he becomes one, without second (*advitīya*). This is the *Brāhmīsthiti*, this can be gradually obtained. This is the *Svarūpa-pratiṣṭhā* or *Dharmapratiṣṭhā* in real sense. The *Dharmavāda* alone can lead to this highest position. The *Dharmavāda* alone can thus establish stability in the entire world and not the *Bhogavāda* or *Apavargavāda*.

धर्मे सर्वं प्रतिष्ठितम्
DHARMA FOR STABILITY OF ALL

(A collection of Articles)

of

The Late Vedaśāstrasampanna Paṇḍita
Jagannath Shridhar Padeshastri

धर्मे सर्वं प्रतिष्ठितम्*

तानि धर्माणि प्रथमान्यासन् (ऋ. १०-९०-१६)

धर्मात् परं नास्ति। (मा.बृ. १-२-२६)

धर्म इति धर्मेण सर्वमिदं परिगृहीतं धर्मान्नातिदुष्करं तस्माह धर्मे रमन्ते इति॥

(तै. आ. १०-७८)

धर्मो विश्वस्य जगतः प्रतिष्ठा लोके धर्मिष्ठं प्रजा उपसर्पन्ति धर्मेण पापमपनुदति
धर्मे सर्वं प्रतिष्ठितं तस्माद् धर्मं परमं वदन्ति। (तै. आ. १०-७९)

धर्मं चर। धर्मान्न प्रमदितव्यम्। (तै. उ. १-११)

तस्माद् धर्मं सहायार्थं नित्यं सञ्चिनुयाच्छनैः।
धर्मेण हि सहायेन तमस्तरति दुस्तरम्॥ (मनु. ४-२४२)

धर्मं पुत्र निषेवस्व। (म.भा.शान्ति. ३२१.४)

स्वधर्मे निधनं श्रेयः। (गी.३-३५)

धर्मसंस्थापनार्थाय सम्भवामि युगे युगे। (गी. ४-८)

इति श्रुति-स्मृतीतिहास-पुराणेषु धर्मिप्रतिष्ठापकत्वेन धर्मः समाम्नायते। यदा यदा धर्मस्य ग्लानिर्भवति, अधर्मस्य चाभ्युत्थानं भवति तदा तदा धर्मसंस्थापनार्थमाचार्या अवतरन्ति धर्मं च प्रस्थापयन्ति। युगे युगे तु भगवान् स्वयमेव धर्मसंस्थापनार्थमवतरतीति स्मर्यते। वैदिकानां हि धर्मात् परं किमपि नास्ति।

'अर्तिस्तुसुहुसृधृभिक्षुभायावापदियक्षिनीभ्यो मन्' (उणादिसू. १-१-४५) इत्युणादिसूत्रेण धृधातोर्मन्प्रत्यये धर्मशब्दो निष्पद्यते। ध्रियते अनेन धर्मी धरति धर्मिणमिति वा धर्मः। वृत्तिमानाधेयो वा पदार्थो धर्मः। वृत्तिमत्त्वं धर्मस्य लक्षणम्। धर्मधर्मिणोरभेदस्तादात्म्यं समवायो वा सम्बन्धः। धर्मभेदे धर्मिभेदो धर्मिभेदे च धर्मभेदः। धर्मधर्मिसम्बन्धो नित्यः। धर्मे नष्टे नाशिते वा धर्मिनाशः। धर्मे प्रतिष्ठिते प्रतिष्ठापिते वा धर्मिप्रतिष्ठा। तस्मात् सिद्धैषा श्रौती प्रतिज्ञा धर्मे सर्वं प्रतिष्ठितमिति। धर्मिप्रतिष्ठासिद्ध्यर्थमेव धर्मरक्षणार्थमधर्मनाशाय च बद्धपरिकरा वैदिका धर्मस्थापनार्थं स्वकीयं जीवनमजस्रं यापयाम्बभूवुः,यापयन्ति यापयिष्यन्ति च।

धर्मस्यास्य ज्ञानं धर्मिज्ञानसापेक्षम्। न ह्यज्ञातस्य धर्मिणो धर्मा ज्ञातुं शक्यन्ते। अत एव धर्मज्ञानार्थं प्रथमं धर्मी ज्ञातव्यो भवति। ज्ञाते च तस्मिन् तस्य सर्वे धर्मा निश्चेतुं शक्यन्ते। लक्षणार्थं प्रथममसाधारणधर्मो निश्चीयते। लक्षिते च धर्मिणि क्रमेण तस्य सामान्या विशेषाश्च सर्वे धर्माः परीक्ष्य निश्चीयन्ते। धर्मिणो यदा सर्वधर्माणां ज्ञानं भवति, तदैव तस्य तत्त्वज्ञानं सम्पद्यते।

* सूर्योदय-वाराणसी-१९६८-१९७३

तत्त्वज्ञानं नाम धर्मिणः सर्वधर्मज्ञानम् । धर्मिणस्तत्त्वज्ञानानन्तरं तस्य धर्माणां प्रतिष्ठापका विनाशकाश्च पदार्था विचार्यन्ते। धर्मप्रतिष्ठापकधर्मनाशकपदार्थविचारानन्तरं ये धर्मप्रतिष्ठापकाः पदार्थास्ते धर्मिप्रतिष्ठापकत्वेन विधीयन्ते। ये धर्मनाशकाः पदार्थास्ते च धर्मिनाशकत्वेन निषिध्यन्त इति द्रव्यगुणकर्मणां पदार्थानां विधिनिषेधसङ्ग्रहपरं शास्त्रं सम्पन्नं भवति । शास्तीति शास्त्रम् । विधिनिषेधानां सङ्ग्रहेण कर्तव्याकर्तव्यमुपदिशति । तथा चोक्तं कुमारिलभट्टैः—

प्रवृत्तिर्वा निवृत्तिर्वा नित्येन कृतकेन वा।
पुंसां येनोपदिश्येत तच्छास्त्रमभिधीयते ।। इति

(मीमांसाश्लोकवार्तिकम्, शब्दपरिच्छेदः, ४)

एतेन धर्मिशास्त्रे धर्मी,तस्य लक्षणप्रतिपादकोऽसाधारणधर्मः,सामान्या विशेषाश्च सर्वे धर्माः, धर्मिस्थापका विधयो, धर्मिनाशका निषेधाः, सहेतुकानां विहितानां निषिद्धानां च द्रव्यगुणकर्मरूपाणां पदार्थानां परिगणनमित्येतेषां संग्रहो भवति । एतन्नियमानुसारेणैव धर्मिणां शास्त्राणि प्रवृत्तानि,प्रवर्तन्ते प्रवर्तिष्यन्ते च । धर्मिणामानन्त्यात् शास्त्राण्यपि अनन्तानि भवन्ति । तस्मात् धर्मिज्ञानानन्तरमेव धर्मज्ञानमिति सिद्धम् ।

यदा अप्रत्यक्षो धर्मी तदा शास्त्रादाप्तवाक्याद्वा लक्षणं ज्ञात्वा स प्रत्यभिज्ञातुं शक्यते । तस्य सर्वधर्माधिगमेन तत्त्वज्ञानमपि भवति। पक्षेऽस्मिन् धर्मज्ञानानन्तरं धर्मिज्ञानम्। धर्मज्ञानमत्र शास्त्रसापेक्षम्। धर्मिज्ञानानन्तरमेव शास्त्रप्रवृत्तिरिति न धर्मिज्ञानानन्तरं धर्मज्ञानमिति सिद्धान्तस्य हानिः।

धर्मज्ञानार्थं धर्मिज्ञानमावश्यकमिति सिद्धान्तितम् । धर्मी हि प्रथमं वेद्यो भवति । तत्र तावद् वेदेष्वेव प्रथमं समाम्नातो धर्म इति वैदिकं दर्शनमनुसृत्य धर्मी निर्णीयते । तत्र वेदेषु तावद् ब्रह्मव्यतिरिक्तस्य पदार्थस्याभावाद् एकमेवाद्वितीयं ब्रह्म वेद्यत्वेन श्रूयते । तदेव केवलं धर्मी । तथा च श्रुतयः—

एकत्वमनुपश्यतः	**(ईश. ७)**
एकमेवाद्वितीयम्।	**(छा. ६-२-१)**
तमेवैकं जानथ आत्मानम्।	**(मुण्ड. २-२-५)**
नेह नानास्ति किञ्चन।	**(बृ. ४-४-१९)**
मृत्योः स मृत्युमाप्नोति य इह नानेव पश्यति।	**(बृ. ४-४-१९)**
यस्मात् परं नापरमस्ति किञ्चित्।	**(श्वे. ३-९)**
नान्योऽतोऽस्ति द्रष्टा नान्योऽतोऽस्ति विज्ञाता।	**(बृ. ३-७-२३)**
नान्यदतोऽस्ति द्रष्टृ नान्यदतोऽस्ति श्रोतृ।	**(बृ. ३-८-८)**
नान्यदतोऽस्ति द्रष्टृ श्रोतृ मन्तृ विज्ञातृ।	**(छा. ६-८-७)**
तदेतद् ब्रह्मापूर्वमनपरमनन्तरमबाह्यम्।	**(बृ. २-५-१९)**
सर्वं तं परादाद् योऽन्यत्रात्मनः सर्वं वेद।	**(बृ. २-४-६)**

यत्र त्वस्य सर्वमात्मैवाभूत् तत् केन कं पश्येत्। (बृ. ४-५-१५)
यत्र वा अस्य सर्वमात्मैवाभूत् तत् केन कं पश्येत्। (बृ. २-४-१४)
आत्मा वा अरे द्रष्टव्यः श्रोतव्यो मन्तव्यो निदिध्यासितव्यः। (बृ. २-४-५)
सोऽन्वेष्टव्यः स विजिज्ञासितव्यः। (छा. ८-७-१)
स एवाधस्तात्। (छा. ७-२५-१)
अहमेवाधस्तात्। (छा. ७-२५-१)
आत्मैवाधस्तात्। (छा. ७-२५-२)
पुरुष एवेदं सर्वम्। (मा.सं. ३१-२)
आत्मैवेदं सर्वम्। (छा. ७-२६-२)
ब्रह्मैवेदं सर्वम् (छा. ७-२५-२)
ब्रह्मैवेदं सर्वम् (मुण्ड.२-२-११)
ब्रह्मैवेदममृतं पुरस्तात्। (मुण्ड. २-२-११)
इदं सर्वं यदयमात्मा। (बृ. २-४-६)
सर्वं खल्विदं ब्रह्म। (छा. ३-१४-१)

इत्येवमादयः। ईश्वरगीतास्वपि—

वासुदेवः सर्वमिति। (गी. ७-१९)
क्षेत्रज्ञं चापि मां विद्धि सर्वक्षेत्रेषु भारत। (गी. १३-२)

ज्ञेयं यत् तत् प्रवक्ष्यामि यज्ज्ञात्वाऽमृतमश्नुते।
अनादिमत् परं ब्रह्म न सत् तन्नासदुच्यते॥ (गी. १३-१२)

सर्वतः पाणिपादं तत् सर्वतोऽक्षिशिरोमुखम्।
सर्वतः श्रुतिमल्लोके सर्वमावृत्त्य तिष्ठति॥ (गी. १३-१३)

सर्वेन्द्रियगुणाभासं सर्वेन्द्रियविवर्जितम्।
असक्तं सर्वभृच्चैव निर्गुणं गुणभोक्तृ च॥ (गी. १३-१४)

बहिरन्तश्च भूतानामचरं चरमेव च।
सूक्ष्मत्वात्तदविज्ञेयं दूरस्थं चान्तिके च तत्॥ (गी. १३-१५)

अविभक्तं च भूतेषु विभक्तमिव च स्थितम्।
भूतभर्तृ च तज्ज्ञेयं ग्रसिष्णु प्रभविष्णु च॥ (गी. १३-१६)

ज्योतिषामपि तज्ज्योतिस्तमसः परमुच्यते।
ज्ञानं ज्ञेयं ज्ञानगम्यं हृदि सर्वस्य विष्ठितम्॥ (गी. १३-१७)

इति। इत्थं श्रुतीनां स्मृतीनां च वेद्यत्वेन धर्मित्वेन चैकस्मिन्नद्वितीये ब्रह्मणि समन्वयः।

वेदप्रतिपादित-धर्मधर्मिविचारार्थं वैदिकैर्मीमांसाशास्त्रं प्रवर्तितम्। रूपाद्यभावान्न ब्रह्म प्रत्यक्षस्य गोचरम्। लिङ्गाद्यभावाच्च नानुमानादीनाम्। आगममात्रसमधिगम्यं

ब्रह्मेति। तस्य धर्मज्ञानमन्तरा ज्ञानं भवितुं नार्हतीति प्रथमम् **अथातो धर्मजिज्ञासेति** धर्मविचार आरब्धः। पश्चाच्च **अथातो ब्रह्मजिज्ञासेति** धर्मिविचार उपक्रान्तः। प्रमेयाणां धर्मिणां प्रथमं धर्मिजिज्ञासा, पश्चाच्च धर्मजिज्ञासा। ब्रह्मणोऽप्रमेयत्वाद् धर्मजिज्ञासानन्तरं धर्मिजिज्ञासा। ब्रह्मव्यतिरिक्तस्य वस्त्वन्तरस्य अभावादुत्तरमीमासायां केवलं ब्रह्मजिज्ञासैव प्रस्तुता, न पुनः पदार्थान्तराणाम्। धर्मिणोऽप्रमेयत्वाद् धर्मोऽप्यप्रमेय एव। नासौ प्रत्यक्षस्य गोचरो नानुमानादीनाम्। केवलं वेदैकगम्यो ब्रह्मवत्। धर्मप्रतिष्ठायां धर्मिप्रतिष्ठायाः सत्त्वेन धर्मनाशे धर्मिणो विनाशेन धर्मधर्मिणोर्धर्मप्राधान्यात् ब्रह्मप्रतिष्ठासिद्ध्यर्थं प्रथमं वेदप्रतिपादित-धर्ममीमांसा समुपक्रान्ता। इत्थं मीमांसाशास्त्रे वेदप्रतिपादितो धर्मो धर्मी च क्रमेण सप्रमाणं सविस्तरं मीमांसितः।

ब्रह्मव्यतिरिक्तः पदार्थो नास्ति। एकमेवाद्वितीयं ब्रह्म वेद्यत्वेन धर्मित्वेन चापि व्यवतिष्ठत इति सप्रमाणं सिद्धान्तितम्। अयमेव सिद्धान्तः शारीरकमीमांसायां ब्रह्मातिरिक्त-वस्तुनिराकरणपरे पराधिकरणे **तथाऽन्यप्रतिषेधादिति** सूत्रे (ब्र. सू. ३-२-३६) भाष्ये च मीमांसितः। तथा हि भाष्यम्—

"तथाऽन्यप्रतिषेधादपि न ब्रह्मणः परं वस्त्वन्तरमस्तीति गम्यते। तथा हि—'स एवाधस्तात्'। (छा. ७-२५-१) 'अहमेवाधस्तात्' (छा. ७-२५-१) 'आत्मैवाधस्तात्' (छा. ७-२५-२) 'सर्व तं परादाद् योऽन्यत्रात्मनः सर्वं वेद' (बृ. २-४-६) 'ब्रह्मैवेदं सर्वम्' 'आत्मैवेदं सर्वम्' (छा. ७-२५-२) 'नेह नानाऽस्ति किञ्चन' (बृ. ४-४-१९) 'यस्मात् परं नापरमस्ति किञ्चित्। (श्वे. ३-९) 'तदेतद् ब्रह्मापूर्वमनपरमनन्तरमबाह्यम्' (बृ. २-५-१९) इत्येवमादिवाक्यानि स्वप्रकरणस्थानि अन्यार्थत्वेन परिणेतुमशक्यानि ब्रह्मव्यतिरिक्तं वस्त्वन्तरं वारयन्ति' इति।

धर्मिणो ब्रह्मणः स्वरूपम्

इदानीं धर्मिणो ब्रह्मण एकस्याद्वितीयस्य स्वरूपं विचार्यते'कीदृशं ब्रह्मेति ? तत्र श्रुतिषु स्वयंज्योतिः-स्वरूपमवधारितं ब्रह्म। स्मृतं च तथैव स्मृतिष्वपि। तथा च श्रुतयः—

ब्रह्म सूर्यसमं ज्योतिः। (मा. सं. २३-४८)

स एषोऽग्निर्वैश्वानरो यत्पुरुषः स यो हैनमेवमग्निं वैश्वानरं पुरुषविधं पुरुषेऽन्तः प्रतिष्ठितं वेदाऽप पुनर्मृत्युं जयति सर्वमायुरेति न हास्य ब्रुवाणं च न वैश्वानरो हिनस्ति। (शत. १०-६-१-११)

येन सूर्यस्तपति पृथिव्यां तेजसेद्धः। (तै. ब्रा. ३-१२-९-७)

यश्चाऽयमस्यां पृथिव्यां तेजोमयोऽमृतमयः पुरुषो यश्चायमध्यात्मं शारीरस्तेजोमयोऽमृतमयः पुरुषोऽयमेव स योऽयमात्मेदममृतमिदं ब्रह्मेदं सर्वम्। (बृ. २-५-१)

यश्चायमात्मा तेजोमयोऽमृतमयः पुरुषः। (बृ. २-५-१४)

अस्तमित आदित्ये याज्ञवल्क्य चन्द्रमस्यस्तमिते शान्तेऽग्नौ शान्तायां वाचि किं ज्योतिरेवायं पुरुष इति ? आत्मज्योतिः सम्राडिति होवाच। आत्मनैवायं ज्योतिषाऽऽस्ते पल्ययते कर्म कुरुते विपर्येतीति। (बृ. ४-११-६)

कतम आत्मेति। योऽयं विज्ञानमयः पुरुषः प्राणेषु हृद्यन्तर्ज्योतिः स समानः सन्नुभौ लोकौ सञ्चरति ध्यायतीव लेलायतीव सधीः स्वप्नो भूत्वेमं लोकमतिक्रामति।

(बृ. ४-११-७)

अत्रायं पुरुषः स्वयंज्योतिर्भवति। (बृ. ४-११-१०; १६)

यस्मादर्वाक् संवत्सरोऽअहोभिः परिवर्तते।
तद्देवात्मज्योतिषां ज्योतिरायुर्होपासतेऽमृतम्॥ (बृ. ४-२-२०)

ब्रह्मैव तेज एव। (बृ. ४-४-७)

ब्रह्मैव लोक एव। (मा.बृ. ४-२-१०)

अथ यदतः परो दिवो ज्योतिर्दीप्यते विश्वतः पृष्ठेषु सर्वतः पृष्ठेष्वनुत्तमेषूत्तमेषु लोकेष्विदं वाव तद्यदिदमस्मिन्नन्तःपुरुषे ज्योतिः। (छा. ३-१३-७)

इदं वाव तद्यदिदमस्मिन्नन्तः पुरुषे ज्योतिः। (छा. ३-१३-७)

भारूपः सत्यसङ्कल्पः। (छा. ३-१४-२)

आत्मानमेवेमं वैश्वानरं सम्प्रत्यध्येषि तमेव नो ब्रूहि। (छा. ४-११-१-६)

यस्त्वेनमेवं प्रादेशमात्रमभिविमानमात्मानं वैश्वानरमुपास्ते स सर्वेषु लोकेषु सर्वेषु भूतेषु सर्वेष्वात्मस्वन्नमत्ति। तस्य ह वा एतस्यात्मनो वैश्वानरस्य मूर्धैव सुतेजाश्चक्षुर्विश्वरूपः प्राणः पृथग्वर्त्मा सन्देहो बहुलो बस्तिरेव रयिः पृथिव्येव पादावुर एव वेदिर्लोमानि बर्हिर्हृदयं गार्हपत्यो मनोऽन्वाहार्यपचन आस्यमाहवनीयः।

(छा. ५-१७-२)

तेजः परस्यां देवतायाम्। (छा. ६-८-६)

तेजसा हि तदा सम्पन्नो भवति। (छा. ८-६-३)

एष सम्प्रसादोऽस्माच्छरीरात् समुत्थाय प!
ज्योतिरुपसम्पद्य स्वेन रूपेणाभि निष्पद्यते। (छा. ७-१२-३)

अङ्गुष्ठमात्रः पुरुषो ज्योतिरिवाधूमकः। ईशानो भूतभव्यस्य स एवाद्य स उ श्वः।
एतद्वै तत्॥ (कठ. २-४-१३)

न तत्र सूर्यो भाति न चन्द्रतारकं नेमा विद्युतो भान्ति कुतोऽयमग्निः।
तमेव भान्तमनुभाति सर्वं तस्य भासा सर्वमिदं विभाति॥
(कठ. २-५-१४; मुण्ड. २-१-१०; श्वे. ६-१४; कौषी. २५-५-१५)

हिरण्मये परे कोशे विरजं ब्रह्म निष्कलम्।
तच्छुभ्रं ज्योतिषां ज्योतिस्तद्यदात्मविदो विदुः॥ (मुण्ड. २-२-९)

सत्येन लभ्यस्तपसा ह्येष आत्मा
सम्यग्ज्ञानेन ब्रह्मचर्येण नित्यम्।
अन्तः शरीरे ज्योतिर्मयो हि शुभ्रो
यं पश्यन्ति यतयः क्षीणदोषा॥

(मुण्ड. ३-१०-५)

महान् प्रभुर्वै पुरुषः सत्त्वस्यैव प्रवर्तकः।
मुनिर्मलामिमां प्राप्तिमीशानो ज्योतिरव्ययः॥ (श्वे. ३-१२)

शारीरमिति कस्मात् ? अग्रयो ह्यत्र श्रियन्ते ज्ञानाग्निर्दर्शनाग्निः कोष्ठाग्निरिति। तत्र कोष्ठाग्निर्नाम अशित-पीत-लेह्य-चोष्यं पचति। दर्शनाग्नी रूपाणां दर्शनं करोति। ज्ञानाग्निः शुभाशुभं च कर्म विन्दति। (गर्भोपनिषत् ५)

—इत्यादयः।

स्मृतयश्च—

ये विनिद्रा जितश्वासाः सत्त्वस्थाः संयतेन्द्रियाः।
ज्योतिः पश्यन्ति युञ्जानास्तस्मै योगात्मने नमः॥

(म० भा० शान्ति० ४७-५५)

योऽन्तः सुखोऽन्तरारामस्तथान्तर्ज्योतिरेव यः।
स योगी ब्रह्मनिर्वाणं ब्रह्मभूतोऽधिगच्छति॥

दिवि सूर्यसहस्रस्य भवेद्युगपदुत्थिता।
यदि भाः सदृशी सा स्याद् भासस्तस्य महात्मनः॥

किरीटिनं गदिनं चक्रिणं च
तेजोराशिं सर्वतो दीप्तिमन्तम्।
पश्यामि त्वां दुर्निरीक्ष्यं समन्ताद्
दीप्तानलार्कद्युतिमप्रमेयम्॥

अनादिमध्यान्तमनन्तवीर्य-
मनन्तबाहुं शशिसूर्यनेत्रम्।
पश्यामि त्वां दीप्तहुताशवक्त्रं
स्वतेजसा विश्वमिदं तपन्तम्॥

नभःस्पृशं दीप्तमनेकवर्णम्॥
तेजोभिरापूर्य जगत् समग्रं
भासस्तवोग्राः प्रपतन्ति विष्णो॥

मया प्रसन्नेन तवार्जुनेदं
रूपं परं दर्शितमात्मयोगात्।

तेजोमयं विश्वमनन्तमाद्यं
यन्मे त्वदन्येन न दृष्टपूर्वम् ॥

ज्योतिषामपि तज्ज्योतिस्तमसः परमुच्यते ।
ज्ञानं ज्ञेयं ज्ञानगम्यं हृदि सर्वस्य विष्ठितम् ॥

न तद् भासयते सूर्यो न शशाङ्को न पावकः ।
यद् गत्वा न निवर्तन्ते तद्धाम परमं मम ॥

यदादित्यगतं तेजो जगद् भासयतेऽखिलम् ।
यच्चन्द्रमसि यच्चाग्नौ तत्तेजो विद्धि मामकम् ॥

अहं वैश्वानरो भूत्वा प्राणिनां देहमाश्रितः ।
प्राणापानसमायुक्तः पचाम्यन्नं चतुर्विधम् ॥

(गी. ५.२४; ११.१२, १७, १९, २४, ३०,
४७; १३.१७; १५.६, १२, १४)

आत्मन्नेवाहमलब्ध्वैतद्धितं सेवस्व नाहितम् ।
अथान्येषु प्रतीच्छामि साधुष्ठानमनपेक्षया ॥

महान्तं तेजसस्कायं सर्वत्र निहितं प्रभुम् ।

(आ.ध. ८ पटलः, ६ सूत्रम्)

एतमेके वदन्त्यग्निं मनुमन्ये प्रजापतिम् ।
इन्द्रमेके परे प्राणमपरे ब्रह्म शाश्वतम् ॥ (मनु० १२-१२३)

द्वासप्ततिसहस्राणि हृदयादभिनिःसृताः ।
हिताहिता नाम नाड्यस्तासां मध्ये शशिप्रभम् ॥

मण्डलं तस्य मध्यस्थ आत्मा दीप इवाचलः ।
स ज्ञेयस्तं विदित्वेह पुनराजायते न तु ॥

अनन्यविषयं कृत्वा मनोबुद्धिस्मृतीन्द्रियम् ।
ध्येय आत्मा स्थितो योऽसौ हृदये दीपवत् प्रभुः ॥

मोहजालमपास्येह पुरुषो दृश्यते हि यः ।
सहस्रकरपन्नेत्रः सूर्यवर्चाः सहस्रकः ॥

स आत्मा चैव यज्ञश्च विश्वरूपः प्रजापतिः ।
विराजः सोऽन्नरूपेण यज्ञत्वमुपगच्छति ॥

अनन्ता रश्मयस्तस्य दीपवद् यः स्थितो हृदि ।
सितासिताः कर्बुरूपाः कपिला नीललोहिताः ॥

ऊर्ध्वमेकः स्थितस्तेषां यो भित्त्वा सूर्यमण्डलम् ।
ब्रह्मलोकमतिक्रम्य तेन याति परां गतिम् ॥

यदस्यान्यद्रश्मिशतमूर्ध्वमेव व्यवस्थितम्।
तेन देवशरीराणि सधामानि प्रपद्यते॥

येनैकरूपश्चाधस्ताद्रश्मयोऽस्य मृदुप्रभाः।
इह कर्मोपभोगाय तैः संसरति सोऽवशः।
ततो ध्येयः स्थितो योऽसौ हृदये दीपवत् प्रभुः॥

(याज्ञ. ३.१०८, ९, ११, १९, २०,
६६-६९, २०१) — इत्यादयः।

सर्वा एताः श्रुतयः स्मृतयश्च ब्रह्म स्वयं ज्योतिःस्वरूपमिति बोधयन्ति। शारीरकमीमांसायां भाष्ये च ब्रह्म स्वयं ज्योतिःस्वरूपमित्येव प्रस्थापितम्। तथा हि—

ब्रह्मण एव ज्योतिःशब्दाभिधेयत्वप्रतिष्ठापनपरे ज्योतिश्चरणाधिकरणे (ब्र० सू० १.१.२४-२७) ज्योतिर्ब्रह्मेति प्रतिष्ठापितम्। परमेश्वरस्यैव वैश्वानरत्वप्रतिपादनपरे वैश्वानराधिकरणे (ब्र० सू० १.२, २४-३२) वैश्वानरः परमेश्वर इति प्रतिपादितम्। चैतन्यस्य सर्वजगद्भासकत्वद्योतनपरे अनुकृत्यधिकारणे (ब्र० सू० १.३.२२-२३) ब्रह्म तु नान्येन ज्योतिषोपलभ्यते, स्वयंज्योतिःस्वरूपत्वादिति सिद्धान्तितम्। ब्रह्मण एव ज्योतिष्ट्वविचारणपरे ज्योतिरधिकरणे (ब्र० सू० १.३.४०) परमेव ब्रह्म ज्योतिःशब्दमिति विचारितम्। तथा 'आत्मा प्रकरणादि'ति सूत्रे (ब्र० सू० ४.४.३) आत्मैवात्र ज्योतिःशब्देनावेद्यते प्रकरणादिति मीमांसितम्।

भाष्यकारैरपि—

इदं तु पारमार्थिकं कूटस्थनित्यं व्योमवत् सर्वव्यापि सर्वविक्रियारहितं नित्यतृप्तं निरवयवं स्वयंज्योतिःस्वभावम्। (शां० भा० १.१.४)

ज्योतिरिति ब्रह्म प्रतिपत्तव्यम्। (शां० भा० १.१.२४)

तथा सति ब्रह्मणोऽपि चैतन्यरूपस्य समस्तजगदवभासहेतुत्वादुपपन्नो ज्योतिःशब्दः। (शां० भा० १.१.२४)

सर्वमिदमित्यविशेषश्रुतेः सर्वस्यैवास्य नामरूपक्रियाकारकफलजातस्य याऽभिव्यक्तिः सा ब्रह्मज्योतिः सत्तानिमित्ता। (शां० भा० १.३.२२)

यतः यदुपलभ्यते तत् सर्वं ब्रह्मणैव ज्योतिषोपलभ्यते। ब्रह्म तु नान्येन ज्योतिषोपलभ्यते स्वयंज्योतिःस्वरूपत्वात्। (शां० भा० १.३.२२)

परमेव ब्रह्म ज्योतिःशब्दम्। (शां० भा० १.३.४०)

अपि च—जागरिते विषयेन्द्रियसंयोगादादित्यादिज्योतिर्व्यतिकराच्चात्मनः स्वयंज्योतिष्ट्वं दुर्विवेचनमिति तद्विवेचनाय स्वप्न उपन्यस्तः। (शां० भा० ३.२.४)

विज्ञानादिशब्दैश्च चैतन्यप्रकाशात्मकत्वमुक्तम्। (शां भा० ४.१.२)

आत्मैवात्र ज्योतिःशब्देनावेद्यते प्रकरणात्। (शां भा० ४.४.३)

— इत्यादिना भाष्येण ब्रह्मणो विस्पष्टं स्वयंज्योतिःस्वरूपत्वं प्रतिपादितम्।

योगशास्त्रे च—

विशोका वा ज्योतिष्मती। (यो० सू० १.३६) एतस्यामवस्थायां गुणसम्बन्धातीतः स्वरूपमात्रज्योतिरमलः केवली पुरुषः। (यो० भा० २.२७)

नाभिचक्रे हृदयपुण्डरीके मूर्ध्नि ज्योतिषि नासिकाग्रे जिह्वाग्रे इत्येवमादिषु देशेषु बाह्ये वा विषये चित्तस्य वृत्तिमात्रेण बन्ध इति धारणा। (यो० भा० ३.१)

मूर्धज्योतिषि सिद्धदर्शनम्। (यो० सू० ३.३२)

शिरःकपालेऽन्तश्छिद्रं प्रभास्वरं ज्योतिः। तत्र संयमात् सिद्धानां द्यावापृथिव्योरन्तरालचारिणां दर्शनम्। (यो० भा० ३.३२) तदा पुरुषः स्वरूपमात्रज्योतिरमलः केवली भवति। (यो० भा० ३.५५)

—इत्यादिष्वात्मनो ज्योतिःस्वरूपत्वमुक्तम्। सर्वाण्येतानि प्रमाणजातानि ब्रह्मणो ज्योतिःस्वरूपं प्रस्थापयन्ति। तस्मादेकमेवाद्वितीयं ब्रह्म एकमेवाद्वितीयं स्वयंज्योतिरित्येव प्रतिपत्तव्यम्। एकमेवाद्वितीयं स्वयंज्योतिरग्निरेव साक्षान्न पदार्थान्तरम्। तेन एक एवाद्वितीयोऽग्निर्ब्रह्मशब्देन व्यपदिश्यत इति सिद्धान्तः। लौकिकाग्नेरग्निशब्देन ग्रहणं मा भूदिति बृहत्वाद् बृंहणत्वाद् विराडग्निग्रहणार्थं ब्रह्मशब्दप्रयोगः। '**अथातो ब्रह्मजिज्ञासे**'ति ब्रह्मशब्देन शारीरकमीमांसारम्भश्च। विराडग्नेः स्वरूपं शतपथब्राह्मणे अग्निरहस्यकाण्डे श्रूयते। तथा हि—

> **तदाहुः, किं छन्दः का देवताऽग्नेः शिर इति ? गायत्री छन्दोऽग्निर्देवता शिरः ॥१॥ किं छन्दः का देवता ग्रीवा इति ? उष्णिक् छन्दः सविता देवता ग्रीवा ॥२॥ किं छन्दः का देवताऽनूकमिति ? बृहतीछन्दो बृहस्पतिर्देवताऽनूकम् ॥३॥ किं छन्दः का देवता पक्षाविति ? बृहद्रथन्तरं छन्दो द्यावापृथिवी देवते पक्षौ ॥४॥ किं छन्दः का देवता मध्यमिति ? त्रिष्टुप् छन्द इन्द्रो देवता मध्यम् ॥५॥ किं छन्दः का देवता श्रोणी इति ? जगती छन्द आदित्यो देवता श्रोणी ॥६॥ किं छन्दः का देवता यस्मादिदं प्राणाद्रेतः सिच्यत इति ? अतिश्छन्दश्छन्दः प्रजापतिर्देवता ॥७॥ किं छन्दः का देवता योऽयमवाङ् प्राण इति ? यज्ञायज्ञियं छन्दो वैश्वानरो देवता ॥८॥ किं छन्दः का देवतोरू इति ? अनुष्टुप् छन्दो विश्वेदेवा देवतोरू ॥९॥ किं छन्दः का देवताऽष्ठीवन्ताविति ? पङ्क्तिश्छन्दो मरुतो देवताऽष्ठीवन्तौ ॥१०॥ किं छन्दः का देवता प्रतिष्ठे इति ? द्विपदा छन्दो विष्णुर्देवता प्रतिष्ठे ॥११॥ किं छन्दः का देवता प्राण इति ? विच्छन्दाश्छन्दो वायुर्देवता प्राणाः ॥१२॥ किं छन्दः का देवता ऊनातिरिक्तानीति ? न्यूनाक्षरा छन्द आपो देवता ऊनातिरिक्तानि। सैषात्मविद्यैव। एतन्मयो हैवैता देवता एनमात्मानमभिसम्भवति। न हात्रान्या लोक्यताया आशीरस्ति ॥१३॥**

(माध्यन्दिनशतपथ-१०.३.२.)

अयमेव ऋग्यजुःसामसु दृष्टः संस्तुतश्च स्वयंज्योतिर्विराडग्निर्वेदान्तेषु बृहत्वाद् बृंहणत्वाच्च ब्रह्मशब्देन व्यपदिश्यते। देहपरिच्छिन्नोऽग्निर्विराडग्निरेक एवेति सिद्धान्तः। अग्नेर्विराट्त्वं द्योतयितुं तस्य ब्रह्मशब्देन परामर्शः। अस्यैव जिज्ञासार्थं शारीरकमामांसाशास्त्रं प्रवृत्तम्।

अद्वितीयस्य ब्रह्मणो लक्षणाभावः।

वैदिकं दर्शनमनुसृत्य समुद्दिष्टो धर्मी। उद्देशो लक्षणं परीक्षा चेति त्रिविधा शास्त्रस्य प्रवृत्तिरिति क्रमेण उद्देशानन्तरं धर्मिणो ब्रह्मणो लक्षणं वक्तव्यम्। ननूक्तमेव लक्षणम्-'स्वयंज्योतिःस्वरूपं ब्रह्म' इति? बाढमुक्तम्; तथापि न तल्लक्षणप्रतिपादनार्थम्। किं तर्हि? उद्देशार्थमेव। 'विराडग्निरि'ति नामधेयान्तरेण ब्रह्मणः सङ्कीर्तनार्थम्। किं प्रयोजनम्? उच्यते।

अत्र केचिद् विवदन्ते—उपनिषत्स्वेव 'एकमेवाद्वितीयं ब्रह्म' श्रूयते। नहि वेदान्ता नाम समग्रा वेदाः। वैदिकैस्तावदुपनयनादारभ्य—

सूर्य आत्मा जगतस्तस्थुषश्च। (मा० सं० १३.४६)

योऽसावादित्ये पुरुषः सोऽसावहम्। (मा० ई० उ० १७)

स यश्चायं पुरुषे यश्चासावादित्ये स एकः। (तै० उ० २.७)

य एष एतस्मिन् मण्डले पुरुषः सोऽग्निस्तानि यजूंषि स यजुषां लोकः। (श० ब्रा० १०.५.२.१)

इत्यादि - श्रुतिप्रतिपादितस्य सवितृमण्डलस्थस्य विराडग्नेः सायंप्रातर्विविक्ते सन्धिकाले प्रत्यहमात्मैकत्वप्रतिपत्त्यर्थमुपासनं विधीयते। व्रतबन्धादारभ्य समावर्तनपर्यन्तं सायं-प्रातः परिचर्यते स एवाऽग्निः। गृहस्थाश्रममारभ्य यावज्जीवं च हूयते सायं-प्रातरग्निहोत्रम्। पञ्चमहायज्ञैः सप्तपाकसंस्थाभिः सप्तहविःसंस्थाभिः सप्तसोमसंस्थाभिश्च अजस्रं सन्तर्प्यते विराडग्निः। तस्मादग्निरेव वैदिकानां धर्मी, न ब्रह्मेति।

तेषां भ्रमं वारयितुं वैदिकैरुपास्यमानो विराडग्निरेव ब्रह्मशब्देन उपनिषत्सु श्रूयते, ब्रह्मणो विराडग्नेश्चाभेद इति च प्रस्थापयितुं ब्रह्मणः स्वयंज्योतिःस्वरूपमुक्तम्, न लक्षणप्रतिपादनार्थम्।

वस्तुतस्तु एकमेवाद्वितीयं ब्रह्म धर्मीति मीमांसितम्। अस्यामवस्थायां लक्षणकर्तुरन्यस्याभावाद् ब्रह्मणो लक्षणमशक्यप्रायमेव। वैदिकैरभेदोपचाराद् ब्रह्मशब्देनैव व्यपदिश्यमाना विज्ञानघना वेदमयी परब्रह्मणः पट्टमहिषी चितिशक्तिः श्रुतिरप्यद्वितीयस्य ब्रह्मणो लक्षणं पृष्टा लज्जावनतमुखी नववधूरिव मौनमेवास्थितवती। पुनः पुनः सनिर्बन्धं पृष्टा प्रतिप्रश्नं पृष्टं धर्ममुत्तमाङ्गविधूननेनैव केवलेन प्रतिषेधन्ती करुणाप्लावितहृदया केवलैर्दृगन्तपातैरेव अन्ते परं ब्रह्म प्रबोधितवतीति महदाश्चर्यम्। तथा च श्रुतयः—

नैनमूर्ध्वं न तिर्यञ्चं न मध्ये परिजग्रभत्। (मा. सं. ३२.२)

योऽस्याध्यक्षः परमे व्योमन्। (तै. ब्रा. २.८९)

स होवाच। एतद्वै तदक्षरं गार्गि ब्राह्मणा अभिवदन्ति। अस्थूलम्। अनणु। अह्रस्वम्। अदीर्घम्। अलोहितम्। अस्नेहम्। अच्छायम्। अतमः। अवायु। अनाकाशम्। असङ्गम्। अस्पर्शम्। अगन्धम्। अरसम्। अचक्षुष्कम्। अश्रोत्रम्। अवाक्। अमनः। अतेजस्कम्। अप्राणम्। अमुखम्। अनाम। अगोत्रम्। अजरम्। अमरम्। अभयम्। अमृतम्। अरजः। अशब्दम्। अविवृतम्। असंवृतम्। अपूर्वम्। अनपरम्। अनन्तरम्। अबाह्यम्। न तदश्नोति कञ्चन। न तदश्नोति कञ्चन।　　(मा.बृ. ३.८.८.)

तद्वा एतदक्षरं गार्गि अदृष्टं द्रष्टृ अश्रुतं श्रोतृ अमतं मन्तृ अविज्ञातं विज्ञातृ। नान्यदस्ति द्रष्टृ। नान्यदस्ति श्रोतृ। नान्यदस्ति मन्तृ। नान्यदस्ति विज्ञातृ। एतद्वै तदक्षरं गार्गि यस्मिन्नाकाश ओतश्च प्रोतश्चेति। (मा० बृ० ३.८.११)

स एव नेति नेत्यात्मा। अगृह्यो नहि गृह्यते। अशीर्यो नहि शीर्यते। असङ्गोऽसितो न सृज्यते न व्यथते। (मा० बृ० ३.९.२८; ३.११.६; ४.२.२७)

यतो वाचो निवर्तन्ते
अप्राप्य मनसा सह।
आनन्दं ब्रह्मणो विद्वान्
न बिभेति कदाचनेति॥　　(तै० उ० २.४)

यस्यामतं तस्य मतं
मतं यस्य न वेद सः।
अविज्ञातं विजानतां
विज्ञातमविजानताम्।　　(केन-उ० २.३)

अन्यदेव तद्विदितादथो अविदितादधि।　　(केन-उ० १.३)

स्मृतिश्च—

अनादिमत्परं ब्रह्म न सत् तन्नासदुच्यते।　　(गी० १३.१२)

ब्रह्मण एकत्वादद्वितीयत्वाद् ब्रह्मव्यतिरिक्तस्य वस्त्वन्तरस्याभावाच्च ब्रह्म अस्तीत्यपि वक्तुं न शक्यते, नास्तीत्यपि वक्तुं न शक्यते। विषयिणो वक्तुः द्वितीयस्याभावात्। दूरे पुनर्लक्षणता।

इयमवरोहक्रमेण श्रौती प्रथमा भूमिका। आरोहक्रमेण अन्तिमा। नात्र धर्मिणो ब्रह्मणो धर्मग्लानिर्भवति। अनुच्छित्तिधर्मत्वाद् ब्रह्मणः। अधर्मस्य वा धर्मिण्यभ्युत्थानं भवति। अविनाशित्वात्, अत एवाऽधर्माभावात्। विनाशधर्मसु हि पदार्थेषु अधर्मोऽवतिष्ठते, नाविनाशिषु। अत एव धर्मप्रतिष्ठापनस्यात्र प्रसङ्ग एव नास्ति। सुप्रतिष्ठितो ह्यत्र धर्मः। तथा हि श्रुतयः—

अविनाशी वा अरे अयमात्मा अनुच्छित्तिधर्मा मात्रासंसर्गस्त्वस्य भवति।
(मा. बृ. ४.३.१५)

अजो नित्यः शाश्वतोऽयं पुराणः। (कठ. २.१८)

स भगवः कस्मिन् प्रतिष्ठित इति स्वे महिम्नि। (छा. ७.२४.१) इति।

स्मृतिश्च—

अविनाशी तु तद्विद्धि येन सर्वमिदं ततम्।
विनाशमव्ययस्यास्य न कश्चित् कर्तुमर्हति॥
वेदाविनाशिनं नित्यं य एनमजमव्ययम्।
नित्यः सर्वगतः स्थाणुरचलोऽयं सनातनः॥
अव्यक्तोऽयमचिन्त्योऽयमविकार्योऽयमुच्यते।
—(गी. २.१७, २१, २४, २५) इति।

देहपातानन्तरमेव भूमिकेयं विदुषा सम्प्राप्यते। भूमिकायामस्याम् एकत्वमद्वितीयत्वं चेति ब्रह्मधर्माः प्राप्यन्ते। विदुषो ब्रह्मभावापत्तिर्भवति। तथा च श्रुतिः—

न तस्या प्राणा उत्क्रामन्ति ब्रह्मैव सन् ब्रह्माप्येति। (बृ. ४.४.९)

विद्यमाने देहे शरीरोपाधिपरिच्छिन्न आत्मा निरुपाधिकेन ब्रह्मणा भिद्यत इति सम्पूर्णा ब्रह्मभावापत्तिर्विदुषोऽपि न भवति।

वस्तुतस्तु ब्रह्मणोऽविकृतस्यैव जीवात्मनाऽवस्थानं ब्रह्मात्मना चेति। उपाध्युत्पत्त्या जीवस्योत्पत्तिः, उपाधिप्रलयेन प्रलयः। लक्षणभेदोऽप्यनयोरुपाधिनिमित्त एव। विद्यमाने देहोपाधौ यद्यप्यात्मैकत्वविद्यया ब्रह्मणा साकमात्मनः सदंशेन चिदंशेन आनन्दांशेन चैक्यं सम्पद्यते, तथापि न पूर्णम्। देहोपाधेर्द्वैतापादकस्य अधर्मस्य विद्यमानत्वात्। तस्यात्मनि समुत्थितस्य देहोपाधिरूपस्य अधर्मस्य प्रलयेनैव द्वैतप्रलयोऽद्वैतभावापत्तिश्च।

नित्यशुद्धबुद्धमुक्तस्वभावं ब्रह्म, शारीरश्चात्मा। देहश्च अनित्योऽशुद्धो जडो बद्धश्च। स्वयंज्योतिःस्वरूप आत्मा। तमःस्वभावो देहः। विरुद्धधर्मावेतौ पदार्थौ। न तत्र धर्मधर्मिसम्बन्ध आस्थातुं शक्यः। तेन देहो नात्मधर्मो भवति, प्रत्युत विरुद्धधर्मत्वाद् अधर्म एव। तस्मादात्मनो देहोपाधिर्नाम आत्मनि अधर्माभ्युत्त्थानमेव।

पाञ्चभौतिको हि देहः। तत्र पृथिवीतत्त्वस्य आकाशतत्त्वस्य च जडेऽपि विद्यमानत्वात् जलतत्त्वमग्नितत्त्वं वायुतत्त्वं चेति महाभूतत्रयमस्य असाधारणो धर्मः। एतदेव पदार्थत्रयं कफः, पित्तं वायुश्चेति समामनन्ति भिषजः। सत्त्वं रजस्तम इति साङ्ख्याः। एतत् त्रैगुण्यमेव साम्यावस्थं प्रकृतिशब्देन साङ्ख्यैर्व्यपदिश्यते। रागद्वेषमोहाः सुखदुःखमोहा वा प्रकृतेर्धर्माः। एवं प्रकृतिरेवास्य शरीरस्य असाधारणो धर्मः।

निस्त्रैगुण्य आत्मा त्रैगुण्येन विरुद्धधर्मेण अत एव अधर्मेण शरीरेण परिच्छिन्न इति स शरीरी देही चेति अविद्याविद्भिरुच्यते। शरीरी देही चेत्यादिप्रयोगेषु शरीरं देहो वा शरीरिणो देहिनो वाऽऽत्मनोऽधर्मः सन्नपि संमूढैर्धर्म इत्युपचर्यते। शरीरं चात्मधर्मो भवति। शरीरधर्माश्च

अविद्ययाऽऽत्मनि अध्यस्यन्ते। एवमत्राऽऽत्मधर्माणां ग्लानिर्भवति। शरीरधर्माणामात्माऽधर्माणामभ्युत्थानं भवति। एवमत्र अधर्मो विपर्ययेण धर्म इत्युपचर्यते।

अयमधर्म एव धर्मिभूतो नीतिरिरिति व्यपदिश्यते। अविद्यादिभिः पञ्चविपर्ययैरत्र नयनं सम्पाद्यते। अविद्ययाऽधर्मो धर्मत्वेन उपचर्यते, धर्मत्वं च नीयते। विपर्ययेण धर्मत्वं नीतोऽधर्म एव नीतिरिरिति च व्यपदिश्यते। नीतिश्च धर्मशब्दपर्याय इत्यास्थीयते।

वस्तुतो धर्मो नीतिश्चेति भिन्नौ पदार्थौ, प्रकृतिभेदादर्थभेदाच्च। अस्यामविद्यावस्थायां धर्मधर्मिणोः संयोगः सम्बन्धः, न समवायो न वाऽभेदः। संयोगसम्बन्धेन विद्यमानो धर्मो धर्मिणा यथाकाममुपादातुं परित्यक्तुं च शक्यत इत्यत्र धर्मधर्मिसम्बन्धोऽशास्त्रीयः, अनित्योऽज्ञानमूलकश्च।

नात्र धर्मनाशे धर्मिनाशः। देहिन आत्मनो धर्मो देह इति देहीशब्देन प्रतीतिरविद्ययैव। अत एवोक्तमीश्वरगीतासु—

अधर्मं धर्ममिति या मन्यते तमसाऽऽवृता।
सर्वार्थान् विपरीतांश्च बुद्धिः सा पार्थ तामसी॥ (गी. १८.३२)

तस्माद् अविद्यया विपर्ययेण च शरीरं विरुद्धधर्ममपि आत्मधर्मत्वेनोपचर्यते। आत्मानात्मविवेकिनो विदुषस्तु देहोऽधर्म एव। सोऽधर्म आत्मधर्मैरुदारैरध्यस्तः शान्तस्तिष्ठति। यावदयमधर्मो न परित्यज्यते तावद् विदुषोऽपि सम्पूर्णा ब्रह्मभावापत्तिर्न भवति। यदा देहावच्छेदरूपोऽधर्मः परित्यज्यते, तदा सर्वधर्माधर्मपरित्यागेन परेण ब्रह्मणा पूर्णमैक्यं सम्पद्यते। तथा चोक्तं गीताशास्त्रे—

सर्वधर्मान् परित्यज्य मामेकं शरणं व्रज। (१८.६६) **इति।**

सर्वे च ते धर्माश्च सर्वधर्मास्तान् सर्वधर्मान्। 'धर्मशब्देनात्र अधर्मोऽपि गृह्यते।' (शां.भा. १८.६६) इति सर्वाधर्मानपि। विनाशिषु पदार्थेषु धर्मेण साकमधर्मोऽपि विद्यते। केवलं धर्म एव नास्ति। स चाधर्मोऽभ्युत्थितो धर्ममभिभूय पदार्थं नाशयति। **धर्मश्च** अभ्युत्थितोऽधर्ममभिभूय धर्मिणं प्रतिष्ठापयति। एवं विनाशिपदार्थेषु धर्माधर्मयोर्द्वन्द्वं नित्यं वर्तते। तस्मात् **सर्वधर्मान् परित्यज्य** इत्यत्र धर्मशब्देन अधर्मोऽप्याकृष्यत इति धर्मशब्देन अधर्मस्यापि ग्रहणम्।

सर्वधर्मा नाम विषयधर्मा देहधर्मा इन्द्रियधर्मा बुद्धिधर्माः प्रकृतिधर्मा आत्मधर्माश्चेति। सर्वाऽधर्मा नाम विषयाधर्मा देहाधर्मा इन्द्रियाधर्मा मनोऽधर्मा बुद्ध्यधर्माः प्रकृत्यधर्मा आत्माधर्माश्चेति।

परित्यज्य त्यक्त्वा। मां परं ब्रह्म। एकमद्वितीयम्। शरणमेकत्वेनाद्वितीयत्वेन च। व्रज गच्छ। एवं सदंशेन चिदंशेन आनन्दांशेन चैकत्वं गतोऽपि विद्वान् देहोपाधिरूपं द्वैतापादकमधर्मं त्यक्त्वाऽद्वितीयत्वं गच्छति। यथा घटाकाशस्य महाकाशादनन्यत्वम्, तथापि घटे विद्यमाने तत्र विद्यमानस्य महाकाशस्य घटाकाशत्वं नापैति, घटावच्छेदस्य विद्यमानत्वात्।

यथा घटे घटाकाशस्य प्रतीतिर्भवति तथा तत्रैव घटे घटाकाशे अनन्यत्वेन विद्यमानस्य महाकाशस्यापि प्रतीतिर्भवति। परन्तु घटे नष्टे उपाधेर्नाशाद् घटाकाशो महाकाश एव सम्पद्यते। आकाशस्य घटावच्छेदो नश्यति। एवं विदुष आत्मनो देहावच्छेदे नष्टे तस्य ब्रह्मभावापत्तिर्भवति। विद्यमाने देहे देहावच्छेदरूपेण विद्यमानं द्वैतं देहपाते निवर्तते। एकमद्वितीयं च ब्रह्म सम्पद्यते। **ब्रह्मैव सन् ब्रह्माप्ये**ति इति। (बृ० ४.४.६)

द्वितीयभूमिकाविचारः-द्विरूपं ब्रह्म, विकारावर्ति, विकारवर्ति च

अवसितः प्रथमभूमिका-विचारः। इदानीं द्वितीयभूमिका-विचार उपक्रम्यते—**द्विरूपं ब्रह्म विकारावर्ति, विकारवर्ति च**। अस्य परब्रह्मणो द्विरूपमवस्थानं श्रूयते-विकारावर्ति विकारवर्ति च। विस्तरेणैतत् मीमांसितमुत्तरमीमांसायाम्। तथा हि, द्विरूपं हि ब्रह्मावगम्यते नाम-रूप-विकारभेदोपाधिविशिष्टं तद्विपरीतञ्च सर्वोपाधिविवर्जितम्।

यत्र हि द्वैतमिव भवति तदितर इतरं पश्यति।
यत्र त्वस्य सर्वमात्मैवाभूत् तत्केन कं पश्येत्॥ (बृ० ४.५.१५)

यत्र नान्यत्पश्यति नान्यच्छृणोति नान्यद्विजानाति स भूमा।
अथ यत्रान्यत् पश्यत्यन्यच्छृणोत्यन्यद्विजानाति तदल्पम्।
यो वै भूमा तदमृतम्। अथ यदल्पं तन्मर्त्यम्। (छा० ७.२४.१)
सर्वाणि रूपाणि विचिन्त्य धीरो
नामानि कृत्वाऽभिवदन् यदास्ते।

(तै० आ० ३.१२)

निष्कलं निष्क्रियं शान्तं निरवद्यं निरञ्जनम्।
अमृतस्य परं सेतुं दग्धेन्धनमिवाऽनलम्॥ (श्वे. ६.१९)

नेति नेति (बृ० २.३.६)। अस्थूलमनणु (बृ० ३.८.८)।

न्यूनमन्यत् स्थानं सम्पूर्णमन्यत्। इति चैवं सहस्रशो विद्याविद्याविषयभेदेन ब्रह्मणो द्विरूपतां दर्शयन्ति।' (शां० भा० १.१.२४)

> सर्वगतस्यापि ब्रह्मण उपासनार्थः प्रदेशविशेषपरिग्रहो न विरुध्यते। ननूक्तं निष्प्रदेशस्य ब्रह्मणः प्रदेशविशेषकल्पना नोपपद्यत इति ? नायं दोषः, निष्प्रदेशस्यापि ब्रह्मण उपाधिविशेषसम्बन्धात् प्रदेशविशेषकल्पनोपपत्तेः। तथा हि—आदित्ये चक्षुषि हृदय इति प्रदेशविशेषसम्बन्धीनि ब्रह्मण उपासनानि श्रूयन्ते। (शां.भा. १.१.२४)

यथैव हि ब्रह्मणो जगदुत्पत्तिः श्रूयत एवं विकारव्यतिरेकेणापि ब्रह्मणोऽवस्थानं श्रूयते। प्रकृतिविकारयोर्भेदेन व्यपदेशात्।

सेयं देवतैक्षत हन्ताऽहमिमास्तिस्रो देवता अनेन जीवेनात्मनाऽनु प्रविश्य नामरूपे व्याकरवाणि। इति (छा. ६.३.२)

तावानस्य महिमा ततो ज्यायांश्च पूरुषः ।
पादोऽस्य सर्वाभूतानि त्रिपादस्यामृतं दिवि ॥ (छा. ३.१२.६)

इति चैवंजातीयकात् तथा हृदयायतनत्ववचनात् सत्सम्पत्तिवचनाच्च । यदि च कृत्स्नं ब्रह्म कार्यभावेन उपयुक्तं स्यात् ।

सता सोम्य तदा सम्पन्नो भवति । (छा. ६.८.१)

इति सुषुप्तिगतं विशेषणमनुपपन्नं स्यात् । विकृतेन ब्रह्मणा नित्यसम्पन्नत्वादविकृतस्य च ब्रह्मणोऽभावात् । तथा इन्द्रियगोचरत्व-प्रतिषेधाद् ब्रह्मणो विकारस्य चेन्द्रियगोचरत्वोपपत्तेः । तस्माद् अस्त्यविकृतं ब्रह्म । (शां. भा. २.१.२७)

विकारावर्ति च तथा हि स्थितिमाह । (ब्र.सू. ४.४.१९)

विकारावर्त्यपि च नित्यमुक्तं पारमेश्वरं रूपं न केवलं विकारमात्रगोचरं सवितृमण्डलाद्यधिष्ठानम् । तथा ह्यस्य द्विरूपां स्थितिमाह आम्नायः—

तावानस्य महिमा ततो ज्यायांश्च पूरुषः ।
पादोऽस्य सर्वा भूतानि त्रिपादस्यामृतं दिवि ॥ (छा. ३.१२.६)
इत्येवमादिः । (शां. भा. ४.४.१९)
दर्शयतश्चैवं प्रत्यक्षानुमाने । (ब्र. सू. ४.४.२०)

दर्शयतश्च विकारावर्तित्वं परस्य ज्योतिषः श्रुतिस्मृती । **न तत्र सूर्यो भाति न चन्द्रतारकं नेमा विद्युतो भान्ति कुतोऽयमग्निः** (कठ. ५.१५, श्वेता. ६.१४, मुण्ड. २.२.१०) इति । **न तद् भासयते सूर्यो न शशाङ्को न पावकः** (गी. १५.६) इति च । तदेवं विकारावर्तित्वं परस्य ज्योतिषः प्रसिद्धमित्यभिप्रायः । (शां.भा. ४.४.२०)

गीताशास्त्रेऽपि परस्य ज्योतिषो द्विरूपमवस्थानं स्मर्यते । तथा हि—

ज्ञेयं यत् तत् प्रवक्ष्यामि यज्ज्ञात्वाऽमृतमश्नुते ।
अनादिमत् परं ब्रह्म न सत् तन्नासदुच्यते ॥ (गी. १३.१२)

इति विकारावर्तित्वं परब्रह्मणो दर्शितम् ।

सर्वतः पाणिपादं तत् सर्वतोऽक्षिशिरोमुखम् ।
सर्वतः श्रुतिमल्लोके सर्वमावृत्य तिष्ठति ॥

सर्वेन्द्रियगुणाभासं सर्वेन्द्रियविवर्जितम् ।
असक्तं सर्वभृच्चैव निर्गुणं गुणभोक्तृ च ॥

बहिरन्तश्च भूतानामचरं चरमेव च ।
सूक्ष्मत्वात् तदविज्ञेयं दूरस्थं चान्तिके च तत् ॥

अविभक्तं च भूतेषु विभक्तमिव च स्थितम् ।
भूतभर्तृ च तज्ज्ञेयं ग्रसिष्णु प्रभविष्णु च ॥

ज्योतिषामपि तज्ज्योतिस्तमसः परमुच्यते।
ज्ञानं ज्ञेयं ज्ञानगम्यं हृदि सर्वस्य विष्ठितम्॥ (गी. १३. १३-१७)

इति विकारवर्तित्वं ब्रह्मणः प्रतिपादितम्।

अथवा बहुनैतेन किं ज्ञातेन तवार्जुन।
विष्टभ्याहमिदं कृत्स्नमेकांशेन स्थितो जगत्॥ (गी. १०.३२)

इत्यत्र विकारवर्ति विकारावर्ति चेति द्विरूपमवस्थानं ब्रह्मणः स्मृतम्। स हि भगवान् महानात्मा वैश्वानररूपेणेदं कृत्स्नं विष्टभ्य स्थितः। तथा हि—

अहं वैश्वानरो भूत्वा प्राणिनां देहमाश्रितः।
प्राणापानसमायुक्तः पचाम्यन्नं चतुर्विधम्॥ (गी. १५.१४)

इति परस्य ब्रह्मणो ज्योतिःस्वरूपेणैव विकारवर्तित्वमुक्तम्।

इत्थमविकृतं विकृतं चेति द्वेधा व्यवतिष्ठते परं ब्रह्म। तत्र विकारावर्तिनो ब्रह्मणोऽप्रमेयत्वात् न तत्र लक्षणप्रवृत्तिर्भवतीति मीमांसितम्। द्वितीयमिदानीं परब्रह्मणो विकारगोचरं स्वरूपं विचार्यते।

विश्वानि भूतान्येकेन अंशेनाभिव्याप्य व्यवतिष्ठते परं ब्रह्म। प्रमेयाणि विश्वानि भूतानि। प्रमेयत्वात् सर्वैर्दार्शनिकैः प्रत्यक्षादिप्रमाणैर्गृह्यन्ते। तेन सर्वेषां दार्शनिकानामयं विषयः प्रमेयो भवति। तत्र दार्शनिकानां प्रमाणविषयभूतानि विश्वान्येतानि भूतानि ब्रह्मेति प्रतिज्ञायते वेदान्तैः। एवमत्र परस्परविरुद्धदर्शनद्वयसम्पातः। ब्रह्मप्रतिज्ञापकं श्रौतम्। इदं सर्वमिति प्रमाणयदश्रौतम्। तत्रैता विकारवर्तिब्रह्मप्रतिपादका श्रुतयो भवन्ति—

पुरुष एवेदं सर्वम्। (मा.सं. ३१.२)
आत्मैवेदं सर्वम्। (छा. ७.२५.२)
ब्रह्मैवेदं सर्वम्। (छा. ७.२५.२ मुण्ड. २.२.११)
ब्रह्मैवेदममृतं पुरस्तात्। (मुण्ड. २.२.११)
इदं सर्वं यदयमात्मा। (बृ. २.४.६.)
सर्वं खल्विदं ब्रह्म। (छा. ३.१४.१)

इति। स्मृतिश्च भवति—

वासुदेवः सर्वम्। इति (गी. ७.१९)

सर्वास्वासु श्रुतिषु स्मृतौ च सर्वमिदं विषयीभूतं दृश्यं जगत् पुरुष इति आत्मेति ब्रह्मेति वासुदेव इति च प्रबोधितम्। सर्वत्र एकवचननिर्देशात् एकमेवाद्वितीयं ब्रह्म इदं सर्वं दृश्यं जगत्। नात्र प्रतिभूतमुपाधिकृत आत्मभेदो न वा विकारावर्तिना ब्रह्मणा भेदः। इदमः सर्वस्य प्रत्याख्यानात् तस्यैव ब्रह्मेति प्रत्यभिज्ञापनादेक एवात्र पदार्थः। स एव इदं सर्वं दृश्यं जगदिति प्रत्यक्षादिप्रमाणैरवैदिकैर्गृह्यते। स एव वेदान्तैर्ब्रह्मेति प्रतिज्ञायते। विवर्तवादमन्तरा इदं सर्वं

ब्रह्मेति कार्यस्य कारणानन्यत्वं भोग्यभोक्त्रादिप्रपञ्चजातस्य ब्रह्मव्यतिरेकेणाभावं प्रबोधयन्तीनां श्रुतीनामुपपत्तिरेव न सम्भवति। ब्रह्मैव जगद्रूपेण विवर्तते। अविजानद्भिरिदं सर्वमिति च गृह्यते। यदा वेदान्तैरिदं सर्वं दृश्यं जगद् ब्रह्मेति प्रबोध्यते तदा तद् ब्रह्मरूपेण विपरिवर्तते। इदमद्वितीयब्रह्मदर्शनमात्मैकत्वप्रतिपत्तिर्वा श्रुतिप्रामाण्यमन्तरा प्रमाणान्तरैः दर्शनान्तरैश्च नैव सम्पद्यते। अत एवोक्तमाचार्यैः अध्यासभाष्ये—

आत्मैकत्वविद्याप्रतिपत्तये सर्वे वेदान्ता आरभ्यन्ते (शां० भा० १.१.१) इति।

वैदिकाऽवैदिक-दर्शन-मीमांसा

"अपरे तु वादिनः पारमार्थिकमेव जैवं रूपमिति मन्यन्ते। अस्मदीयाश्च केचित् तेषां सर्वेषामात्मैकत्व-सम्यग्दर्शनप्रतिपक्षभूतानां प्रतिबोधायेदं शारीरकमारब्धम्" इति च। (शां० भा० १.३)

इत्थं प्रमाणान्तराप्रमेयस्यापि परब्रह्मणो वेदान्तैः प्रबोधितं विकारगोचरमवस्थानम् अवधारितम्। अत्रैकस्यैव पदार्थस्य दर्शनद्वयं सम्पन्नम्-श्रौतमेकम्, अपरमश्रौतम्। एकस्यैव पदार्थस्य परस्परविरुद्धमेतद् दर्शनद्वयमिति स्पष्टप्रतिपत्त्यर्थमत्रैव संक्षेपतः परामृश्यते प्रसङ्गागतत्वात्। विस्तरस्तु यथास्थानमेव करिष्यते। प्रसङ्गागतदर्शनद्वयविचारानन्तरं प्रकृतं क्रमप्राप्तं ब्रह्मणो लक्षणं विस्तरेण उपपादयिष्यते।

पादोऽस्य विश्वा भूतानि। (मा. सं. ३१.३) विष्टभ्याऽहमिदं कृत्स्नमेकांशेन स्थितो जगत्। (गी. १०.४२) इत्यादिषु श्रुतिस्मृतिषु ब्रह्मणो विकारवर्ति स्वरूपं प्रतिपादितम्। सर्वाणि भूतानि परस्य ब्रह्मणः सोपाधिकं स्वरूपम्। भूतानि हि द्विविधानि—स्थावराणि जङ्गमानि च। सर्वाणि पाञ्चभौतिकानि। तत्राऽऽकाशः पृथिवी चेति महाभूतद्वयं जडेऽपि विद्यते। अवशिष्टं महाभूतत्रयम् अग्निर्वायुर्जलं चेति चेतनानां भूतानाम् असाधारणो धर्मः। एतन्महाभूतत्रयमेव सर्वेषां भूतानां लक्षणम्। तत्र मध्यस्थो वायुः योगवाह इत्यग्निना युक्त उष्णो भवति, जलेन युक्तश्च शीतो भवति। तथा चोक्तं चरके—

योगवाहः परं वायुः संयोगादुभयार्थकृत्।
दाहकृत् तेजसा युक्तः शीतकृत् सोमसंश्रयात्॥ (चिकित्सास्थानम् ६.२८)

एवम् अग्निर्जलं चेति महाभूतद्वयमेव प्राधन्यतोऽवशिष्यते इति महाभूतद्वयात्मकान्येव सर्वाणि भूतानि—आग्नेयानि आप्यानि च। तैजसानि जलानि चेति वा। डलयोरभेद इति तैजसानि जडानि च। चेतनान्यचेतनानीति यावत्। चेतन आत्मा, शरीरं चाचेतनम्। तत्रात्मनः प्रत्यक्षेणाग्रहणात् शरीरस्य च प्रत्यक्षेण ग्रहणात् सर्वाणि भूतानि इदं सर्वमिति व्यपदिश्यन्ते। चेतनेनात्मना परित्यक्ते शरीरे अग्नितत्त्वव्यतिरेकेण चत्वारि महाभूतानि विद्यन्त एवेति अग्निरेव भगवान्—

अहं वैश्वानरो भूत्वा प्राणिनां देहमाश्रितः। (गी. १५.१४) इति स्मृतेः स्वयंज्योतिःस्वरूप

आत्मा। तथा चोक्तम् उत्तरमीमांसायां सूत्रे भाष्ये च—

अस्यैव चोपपत्तेरेष ऊष्मा। **(ब्र० सू० ४.२.११)**

'अस्यैव च सूक्ष्मस्य शारीरस्यैव ऊष्मा यमेतस्मिञ्छरीरे संस्पर्शेनोष्माणं विजानन्ति। तथा हि—मृतावस्थायामवस्थितेऽपि देहे विद्यमानेष्वपि च रूपादिदेहगुणेषु नोष्मा उपलभ्यते, जीवदवस्थायामेव तु उपलभ्यत इत्यत उपपद्यते प्रसिद्धशरीरव्यतिरिक्तव्यपाश्रय एवैष ऊष्मेति। तथा च श्रुतिः—

'उष्ण एव जीविष्यत् शीतो मरिष्यत्' इति। **(शां० भा० ४.२.११)**

आत्मा हि नित्योऽविनाशी च। भूतचतुष्टयात्मकं जलप्रधानं जडं शरीरमनित्यं विनाशी च। तस्मादिह सर्वं दृश्यं जगदविनाशिस्वरूपेण ब्रह्मेति आत्मेति पुरुष इति वासुदेव इति च श्रुतिभिरवधार्यते। इत्थमेकस्यैव पदार्थस्य दर्शनद्वयं सम्पद्यते—विवेकेन आत्मा, अविवेकेनेदं सर्वमिति।

(१)

ब्रह्मदर्शनमात्मैकत्वदर्शनं वा वैदिकम्, ब्रह्मणो वेदैकगम्यत्वात्, केवलायां चितिशक्तौ प्रकाशमानत्वाच्च। चितिर्ज्ञानं वेदाश्चेति पर्यायाः। अत एव ब्रह्म चिन्मयं विज्ञानघनं त्रयीमयं वेदमयं चोच्यते। ब्रह्मधर्मश्चिच्छक्तिः। धर्मेणैव धर्मी परिज्ञायत इति चिच्छक्त्या वेदैर्वा ब्रह्म ज्ञातुं शक्यते। शक्तिशक्तिमतोरभेदः सम्बन्धः। अयमेवार्थः **शास्त्रयोनित्वात्** इति सूत्रेण (ब्र-सू. १.१.३) ज्ञाप्यते। शास्त्रं वेदाः चितिशक्तिर्वा योनिः कारणं प्रमाणमस्य ब्रह्मणो यथावत् स्वरूपाधिगमे। शास्त्रस्य वेदानां चितिशक्तेर्योनिः कारणं ब्रह्म। व्युत्थाने आनन्दांशादेव चितिशक्तेरुद्भवः, समाधौ आनन्दांशे चितिशक्तेर्विलयश्च। श्रुतेरक्षुण्णं श्रूयमाणत्वाद्। अस्मिन् पक्षे प्रत्यक्षं प्रमाणं वेदाः स्वतःप्रमाणं च।

अस्य सर्वस्य दृश्यस्य विषयीभूतस्य जगतो दर्शनमनात्मदर्शनं वा अवैदिकं तार्किकं च, वेदनिरपेक्षप्रमाणविषयत्वात्। अवैदिकास्तार्किका द्विविधाः—तर्कानुकूलं वेदान् शब्दप्रमाणत्वेन प्रमाणयन्तो भूतेन्द्रियात्मकस्य दृश्यस्यापवर्जनानन्तरं देहव्यतिरिक्तस्य चिदात्मनोऽस्तित्वं मोक्षकाले प्रत्यक्षीकुर्वाणा भोगापवर्गवादिनो वैदिकभिन्ना वैदिकसदृशाः। वेदानप्रमाणयन्तो देहव्यतिरिक्तस्य चिदात्मनोऽस्तित्वमनङ्गीकुर्वन्तः अपवर्गवादिनो भोगवादिनश्च वेदबाह्याः।

(२)

ब्रह्मदर्शनं देवानाम्। देहात्मदर्शनं इदं सर्वमिति दृश्यस्य जगतो वा दर्शनमसुराणाम्। तथा हि—

देवाश्च वा असुराश्च। उभये प्राजापत्याः पस्पृधिरे।

(मा. श. १.२.५.१; ५.१.१.१; ११.१.८.१)

द्वया ह प्राजापत्याः। देवाश्चासुराश्च, ततः कानीयसा एव देवा ज्यायसा असुरास्त एषु लोकेष्वस्पर्धन्त। (मा. बृ. १.१.१; १.३.१)

इति प्राजापत्यानां भूतानां देवासुरविभागः, तेषु स्पर्धा च श्रूयते। गीताशास्त्रेऽपि—

द्वौ भूतसर्गौ लोकेऽस्मिन् दैव आसुर एव च। (१६.६)

इति लोके सृज्यमानानि भूतानि दैवासुरसम्पद्युक्तानि प्रोक्तानि। सर्वेषां भूतानां द्वैविध्योपपत्तेः। विभागोऽयं सनातनः, इदानीमपि लोकेषु दर्शनात्। भगवता स्वयमेवायं विभागः सविस्तरं गीताशास्त्रे षोडशाध्याये प्रपञ्चितः। दैवी सम्पदुपादानार्थमासुरीसम्पच्च परिवर्जनार्थं महता कौशल्येन प्रदर्शिता।

तत्र देवानामिन्द्रो विरोचनश्चासुराणां ब्रह्मज्ञानार्थं प्रजापतिं जग्मतुः। प्रजापतिना प्रथमं देहात्मवाद एव प्रोक्तः। विरोचनेन च यथाश्रुतं गृहीतः, असुरेभ्यश्च प्रोक्तः। असुरास्तेन अनात्मवादिनः संवृत्ताः। इन्द्रेण तु यथाश्रुतं न गृहीतः। पुनःपुनरागत्य एकशतं वर्षाणि ब्रह्मचर्येण प्रजापतिं परितोष्य ततो ब्रह्मज्ञानं गृहीतम्। देवेभ्यश्च प्रोक्तमिति देवा ब्रह्मवादिनः संवृत्ताः इति छान्दोग्ये अष्टमाध्याये श्रूयते। तत आरभ्यैव अनात्मवादोऽसुराणाम्, आत्मवादश्च देवानामिति विभागः प्रवृत्तः।

दिवु क्रीडा-विजिगीषा-व्यवहार-द्युति-स्तुति-मोद-मद-स्वप्न-कान्ति-गतिषु (११०७ सि० कौ०) इति। दीव्यन्तीति देवाः। **पचादिषु पाठात्** (३.१.१३४ पा० सू०) अच्। द्युतिमन्तो द्योतमाना वा देवाः। द्योतमानत्वं च स्वयंज्योतिःस्वरूपेण आत्मनैव। शोभनं राजन्ते इति सुराः। राज्दीप्तौ। **अन्येभ्योऽपि** (वा० ३.२.१०१) इति डः। न सुरा असुराः सुरविरुद्धाः, देहात्मवादिनो जडास्तामसा वा।

(३)

ब्रह्मणोऽविनाशित्वाद् अनुच्छित्तिधर्मत्वात् **अस्तीत्येवोपलब्धव्यः।** (कठ० ६.१३) इति श्रुतेश्च नित्यमस्तित्वम्। अत एव ब्रह्मवादिन आस्तिकाः।

सर्वं परिदृश्यमानं जगद् विनाशीत्यनित्यम्। आद्यन्तवच्च। पूर्वं नासीत् भविष्ये च न स्यात्। कालद्वये अभावाद् वर्तमानकाले एव केवलमस्तित्वदर्शनाद् भावस्याप्युभयतोऽभावेन ग्रस्तत्वाद् ब्रह्मण्येकस्मिन् अविद्याध्यस्तं जगद् वर्तमानकालेऽपि नास्तीत्येव उच्यते। तेन अनात्मवादिनो नास्तिकाः। आत्मनोऽस्तित्वाङ्गीकाराभावात् जगदसत्यमप्रतिष्ठितं च भवति। तथा चोक्तं गीतायाम्—

असत्यमप्रतिष्ठं ते जगदाहुरनीश्वरम्। (१६.१) **इति।**

(४)

ब्रह्मणो ध्रियमाणत्वाद्, अत एवाविनाशित्वाद् ब्रह्म धर्मः। जगतोऽध्रियमाणत्वात्, अत एव विनाशित्वात् जगदधर्मः। अत एव ब्रह्मवादिनो धार्मिकाः। जडवादिनोऽधार्मिकाः कामुका वा।

ब्रह्मदर्शने ब्रह्मणोऽजत्वादविनाशित्वादत एव नित्यत्वाद् उत्पत्तिप्रलयचिन्ता नास्ति। अनुत्पद्यमानत्वादत एव अकार्यत्वाच्च कारणविचारोऽपि नास्ति।

इदं सर्वमित्यनात्मदर्शनम्। इदं सर्वं परिदृश्यमानं जगत् कार्यत्वात् कथमुत्पन्नं कस्माच्चोत्पन्नमिति जगत्-कारणवादः समुज्जृम्भते। वेदबाह्या अवैदिकाश्च सर्वेऽपि तार्किकाः सप्रमाणं जगत्कारणं तर्कयन्ति। तथापि न तत्र कस्याप्यैकमत्यमिति महदाश्चर्यम्। ऐकमत्याभावात् तार्किकाणां विभिन्ना जगत्कारणवादाः प्रवर्तन्ते। सर्वेऽप्येते वादिनो महताऽभिनिवेशेन परतन्त्रसिद्धान्तान् दूषयित्वा स्वसिद्धान्तं प्रतिष्ठापयन्ति। एवं तार्किकाणां सर्वेऽपि जगत्कारणवादा दूषिताः खण्डिताश्च भवन्तीति तेषु प्रामाण्यं न प्रतिष्ठते। तार्किकाः परस्परमेवं दूषयित्वा जगत्कारणवादस्तर्केण सर्वथा दुरुपपाद इत्येव साधयन्ति। तर्केणैव कार्यकारणभावस्य अप्रतिष्ठितत्वात् कार्यकारणभाव एव जगदन्तरेण प्रतिष्ठते इत्येव निगमयन्ति। अत एव ब्रह्मवादिनां तैः सार्धं विवादस्य प्रसङ्ग एव नोपतिष्ठते। अत एवोक्तं गौडपादाचार्यैः।

भूतस्य जातिमिच्छन्ति वादिनः केचिदेव हि।
अभूतस्यापरे धीरा विवदन्तः परस्परम्॥

भूतं न जायते किञ्चिदभूतं नैव जायते।
विवदन्तोऽद्वया ह्येवमजातिं ख्यापयन्ति ते॥

ख्याप्यमानामजातिं तैरनुमोदामहे वयम्।
विवदामो न तैः सार्धमविवादं निबोधत॥ **(गौ. का. ४.३-५)**

ब्रह्मसूत्रेषु उपन्यस्तो जगत्कारणवादो ब्रह्मात्मभावप्रतिपादनपर एव, न सृष्टिप्रतिपादनपर इति स्थाने स्थाने आचार्यैर्भाष्ये उक्तम्। तथा हि—

'अपि च यदा तत्त्वमसीत्येवंजातीयकेन अभेदनिर्देशेन अभेदः प्रतिबोधितो अपगतं भवति तदा जीवस्य संसारित्वं ब्रह्मणश्च स्रष्टृत्वम्। समस्तस्य मिथ्याज्ञानविजृम्भितस्य भेदव्यवहारस्य सम्यग्ज्ञानेन बाधितत्वात्। तत्र कुत एव सृष्टिः, कुतो वा हिताकरणादयो दोषाः? अविद्याप्रत्युपस्थापितनामरूपकृतकार्यकारणसङ्घातोपाध्य-विवेककृता हि भ्रान्तिः हिताकरणादिलक्षणः संसारो न तु परमार्थतोऽस्तीत्यसकृदवोचाम। जन्ममरणच्छेदन-भेदनाद्यभिमानवत्।' (शां. भा. २.१.२२)

'न चेयं परमार्थविषया सृष्टिश्रुतिः। अविद्याकल्पित-नामरूपव्यवहारगोचरत्वात् ब्रह्मात्मभावप्रतिपादनपरत्वाच्चेत्येतदपि नैव विस्मर्तव्यम्।' (२.१.३३)

'आत्मैकत्ववादे जगदेव नास्ति। का तस्योत्पत्तिचिन्ता। अत एवाचार्यैः **वैषम्यनैर्घृण्याधिकरणं** (ब्र.सू.२.१.३४-३६) श्रुतिप्रामाण्येन यथाकथञ्चित् प्रस्थापितमपि '**तत्तु समन्वयात्**' इति सूत्रे भाष्ये (ब्र. सू. १.१.४) '**पत्युरसामञ्जस्यात्**। इति सूत्रे भाष्ये (२.२.३७) प्रत्याख्यातम्।'

आत्मैकत्ववादे एकमद्वितीयं कूटस्थं नित्यं च ब्रह्म। श्रुतिभिर्ब्रह्मव्यतिरिक्तस्य प्रपञ्चस्य निराकरणाद् ब्रह्ममात्रपरिशेषाच्च एक एव पदार्थः। पदार्थान्तरस्याभावात् कामभेदानां धर्मार्थकाममोक्षाणां भोगापवर्गवादिभिर्द्वैतिभिः परिकल्पितानां स्थानमेव नास्ति। ब्रह्मैव धर्मी। तस्याविनाशित्वाद् अनुच्छिन्नधर्मत्वात् तस्मिन्नधर्माभावः। केवलं धर्म एव। ब्रह्मणो नित्यं ध्रियमाणत्वाद् अवतिष्ठमानत्वाद्वा ब्रह्म धर्मरूपमेव। अभेदोपचाराद् धर्म इत्येव व्यपदिश्यते। अत एव ब्रह्मवादो धर्मवाद इत्याख्यायते। अत्र धर्मी सनातन इति धर्मोऽपि सनातन उच्यते। अयं धर्मधर्मिविचारो वैदिकैः सर्वत्र नित्यानित्येषु पदार्थेषु प्रवर्तितः। अनन्तानि च धर्मिशास्त्राणि निर्मितानि। भोगापवर्गवादस्य केवलापवर्गवादस्य भोगवादस्य स्वभाववादस्य च बहुभिः प्रचारणात् स्वीकाराच्च तानि सर्वाणि शास्त्राणि नष्टानि नाशितानि च। केवलं भोगापवर्गप्रस्थापकानि शास्त्राणि प्रवर्तन्ते। धर्मनाशे धर्मिनाशो धर्मप्रतिष्ठायां धर्मिप्रतिष्ठेति धर्मिप्रतिष्ठार्थं सर्वत्र धर्मप्रतिष्ठापनमेव वैदिकानां धर्मः संवृत्तः। धर्मविचारार्थं धर्मी एक एवापेक्ष्यत इति एकत्वे अद्वितीयत्वे च धर्मविचारः। द्वैते भोगविचारः भोक्ता भोग्यश्चेति पदार्थद्वयनिष्ठत्वात्।

वेदोक्तस्य धर्मधर्मिणोर्विचारार्थमेव मीमांसाशास्त्रं प्रवृत्तम्। पूर्वमीमांसायाम् **अथातो धर्मजिज्ञासा** (पू० मी० १.१.१) इति धर्मविचार आरब्धः। उत्तरमीमांसायां च **अथातो ब्रह्मजिज्ञासा** इति (ब्र. सू. १.१.१) धर्मिविचार उपक्रान्तः। धर्मी एकमेवाद्वितीयं ब्रह्म। तस्याप्रमेयत्वात् प्रथमं धर्मजिज्ञासैव। धर्मश्च देहोपाधिकश्चिदात्मा। **स्वरूपप्रतिष्ठा वा चितिशक्तिः** (यो. सू. ४.३४) इति चितिशक्तौ देहोपाधिके चिदात्मनि स्वरूपावस्थाने वा योगदर्शनस्य परिसमाप्तिदर्शनात्।

ब्रह्मणो विकारवर्ति प्रमेयं रूपमेव धर्मशब्देनोच्यते। तच्च **पादोऽस्य विश्वा भूतानि** (मा. सं. ३१.३) इति मन्त्र एवोक्तम्। विषयोऽयं भावनोपनिषद्भाष्ये भास्कररायैः स्वसम्प्रदायानुसारं परिष्कृतः। तथा हि—

'**निरुपाधिकी संविदेव कामेश्वरः।** **(भावनोप०, २६)**

"उपाधिरहितं शुद्धं चैतन्यमेव बिन्दुरूपः कामेश्वरः। 'संविद् कामेश्वरः स्मृतः' इत्युपबृंहणात्।" (भाष्यम्, २६)

सदानन्दपूर्णा स्वात्मैव परदेवता ललिता **(भावनोप०, २७)**

"संविदो निरुपाधिकत्वविशेषणबलात् तदङ्कनिलयायाः परदेवतायाः किञ्चिदुपाधिविशिष्टत्वमात्रेण ततो भिन्नतयोपास्यत्वम्। तादृशश्च स्वात्मैव। स्वाभिन्न एव

परदेवता उपास्तिरूपज्ञानविशेषनिरूपितमुख्यविशेष्यताशालिनी। तामेव असाधारणनाम्ना निर्दिशति ललितेति। अत्र सदानन्दपूर्णेत्युपाधिकथनम्। तेन अन्तःकरणावच्छिन्नस्य न ललितात्वं तस्योपासककोटौ प्रवेशात्। अत एव स्वात्मेत्युक्तम्। स्वस्योपासकस्य आत्माऽन्तर्यामीति तदर्थत्वात्। इत्थं च एक एवात्मा अन्तःकरणोपाधिकः सन्नुपासको भवति। सत्त्वचित्त्वानन्दत्वरूप-धर्मत्रयविशिष्टवेषेण ललिता भवत्युपास्या। धर्मत्रयविनिर्मुक्तं धर्मिमात्रमुपास्यदेवताधारभूतः कामेश्वरो भवतीति विवेकः।......" (भावनोपनिषद्भाष्यम्, २७) "अत्रेदं गुरुमुखैकवेद्यं रहस्यम्। निरुपाधिकपदेन केवलत्वस्य सदानन्दपूर्णपदेन धर्मविशिष्टत्वस्य च कथनेन विशिष्टकेवलयोरवयवावयविनोरिव अयुतसिद्धयोस्तादात्म्यरूप एव सम्बन्धः न, संयोगादिरूपो भेदघटितः"... (भावनोपनिषद्भाष्यम्, २८)

आत्मनो देहपरिच्छिन्नस्य ब्रह्मणश्च धर्मधर्मिणोरभेदः सम्बन्धः। तयोरनन्यत्वम्—

तदनन्यत्वमारम्भणशब्दादिभ्यः (ब्र० सू० २.१.१४)

इत्यारम्भणाधिकरणे प्रस्थापितम्। धर्मनाशे धर्मिनाशः। यद्यप्यात्मनो नाशो न भवति अविनाशित्वात्; तथापि देहात्मवादे अविद्यया समुत्थिते देहव्यतिरिक्तस्यात्मनोऽस्तित्वस्य भानमेव न भवति। अयमेवाविद्यया आत्मनाश उच्यते। अत एव गीताशास्त्रे—

नष्टात्मानोऽल्पबुद्धयः।

इत्यसुरा नष्टात्मान उक्ताः। य एवमात्मनाशं कुर्वन्ति, ते आत्महन इत्युच्यन्ते। तथा चोक्तम् ईशोपनिषदि—

असुर्या नाम ते लोका अन्धेन तमसाऽऽवृताः।
तांस्ते प्रेत्यापि गच्छन्ति ये के चात्महनो जनाः॥ (ईश. ३)

आत्मनाशे चैवमन्तर्यामित्वेन प्रतीतस्य ब्रह्मणोऽपि नाशो भवति। ब्रह्मणः प्रतीतिरेव न भवति। धर्मप्रतिष्ठायां धर्मिप्रतिष्ठेति सिद्धान्तात् देहात्मवादे नष्टे आत्मबोधे संवृत्ते आत्मप्रतिष्ठायां तस्मिन्नेवात्मनि प्रथममनन्यत्वेन अन्तर्यामित्वेन च विद्यया ब्रह्मप्रतीतिर्भवति। इयमेव ब्रह्मप्रतिष्ठा। अत एवोक्तं गीताशास्त्रे—

ब्रह्मणो हि प्रतिष्ठाऽहममृतस्याव्ययस्य च।
शाश्वतस्य च धर्मस्य सुखस्यैकान्तिकस्य च॥ (गी० १४.२७)

अत्राहंशब्देन ब्रह्मणो विकारवर्ति एकमद्वितीयं स्वरूपमीश्वर इति व्यपदिश्यमानं सोपाधिकं सगुणं च गृह्यते। तत्रैव ब्रह्मणः प्रतिष्ठा। देहोपाधिके आत्मन्येव ब्रह्मप्रतीतिरनन्यत्वेन भवति। तथा च श्रुतिः—

आत्मन्येवात्मानं पश्येत्। (बृ० उ० ४.२.२८)

'अमृतस्याव्ययस्य चे'ति (गीता १४.२७) ब्रह्मधर्मा उक्ताः। शाश्वतस्य नित्यस्य धर्मस्यापि प्रतिष्ठा सोपाधिक आत्मैव। तथा 'ऐकान्तिकस्य सुखस्यापि देहोपाधिकः सगुण आत्मा विकारवर्तिस्वरूपो वा ईश्वरःप्रतिष्ठा'। अत्र सुखशब्दःप्रयुक्तो नानन्दशब्दः। आनन्दस्तु ब्रह्मधर्म

एव। ब्रह्मप्रतीतावेव आनन्दांशस्य प्राकट्यं भवति। श्लोकोऽयं परवैराग्यप्रतिपादनपरे चतुर्दशाध्याये उक्तः।

तत्परं पुरुषख्यातेर्गुणवैतृष्ण्यम्। **(यो० सू० १.१६)**

इति परवैराग्यं गुणातीतत्वं वा देहव्यतिरिक्ताऽऽत्मदर्शनेनैव जायते। आत्मबोधानन्तरं महावाक्यनामुपदेशेन तेषां मननेन च ब्रह्मप्रतीतिरिति विकारवर्तिब्रह्मणो रूपमधिकृत्यैवायं श्लोकः।

ब्रह्मप्रतीत्यनन्तरं अहमात्मनो ब्रह्मणा साकं सत्तांशेन चिदंशेन आनन्दांशेन मीलने तादात्म्योऽभेदो वा सम्बन्धः सुस्थिरो भवति। देहपातानन्तरमेकत्वं सम्पद्यते। यावद्देहोपाधिर्विद्यते, तावदात्मा ब्रह्म चेति पदार्थद्वयमनन्यत्वेन अभेदसम्बन्धेन वाऽवतिष्ठते इति तत्र धर्म-धर्मि-सम्बन्धः। आत्मा च ब्रह्मधर्मो भवति। तस्माद्धर्मशब्देन आत्मा गृह्यते। स च सच्चिद्रूपः। अत एव चिदात्मेति व्यपदिश्यते। आनन्दांशस्य ब्रह्मधर्मत्वादात्मैकत्व-बोधप्राकट्यम्। आत्मैकत्वप्रतिपत्तिः ब्रह्मप्रतिपत्तिर्वा वेदान्तशास्त्रादेव। तस्मादात्मजिज्ञासैव पूर्वमीमांसाया विषयः। ब्रह्मजिज्ञासा च उत्तरमीमांसायाः। धर्मस्य आत्मनो वा लक्षणम्—

चोदनालक्षणोऽर्थो धर्मः। **(पू० मी० १.१.२)**

अत्र धर्मशब्देन देहपरिच्छिन्न आत्मा उच्यते, तस्यैव ब्रह्मधर्मत्वात्। स च अर्थ्यमानत्वादर्थो भवति। तथा च श्रुतिः—

आत्मा वा अरे द्रष्टव्यः श्रोतव्यो मन्तव्यो निदिध्यासितव्यः (मा० बृ० २.४.५)

तस्य लक्षणम् अस्तित्वद्योतकोऽसाधारणधर्मश्चोदना। 'इदं कार्यमिदं न कार्यम्' इति चोदयत्येवात्मा। अयं हि तस्यासाधारणो धर्मः सर्वैरनुभूयते। आत्मनश्चोदनेयं सर्वैः श्रूयत इति सा श्रुतिरिति व्यपदिश्यते। आत्मन इदमपौरुषेयं वाक्यं श्रूयत इति श्रुतेरपौरुषेयत्वम्। प्रत्यक्षं श्रूयत इति श्रुतेः प्रत्यक्षत्वम्। अत एव उत्तरमीमांसायां श्रुतिप्रामाण्यस्य सूत्रकारेण भगवता प्रत्यक्षशब्देनैव निर्देशः कृतः। तथा हि—

दर्शयतश्चैवं प्रत्यक्षानुमाने। **(ब्र० सू० ४.४.२०)**

आचार्यैश्च—'दर्शयतश्च विकारावर्तित्वं परस्य ज्योतिषः श्रुति-स्मृती' इति श्रुतिशब्दनैव प्रत्यक्षशब्दो व्याख्यातः। वैदिकानां श्रुतिः शब्दो वेदो वा प्रत्यक्षमेव प्रमाणम्। विधि-निषेधात्मकः शब्दश्चिदात्मनः श्रूयते। चित् ज्ञानं वेद इति पर्यायाः। तस्माद् वेदात्मान एव श्रूयते। वेदानामेवेदं वाक्यं श्रूयते। इयं चोदनैव आत्मास्तित्वे प्रमाणमिति चोदनालक्षण आत्मा उच्यते। तथापि—

अवजानन्ति मां मूढा मानुषीं तनुमाश्रितम्। **(गीता ९.११)**

इति कामान्धैरसुरैः मानुषीं तनुमाश्रितस्याऽऽत्मनः तद्विधिनिषेधरूपस्य चोदनारूपस्य वाऽपौरुषेयस्य श्रुतिवाक्यस्य, अवज्ञैव क्रियते। अत एव मनुनोक्तम्—

माऽवमंस्थाः स्वमात्मानं नृणां साक्षिणमुत्तमम्। (८.८४)

तथा च—**एकोऽहमस्मीत्यात्मानं यत्त्वं कल्याण मन्यसे।**

नित्यं स्थितस्ते हृद्येषः पुण्यपापेक्षिता मुनिः। (८.९१)

यमो वैवस्वतो देवो यस्तवैष हृदि स्थितः।

तेन चेदविवादस्ते मा गङ्गां मा कुरून् गमः॥ (८.९२)

देवस्य त्वा सवितुः प्रसवे (मा० सं० १.१०, २१, २४; ५.२२,२६; ६.१,९,३०; ९.३०,३८; ११.९,२८; १८.३७; २०.३; ३७.१, ३८.१)। **देवः सवितः प्रसुव यज्ञम्** (मा० सं० ९.१; ११.७; ३०.१) इत्यादिभिः मन्त्रवर्णैः वेदात्मनः सवितुश्चोदनानुसारमेव विद्यावतां वैदिकानां क्रियाः प्रवर्तन्ते, न स्वेच्छया। कामचाराभावात् आत्मनश्चोदनानुसारमेव क्रियाप्रवृत्तेरियं क्रिया राग-द्वेष-मोहैः विमुक्ता निर्दोषा धर्मरूपैव। फलमस्याः कर्मगाम्येव, न कर्तृगामि।

नवानामात्मगुणानामत्यन्तानुत्पादो मोक्ष इति काणादाः (शां० भा० २.३.५०) इति काणाददर्शनानुसारमेते वैदिका मुक्ता एव। योगदर्शनानुसारमपि **ततः क्लेशकर्मनिवृत्तिः** (यो० सू० ४.३०) इति क्लेश-कर्मनिवृत्त्यनन्तरमेव चोदनानुसारं धर्मानुष्ठानमिति वेदितव्यम्।

आत्मैकत्वपक्षे कामस्याभावात् काम एव नास्ति। कामश्च नात्मधर्मः। बुद्धिपर्यन्तमेव कामः। तस्मादपीयं क्रिया धर्मरूपैव। स्वेच्छाचाराभावाद् आत्मनश्चोदनानुसारं क्रियाप्रवृत्तेरियं क्रियैव कर्मसंन्यासः।

कर्मसन्न्यासो गीताशास्त्रे विस्तरेण प्रपञ्चितः। कर्मसन्न्यासेऽस्मिन् **काम्यानां कर्मणां न्यासं संन्यासं कवयो विदुः** (गी० १८.२), **सर्वकर्माणि मयि संन्यस्य** (१८.५७) इति प्रकारद्वयरूपे। **करिष्ये वचनं तव** (गी० १८.७३) इत्येव धर्मो भवति। भगवत आत्मन्यन्तर्यामित्वेन अनन्यत्वेन अवस्थितस्य चोदनानुसरणमेव धर्मः। येषामविद्यया आत्मबोधो नास्ति तेषां भगवतः परब्रह्मणो विज्ञानघनायाश्चितिशक्तेः वेदमय्यास्त्रयीरूपेण अवस्थितायाः चोदनानुसरणं धर्म इति तेषां गुरुपरम्परागतैः वेदैः प्रतिपादितो धर्मो भवति। इत्थं मीमांसासूत्रमिदं विद्याऽविद्याविषयभेदेन प्रकारद्वयेन द्वेधा व्याख्यायते विद्वदविद्वद्भूमिकानुसारेण। तथा चोक्तं गीताशास्त्रे (१६.२४)—

तस्माच्छास्त्रं प्रमाणं ते कार्याकार्यव्यवस्थितौ।

ब्रह्मविद्याप्रतिपादकं गुह्यतमं शास्त्रं पञ्चदशाध्यायपर्यन्तमुक्तं भगवता। षोडशाध्याये आत्मविमुखानामिदं सर्वं दृश्यं प्रत्यक्षीकुर्वाणानां देहात्मवादिनाम् असुराणामासुरीसम्पत्परिवर्जनाय अयमुपदेशः। वेदोक्तधर्मचर्ययैव कामनाशनेन वैराग्यप्राप्तौ आत्मबोधो भवतीति। इत्थं विद्यावतां कृते '**करिष्ये वचनं तव**' इति धर्मो व्यवस्थितः। अविद्यावतां कृते '**तस्माच्छास्त्रं प्रमाणं ते.....**' इति च भगवतोपदिष्टम्। एवं '**चोदनालक्षणोऽर्थो धर्मः**' इति सूत्रं गीताशास्त्रे द्वेधा व्याख्यातम्। इत्थं ब्रह्मवादे चिदात्मा धर्मो ब्रह्म च धर्मीति स्थितम्।

अनात्मवादे जगतो विनाशित्वात् जगत उत्पत्तिस्थिति-प्रलया वितर्क्यन्ते। जगत इत्थमध्रियमाणत्वात् अनवतिष्ठमानत्वात् च जगदधर्मस्वरूपमेव अधर्म इत्युच्यते। तस्माद् आत्मैकत्ववादो ब्रह्मवादो वा धर्मवादः, अनात्मवादो जडवादो वाऽधर्मवादः। देहात्मवादिभिः अधर्मस्यैव धर्मत्वेन नयनाद् अधर्म एव नीतिः। अविद्यादिपञ्चपर्वणो विपर्ययस्य स्वरूपमेव नीतिः, कामवादः पुरुषार्थवादो वा।

देहात्मवादे कामो देहधर्म इति कामः पुरुषार्थो भवति। देहस्य असाधारणो धर्मस्त्रैगुण्यं प्रकृतिश्चेति कामोऽपि त्रैगुण्यानुरोधेन त्रिविधः सम्पद्यते। तथा चोक्तं मनुना—

तमसो लक्षणं कामो रजसस्त्वर्थ उच्यते।
सत्त्वस्य लक्षणं धर्मः श्रैष्ट्यमेषां यथोत्तरम्॥ (२.३८)

सत्त्वं ज्ञानं तमोऽज्ञानं रागद्वेषौ रजः स्मृतम्।
एतद् व्याप्तिमदेतेषां सर्वभूताश्रितं वपुः॥ (२.२६)

त्रिविधोऽयं कामो धर्मोऽर्थः कामश्चेति क्रमेण व्यपदिश्यते। काम्यं जगत् सुख-दुःख-मोहात्मकम्। कामफलं भोगः। स च सुख-दुःखान्यतरसाक्षात्कारः। तत्र कामो नाम इष्टार्थप्रार्थना। तामसः कामो नाम अनिर्ज्ञातप्राप्येष्टार्थप्रार्थना। निर्ज्ञातप्राप्येष्टार्थप्रार्थना अर्थः। राजसः कामो वा। दृष्टोपायैरशक्यप्राप्तेः इष्टार्थस्य वैदिकैरुपायैः प्राप्तेरिच्छा सात्त्विकः कामो धर्मो वा। तेनास्मिन् पक्षे इह भोगाय अमुत्र भोगाय वा क्रियमाणं काम्यं वैदिकं कर्म 'धर्म' इति व्यपदिश्यते। अवैदिकानामेवं धर्मोऽपि काम एव। वैदिकानां पुनः कामोऽपि धर्म एवेति विशेषः। देहो जडस्वरूपस्तमःस्वरूपो वेति तामसा जडाश्च देहात्मवादिनः। ते हि काममधर्मं धर्ममिति मन्यन्ते। तथा चोक्तम् ईश्वरगीतासु— (१८.३२)

अधर्मं धर्ममिति या मन्यते तमसाऽऽवृता।
सर्वार्थान् विपरीतांश्च बुद्धिः सा पार्थ तामसी॥

काम आत्मधर्म इति वैशेषिकाः। बुद्धिः, सुखम्, दुःखम्, इच्छा, द्वेषः, प्रयत्नः, धर्मः, अधर्म इत्यष्टौ आत्मगुणास्तैः प्रोक्ताः। तथा हि—

सुखदुःखेच्छाद्वेषप्रयत्नाश्चात्मनो लिङ्गानि। (वै० सू० ३.२.४)
इच्छाद्वेषप्रयत्नसुखदुःखज्ञानान्यात्मनो लिङ्गमिति। (न्या० सू० १.१.१०)

चरकेऽपि (शारीरस्थाने ४.१.७२)—

इच्छा द्वेषः सुखं दुःखं प्रयत्नश्चेतना धृतिः।
बुद्धिः स्मृतिरहङ्कारो लिङ्गानि परमात्मनः॥

इति वैशेषिकसिद्धान्त एवाऽनूदितः। सुश्रुते (शारीरस्थाने १.१७) च तथैवोक्तम्। यथा—

तस्य सुखदुःखे इच्छाद्वेषौ प्रयत्नः प्राणापानावुन्मेषनिमेषौ बुद्धिर्मनः सङ्कल्पो विचारणा स्मृतिर्विज्ञानमध्यवसायो विषयोपलब्धिश्च गुणाः।

भगवता तु प्रत्याख्यातोऽयं वैशेषिकसिद्धान्तो गीताशास्त्रे। तथा हि—

इच्छा द्वेषः सुखं दुःखं सङ्घातश्चेतना धृतिः।
एतत् क्षेत्रं समासेन सविकारमुदाहृतम्॥ (१३.६)

इत्येते क्षेत्रस्य देहस्य धर्माः, न तु क्षेत्रज्ञस्य आत्मन इति। तार्किकैरेते आत्मधर्मत्वेन परिगणिताः। देहधर्मानिवैते आत्मन्यध्यस्यन्ति। आत्माऽधर्मान् आत्मधर्मत्वेन परिगणयन्तीति देहव्यतिरिक्तस्य आत्मनोऽस्तित्वमङ्गीकुर्वाणा अप्येते अनात्मवादिनो नास्तिका असुरा अवैदिका इति चोच्यन्ते, आत्मनो यथार्थज्ञानाभावात्। तामसत्वादेषाम् आत्मनो यथार्थज्ञानं न भवति, धर्मज्ञानाभावादात्मनः। आत्माऽधर्मानिव आत्मधर्मत्वेनाभिमन्यन्त इत्याऽऽत्मबोध एषां नास्ति। तस्माद् देहव्यतिरिक्तेऽप्यात्मनि अभ्युपगम्यमाने एते आत्मनः स्वरूपज्ञानाभावात् आत्मनो बोधाभावाच्च अनात्मविद एवोच्यन्ते।

बृहदारण्यकोपनिषद्भाष्ये आचार्यैरपि प्रत्याख्यातोऽयं पक्षः। तथाहि—

यथेच्छादीनामप्यात्मधर्मं कल्पयन्तो वैशेषिका नैयायिकाश्च उपनिषच्छास्त्रार्थेन न सङ्गच्छन्त इति। (बृ० भा० ४.३.२२)

एवं चात्र पक्षद्वयम्। कामो देहधर्म इति वैदिकानां पक्षः। काम आत्मधर्म इति तार्किकाणां पक्षः। तार्किकाणां पक्षे कामस्य फलं सुखं दुःखं च। सुखदुःखान्यतरसाक्षात्कारो भोगो वा। सोऽपि आत्मधर्म एव। सुखदुःखहेतू पुण्यापुण्ये चात्मधर्म एव। धर्मात् सुखमधर्माद् दुःखमिति सिद्धान्तात्। अनुक्षणविनाशिनः कर्मणः कालान्तरभावि सुखं दुःखं वा फलं भवतीत्यनुपपन्नम्। अभावाद्भावानुत्पत्तेः। अपूर्वस्याचेतनस्य प्रवृत्त्यनुपपत्तेः। अत ईश्वरः फलं ददातीति—

फलमत उपपत्तेः। (ब्र० सू० ३.२.३८) इति फलाधिकरणे उत्तरमीमांसायां सिद्धान्तितम्। सृज्यमान-प्राणिधर्माधर्मापेक्षया ईश्वरः फलं ददातीति ईश्वरस्य वैषम्य-नैर्घृण्यदोषप्रसक्तिः **वैषम्य-नैर्घृण्याधिकरणे** (ब्र० सू० २.१.३४-३६) परिहृता।

एतदुक्तं भवति—तार्किकाणां पक्षे सुखं दुःखं चात्मधर्मः। सुखदुःख-प्राप्तिकारणं पुण्यापुण्ये। सुखदुःख-फलप्रदाता च ईश्वरः। सिद्धान्तोऽयं तर्के प्रतिष्ठितः। तथापि पक्षेऽस्मिन्नाद्या सृष्टिस्तुल्यैव प्राप्नोति कर्माविभागात्। अत्र तर्केणोत्तरं दातुं न शक्यत इति सूत्रकारैः भाष्यकारैश्च **उपपद्यते चाप्युपलभ्यते च** (ब्र० सू० २.१.३६) इति सूत्रे श्रुतिप्रामाण्यमेव उपन्यस्तम्। श्रुतिप्रामाण्योपन्यासात् श्रुतिप्रामाण्यमन्तरा प्रमाणान्तरैः वैषम्यनैर्घृण्य-दोषपरिहारोऽशक्य एवेति ध्वनितम्। श्रौता एव श्रुतिप्रामाण्योपन्यासेन परिहारमङ्गीकरिष्यन्ति न तार्किका इति वैषम्य-नैर्घृण्यदोषस्तदवस्थ एव। तस्माद् देहात्मवादे प्रतिष्ठितोऽयं सिद्धान्तः प्रत्याख्यानयोग्य एव।

कामो देहधर्म इति वैदिकानां पक्षे तु सुख-दुःखान्यतरसाक्षात्कारो भोगोऽपि देहधर्म एव। तदर्थं हेतुत्वेन पुण्यापुण्यत्व-कल्पना फलप्रदत्वेन ईश्वराभ्युपगमोऽपि देहात्मवाद एव। आत्मवादे कामस्याभाव एव।

पाप्मानं प्रजहि ह्येनं ज्ञानविज्ञाननाशनम्।

इति गीताशास्त्रे (३.४१) ज्ञान-विज्ञाननाशनः तामसः कामो राजसश्चार्थरूपः कामः सर्वपापमूलभूतः हन्तव्य एवेत्युपदिष्टम्।

जहि शत्रुं महाबाहो कामरूपं दुरासदम्। (गी. ३.४३)

इत्यत्र सात्त्विकस्य कामस्य इहामुत्रभोगाय क्रियमाणस्य काम्यस्य धर्मस्यापि घात उक्तः। नहि कामो द्रव्यमिति कामस्य घातेन काम्यस्य जगत एव घात उक्तः। एवं निस्त्रैगुण्ये आत्मधर्मे अवस्थानमुक्तम्। मोक्षोऽपि बद्धस्य दुःखितस्य सात्त्विकः काम एवेति तस्यापि परित्याग उक्तः। एवं त्रिविधोऽपि कामः समूलघातं हत एव। एतेन तार्किकाणां धर्मार्थकाममोक्षाश्चतुर्विधाः पुरुषार्था भगवता समूलघातं घातिताः, वैदिकश्च धर्मधर्मि-सिद्धान्तः प्रस्थापित इति द्रष्टव्यम्।

कामो बुद्धिपर्यन्तमेवाऽवतिष्ठते। आत्मना साकं तस्य सम्बन्ध एव नास्तीति नात्मधर्मः। तथा हि ईश्वरगीतासु—

इन्द्रियाणि मनो बुद्धिरस्याधिष्ठानमुच्यते। (गी० ३.४०)

इति आत्मैकत्ववादे कामस्य आत्मधर्मत्वाभावात् सुखदुःखकल्पना तद्धेतुत्वेन पुण्यापुण्यकल्पना ईश्वराभ्युपगमश्च नास्ति। वैषम्य-नैर्घृण्यदोषपरिहारार्थं च संसारस्य अनादित्वकल्पनमपि नास्ति, संसारस्य मिथ्यात्वाभ्युपगमात्। वैषम्यनैर्घृण्याधिकरणं सूत्रकारैरुपन्यस्तमपि अविद्यावद्विषयमिति यथासूत्रं व्याख्याय स्थानद्वये प्रत्याख्यातमाचार्यैः स्वकीये भाष्ये, वैदिकश्च सिद्धान्तः प्रस्थापितः। तथा हि—

हीनमध्यमोत्तमभावेन हि प्राणिभेदान् विदधत ईश्वरस्य रागद्वेषादि-दोषप्रसक्तेरस्मदादिवदनीश्वरत्वं प्रसज्येत। प्राणिकर्मापेक्षितत्वाददोष इति चेन्न। कर्मेश्वरयोः प्रवर्त्य - प्रवर्तयितृत्वे इतरेतराश्रयदोषप्रसङ्गात्। न अनादित्वादिति चेन्न। वर्तमानकाल-वदतीतेष्वपि कालेष्वितरेतराश्रयदोषाविशेषाद् अन्ध-परम्परान्यायापत्तेः।

(शां० भा० २.२.३७)

न ह्यात्मनः शरीरात्माभिमानलक्षणं मिथ्याज्ञानं मुक्त्वाऽन्यतः सशरीरत्वं शक्यं कल्पयितुम्। नित्यमशरीरत्वमकर्मनिमित्तत्वादित्यवोचाम। तत्कृतधर्माधर्मनिमित्तं सशरीर-त्वमिति चेन्न। शरीरसम्बन्धस्यासिद्धत्वाद् धर्माधर्मयोरात्मकृतत्वासिद्धेः। शरीरसम्बन्धस्य धर्माधर्मयोस्तत्कृतत्वस्य चेतरेतराश्रयत्वप्रसङ्गादन्धपरम्परैषाऽ-नादित्वकल्पना। क्रियासमवायाभावाच्चात्मनः कर्तृत्वानुपपत्तेः। (शां० भा० १.१.४) इति।

योगसूत्रेऽपि—

क्लेशमूलः कर्माशयो दृष्टादृष्टजन्मवेदनीयः। (यो० सू०, २.१२.)
सति मूले तद्विपाको जात्यायुर्भोगाः। (यो० सू०, २.१३)
ते ह्लादपरितापफलाः पुण्यापुण्यहेतुत्वात्। (यो० सू०, २.१४)

इति अविद्यादिक्लेशमूलः कर्माशयस्तद्विपाको जात्यायुर्भोगास्तेषां फलं ह्लादः परितापश्चेत्युक्तम्। अविद्याभावे कर्माशयाभावो भोगाभावः सुखदुःखाभावश्च। तस्माद्विद्यावतामात्मवादिनां धर्मधर्मिवादः। प्रतिपदार्थमधर्मनाशनं धर्मप्रतिष्ठा च। तथा चोक्तं योगशास्त्रे—**प्रसंख्यानेऽप्यकुसीदस्य सर्वथा विवेकख्यातेर्धर्ममेघः समाधिः** (यो० सू० ४.२९)। **ततः क्लेशकर्मनिवृत्तिः**। (४.३०)।

अनात्मवादे सात्त्विकः कामः इहामुत्रभोगार्थं क्रियमाणं कर्मैव धर्मः। स चाधर्मोऽपि धर्म इत्युपचर्यते। फलमिहामुत्र भोगः। मीमांसकैः काम्यं कर्म निषिद्धमेव। नित्यनैमित्तिकस्यापि कर्मणो न ममेति **प्रवृत्तिदोषजनितोऽर्थः फलम्** (न्या० सू० १.१.२०) इति कर्तृगामिफलत्याग एव विहितः।

वस्तुतस्तु क्रियायाः फलं कर्मगाम्येव, न कर्तृगामि। क्रियायाः कर्तृगामिफलस्य हेतुः काम एव, न क्रिया। अत एव कामुकानां क्रियायाः अपि स्वेष्टस्य फलस्य कर्तृगामित्वमिच्छतां कृते फलत्यागोपदेशः। फलेच्छा फलप्राप्तिश्च क्रियाया अभिसन्धिपूर्वको विनिमय एव, न क्रियायाः फलम्। अत एव गीताशास्त्रे (१८.२)—

सर्वकर्मफलत्यागं प्राहुस्त्यागं विचक्षणाः।

इति नित्य-नैमित्तिकानामपि कर्मणां फलत्याग उक्तः। अत्र फलत्यागो नाम फलेच्छायास्त्यागः। क्रियाफलस्य कर्मगामित्वात् कर्तृगामित्वाभावात्। तथापि द्वैतिनां देहात्मवादिनां क्रियासु प्रवृत्तिर्न भवेदिति प्ररोचनार्थं नित्यनैमित्तिककर्मणामपि फलमर्थवादवाक्यैः श्रुत्या श्रावितम्।

तस्माद् धर्मस्य फलं धर्मिप्रतिष्ठैव। कर्मणः फलवत्त्वनियमात्। **फलयुक्तानि कर्माणि** (का० श्रौ० सू० १.१.२) इति सूत्रेण निर्धारितः क्रियाफलयोरविनाभावः सम्बन्धः। स च कर्मणा साकमेव। फलाश्रयं कर्म, व्यपाराश्रयः कर्तेति सिद्धान्तात्। क्रियाफलस्य कर्त्रा सह सम्बन्धभावात् कामुकैरेव क्रियाफलस्य कर्तृगामित्वसम्भावनात् कामनाशाय कर्मफलत्यागः सर्वत्र वैदिकानाम्। कर्म त्यागार्थं धर्मिप्रतिष्ठार्थमेव, नेष्टफलभोगार्थम्। गीताशास्त्रेऽपि पुरुषार्थरूपस्य धर्म इत्युपचर्यमाणस्य कामस्य निन्दैव कृता। तथाहि (गी० २.४२-४४)—

यामिमां पुष्पितां वाचं प्रवदन्त्यविपश्चितः।
वेदवादरताः पार्थ नान्यदस्तीति वादिनः॥

कामात्मानः स्वर्गपरा जन्मकर्मफलप्रदाम्।
क्रियाविशेषबहुलां भोगैश्वर्यगतिं प्रति॥

भोगैश्वर्यप्रसक्तानां तयाऽपहृतचेतसाम्।
व्यवसायात्मिका बुद्धिः समाधौ न विधीयते॥

अत्र मीमांसकमतं दूषितं भगवतेति न भ्रमितव्यम्। धर्मवादिभिः मीमांसकैर्निषिद्धमेव

काम्यं कर्म,न धर्म इति स्वीकृतम् । कामहतानामधर्मं धर्म इत्युपचरतां भोगापवर्गप्रतिष्ठापकानां पुरुषार्थवादिनां तार्किकाणामेव मतमत्र दूषितमित्यवगन्तव्यम् । ते हि भोगैश्वर्यप्रसक्ताः (गी. २.४४), त्यागिनो हि वैदिकाः धर्मप्रतिष्ठापकाः ।

कामहताकामहतानामानन्दपरम्परा

कामहतानाम् अनात्मवादिनामिह भोगः त्रैलोक्याधिपत्यप्राप्त्या सम्पद्यते । तथा हि—

पुराशुम्भनिशुम्भभ्यामसुराभ्यां शचीपतेः ।
त्रैलोक्यं यज्ञभागाश्च हता मदबलाश्रयात् ॥

मम त्रैलोक्यमखिलं मम देवा वशानुगाः ।
यज्ञभागानहं सर्वानुपाश्नामि पृथक् पृथक् ॥
सत्यमुक्तं त्वया नात्र मिथ्या किंचित् त्वयोदितम् ।
त्रैलोक्याधिपतिः शुम्भो निशुम्भश्चापि तादृशः ॥ (सप्तशती ५.१, ५९, ६७) इति ।

अमुत्र भोगश्च प्राजापत्यप्राप्त्या सम्पद्यते । कामहतानामिहामुत्र-भोगपरम्परा अकामहतानाम् आनन्दपरम्परा च बृहदारण्यके तैत्तिरीये च विस्पष्टं श्रूयते । तथा हि—

स यो मनुष्याणां राद्धः समृद्धो भवत्यन्येषामधिपतिः ।
स वै मानुष्यकैः कामैः सम्पन्नतमः स मनुष्याणां परम आनन्दः ॥३२ ॥

अथ ये शतं मनुष्याणामानन्दाः, स एकः पितृणां जितलोकानामानन्दः ॥३३ ॥

अथ ये शतं पितृणां जितलोकानामानन्दाः, स एकः कर्मदेवानामानन्दो ये कर्मणा देवत्वमभिसम्पद्यन्ते ॥३४ ॥

अथ ये शतं कर्मदेवानामानन्दाः, स एक आजानदेवानामानन्दो यश्च श्रोत्रियोऽवृजिनोऽकामहतः ॥३५ ॥

अथ ये शतमाजानदेवानामानन्दाः स एको देवलोक आनन्दो यश्च श्रोत्रियोऽवृजिनोऽकामहतः ॥३६ ॥

अथ ये शतं देवलोक आनन्दाः, स एको गन्धर्वलोक आनन्दो यश्च श्रोत्रियोऽवृजिनोऽकामहतः ॥३७ ॥

अथ ये शतं गन्धर्वलोक आनन्दाः, स एकः प्रजापतेरानन्दो यश्च श्रोत्रियोऽवृजिनोऽकामहतः ॥३८ ॥

अथ ये शतं प्रजापतिलोक आनन्दाः, स एको ब्रह्मलोक आनन्दो यश्च श्रोत्रियोऽवृजिनोऽकामहतः । एष ब्रह्मलोकः सम्राडिति हैतमनुशशासैतदमृतम् । सोऽहं भगवते सहस्रं ददामि । अत ऊर्ध्वं विमोक्षायैव ब्रूहीति ॥३९ ॥

(मा० बृ० उ० ४-१०-३२, ३९, का०बृ० ४.३.३३)

युवा स्यात् साधु युवाध्यायकः । आशिष्टो दृढिष्ठो बलिष्ठः । तस्येयं पृथिवी सर्वा

वित्तेन पूर्णा स्यात्। स एको मानुष आनन्दः। ते ये शतं मानुषा आनन्दाः, स एको मनुष्यगन्धर्वाणामानन्दः। श्रोत्रियस्य चाकामहतस्य।

ते ये शतं मनुष्यगन्धर्वाणामानन्दाः, स एको देवगन्धर्वाणामानन्दः। श्रोत्रियस्य चाकामाहतस्य। ते ये शतं देवगन्धर्वाणामानन्दाः,

स एकः पितृणां चिरलोकलोकानामानन्दः। श्रोत्रियस्य चाकामहतस्य।

ते ये शतं पितृणां चिरलोकलोकानामानन्दाः, स एक आजानजानां देवानामानन्दः। श्रोत्रियस्य चाकामहतस्य।

ते ये शतमाजानजानां देवानामानन्दाः, स एकः कर्मदेवानां देवानामानन्दः। ये कर्मणा देवानपियन्ति। श्रोत्रियस्य चाकामहतस्य।

ते ये शतं कर्मदेवानामनन्दाः, स एको देवानामानन्दः। श्रोत्रियस्य चाकामहतस्य।

ते ये शतं देवानामानन्दाः, स एक इन्द्रस्यानन्दः। श्रोत्रियस्य चाकामहतस्य।

ते ये शतमिन्द्रस्यानन्दाः, स एको बृहस्पतेरानन्दः। श्रोत्रियस्य चाकामहतस्य।

ते ये शतं बृहस्पतेरानन्दाः, स एकः प्रजापतेरानन्दः। श्रोत्रियस्य चाकामहतस्य।

ते ये शतं प्रजापतेरानन्दाः, स एको ब्रह्मण आनन्दः। श्रोत्रियस्य चाकामहतस्य।

स यश्चायं पुरुषे। यश्चासावादित्ये। स एकः। स य एवंवित्। (तै० उ० २.७)

वेदान्तद्वयेऽपि कामहतानां तार्किकाणामासुरीं सम्पदमभिजातानाम् इहामुत्रभोगो भोगानन्दपरम्परा च प्रदर्शिता। साऽऽनन्दपरम्परा ब्रह्मानन्दे पर्यवस्यति। अकामहतानां निस्त्रैगुण्यानां श्रोत्रियाणां तु ब्रह्मानन्द एव। श्रोत्रियाणमाजानदेवैः साम्यं बृहदारण्यके प्रदर्शितम्। अत एव श्रोत्रिया भूदेवाः। ब्रह्मनिष्ठानां श्रोत्रियाणामानन्दपरम्परा नास्ति, ब्रह्मानन्दस्य निरतिशयत्वात्। कामहतानामिह भोगस्य परिसमाप्तिः सर्वस्याः पृथिव्याआधिपत्यप्राप्त्या परिसमाप्यते। अमुत्र भोगः प्राजापत्यप्राप्त्या पर्यवस्यति। वैदिकानामकामहतत्वाद् भोगो नास्ति। सुखं दुःखं च देहधर्मो नात्मधर्म इत्यात्मैकत्ववादिनां वैदिकानां देहधर्मः सुखदुःखान्यतरसाक्षात्काररूपो भोगोऽपि नास्ति, अशरीरत्वात्। तथा चोक्तम् आचार्यैर्भाष्ये—'तस्मात् मिथ्याप्रत्ययनिमित्तत्वात् सशरीरस्य सिद्धम्, जीवतोऽपि विदुषोऽशरीरत्वम्। तथा च ब्रह्मविद्विषया श्रुतिः— 'तद्यथाऽहिनिर्ल्वयनी वल्मीके मृता प्रत्यस्ता शयीत एवमेवेदं शरीरं शेते। अथाऽयमशरीरीऽमृतः प्राणो ब्रह्मैव तेज एव" (बृ० ४.४.७)। (शां० भा० १.१.४) इति। केवलं धर्म एव स चानन्दः। आनन्दो हि ब्रह्मधर्मः। आनन्दमयं ब्रह्मेति निर्णीतम् आनन्दमयाधिकरणे ब्रह्मधर्मप्राकट्यात् श्रोत्रियस्य देहपरिच्छिन्नस्यापि आत्मनो ब्रह्मसम्पत्तिर्ब्रह्मभावापत्तिर्वा वेदान्तद्वयेऽपि प्रदर्शिता।

'श्रोत्रिय'शब्देनात्र अधीतवेदा अश्रान्तश्रुतिपाठं कुर्वन्तो वेदानामखण्डं श्रवण-मनन-निदिध्यासनादिकं कुर्वाणा ब्राह्मण-क्षत्रिय-वैश्या गृह्यन्ते। तेषामेव श्रोत्रियत्वं सम्भवति। तथा च पाणिनिसूत्रम्—

श्रोत्रियश्छन्दोऽधीते (५.२.८४)

इति। यच्छन्दोऽधीते स श्रोत्रियो भवति। ब्राह्मण-क्षत्रिय-वैश्यानां वेदाध्ययनं प्रत्यहं ब्रह्मयज्ञश्च विहित इति ते श्रोत्रिया भवन्ति। अकामहतत्वं श्रोत्रियधर्म उक्तः। कामश्च शरीरधर्मो नात्मधर्म इति प्रपञ्चितं प्राक्। श्रोत्रियाणां विद्यमानेऽपि देहोपाधौ शरीरात्माभिमानलक्षणस्य मिथ्याज्ञानस्याभावात् सशरीरत्वं नास्ति। नित्यमशरीरत्वमेव, सशरीरत्वस्य मिथ्याज्ञाननिमित्तत्वात्। तथा चोक्तम् आचार्यैर्गीताभाष्ये—**क्षेत्रक्षेत्रज्ञसंयोगात्** (गी० १३.२६) इत्यस्य व्याख्याने।

कः पुनरयं क्षेत्र-क्षेत्रज्ञ-संयोगोऽभिप्रेतः? न तावद् रज्ज्वेव घटस्य अवयवसंश्लेषद्वारकः; सम्बन्धविशेषः संयोगः क्षेत्रेण क्षेत्रज्ञस्य सम्भवति, आकाशवन् निरवयवत्वात्। नापि समवायलक्षणस्तन्तुपटयोरिव क्षेत्रक्षेत्रज्ञयोः सम्बन्धः, इतरेतरकार्यकारणभावानभ्युपगमादिति।

अत्रोच्यते—क्षेत्र-क्षेत्रज्ञयोः विषय-विषयिणोः भिन्नस्वभावयोः इतरेतराध्यासलक्षणः संयोगः क्षेत्रक्षेत्रज्ञस्वरूपविवेका-ऽभावनिबन्धनो रज्जु-शुक्तिकादीनां तद्विवेकज्ञानाभावाद् अध्यारोपित-सर्परजतादिसंयोगवत्। सोऽयमध्यासस्वरूपः क्षेत्रक्षेत्रज्ञसंयोगो मिथ्याज्ञानलक्षणः। यथाशास्त्रं क्षेत्र-क्षेत्रज्ञलक्षण-भेदपरिज्ञानपूर्वकं प्राग्दर्शितरूपात् क्षेत्रात् गुञ्जादिवेषीकां यथोक्तलक्षणं क्षेत्रज्ञं प्रविभज्य—

न सत् तन् नासदुच्यते। (गी. १३.१२) इत्यनेन निरस्तसर्वोपाधिविशेषं ज्ञेयं ब्रह्म स्वरूपेण यः पश्यति, क्षेत्रं च मायानिर्मित-हस्तिस्वप्नदृष्टवस्तु-गन्धर्वनगरादिवद् असदेव सदिवाऽवभासत इत्येवं निश्चितविज्ञानो यस्तस्य यथोक्तं सम्यग्दर्शनविरोधादपगच्छति मिथ्याज्ञानं तस्य जन्महेतोरपगमात्।

> **'य एवं वेत्ति पुरुषं प्रकृतिं च गुणैः सह'** (गी. १३.२३) इत्यनेन **'विद्वान् भूयो नाभिजायते'** (१३.२३) इति यदुक्तं तदुपपन्नमुक्तम्।' (शां, भा० गी० १३.२६)

मिथ्याज्ञानापायश्च श्रोत्रियाणाम् उपनयनसंस्कारेणैव भवति। तस्मादुपनयनसंस्कारेण मिथ्याज्ञानापाये मुक्तिः सम्प्राप्यते। मुक्तोपसृप्यं च ब्रह्म। तथा च सूत्रम्—

मुक्तोपसृप्यव्यपदेशात् (ब्र० सू० १.३.२) इति। उपनयनसंस्कारश्च ब्रह्मविद्याप्रदानार्थम्। ब्रह्मविद्याप्रतिपत्तेश्च **सोऽमृतो भवति मृत्युर्ह्यस्यात्मा भवति** (मा. शत. १०.५.२.२३)। **शुद्धः पूतोऽजरोऽमृतः सम्भवति** (मा० बृ० ५.१५.१२, का० बृ० ५.१४.८) इति अमृतत्वफलश्रवणात्। तस्मात् उपनयनसंस्कारसमये सावित्रीमन्त्रोपदेशेन आत्मैकत्वविद्याप्रतिपत्त्या सद्य एव ब्रह्मभावापत्तिर्भवतीति अकामहतत्वमानन्दमयत्वं चेति ब्रह्मधर्माः प्रकटीभवन्ति। ब्रह्मसाक्षात्कारानन्तरं श्रवण-मनन-निदिध्यासनार्थं वेदाध्ययनम्। **आत्मा वाऽरे द्रष्टव्यः श्रोतव्यो मन्तव्यो निदिध्यासितव्यः** (बृ० २.४.५) इति श्रुतेः।

पदार्थदर्शनानन्तरमेव तस्य सर्वधर्मज्ञानेन तत्त्वज्ञानं लभ्यत इति तत्त्वज्ञानार्थं वेदाध्ययनम्। श्रोत्रियाणां नित्यमशरीरत्वादेव अकामहतत्वमिति विशदीकरणाय अवृजिनत्वं धर्मो बृहदारण्यके उक्तः। अवृजिन इति श्रोत्रियो विशेषितः। वृजिनशब्देनात्र देह एवोच्यते,

तस्यैव वृजिनरूपत्वात्, विनाशित्वेन अधर्मरूपत्वाद् अशुचित्वाच्च। जडत्वेन तमःस्वभावत्वाद् दुःखरूपत्वाच्च। तस्मादवृजिनो नाम अशरीरः।

एतदुक्तं भवति—**यश्च श्रोत्रियोऽवृजिनोऽकामहतः** (मा० बृ० ४.१) इत्यत्र श्रोत्रियशब्देन उपनयनसंस्कारेण प्रतिपन्नब्रह्मविद्या अश्रान्तं वेदाध्ययनशीला ब्राह्मण-क्षत्रिय-वैश्या गृह्यन्ते। अवृजिनशब्देन तेषां ब्रह्मविद्याप्राप्त्या मिथ्याज्ञानापायेन नित्यमशरीरत्वम्। तथा च श्रुतिः—

अशरीरं वाव सन्तं न प्रियाप्रिये स्पृशतः। (छा० ८.१२०)

इति। शरीरत्वाभावादेव अकामहतत्वम्। अत एव ब्रह्मधर्मस्य आनन्दस्य प्राकट्यम्। साधनत्रयमेतत् ब्रह्मधर्मप्रतिपत्त्यर्थमुक्तम्। तथा हि भाष्ये—

'अत्रैतानि साधनानि श्रोत्रियत्वाऽवृजिनत्वाऽकामहतत्वानि तस्य तस्याऽऽनन्दस्य प्राप्तौ अर्थादभिहितानि।' (बृ० उ० भा० ४.३.३३)

वेदान्तद्वयेऽपि श्रोत्रियशब्देन धर्मप्रतिष्ठापनार्थं गृहीतसन्न्यासस्य वैदिकस्य ब्राह्मणपरिव्राजकस्य ग्रहणे किमपि लिङ्गं नास्ति। प्रयोजनमपि नास्ति। संन्यासस्तु सर्वथा देहात्मवादिनामवैदिकानां भोगिनामसुराणामेव।

यदहरेव विरजेत् तदहरेव प्रव्रजेत्।

(जाबा० ४, प० प० उ० २,
नारदप० ३७७, याज्ञव० १)

इति संन्यासश्रुतौ रागिणां कामुकानामेव वैराग्यप्राप्तौ सन्न्यासोपदेशः, न निष्कामाणाम्।

वैदिकैस्तु धर्मसंस्थापनार्थमेव पारिव्राज्यम्, तदपि ब्राह्मणानामेवाऽङ्गीकृतम्। पारिव्राज्यमन्तरा सर्वत्र धर्मस्थापनाया अशक्यत्वात्। क्षत्रियादीनां परिव्राज्यमन्तराऽपि **अभयं वै जनक प्राप्तोऽसि** (मा० बृ० ३.११.६) इत्यभयप्राप्तिदर्शनात्। भोगापवर्गवादस्य भोगसन्न्यासवादस्य वा अवैदिकत्वात्। आत्मैकत्वविद्याया ब्रह्मविद्याया वा वेदान्तेष्वेव श्रवणात्।

भोगापवर्गवादिभिश्च आत्मभेदाभ्युपगमाद् वैदिकस्य दर्शनस्य प्रत्यासन्नमपि योगदर्शनम्—

स्वरूपप्रतिष्ठा वा चितिशक्तेः। (यो० सू० ४.३४)

इत्यात्मनः चितिशक्तिपर्यन्तमेव गच्छति। चित् ज्ञानमिति च पर्यायाः। ज्ञानपर्यन्तमेव गच्छति, नाऽऽनन्दांशपर्यन्तमिति यावत्। स्वरूपप्रतिष्ठायां वा चितिशक्तौ दर्शनेऽस्मिन् कर्मणोऽन्तो भवति। तथा हि भगवद्गीतासु—

सर्वं कर्माऽखिलं पार्थ ज्ञाने परिसमाप्यते। (४.३३) ज्ञाने इति। यदा स्वरूपप्रतिष्ठा चितिशक्तिर्भवति तदा व्युत्थाने वृत्तिसारूप्ये क्रियाः प्रवर्तन्ते। अखिलमिति। आशयसहितम् कर्माशयोऽपि नावशिष्यते।

अत एवेदं **'कृतान्तम्'** इति व्यपदिश्यते। तथा हि गीताशास्त्रे—

सांख्ये कृतान्ते प्रोक्तानि। (८.१३)

कृतान्ते सांख्ये ज्ञानप्रतिपादकशास्त्रे प्रोक्तानि। यदा चितिशक्तेर्ज्ञानस्य वेदस्य वाऽऽनन्दांशे लयो भवति, योगी चाऽऽनन्दमयः सम्पद्यते, तदा वेदस्य ज्ञानस्य चितिशक्तेर्वा अन्तो भवति। भूमिकायामस्यां वेदान्तो भवतीति ब्रह्मप्रतिपादकशास्त्रम् आत्मैकत्वप्रतिपादकशास्त्रं वा वेदान्तशास्त्रमिति व्यपदिश्यत इति दार्शनिकैरवगन्तव्यम्। आत्मैकत्वाभावाद् आनन्दाशस्य ब्रह्मधर्मस्य द्वैतिनां योगिनामपि समाधौ प्रतीतिर्न भवति।

वेदान्तद्वयेऽपि श्रोत्रियस्य ब्रह्मानन्द उक्त इति वैदिकमेव दर्शनं तत्र प्रतिपादितम्। न द्वैतिनां भोगिनामपवर्गदर्शनं संन्यासदर्शनं वा। एवमत्र कामहतानामवैदिकं दर्शनम्, अकामहतानां च वैदिकं दर्शनमिति दर्शनद्वयं प्रतिपादितम्। न पुनरवैदिकानां भोगापवर्गवादिनां भोगसन्न्यासवादिनां वा भोगवादः सन्न्यासवादश्च। कामहतानां तार्किकाणामयं भोगवादो गीताशास्त्रेऽपि निन्दित एव। तथा हि—

त्रैविद्या मां सोमपाः पूतपापा
यज्ञैरिष्ट्वा स्वर्गतिं प्रार्थयन्ते।
ते पुण्यमासाद्य सुरेन्द्रलोक-
मश्नन्ति दिव्यान् दिवि देवभोगान्॥
ते तं भुक्त्वा स्वर्गलोकं विशालं
क्षीणे पुण्ये मर्त्यलोकं विशन्ति।
एवं त्रयीधर्ममनुप्रपन्ना
गतागतं कामकामा लभन्ते॥ (९.२०, २१) इति।

किञ्चान्यत्—**करिष्ये वचनं तव** (गी० १८.७३) इति गुरुपरिचर्या इहामुत्रभोगविरागमन्तरा न भवति। कर्मसन्न्यास एवाऽत्र विधीयते। गुरोराज्ञयैव कर्माण्यनुष्ठीयन्ते इति आत्मनः कामस्य कामाचारस्य च अवकाश एव नास्ति। योगशास्त्रप्रोक्तम्—

दृष्टानुश्रविकविषयवितृष्णस्य वशीकारसंज्ञावैराग्यम्। (यो० सू० १.१५)

इति वशीकारसंज्ञावैराग्यम् ब्रह्मविद्याप्राप्त्या च पुरुषख्यातेः—

तत्परं पुरुषख्यातेर्गुणवैतृष्ण्यम्। (यो० सू० १.१६)

इति परं वैराग्यं चेति वैराग्यद्वयम् आबाल्यादेव सिद्ध्यति। गुरुपरिचर्या च मन्त्रे एव श्रूयते। तथा हि—

मम व्रते ते हृदयं दधामि
मम चित्तमनु चित्तं तेऽस्तु।
मम वाचमेकमना जुषस्व
बृहस्पतिष्ट्वा नियुनक्तु मह्यम्॥

(पार०-गृ० २.२.१६)

अत्र मम चित्तमनु चित्तं तेऽस्तु इति गुरुशिष्ययोश्चिदंशेन मीलनं सम्पद्यते। अभ्यस्तेऽस्मिन् मीलने योगे वा—**मच्चित्तः सततं भव** (गी० १८.५७), **मन्मना भव** (गी० ९.३४; १८.६५) इति ब्रह्मणा साकं चिदंशेन मीलनं सरलं सम्पद्यते। अवैदिकेन **योगश्चित्तवृत्तिनिरोधः** (यो० सू० १.२) इति वृत्तिनिरोधमार्गेण वैराग्यद्वयमनेकजन्मसाध्यमेव। का कथा पुरुषख्यातेः?

अत्रैके प्रत्यवतिष्ठन्ते—

यश्च श्रोत्रियोऽवृजिनोऽकामहतः। **(बृ० ४.३.३३. मा. बृ० ४.१.३५)**
श्रोत्रियस्य चाकामहतस्य। **(तै० उ० २.७)**

इति वेदान्तद्वयेऽपि श्रोत्रियः 'अकामहत' इति विशेषितः। विशेषणं भेदकं भवतीति कामहतोऽपि श्रोत्रियो भवति। कामहतानां श्रोत्रियाणां मनुष्यानन्दादारभ्य आनन्दपरम्परोक्ता। कामहता अपि श्रोत्रिया उपनयनसंस्कारेण संस्कृता एव। उपनयनसंस्कारश्च अविद्यानिवृत्त्यर्थमात्मैकत्वप्रतिपत्त्यर्थमेवोक्तः। तथापि कामहतानां तेन मिथ्याज्ञानापायो न भवति। इहामुत्र भोगरागस्तथैव अवतिष्ठत इति वेदान्तद्वयेऽपि स्पष्टम्। तेन एषामुपनयनसंस्कारेणाऽपि मिथ्याज्ञाननिवृत्तिर्नैव भवतीति गम्यत इति।

तत्रोच्यते—एते कामहता भोगापवर्गवादिनस्तार्किकाः तर्केणैव शास्त्रार्थं व्यवस्थापयन्ति। तर्कानुकूलञ्च वेदं प्रमापयन्ति। वेदाः प्रत्यक्षं प्रमाणमिति नातिष्ठन्ते। ईश्वरोक्तत्वात् शब्दप्रमाणत्वेन ग्रन्थप्रामाण्यमाद्रियन्ते। अविद्यावस्थायां व्याख्यानविपर्ययञ्च कुर्वन्ति। भोगापवर्गवादिभिस्तार्किकै उपनयनसंस्कार आत्मैकत्वविद्याप्रतिपत्त्यर्थं नैवाऽङ्गीकृतः। अपि तु वेदाध्ययनाधिकारसिद्ध्यर्थमेव उपनयनमित्येव एषामभ्युपगमः। वेदाश्च त्रैगुण्यविषयाः। त्रैगुण्यं सुख-दुःख-मोहात्मकं जगत् तत्कारणं प्रधानञ्च भोग्यमिति इह भोगोऽमुत्र भोगश्च वेदानां विषयः।

ईश्वरगीतास्वपि—**त्रैगुण्यविषया वेदाः** (गी. २.४५) इति कामहतानाम् अवैदिकानामसुराणां मतमुपन्यस्तम्। उपनयनं विना न वेदाध्ययनम्। अत एव आत्मैकत्वप्रतिपत्त्यर्थमुपनयनाभ्युपगमे आत्मैकत्वप्रतिपत्त्यनन्तरं त्रैगुण्यविषयक-वेदाध्ययनं वृथैवेति आत्मैकत्वप्रतिपत्त्यर्थमुपनयनं नास्ति। अपि तु वेदाध्ययनाधिकारसिद्ध्यर्थमेव। एवमुपनयनं वेदाध्ययनाधिकारसिद्ध्यर्थम्। वेदाश्च भोगप्रतिपत्त्युपायप्रदर्शनमित्येवैषां दर्शनमिति तामसानां भोगैकप्रवणानामेषां मिथ्याज्ञानापाय उपनयनेन न भवतीति तैः दुःखत्रयाभिघातानन्तरं पृथक् सन्न्यासो गुरूपसदनं गुरूपदेशश्च उपदिष्टः। विभिन्नानि मोक्षशास्त्राणि प्रणीतानि। मोक्षोऽपि काम एव भोग एव वा इति वेदाश्च भोगप्रतिपादनपरा इति व्यवस्थाप्य भोगशास्त्रं वेदा इत्येव सिद्धान्तितम्। इत्थमेते अवैदिका वेदाधर्मपरा इति वैदिकमतविरुद्धं वेदा भोगपरा इति मतं प्रतिष्ठापयन्ति। वेदविरुद्धानि वेदनिन्दकानि च तन्त्राणि प्रमाणयन्ति।

वैदिकानां तु निस्त्रैगुण्यविषयाः वेदाः। आत्मविषया इति यावत्। अत एव **चोदनालक्षणोऽर्थो धर्मः** (पू० मी० १.१.२) इति धर्मरूपस्य आत्मनो लक्षणं सङ्गच्छते। वेदा ब्रह्मविषयाश्च। आत्मैकत्वं ब्रह्म निस्त्रैगुण्यमेव। तस्मादुपनयनमपि निस्त्रैगुण्यस्यात्मनो ब्रह्मणश्च प्रतिपत्तिपरमेवेति वैदिकाऽवैदिकव्याख्याने महान् भेदः। आत्मैकत्वप्रतिपत्तेः

ब्रह्मप्रतिपत्तेर्वा उपनयनेन तत्र च सावित्र्युपदेशेन सिद्धत्वात् दर्शनेऽस्मिन् सार्ववर्णिकः संन्यासो नास्ति। अत एव गीताशास्त्रे—

काम्यानां कर्मणां न्यासं संन्यासं कवयो विदुः। (१८.२)

इति संन्यासशब्देन काम्यानां कर्मणां न्यास एवोक्तः। धर्मप्रतिष्ठापकानां कर्मगामिफलानां कर्मणां विधिश्चोक्तः। मीमांसकैः काम्यानि कर्माणि निषिद्धान्येवेति मीमांसकमतमेव उपन्यस्तं भगवता। अवैदिकः संन्यासः प्रत्याख्यातश्च।

इत्थं वेदान्तद्वयेऽपि कामहतानामवैदिकानां भोगापवर्गवादिनां श्रोत्रियाणामानन्दपरम्परा धर्मवादिनामकामहतानां श्रोत्रियाणां ब्रह्मानन्दः प्रतिपादितो वैलक्षण्यप्रदर्शनार्थमित्येव सिद्धान्तः। कामहतानां भोगिनामकामहतानामपवर्गवतां संन्यासिनां वैलक्षण्यमत्रोपन्यस्य भोगापवर्गवाद एव प्रस्थापित इति व्याख्यानमविद्याविलास इति तत् नादर्तव्यम्।

यत्तु—उच्यते श्रोत्रियपदेन संन्यासी ग्राह्य इत्यत्र अकामहत इति विशेषणमेव गमकमिति। तत्रोच्यते; अकामहतत्वं सन्न्यासमन्तराऽपि व्रतबन्धादारभ्यैव प्रकटीभवतीति तदर्थं सन्न्यासो नापेक्ष्यत इति निरूपितं प्राक्। श्रोत्रियपदेन संन्यासी ग्राह्य इति विवक्षाऽभविष्यत् तर्हि श्रोत्रियपदस्थाने संन्यासिनः परिव्राजकस्य वेति पदमश्रोष्यत्। तस्मादवैदिकानां भोगापवर्गवादिनां व्याख्यानमसमञ्जसमेव।

(५)

अवसितः प्रासङ्गिको विचारः। प्रकृतमनुसरामः। धर्मार्थकामस्वरूपस्त्रिविधोऽप्ययं कामो भोगफलो भूतानामुपघातायैव। तथा चोक्तं योगशास्त्रे—

नानुपहत्य भूतान्युपभोगः संभवतीति। (यो० भा० २.१५)

ईश्वरगीतास्वपि भोगवादिनामसुराणां सविस्तरवर्णनप्रसङ्गे षोडशाध्याये —

प्रभवन्त्युग्रकर्माणः क्षयाय जगतोऽहिताः। (१६.९)

इति प्रतिपादितम्। भोगवादे चैवं जगतो विनाश एव, न प्रतिष्ठा। भोगवादिनो जगतः शत्रवो जगतः क्षयायैव भोगार्थं प्रवर्तन्ते। तस्मात् जगतः प्रतिष्ठार्थं भोगवादः सर्वथा परिहर्तव्य एव।

ये हि संस्पर्शजा भोगा दुःखयोनय एव ते।
आद्यन्तवन्तः कौन्तेय न तेषु रमते बुधः॥ (गी० २.२२)

इति गीताशास्त्रे भोगा दुःखयोनय एवेत्युक्तम्। योगशास्त्रेऽपि—

परिणामतापसंस्कारदुःखैर्गुणवृत्तिविरोधाच्च दुःखमेव सर्वं विवेकिनः।
(यो० सू० २.१५)

इति संसारो दुःखबहुल इत्युक्तम्। त्रिविधं सुखमपि परिणाम-तापसंस्कार-

दुःखसम्भिन्नमिति दुःखमेव। अस्य दुःखस्य प्रहाणाय अपवर्गवादः प्रवर्तितः। तथा च योगसूत्रम्—

प्रकाशक्रियास्थितिशीलं भूतेन्द्रियात्मकं भोगापवर्गार्थं दृश्यम् (यो० सू० २.१८)

इदं सर्वं दृश्यं जगद् भोग्यं भोगार्थम्। भोगाश्च दुःखयोनय इतीदं सर्वं दृश्यं जगदेव दुःखकारणम्। तस्योपादाने भोगो दुःखं च। तस्यैवापवर्जने सन्न्यासे वा दुःखस्य आत्यन्तिकी निवृत्तिः।

सांख्यशास्त्रप्रवृत्तिरपि दुःखत्रयाभिघातायैव। तथा हि—

दुःखत्रयाभिघाताज्जिज्ञासा तदभिघातके हेतौ।
दृष्टे साऽपार्था चेन्नैकान्तात्यन्ततोऽभावात्॥ (सां० का० १)

दुःखं च शरीरधर्मो नात्मधर्म इति प्रतिपादितं प्राक्। एवं देहात्मवादिनां कृते एव सर्वेषां मोक्षशास्त्राणां प्रवृत्तिः।

दृष्टवदानुश्रविकः स ह्यविशुद्धिः क्षयातिशययुक्तः।
तद्विपरीतः श्रेयान् व्यक्ताव्यक्तज्ञविज्ञानात्॥ (सां० का० २)

इति वेदनिन्दाश्रवणात् आत्मैकत्वप्रतिपत्तेरभावात् सांख्यानामवैदिकत्वम्। दर्शनेऽस्मिन् प्रकृतिपर्यन्तमपवर्गेण देहात्मवादनिवृत्तिरात्मबोधश्च। ततो मोक्षः। अपवर्गप्रतिपादकमेतच्छास्त्रम्।

यथा जगदुत्पत्तिवादे तार्किकाणामैकमत्यं नास्ति तथा मोक्षेऽपि तेषां नैकमत्यम्। प्रतिदर्शनं मोक्षकल्पना भिद्यते। मोक्षकल्पनाभेदात् प्रतिदर्शनं तत्त्वज्ञानमपि भिद्यते। एवं द्वैतिनां तार्किकाणां दर्शनेषु पराऽनवस्था सम्पद्यते सर्वेऽप्येते वादिनः परसिद्धान्तान् दूषयित्वा स्वसिद्धान्तान् प्रस्थापयन्तीति सर्वाण्येतानि दर्शनानि खण्डितानि सम्पद्यन्ते।

वस्तुतस्तु—तत्त्वज्ञानमेकरूपमेव भवितुमर्हति, वस्तुतन्त्रत्वात्। तथापि प्रतितन्त्रं भिद्यत इति अप्रमाणमेव भवति द्वैतिनाम्। सांख्यसिद्धान्ते आत्मनः शुद्धावस्थैव मोक्षः। न्यायवैशेषिकसिद्धान्ते जीवस्य अदृष्टकारितात् परमाणुरूपमनःसम्बन्धरूपाद् बन्धनात् मोक्षो जीवस्य। मनस्तस्मिन् समये जडतां धारयति। तस्मात् मनसो जडतैव मोक्षः। तथा चोक्तमाचार्यपादैर्भाष्ये—

> सति बहुत्वे विभुत्वे च घटकुड्यादिसमाना द्रव्यमात्रस्वरूपाः स्वतोऽचेतना आत्मानस्तदुपकरणानि चाणूनि मनांस्यचेतनानि। तत्र आत्मद्रव्याणां मनोद्रव्याणां च संयोगात् नवेच्छादयो वैशेषिका आत्मगुणा उत्पद्यन्ते। ते चाव्यतिरेकेण प्रत्येकमात्मसु समवयन्ति स संसारः। तेषां नवानामात्मगुणानामत्यन्तानुत्पादो मोक्ष इति काणादाः।

—(ब्रह्म० शां० भा० २.३.५०)

वैष्णव-शैव-शाक्त-गाणपत-सौराणां तत्तल्लोकप्राप्तिर्मोक्षः। तत्र मुक्तेश्चातुर्विध्यम्—सलोकता, सरूपता, समीपता, सायुज्यं चेति। भोगः कामचारश्च फलम्। ब्रह्मत्वेनाभिमतस्य पदार्थस्यापि भेदः।

इत्थं प्रतिपर्णां मोक्षकल्पनाभेदात् मोक्ष एवाप्रमाणम्। यथा बन्धो नात्मधर्मस्तथा मोक्षोऽपि। मोक्षकल्पना चैवमविद्यावतां तामसानामसुराणाम्। तमोगुणेन ते नायन्त इति मोक्षं कल्पयन्ति। पञ्चपर्वणो विपर्ययस्य स्वरूपं नीतिः। सा च नीतिरित्थं त्रिविधा—सात्त्विकी, राजसी, तामसी चेति भेदात्। सामान्यतः सर्वेषामपवर्गवादिनां मतेन मोक्षो नाम एकविंशतिप्रभेदभिन्नस्य दुःखस्य आत्यन्तिकी निवृत्तिरेव। दुःखस्य एकविंशतिप्रभेदाः। शरीरं, षडिन्द्रियाणि, षड्विषयाः, षड्बुद्धयः, सुखं दुःखं चेति। सुखं दुःखमेव, दुःखसम्भिन्नत्वात्। एकविंशतिप्रभेदभिन्नस्य दुःखस्य आत्यन्तिकी निवृत्तिस्तु सर्वस्यास्य दृश्यस्य विषयीभूतस्य प्रकृतिपर्यन्तस्य जगतः संन्यासेन अपवर्गेण वा भवतीति सन्न्यास एव मोक्षहेतुः। इत्थं जगतः सन्न्यासाद् अपवर्गवादोऽपि न जगतः प्रतिष्ठायाः कारणं भवति। प्रत्युत जगतः परित्यागेन तस्य विनाशायैव कारणं भवति। एवमवैदिकानामसुराणां भोगापवर्गवाद उक्तः।

भोगापवर्गसिद्धान्तानुरूपमेव तैर्भोगापवर्गप्रतिष्ठापकं धर्मलक्षणं सूचितम्। तथा हि तेषां सूत्रम्—

यतोऽभ्युदयनिःश्रेयससिद्धिः स धर्मः। (वै० सू० १.१.२)
प्रवृत्तिर्वाग्बुद्धि-शरीरारम्भः। (न्या० सू० १.१.१७)
प्रवर्तनालक्षणा दोषाः। (न्या० सू० १.१.१८)
प्रवृत्तिदोषजनितोऽर्थः फलम्। (न्या० सू० १.१.२०)

इति न्यायवित्समयानुसारं कायिकं वाचिकं मानसिकं चेति त्रिविधं कर्म राग-द्वेष-मोहपूर्वकमेवेति काम्यं सदोषं च। प्रवृत्तिर्निष्कामा निर्दोषा चेति सर्वथाऽशक्यप्रायमेव। नहि कश्चिद् रागद्वेषवियुक्तः स्वार्थे परार्थे वा प्रयतमानो दृश्यते। स्वार्थप्रयुक्त एव सर्वो जनः परार्थेऽपि प्रवर्तत। तस्माद् धर्मप्रवृत्तिरपि काम्या सदोषा च। प्रवृत्तिसत्त्वे जन्मसत्त्वात् प्रवृत्त्यपाये जन्मापायाद् अपवर्गार्थं सर्वा प्रवृत्तिः परित्यक्तव्येति सिद्धान्तितम्। तथा च आचार्यस्य न्यायोपबृंहितं सूत्रम्—

दुःख-जन्म-प्रवृत्ति-दोष-मिथ्याज्ञानानामुत्तरोत्तरापाये तदनन्तरापायादपवर्गः।
(न्या० सू० १.१.२)

तार्किकाणां सिद्धान्तोऽयं गीताशास्त्रे प्रत्याख्यातः। तथा हि—

त्याज्यं दोषवदित्येके कर्म प्राहुर्मनीषिणः।
यज्ञ-दान-तपः कर्म न त्याज्यं कार्यमेव तत्॥ (१८.३)

एके मनीषिणो मनश्चैतन्यवादिनो नैयायिकाः सर्वे चापवर्गवादिनः। कर्म त्याज्यं प्राहुः प्रवृत्त्यपाये जन्मापायात् जन्मापाये च दुःखापायात् दोषवदिति। '**प्रवर्तनालक्षणा दोषाः**' (न्या०

सू० १.१.१८)। दोषापाये च प्रवृत्त्यपायः '**प्रवृत्तिर्वाग्बुद्धिशरीरारम्भः**' (१.१.१७) इति कायिकं वाचिकं मानसिकं च कर्म त्याज्यमिति वदन्ति। अपरे मीमांसकाः यज्ञ-दान-तप-कर्म न त्याज्यमिति वदन्ति। मीमांसकमतमेव तत्र सिद्धान्ततया उपन्यस्तं भगवता। तथा हि—

निश्चयं शृणु मे तत्र त्यागे भरतसत्तम।
त्यागो हि पुरुषव्याघ्र त्रिविधः संप्रकीर्तितः॥

यज्ञो दानं तपः कर्म न त्याज्यं कार्यमेव तत्।
यज्ञो दानं तपश्चैव पावनानि मनीषिणाम्॥

एतान्यपि तु कर्माणि सङ्गं त्यक्त्वा फलानि च।
कर्तव्यानीति मे पार्थ निश्चितं मतमुत्तमम्॥　　　　(गी० १८.४-६)

मिथ्याज्ञानविहीनानाम् आत्मैकत्ववादिनां वैदिकानां कर्मणि प्रवृत्तिर्धर्मतो कर्मगामिफलाय, न दोषतः कर्तृगामिफलेच्छया। जन्म शरीरस्य नात्मन इत्यात्मैकत्ववादिनां जन्म नास्ति, दुःखमपि नास्ति। अतो 'दुःखतन्मे'ति सूत्रं (न्या० सू० १.१.२) देहात्मवादिपरमेव। तार्किकाणां तु इहामुत्रभोगाय धर्मानुष्ठानम्। स भोग एव 'अभ्युदय'शब्देन व्यपदिश्यते। अभ्युदयो नाम ममत्वेन स्वामित्वेन ऐश्वर्यत्वेन वाऽभिमतानां भोग्यानां विषयाणां प्राप्तिः। तस्या अभिवृद्धिर्यथा यथा भवति, तथा तथा अभ्युदयो वर्धते। इतरापेक्षया अभितः = सर्वतः सर्वप्रकारैः, उद् = उत्कृष्टा, अयो गतिरभ्युदयः। एवं विषया एव अभ्युदयहेतवो भवन्ति। इहाभ्युदयसमाप्तिस्तु त्रैलोक्याधिपत्यप्राप्त्या भवति। अमुत्र चाभ्युदयपरिसमाप्तिः क्षत्रियाणाम् इन्द्रपदप्राप्त्या ब्राह्मणानां च प्राजापत्यप्राप्त्या भवति, प्रजापतेः इन्द्रस्य च क्रमशो ब्राह्मणक्षत्रियरूपत्वात्। इन्द्रपदप्राप्त्यर्थम् अश्वमेधशतं बहुभिः क्षत्रियैरनुष्ठितमिति इतिहास-पुराणेषु स्मर्यते।

इत्थं विषया एव अभ्युदयहेतवो भवन्ति। तेषां स्वामित्वेनोपादाने भोगोऽभ्युदयश्च सिद्ध्यति। भोगोऽभ्युदयो वा दुःखयोनिरिति दुःखायैवेति दुःखपरिहारार्थं दुःखयोनीनां भोग्यानां विषयाणामपवर्जनेन संन्यसनेन वा मोक्षोऽपवर्गो निःश्रेयसं वा सिद्ध्यति। तस्माद् विषया एव निःश्रेयसहेतवो भवन्ति। इत्थमभ्युदय-निःश्रेयससिद्धिः विषयाधीनैव। अत एव विषया एवाभ्युदय-निःश्रेयससिद्धिहेतुत्वाद् धर्मपदेन व्यपदिश्यन्ते।

ननु विषय-विषयिणोः संयोगः सम्बन्धो नाऽभेदः। स चेतरेतराध्यासलक्षणः। तेन तयोर्धर्मधर्मिसम्बन्धो नास्ति, नोपपादयितुं शक्यते चेति।

सत्यम्; तथापि तामसैरवैदिकैः अत्राऽधर्म एव धर्म इत्युपचर्यते। किं चान्यत्; विषया यदा विषयिणो बुद्ध्यारूढा भवन्ति, विषयी च यदा विषयैरुपरक्तो जायते, तदैव तस्य विषयित्वं सम्पद्यते। अस्यामवस्थायां विषया विषयिणि तादात्म्यसंबन्धेन अवतिष्ठन्ते इति तत्र धर्मधर्मिसंबन्धस्तार्किकैः प्रतिष्ठापितः। तस्मादवैदिकैस्तार्किकैः परिदृश्यमानमिदं सर्वं विषयीभूतं दृश्यं जगदेव धर्मशब्देन व्यपदिश्यत इति विद्यावद्भिर्वैदिकैः विभावनीयम्।

जगतो विनाशित्वाद् अनवतिष्ठमानत्वाद् अध्रियमाणत्वाद्वा जगदधर्म इति सिद्धान्तितं वैदिकैः। वैदिकानां देहोपाधिपरिच्छिन्न आत्मा धर्मो ब्रह्म च धर्मी। अवैदिकानां पुनर्विषया जगद्वा धर्मो विषयी च बुद्धिचैतन्यवादी विज्ञानमयो मनश्चैतन्यवादी मनोमयः इन्द्रियचैतन्यवादी प्राणमयो देहचैतन्यवादो अन्नमयो ना पुरुषो धर्मी। वैदिकानां धर्मः सनातनः, अवैदिकानां पुनर्विनाशी। 'धर्म'शब्देन व्यपदिश्यमानं प्रकृतिपर्यन्तं दृश्यं जगत् त्रिगुणात्मकमिति धर्मोऽपि धर्मार्थकामरूपेण त्रिविधः सम्पद्यते, 'पुरुषार्थ'शब्देन व्यपदिश्यते च। अयं परस्परविरुद्धो वैदिकदर्शनसिद्धान्तोऽवैदिक-दर्शनसिद्धान्तश्च धर्मप्रतिष्ठापकैः निपुणमतिभिरवश्यं चिन्तनीय इत्यस्माकं विनीत आग्रहः।

मोक्षो बद्धस्य काम एव, न धर्मः। नहि बन्धोऽपि धर्मः। बन्धनान् मोक्षो न स्यात्। तस्मात् कामकृतं बन्धनं मोक्षोऽपि काम एव। तस्मात् कामहतानामयं मोक्षवादो नाकामहतानां धर्मवादिनां वैदिकानाम्। भोगापवर्गवादिनां सर्वेषां द्वैतिनां मोक्ष एव परमपुरुषार्थः। तथापि मोक्षस्वरूपे न तेषामैकमत्यमिति निरूपितं प्राक्। इत्थं मोक्षपदार्थस्याऽनवस्थानात् मोक्षस्य याथाकाम्यम्। नायं शास्त्रीयः पदार्थः। यथा जगत् मिथ्या, तथा मोक्षोऽपि। मोक्षवादेऽभ्युपगम्यमाने—

> 'ये संसारिणः संसारान् मुच्यन्ते, तेषां संसारोऽन्तवान्। संसारित्वं च तेषामन्तवत्। एवमितरेष्वपि क्रमेण मुच्यमानेषु संसारस्य संसारिणां चान्तवत्त्वं स्यात्। (शां० भा० २.२.४)

इत्यादिभाष्येण आचार्यैः मोक्षवादस्य तार्किकपरिगृहीतेश्वर-कारणवादस्य चासङ्गतत्वं प्रतिष्ठापितम्।

मोक्षार्थं द्वैतिभिः अपवर्गः संन्यासो वा विधीयते। स च सर्वेषां मुमुक्षूणां स्त्री-पुरुषाणामनुज्ञायते। यथा भोगवादो जगतो विनाशायैव, एवमेव अपवर्गवादः संन्यासवादो वा प्रकृतिपर्यन्तस्य जगतः शरीरस्यापि च उपेक्षया विनाशायैवेति द्वैतिनां तार्किकाणां भोगापवर्गवादो जगतो विनाशार्थम्, न प्रतिष्ठापनार्थम्।

आत्मैकत्ववादे ब्रह्मवादे वा द्वैताभावाद् भोगो नास्ति। भोगाभावाद् धर्मार्थकामाः पुरुषार्थाः दुःखं च नास्ति। दुःखाभावात् मोक्षो नास्ति। मोक्षाभावात् मोक्षार्थमुपदिश्यमानः संन्यासो दर्शनं च नोपपद्यत एव। नहि धर्मः संन्यसितुं शक्यः, भोग-संन्यासयोर्द्वन्द्वाद् भोगस्य भोग्यस्यैव वा संन्यासः। तस्माद् वैदिकानामात्मैकत्ववादे धर्मवादे वा संन्यासो नास्ति। तथा चोक्तं बौधायनेन—

> **ऐकाश्रम्यं त्वाचार्या अप्रजननत्वादितरेषाम्।** (बौ० ध० सू० २.६.२९)

तत्रोदाहरन्ति—

> **प्राह्लादिर्ह वै कपिलो नामासुर आस। स एतान् भेदांश्चकार देवैः सह स्पर्धमानः। तान् मनीषी नाद्रीयेत।** (बौ० ध० सू० २.६.४०)

गौतमोऽप्याह—

तस्याश्रमविकल्पमेके ब्रुवते।
ब्रह्मचारिगृहस्थो भिक्षुर्वैखानसः।
तेषां गृहस्थो योनिरप्रजननत्वादितरेषाम्।
ऐकाश्रम्यं त्वाचार्याः प्रत्यक्षविधानाद् गार्हस्थ्यस्य गार्हस्थ्यस्य।

(गौ० ध० सू० १.३.१-३;३५)

इत्थं देहात्मवादिभिरसुरैरेव पुरस्कृतोऽयमाश्रमविकल्पः स्मृतिषु स्मर्यते। तथापि वेदविरुद्धाः स्मृतयोऽप्रमाणमिति व्यवस्थापितं मीसांसकैः। तथा हि—

विरोधे त्वनपेक्षं स्यादसति ह्यनुमानम्।

इति सूत्रे (पू० मी० १.३.३) भाष्ये अष्टाचत्वारिंशद्-वर्षाणि वेदब्रह्मचर्यचरणम् **जातपुत्रः कृष्णकोशोऽग्नीनादधीत** इत्यनेन विरुद्धमिति श्रुतिस्मृत्योर्विरोधं प्रदर्श्य **हेतुदर्शनाच्च** (पू० मी० १.३.४) इति सूत्रे भाष्ये **अपुंस्त्वं प्रच्छादयन्तश्चाष्टचत्वारिंशद् वर्षाणि वेदब्रह्मचर्यं चरितवन्तः, तत एषा स्मृतिरित्यवगम्यते** इति।

ब्रह्मचर्यं वाऽष्टाचत्वारिंशकम्।
द्वादशकेऽप्येके। **(पार० गृ० सू० २.५.२-३)**
प्रतिवेदं ब्रह्मचर्यं द्वादशाब्दानि पञ्च वा।
ग्रहणान्तिकमित्येके केशान्तश्चैव षोडशे॥ **(याज्ञ० स्मृ० १.३६)**

षड्त्रिंशदाब्दिकं चर्यं गुरौ त्रैवेदिकं व्रतम्।
तदर्धिकं पादिकं वा ग्रहणान्तिकमेव वा॥ **(मनु० ३.१) इति।**

कल्पसूत्रकारैः स्मृतिकारैश्च प्रोक्तस्य श्रुतिविरुद्धस्य अष्टचत्वारिंशद्वर्षाणि वेदब्रह्मचर्यचरणस्य निन्दैव कृता। का पुनर्वार्ता नैष्ठिकब्रह्मचर्यस्य।

सांख्यसिद्धान्तपरिग्रहो मन्वादिस्मृतिषु स्पष्टमुपलभ्यते। स्मृतिर्हि चित्तस्य वृत्तिः। तथा च योगसूत्रम्—

प्रमाणविपर्ययविकल्पनिद्रास्मृतयः। (१.६) स्मृतीनां देहधर्माणामेव प्रतिपादकत्वात्। स्मृतीनां धर्मी देहपरिच्छिन्नआत्मा। देहोपाधिविशिष्टमात्मानं धर्मिणमाश्रित्यैव वर्णाश्रमधर्माः प्रवर्तन्ते, न निरुपाधिकमात्मानम्। अत एव वर्णाश्रमधर्माः स्मृतिप्रोक्ता देहपरिच्छिन्नस्य आत्मन एव। सांख्यैः देहस्यैव प्रकृतिपर्यन्तं सूक्ष्मो विचारः कृतः। अत एव तस्य परिग्रहः स्मृतिकारैः कृतः, न वैदिकानां निरुपाधिकात्मवादस्य। सांख्ययोगैश्च दुःखत्रयविघाताय संन्यासः प्रतिपादितः। तथा चोक्तमाचार्यैः—

सांख्ययोग-शास्त्रेषु च संन्यासो ज्ञानं प्रति प्रत्यासन्न उच्यते।
कामप्रवृत्त्यभावाच्च। (बृ० ४.५. शाङ्करभाष्यम्)

इत्थञ्च मोक्षप्रतिपादकानि हि सर्वाणि द्वैतानि सांख्य-योग-न्याय-वैशेषिकादि- दर्शनानि। मोक्षो हि परमपुरुषार्थस्तेषाम्। मोक्षश्च काम एव, न धर्म इति कामप्रतिष्ठापकानि द्वैतानि दर्शनानि। मोक्षश्च दुःखस्यात्यन्तिकी निवृत्तिः। भोगफलं दुःखं च शरीरधर्म इति देहात्मवादिनो दुःखितान् असुरानधिकृत्य इमानि दर्शनानि प्रवृत्तानि। आचार्याश्चैते प्रवृत्ताः।

वैदिकं दर्शनं पुनः धर्म-धर्मिप्रतिपादकम्। धर्मप्रतिष्ठापनार्थमेव आचार्याणां जगद्गुरूणां भगवतोऽवतारः स्मर्यते, न मोक्षप्रतिष्ठापनार्थम्, न वा भोगरूप-धर्मार्थकामप्रतिष्ठापनार्थम्। तथा हि—

यदा यदा हि धर्मस्य ग्लानिर्भवति भारत।
अभ्युत्थानमधर्मस्य तदाऽऽत्मानं सृजाम्यहम्॥

परित्राणाय साधूनां विनाशाय च दुष्कृताम्।
धर्मसंस्थापनार्थाय सम्भवामि युगे युगे॥ (गी. ४.७-८)

धर्मस्थापनं प्रकारद्वयेन भवति। प्रथमं को धर्मी, कश्च तस्य धर्मः, कश्च अधर्म इति धर्म-धर्मिनिर्णयः कर्तव्यो भवति। धर्मिणो धर्माधर्मनिर्णयं विधाय शास्त्रप्रणयनं सशास्त्रं च सनातनधर्मानुशासनं रजस्तमोभ्यां निर्मुक्तैः **ज्ञानं विज्ञानम्** (गी. १८.४२) इति येषां धर्मस्तैः ब्राह्मणैरेव कर्तुं शक्यत इति धर्माधर्मव्यवस्थापनमाचार्यैः क्रियते। अयं प्रथमो धर्मप्रतिष्ठापन-प्रकारः।

धर्मप्रतिष्ठाऽधर्मनाशश्च ईश्वरभावमन्तरा न भवतीति ईश्वरभावो (गी. १८.४३) येषां धर्मस्तैः क्षत्रियैरेव यथाशास्त्रं धर्मप्रतिष्ठा अधर्मनाशश्च कर्तुं शक्यते। अत एव ब्राह्मणानां गेहे क्षत्रियाणां गेहे चेति भगवतोऽवतारद्वयं गीताशास्त्रे श्लोकद्वये स्मर्यते।

एवमेव योगभ्रष्टस्यापि योगिनां ब्राह्मणानां गेहे श्रीमतां क्षत्रियाणां गेहे चेत्यवतारद्वयं स्मर्यते। तथा हि—

शुचीनां श्रीमतां गेहे योगभ्रष्टोऽभिजायते।
अथवा योगिनामेव कुले भवति धीमताम्॥ (गी. ६.४१-४२) इति।

यदा यदा हीति। धर्मस्य आत्मैकत्ववादस्य एकत्वस्य अद्वितीयत्वस्य च ग्लानिर्भवति। अधर्मस्य द्वैतस्य देहवादस्य च अभ्युत्थानं भवति। धर्मवादः क्षीणो भवति, भोगापवर्गवादस्य च सर्वतोऽभ्युत्थानं भवतीति यावत्। दैवीसम्पत्तेस्तिरोधानम्, आसुरीसम्पत्तेश्च अभ्युत्थानं भवति। शास्त्रीयस्य धर्माधर्मव्यवस्थापनस्य लोपो भवति। सर्वत्र चाशास्त्रीयः कामचारः प्रवर्तते। कर्मगामिक्रियाफलवादः क्षीयते, कर्तृगामिक्रियाफलवादश्च समुज्जृम्भते।

द्व्यक्षरस्तु भवेन्मृत्युस्त्र्यक्षरं ब्रह्म शाश्वतम्।
ममेति च भवेन्मृत्युर्न ममेति च शाश्वतम्। (म० भा० १४.१३.३)

इति महाभारतोक्तस्य सनातनस्य सिद्धान्तस्य ग्लानिर्भवति। तदा तस्मिन् काले। अहं

पितृत्वेनावस्थितो देहोपाधिकः 'अहं ब्रह्मास्मि' इति प्रबुद्धः, अत एव परेण ब्रह्मणा साकं सत्तांशेन चिदंशेन आनन्दांशेन चैक्यं गतो देहोपाधिनैव केवलेन द्वैतभावेनावस्थितः। आत्मानम् जन्मत एव अविद्यारहितं देहोपाधावपि अशरीरं नित्यशुद्धबुद्धमुक्तस्वभावं धर्माधर्मव्यवस्थापनार्थम्। सृजामि उत्पादयामि। अवतारेऽस्मिन् धर्माधर्मव्यवस्थार्थं सत्त्वगुणाध्यासो वृत्तिसारूप्यं च कर्तव्यं भवति। तथापि कार्ये निवृत्ते पुनः स्वाभाविकी स्वरूपावस्थितिर्ब्रह्मभावापत्तिश्च भवतीति क्लेशाभावादयमवतारो यदा यदा धर्मग्लानिः, अधर्मस्य चाभ्युत्थानं भवति। तदा तदा भवति, वारं वारं भवतीत्यर्थः। अनेकवारमाचार्यरूपेण ईश्वरोऽवतरति, धर्मस्थापनं च करोति।

परित्राणायेति। परित्राणाय रक्षणाय। साधूनाम् आत्मैकत्ववादिनां धार्मिकाणाम् अकामहतानाम्, अत एव क्रियाफलस्य कर्मगामित्वमातिष्ठमानानाम्। विनाशाय संहाराय च। दुष्कृतां द्वैतिनां देहात्मवादिनाम्, अत एव अधार्मिकाणां कामुकानां रागद्वेषमोहात्मकानां भोगापवर्गवादिनामसुराणाम् प्रवृत्तिदोषजनितार्थं फलं कर्तृगामीति सिद्धान्तयताम्। रागद्वेषमोहैः सर्वा कृतिः क्रिया दुष्टैवेतेषाम्, अत एव ते दुष्कृत इति व्यपदिश्यन्ते। दुष्कृतां कामचाराणामिति यावत्। साधूनां रक्षणं दुष्कृतां विनाशश्च ईश्वरभावमन्तरा न भवतीत्ययमवतारः **'क्षत्रियस्य च रक्षणम्'** (मनु० १०.८), **'ईश्वरभावश्च क्षत्रकर्म स्वभावजम्'** (गी० १८.४३) इति क्षत्रियगेहे भवति। क्षत्रियेणैव आचार्याणामनुशासनानुसारं धर्मव्यवस्था कर्तुं शक्यत इति धर्मसंस्थापनार्थम्। सम्भवामि नित्यशुद्धबुद्धमुक्तस्वभावः अजोऽपि देहवानिव भवामि। युगे युगे प्रतियुगं, न पूर्ववद् वारं वारम्। संभवः प्रकृतिमधिष्ठाय भवति। त्रैगुण्याधिष्ठानमन्तरा साधूनां रक्षणं दुष्कृतां विनाशश्च न सम्भवति इति त्रैगुण्याधिष्ठानं सततम्। निस्त्रैगुण्यावस्था कार्याभाव एव। नित्यं त्रैगुण्याध्यासः प्रवृत्तिर्वा नित्यशुद्धबुद्धमुक्तस्वभावाय परमात्मने न रोचते इति न वारं वारं क्षत्रियकुलेऽवतारः। क्षत्रियस्येश्वरभावेन नित्यमवस्थानाद् द्वैतेऽवस्थानं नाद्वैते इत्यत्र क्षत्रियस्य पितुरुल्लेखो नास्ति, प्रत्युताऽपह्नव एव। अत एव 'सम्भवामी' त्युक्तम्। सम्यक् स्वयमेव भवामीति यावत्। एवं ब्राह्मणानां क्षत्रियाणां चैकत्व एव धर्मप्रतिष्ठापनं शक्यं न द्वैते। अत एवोक्तम्—

यत्र ब्रह्म च क्षत्रं च सम्यञ्चौ चरतः सह।
तं लोकं पुण्यं प्रज्ञेषं यत्र देवाः सहाऽग्निना॥ (मा० सं० २०.२५)

नाब्रह्म क्षत्रमृध्नोति नाक्षत्रं ब्रह्म वर्धते।
ब्रह्म क्षत्रं च संपृक्तमिह चामुत्र वर्धते॥ (मनु० ९.३२२) इति।

(६)

स्वयंज्योतिःस्वरूपं ब्रह्मेति ब्रह्मवादिनः सूर्यमण्डलस्थस्याऽग्नेः सायं-प्रातरुपासनाम् अग्निहोत्रस्य च परिचरणं सायं प्रातः कुर्वन्ति, महायज्ञैश्च यज्ञैश्च अग्निमेव सन्तर्पयन्ति।

देहात्मवादिभिस्तु मूर्तिपूजा क्रियते। प्रकृतिवादाद् देहात्मवादाच्च मूर्तिपूजाया उद्गमः। प्रकृतिवादे देवताया मूर्तिरुपासनार्थं क्रियते। तत्र चाऽऽत्मप्रतिष्ठा क्रियते। एवं सांख्यसिद्धान्तानुसारेण प्रतिमूर्ति आत्मभेदो भवति। केवलं शिवलिङ्गे सर्वस्त्री-पुरुषात्मके सकिलस्य आत्मैकत्वस्य स्थापना भवति। तस्मात् महादेवमूर्तिरिव वैदिकी। ब्रह्मणो विराट्शरीरस्य स्त्री-पुरुषात्मकस्य एकत्वं गतस्य प्रतीकरूपत्वात्, तत्र च आत्मैकत्वस्य प्रतिष्ठापनाच्च। ब्रह्मस्वरूपमेव शिवलिङ्गम्। तत्र धर्मस्वरूपो वृषभः। **वृषो हि भगवान् धर्मः** (८.१६) इति मनूक्तेः। तत्र वैदिकस्य धर्मस्य धर्मिणश्च प्रतीकमेव शिवालये परिदृश्यते। प्रकृतीनामानन्त्यात् मूर्तीनामानन्त्यं भवति। तथा चोक्तं चरके—

'भूतानां चतुर्विधा योनिर्भवति जराय्वण्डस्वेदोद्भिदः। तासां खलु चतसृणामपि योनीनामेकैका योनिरपरिसंख्येयभेदा भवति। भूतानामाकृतिविशेषापरिसंख्येयत्वात्। (चरक० शारीर० ३.२६) 'तत्र शरीरं योनिविशेषाच्चतुर्विधमुक्तमग्रे। त्रिविधं खलु सत्त्वं शुद्धं राजसं तामसमिति। तत्र शुद्धमदोषमाख्यातं कल्याणांशत्वात्। राजसं सदोषमाख्यातं रोषांशत्वात्। तामसमपि सदोषमाख्यातम्, मोहांशत्वात्। तेषां तु त्रयाणामपि सत्त्वानामेकैकस्य भेदाग्रमपरिसङ्ख्येयं तरतमयोगाच्छरीरयोनिविशेषेभ्यश्च अन्योन्यानुविधानत्वाच्च।' (४.४३-४४)

'इत्येवं शुद्धस्य सत्त्वस्य सप्तविधं भेदांशं विद्यात् कल्याणांशत्वात्।' (४.५२)
'इत्येवं खलु राजसस्य सत्त्वस्य षड्विधं भेदांशं विद्यात् रोषांशत्वात्।' (४.५९)
'इत्येवं तामसस्य सत्त्वस्य त्रिविधं भेदांशं विद्यात्, मोहांशत्वात्।' (४.६३)
'इत्यपरिसंख्येयभेदानां त्रयाणामपि सत्त्वानां भेदैकदेशो व्याख्यातः। शुद्धस्य सत्त्वस्य सप्तविधो ब्रह्मर्षि-शक्र-यम-वरुण-कुबेर-गन्धर्व-सत्त्वानुकारेण। राजसस्य षड्विधो दैत्य-राक्षस-पिशाच-सर्प-प्रेत-शकुनि-सत्त्वानुकारेण। तामसस्य त्रिविधः पशुमत्स्यवनस्पतिसत्त्वानुकारेण। कथं च यथासत्त्वमुपचारः स्यादिति।' (४.६४-६५)

योनयः —४। सत्त्वस्य शुद्धस्य—७। राजसस्य सत्त्वस्य—६। तामसस्य सत्त्वस्य—३ भेदांशम्। ७+६+३ = १६ भेदाः। ४×१६ = ६४ भेदाः। अत एव चतुष्षष्टियोगिन्य आभ्युदयिके पूज्यन्ते। तासामपरिमितभेदात् चतुष्षष्टिकोटियोगिन्यः। प्रकृतिश्च चतुष्षष्टिकोटि-योगिनी-नायिका। तथा चोक्तं 'ललितासहस्रनाम'-स्तोत्रे—

महाचतुष्षष्टिकोटि-योगिनी गणसेविता (१०९)

एवं सत्त्व-रज-स्तमसामनन्तभेदान् मूर्तीनामपि अनन्तभेदा भवन्ति। तत्र **यथाभिमतध्यानाद्वा** (यो० सू० १.३९) इति सूत्रानुसारम् अभिमताया एव मूर्तेर्ग्रहणमुपासनार्थं भवति। देहात्मवादे चाचार्याणां महात्मनां च मूर्तिरुपासनार्थं प्राणप्रतिष्ठा-विधिमन्तरेण

प्रतिष्ठाप्यते। अस्मिन् पक्षे देहव्यतिरिक्तस्य आत्मनोऽभावात्। एवं मूर्तिपूजा असुराणामेव। अनार्याणां सकाशान् मूर्तिपूजायाः प्रचार इति केषाञ्चिदुद्घोषः संप्रदायविरुद्ध एव। असुराणामेवाऽयं पक्षः। मूर्तिपूजाया अवैदिकत्वाद् वैदिकैः कल्पसूत्रकारैर्देवपूजाप्रयोगो न सूत्रितः। यः किल दृश्यते बोधायनसूत्रादिषु, सोऽपि प्रकृतिवादमाश्रित्यैव। प्रकृतिवादमाश्रित्यैव प्रवृत्तानि धर्मसूत्राणि स्मृतयश्च देहधर्मान् विषयधर्मांश्च व्यवस्थापयन्ति। अत एव तैः सांख्यसिद्धान्त एव स्वीकृत इत्यवगन्तव्यम्। स्मृतिर्हि चित्तस्य वृत्तिः, न चितः। चिदेवाऽऽत्मधर्मो न चित्तम्। वृत्तिसरूपं हि चित्तमुच्यते। अवृत्तिका चिदुच्यते।

(७)

आत्मैकत्ववादिनां धर्मः सत्ये प्रतिष्ठितः। सत्तास्वभावं हि ब्रह्म। सत्यं ब्रह्मधर्मः। तस्मात् सत्यमेव धर्मः। तथा चोक्तं बृहदारण्यके (१.२.२६)— **यो वै स धर्मः। सत्यं वै तत्। तस्मात् सत्यं वदन्तमाहुर्धर्मं वदतीति। धर्मं वा वदन्तं सत्यं वदतीति।** मुण्डकेऽपि (३.६)—

सत्यमेव जयते नानृतम्,
सत्येन पन्था विततो देवयानः।
येनाऽऽक्रमन्त्यृषयो ह्याप्तकामाः,
यत्र तत् सत्यस्य परमं निधानम्॥

देहात्मवादिनां धर्मोऽसत्ये प्रतिष्ठितः। इदं सर्वं परिदृश्यमानं विश्वं शरीरं च विनाशि। विनाशित्वात् तस्य सत्ता नास्ति। मिथ्या हि सर्वम्। विषया मिथ्याः, त एव धर्म इति धर्मोऽपि मिथ्यात्वे प्रतिष्ठितः। शरीरं धर्मीति हिंसया तस्य नाशः, अहिंसया प्रतिष्ठेति देहात्मवादिनां धर्मोऽहिंसायां प्रतिष्ठितः। अहिंसा च हिंसाया अभाव एवेति अभावे प्रतिष्ठितो भावरूपो धर्मपदार्थ इति विपर्ययस्य पराकाष्ठा देहात्मवादिनाम्। इत्थमहिंसया सुप्रतिष्ठितमपि देहं जगद्वा कालो हिनस्त्येवेति महदाश्चर्यम्! तथा चोक्तं महाभारते—

अस्मिन् महामोहमये कटाहे
सूर्याग्निना रात्रिदिवेन्धनेन।
मासर्तु - दर्वी - परिघट्टनेन
भूतानि कालः पचतीति वार्ता॥

(वनपर्वणि, ३१३.११८)

इत्थमहिंसया सुप्रतिष्ठितस्य जगतः शरीरस्यापि कालेनाभावः सम्पाद्यते। भावरूपो धर्मी देहो जगच्च कालेनाभावे पर्यवस्यति। परिदृश्यमानस्य जगतोऽहिसायां प्रतिष्ठितत्वात् योगशास्त्रे अविद्यावतां व्युत्थितचित्तानां देहात्मवादिनां भोगिनां कृते समारब्धे साधनपादे अहिंसयैव यमानामारम्भः। अहिंसाधिष्ठितत्वं च तेषाम्। तथा हि—

अहिंसासत्यास्तेयब्रह्मचर्यापरिग्रहाः यमाः। (यो० सू० २.३०)

उत्तरे च यम-नियमास्तन्मूलाः तत्सिद्धिपरतया तत्प्रतिपादनाय प्रतिपाद्यन्ते। तदवदानरूपकरणायैव उपादीयन्ते। तथा चोक्तम्—

'स खल्वयं ब्राह्मणो यथा यथा व्रतानि बहूनि समादित्सते तथा तथा प्रमादकृतेभ्यो हिंसानिदानेभ्यो विवर्तमानस्तामेव अवदानरूपामहिंसां करोति।'

(यो० भा०,२.३०)

यद्यपि इत्थमहिंसया शरीरं विषयाश्च प्रतिष्ठिता भासन्ते; तथापि धर्मेण सुप्रतिष्ठतानामपि तेषां विनाशित्वात् सहजेन अधर्मेण कालप्रभावेण च हिंसिता भवन्ति, क्रमेण विनाश्यन्ते च। तस्मादहिंसया सुप्रतिष्ठितमपि इदं सर्वं कालेन कवलीक्रियत एव। अहिंसावाद इत्थं विशीर्यत एव। हिंसा तु भवत्येव। तस्मात् हिंसैव शरीरधर्मो सर्वस्य इदमश्च धर्मो नाऽहिंसा। सर्वथाऽहिंसया यथाकथञ्चिद् रक्ष्यमाणमपि हिंस्यत एव। हिंसायाः शरीरधर्मत्वात् वैदिकैः धर्मार्थं शरीरमपि हिंस्यत एव। अत एवोक्तं महाभारते—

धर्मं न त्यजेज्जीवितस्यापि हेतोः। (१८.५.६३)

किञ्चान्यत्-अहिंसा नाम हिंसाया अभावः। न ह्यभावात्मकः पदार्थो धर्मो भवितुमर्हति, धर्मस्य भावरूपत्वादिति पूर्वमुक्तम्। तस्मात् हिंसैव धर्मः। तथा च श्रुतयः—

भीषाऽस्माद्वातः पवते, भीषोदेति सूर्यः।
भीषाऽस्मादग्निश्चेन्द्रश्च, मृत्युर्धावति पञ्चमः॥ (तै० उ० २.८)

महद्भयं वज्रमुद्यतम्। (कठ० ६.२)

भयादस्याग्निस्तपति, भयात् तपति सूर्यः।
भयादिन्द्रश्च वायुश्च, मृत्युर्धावति पञ्चमः॥ (कठ० ६.३)

स्मृतिश्च—

तस्य सर्वाणि भूतानि स्थावराणि चराणि च।
भयाद्भोगाय कल्पन्ते स्वधर्मान्न चलन्ति च॥ (मनु० ७.१५)

सर्वो दण्डजितो लोको दुर्लभो हि शुचिर्नरः।
दण्डस्य हि भयात्सर्वं जगद् भोगाय कल्पते॥ (मनु० २०.२२)

हिंसैव हिंस्राणां पशूनां धर्मो भवति। दुष्कृतां विनाशश्च धर्मो भवति राज्ञाम्।

गीताशास्त्रेऽपि देहात्मवादमाश्रित्य अर्जुनेन **पृच्छामि त्वां धर्मसंमूढचेताः** (गीता २.७) इति धर्मः पृष्टः। स च युद्धं धर्म उत युद्धविरामो धर्म इत्येव। अथवा दार्शनिकपरिभाषया हिंसा धर्म उत अहिंसा धर्मः? इति। भगवता च प्रश्नस्यास्य आत्मवादमाश्रित्यैव उत्तरं दत्तम्। हिंसाऽहिंसाकल्पना आत्मवादे नास्तीति। तथा हि—

नैनं छिन्दन्ति शस्त्राणि नैनं दहति पावकः।

न चैनं क्लेदयन्त्यापो न शोषयति मारुतः ॥

अच्छेद्योऽयमदाह्योऽयमक्लेद्योऽशोष्य एव च ।
नित्यः सर्वगतः स्थाणुरचलोऽयं सनातनः ॥ (गी. २.२३-२४)

अत एव—**असतो मा सद् गमय । तमसो मा ज्योतिर्गमय । मृत्योर्मा अमृतं गमय ।** (बृ० १.१.३०)

इत्यत्र देहात्मवादाद् आत्मैकत्ववादं गमयेति प्रार्थ्यते । विनाशी देह इदं सर्वं दृश्यं जगत् च । सत्तास्वभावोऽविनाशी आत्मा । ज्योतिःस्वरूप आत्मा, तमःस्वभावो देहो विषयीभूतं जगच्च । अन्तवान् देहः । तथा च श्रुतिः—

मघवन् मर्त्यं वा इदं शरीरमात्तं मृत्युना तदस्यामृतस्याशरीरस्याऽऽत्मनोऽधिष्ठानमात्रो वै सशरीरः प्रियाऽप्रियाभ्याम् । न वै सशरीरस्य सतः प्रियाऽप्रिययोरपहतिरस्ति । अशरीरं वाव सन्तं न प्रियाऽप्रिये स्पृशतः । (छा० ८.१२.१)

देशतः कालतः स्वभावतश्च अनन्तं ब्रह्मेति तत्राऽमृतत्वम् । अत्र स्वयंज्योतिःस्वरूपं ब्रह्मणः स्पष्टमुक्तम् । तस्मात् **सत्यं ज्ञानमनन्तं ब्रह्म** (तै० उ० २.१.१) इत्यत्र सत्यमेव ब्रह्मधर्मः । ज्ञानं स्वयंज्योतिर्वा ब्रह्म-पदार्थः । अनन्तत्वं सत्ताया एव व्याख्यानम्, सत्तायाः सनातनत्वात् । अत एव **सत्यमेव जयते नानृतम्** (मुण्ड० ३.१.६) इति सिद्धान्तितम् ।

(८)

देहात्मवादे भोगापवर्गवादे वा अस्मिन् जगति स्त्रीसदृशो भोग्यः पदार्थ एव नास्ति । षडिन्द्रियाणां भोग्यो विषयः स्त्री । स्त्रीसदृशम् एकसमयावच्छेदेन षडिन्द्रियाणामाकर्षकं भोग्यं च वस्त्वन्तरं नास्ति । गन्ध-रस-रूप-स्पर्श-शब्दाः क्रमेण पञ्चेन्द्रियाणि आकर्षयन्ति । स्त्रिय आनन्दप्रदत्वं मन आकर्षयति । एवं सर्वेन्द्रियाणामाकर्षणं सन्तर्पणं चैकेनैव पदार्थेन भवतीति षडिन्द्रियाणां विषयो योषिद् भवति । अत एव भोगिनां स्त्रीसदृशो भोग्यः पदार्थ एव नास्ति । स्त्रियं दृष्ट्वा भोगिनः कामुकाः कामान्धाश्च भवन्तीति प्रसिद्धमेव । अपवर्गवादिनां योगिनां चित्तनिरोधोऽपि स्त्रीदर्शनपर्यन्तमेव । स्त्रियं दृष्ट्वा तेऽपि वृत्तिसरूपा भवन्तीति महदाश्चर्यम् । इत्थं स्त्री भोग्यः पदार्थ इति भोगवादिनां सिद्धान्तः । अत एव तैः सा यथेष्टं भोगायैव उपयुक्ता । तस्याः स्वातन्त्र्यं नास्ति ।

कामान्धानां कामुकत्वात् तेषां कामपूर्तेश्च स्त्र्यधीनत्वात् ते स्त्रीजिता भवन्तीति भोगवादे स्त्रियाः पुंवद्भावो भवति । सैव च कर्त्री भवति । यथा—रामायणे कैकेयी । भोगवादे कामाचार इति पातिव्रत्यं नास्ति । इत्थं स्त्रियं भोग्यां विधाय सा कदर्थीकृता भोगवादिभिः । प्रत्यक्षप्रमाणवादिभिः लौकायतिकैस्तु मातृत्वस्य अप्रत्यक्षत्वात्, अत एवाऽप्रमाणत्वाच्च

मातृगमनमपि न प्रतिषिद्धं प्रत्युत प्रमाणितम्। तथा च श्रूयते—**अपि वा मातरमियात्, अपि वा स्वसारम्** (?)।

अपवर्गवादिनो द्विविधाः—एके भोगानन्तरं संसारस्य दुःखमयत्वात् संसारमपवर्जयन्ति। वार्धक्य एतेषां संन्यासः। इतरे पुनः संसारस्य दुःखमयत्वाद् ब्रह्मचर्यादेव संन्यस्यन्ति। इन्द्रियाणाम् अतियोगाऽयोग-मिथ्यायोगा अधर्मः। योग एव धर्मः। अत एव गीताशास्त्रे (६.१७)—

युक्ताहार-विहारस्य युक्तचेष्टस्य कर्मसु।
युक्तस्वप्नाऽवबोधस्य योगो भवति दुःखहा॥

योग एव धर्मत्वेनोक्तः। एवं विवाह एव इन्द्रियधर्मः। ब्रह्मचर्यात् संन्यास इन्द्रियनिरोध इन्द्रियायोग इन्द्रियाधर्मः काम एव सा। अत एव संन्यासोऽयमधर्मः कामो वा। नहि धर्मः संन्यस्यते। ममत्वाभिमानेन स्वामित्वसम्बन्धेन भोग्यत्वेन वा विद्यमाना भोग्या विषया एव प्रकृतिपर्यन्ताः संन्यस्यन्ते। संन्यासेऽस्मिन् कामतो निरोधाद् इन्द्रियाणां स्त्रीणां च एकसमयावच्छेदेन षडिन्द्रियाणामाकर्षकत्वात् स्त्रियं दृष्ट्वैव एते योगभ्रष्टा भवन्ति। अत एव एभिश्चित्रस्थमपि स्त्रीदर्शनं निषिद्धं वर्जितं च। स्त्रीणां च मोहापादकत्वात् निन्दैव कृता। वस्तुतस्तु एत एवाऽधर्मचारिणो निन्द्या भवन्ति।

धर्मवादे स्त्री धर्मः,पुरुषश्च धर्मी। दम्पत्योरभेदः सम्बन्धः। तेनात्र विच्छेदो नास्ति। पदार्थ एक एव। यथा ब्रह्मणि आनन्दांशः परमशिवो धर्मी, चिदंशो भगवती चितिशक्तिर्धर्मः। धर्मधर्मिणोश्च अभेदः सम्बन्धः। तथापि धर्म-धर्मिणोः धर्मप्राधान्यात् चिच्छक्तिरेव मुख्या, गौण आनन्दांशः। जगदिदं चिद्विलास एव। तथा दम्पत्योरपि स्त्री मुख्या, पुरुषो गौणः। तेन दम्पती-पूजने स्त्रियः सम्पूर्णाः पूज्याः, पुरुषस्य तु यथा कथञ्चित् फलादिदानेन। **गौणमुख्ययोर्मुख्ये कार्यसम्प्रत्ययः** इति न्यायात् (परिभाषेन्दुशेखरे, परि० १४)। न्यायोऽयं ब्रह्मण्यपि समानः। ब्रह्मणश्चिदंश एव ज्योतिःस्वरूपः। स एव विराडग्निः। स एव महायज्ञैश्च यज्ञैश्च सन्तर्प्यते वैदिकैः।

अत एव पत्न्याः सद्भाव एव अग्निहोत्रादिधर्मः। तत्र पत्न्याः एव प्राधान्यम्। यजमानप्रवासे यजमानपत्न्या अग्निहोत्रपरिचर्या विधीयते। पत्नीप्रवासे तु सहैवाऽग्नयो नीयन्त इति धर्मे धर्मस्वरूपायाःपत्न्याःप्राधान्यम्। पूज्यस्य दक्षिणतःस्थानमिति धर्मकार्येषु पत्युर्दक्षिणतःपत्न्याः स्थानम्। माङ्गलिकेषु स्त्रीरग्रतः कृत्वा गच्छन्ति। तथा च महाभारते—

अग्नीन् प्रदक्षिणीकृत्य ब्राह्मणांश्च तपोधनान्।
याज्ञसेनीं पुरस्कृत्य षडेवाऽथ प्रवव्रजुः॥ **(विराट० ४.४.५६)**

व्याकरणशास्त्रेऽपि 'मातापितरौ, पार्वतीपरमेश्वरौ, सीतारामचन्द्रौ' इत्यादिषु स्त्रियाः पूर्वनिपात इष्यते। 'अभ्यर्हितं च' (पा० २.२.३४) इति वार्तिकेण स्त्रीणामभ्यर्हितत्वात्। एते सिद्धाः प्रयोगाः स्त्रीणामभ्यर्हितत्वं साधयन्ति। श्रुतावपि—

मातृदेवो भव। पितृदेवो भव। **(तै० उ० १.११.२)**

इत्यत्र मातुरेव अभ्यर्हितत्वात् प्रथममुपन्यासः। भगवता मनुनाऽपि स्त्रीणां प्रशंसैव कृता। तथा हि—

पितृभिर्भ्रातृभिश्चैताः पतिभिर्देवरैस्तथा।
पूज्या भूषयितव्याश्च बहुकल्याणमीप्सुभिः॥
यत्र नार्यस्तु पूज्यन्ते रमन्ते तत्र देवताः।
यत्रैतास्तु न पूज्यन्ते सर्वास्तत्राफलाः क्रियाः॥
शोचन्ति जामयो यत्र विनश्यत्याशु तत्कुलम्।
न शोचन्ति तु यत्रैता वर्धते तद्धि सर्वदा॥
जामयो यानि गेहानि शपन्त्यप्रतिपूजिताः।
तानि कृत्याहतानीव विनश्यन्ति समन्ततः॥
तस्मादेताः सदा पूज्या भूषणाच्छादनाशनैः।
भूतिकामैर्नरैर्नित्यं संस्कारेषूत्सवेषु च॥ **(मनु० ३.५५-५९)**

महाभारते मातृसमो गुरुर्नास्तीत्युक्तम्। तथा हि—

पितॄन् दश तु मातैका सर्वां वा पृथिवीमपि।
गुरुत्वेनाऽभिभवति नास्ति मातृसमो गुरुः॥ **(म.भा. शान्ति., १०८.१६)**

वैदिकस्य अग्निहोत्रादि-धर्मजातस्य स्त्रियमन्तरेणाऽप्रवृत्तेः स्त्रीणां धर्मरूपत्वम्। तासां च प्राधान्यं वैदिके धर्मे।

(९)

देहात्मवादिनो भोगापवर्गवादिनो वा दुष्कृतिनः। आत्मैकत्ववादिनो धर्मवादिनो वा सुकृतिनः। विभागोऽयं गीताशास्त्रे उक्तः। तथा हि—

न मां दुष्कृतिनो मूढाः प्रपद्यन्ते नराधमाः।
माययाऽपहृतज्ञाना आसुरं भावमाश्रिताः॥ **(७.१५)**

आसुरं भावमाश्रिताः देहात्मवादिनो भोगवादिनो वा।

प्रवृत्तिं च निवृत्तिं च जना न विदुरासुराः।

इति गीताशास्त्रे षोडशाध्याये (७ सप्तमश्लोके) सविस्तरमासुरी सम्पदुक्ता, तामाश्रिताः। ते इदं सर्वं दृश्यं जगदेव विषयीभूतं भोगार्थं प्रपद्यन्ते, नात्मानम्। त्रिगुणात्मिकाया महामायाया उपासका एते। तथा हि—**मायेत्यसुराः** (शत० ब्रा० १०.५.२.२०) इति परिदृश्यमानायास्त्रिगुणात्मिकाया मायाया एवोपासकत्वमसुराणाम्।

त्रिभिर्गुणमयैर्भावैरेभिः सर्वमिदं जगत्।

मोहितं नाभिजानाति मामेभ्यः परमव्ययम् ॥ (गी० ७.१३)

इत्येते मायामोहितत्वात् मायां प्रपद्यन्ते, नात्मानम्। प्रकृतेश्च भेदा अनन्ता भवन्तीति उपासनाप्रकाराश्चानन्ता असुराणाम्। ते च सर्वे तन्त्रशास्त्रेषु पुराणेषु चोपवर्णिताः। प्रकृत्युपासका मूर्त्युपासका वा एते। प्रकृतिवाद एव मूर्तीनामानन्त्यम्, उपासनाप्रकाराणां चानन्त्यम्।

एते हि तमःप्रधानत्वात् **सुहन्मित्रार्युदासीनमध्यस्थद्वेष्यबन्धुषु** इति (६.९) श्लोके १. सत्त्वप्रधाना **सुहृच्छ**ब्देन, २. रजःप्रधाना **मित्र**शब्देन, ३. तमःप्रधाना **अरि**शब्देन, ४. त्रिगुणात्मका **उदासीनशब्देन,** ५. सत्त्वतमःप्रधाना **मध्यस्थ**शब्देन, ६. रजस्तमःप्रधाना **द्वेष्य**शब्देन, ७. सत्त्वरजःप्रधाना **बन्धु**शब्देन इत्येवं ये सप्त प्रकृतिभेदा उक्तास्तत्रैते अरिस्वभावाः सर्वेषामरयो भवन्ति।

अयम्—आरोहक्रमेण दुष्कृतिनां प्रथमः प्रकारः। अवरोहक्रमेण चान्तिमः। एते विषयिणः।

मायया त्रैगुण्यात्मिकया।

दैवी ह्येषा गुणमयी मम माया दुरत्यया। (गी० ७.१४)

त्रैगुण्यं देहस्याऽसाधारणो धर्मः। मायया अपहृतं सन्मुषितं ज्ञानं येषां ते।

प्रमादमोहौ तमसो भवतोऽज्ञानमेव च।

(गी० ७.२०) इत्युक्तेः। ज्ञानं क्षेत्रज्ञरूपस्य आत्मनः प्रकाशरूपस्य धर्मः। **अमानित्वमदम्भित्वम्** (गी० १४.७) इत्यारभ्य—

एतज्ज्ञानमिति प्रोक्तमज्ञानं यदतोऽन्यथा।

(गी० १३.११) इत्यन्तमुक्तः। अज्ञानं मानित्वं दाम्भित्वमित्यादयः क्षेत्रधर्माः। देहात्मवादिनोऽसुरा विज्ञानवन्तो विपरीतज्ञानयुक्ता अज्ञानिन इति यावत्। नञोऽत्र विरुद्धार्थता। अत्र मायया दृश्येन विश्वेन अपहृतं ज्ञानं अभेदोपचारात् प्रमाकरणानि इन्द्रियाणि येषां ते। देहिनोऽन्नमयकोशस्था देहात्मवादिन इति यावत्। आरोहणक्रमेणायं द्वितीयः प्रकारः।

नराधमाः, नराणां मध्ये अधमाः निकृष्टाः, तमःप्रधानत्वात् कामहताः। विषय-विषयाणि येषामिन्द्रियाणि। येषां मन इन्द्रियाणां पश्चादेव धावति ते इन्द्रियचैतन्यवादिनो नराधमाः प्राणमयकोशस्थाः प्राणिन इति यावत्। आरोहणक्रमेणायं तृतीयः प्रकारः।

मूढाः बुद्धिहीनाः। तमःप्रधानाः मोहप्रधानाः कामान्धा इति यावत्।

इन्द्रियाणि मनोबुद्धिरस्याधिष्ठानमुच्यते।

इति (गी० ३.४०) बुद्धिपर्यन्तं कामस्याधिष्ठानात् विषयिणो विषयमापन्नाः।

इच्छाद्वेषसमुत्थेन द्वन्द्वमोहेन भारत।
सर्वभूतानि सम्मोहं सर्गे यान्ति परन्तप ॥

इति (गी० ७.२७) सम्मोहेन मायापर्यन्तान् विषयानेव प्रपद्यन्ते। तेषामिन्द्रियाणि मनो बुद्धिश्च विषयैराक्रान्ता भवतीति नेदिष्ठस्याप्यात्मनो बोधो नास्ति। अत एव ते मूढा

मनोमयकोशस्था मनश्चैतन्यवादिनो मनीषिण इति यावत्। आरोहणक्रमेणायं चतुर्थप्रकारः।

एते चत्वारोऽपि दुष्कृतिनः पापकारिणः।

प्रवृत्तिर्वाग्बुद्धिशरीरारम्भः। (न्या० सू० १.१.१७)
प्रवर्तनालक्षणा दोषाः। (१.१.१८)
दोषा रागद्वेषमोहाः। (न्या० भा० १.१.१८)
प्रवृत्तिदोषजनितोऽर्थः फलम्। (१.१.१९)

इति न्यायवित्समयानुसारेण सर्वा प्रवृत्तिः सदोषैव भवति। क्रियायाः सदोषत्वात् सा दुष्कृतिरित्येवोच्यते। मिथ्याज्ञानापायाभावे देहात्मवादिनां क्रिया दुष्कृतिरेव। अत एव ते दुष्कृतिन इत्यभिधीयन्ते। तेषां क्रियाफलं कर्तृगामि, तच्चार्थरूपम्। वस्तुतस्तु क्रियाफलं कर्मगामि। तच्च धर्मरूपम् अर्थरूपं फलमेभिस्तु कामस्यैव लभ्यते, न क्रियायाः। नष्टे कामे फलमर्थरूपं नास्ति।

एते सर्वे। न माम् अन्तर्यामिणं परमेश्वरं सर्वभूतस्थितं (गी० ६.३१), **पादोऽस्य विश्वाभूतानि** (मा० सं० ३१.३) इति परब्रह्मणः पादस्वरूपत्वम्। प्रपद्यन्ते। कामहतत्वात्। भगवानप्यत्र भक्तानुग्रहार्थं परिदेवयते।

आत्मैकत्ववादिनः सुकृतिनः। तथा हि—

चतुर्विधा भजन्ते मां नराः सुकृतिनोऽर्जुन।
आर्तो जिज्ञासुरर्थार्थी ज्ञानी च भरतर्षभ॥ (गी० ७.१६)

चतुर्विधाः चतुष्प्रकाराः आर्तः, जिज्ञासुः, अर्थार्थी ज्ञानी चेति। भजन्ते सेवन्ते। मनसा वाचा क्रियया च। मनसा एकमेवाद्वितीयं ब्रह्म धर्मीति चिन्तयन्ति। वाचा एकत्वमद्वितीयत्वं च प्रस्थापयन्ति। द्वैतं च समूलमुन्मूलयन्ति। क्रियया एकत्वप्रस्थापनार्थं न ममेति त्यागं कुर्वन्ति, न भोगं ममेति भुञ्जन्ति। क्रियाफलं कर्मगामि, स च धर्म इति प्रस्थापयन्ति। क्रियाफलं कर्तृगामि, स चार्थः कामफलं न क्रियाफलमिति तस्य त्यागं प्रतिपादयन्ति। कर्ता केवलं निमित्तकारणमित्यन्यथासिद्धः। अन्यथासिद्धत्वात् फलं प्रति तस्य हेतुत्वं नास्ति। तथाऽन्यथासिद्धत्वात् कर्तृत्वमपि नास्ति। कर्तृत्वमेकस्यैव। अथवा समवायिकारणाऽसमवायिकारणनिमित्तकारणानामेकीभूतानामेव। मां सर्वभूतस्थितमेकमद्वितीयं चित्स्वरूपमीश्वरम्। नराः जनाः सुकृतिनः पुण्यकर्माणः। तथा चोक्तं गीतासु (७.२८)—

येषां त्वन्तगतं पापं जनानां पुण्यकर्मणाम्।
ते द्वन्द्वमोहनिर्मुक्ता भजन्ते मां दृढव्रताः॥

येषां तु। अन्तगतं समाप्तप्रायं क्षीणम्। पापं कामः काम्यं जगदिति यावत्। तथा चोक्तं गीताशास्त्रे—

काम एष क्रोध एष रजोगुणसमुद्भवः।

महाशनो महापाप्मा विद्ध्येनमिह वैरिणम्॥ (३.३७)

पाप्मानं प्रजहि ह्येनं ज्ञानविज्ञाननाशनम्। (३.४१)

ध्यायतो विषयान् पुंसः सङ्गस्तेषूपजायते।
सङ्गात् सञ्जायते कामः कामात् क्रोधोऽभिजायते॥ (२.६२)

कामश्च बुद्धिपर्यन्तमेव अवस्थितः, विषयसम्बद्धत्वात्। विषया अपि बुद्धिपर्यन्तमेव अवस्थिताः। तथा चोक्तं गीताशास्त्रे (३.४२)—

इन्द्रियाणि मनोबुद्धिरस्याधिष्ठानमुच्यते।

बुद्धेः परश्चात्मा। तथाहि–

इन्द्रियाणि पराण्याहुरिन्द्रियेभ्यः परं मनः।
मनसस्तु परा बुद्धिर्यो बुद्धेः परतस्तु सः॥

जनानां लोकानाम्। पुण्यकर्मणां नित्यं नैमित्तिकं चैव कुर्वताम्। काम्यं निषिद्धं च कर्म संन्यस्यताम्। कर्मगामि क्रियाफलं न कर्तृगामीति सिद्धान्तयताम्। धर्मः फलं नार्थ इत्यभ्युपगच्छताम्। कर्तृगामि क्रियाफलं कामस्यैवेति काममेव न क्रियां परित्यजताम्। ते। द्वन्द्वमोहनिर्मुक्ताः। तथा चोक्तम्—

इच्छाद्वेषसमुत्थेन द्वन्द्वमोहेन भारत।
सर्वभूतानि सम्मोहं सर्गे यान्ति परन्तप॥ (गी. ७.२७)

इच्छाद्वेषमोहैर्निर्मुक्ता गुणत्रयातीता इति यावत्। भजन्ते सेवन्ते। मां परमात्मानम्। दृढव्रताः एकमेवाद्वितीयं ब्रह्मेति परमार्थतत्त्वं नान्यथेति निश्चितविज्ञानाः। एकत्वाद्वितीयत्वप्रस्थापकाः। एकत्वमेव दृढं व्रतं येषां ते। एकत्विनः। तस्मादत्र सुकृतिनो गुणातीताः। तेषामेव आत्मख्यातिः। तथा च योगसूत्रम्—

तत्परं पुरुषख्यातेर्गुणवैतृष्ण्यम्। (१.१६)

अत एव गुणातीता मां भजन्ते। अर्जुन। आत्मज्ञाने जाते तत्रैव अन्तर्यामित्वेन परमात्मज्ञानमिति परमात्मभजनमात्मज्ञानमेव।

आर्तो दुःखाभिभूतो विषया एव दुःखहेतव इति इहामुत्रभोगविरागसम्पन्नः कामाभावाद् गुणातीतो नित्यानित्यवस्तुविवेकज्ञश्च। नित्यानित्यवस्तुविवेकश्च त्रयोदशाध्याये, गुणवैतृष्ण्यं चतुर्दशाध्याये, वशीकारसंज्ञावैराग्यं पञ्चदशाध्याये गीतायामुक्तम्। आत्मैकत्वविद्या चावरोहक्रमेण परिसमापिता। तत्रैव निस्त्रैगुण्यप्रतिपादनपरगुह्यतमशास्त्रस्य समाप्तिः। अन्तिममध्यायत्रयं त्रैगुण्यविषयं देहात्मवादिनां कृते। एवम् आर्तो नाम आत्मज्ञः। विज्ञानमयकोशस्थो बुद्धिचैतन्यवादी बुद्धिमान् इति यावत्। अत एवोक्तं भगवद्गीतासु (१५.२०)—

एतद् बुद्ध्वा बुद्धिमान् स्यात् कृतकृत्यश्च भारत। इति।

एवञ्च आर्तो नाम विज्ञानमयकोशस्थो नित्यसत्त्वस्थः सिद्ध्यति। **सत्त्वात् सञ्जायते ज्ञानम्**(गी० १४.१७)इति सञ्जातात्मतत्त्वज्ञान इति यावत्। आत्मैकत्वज्ञानस्य दृढीकरणार्थमेव विज्ञानमय-कोशस्थानां महत्तत्त्वम्, अहङ्कारः, तन्मात्रपञ्चकं चेति सप्तपदार्थानां वैगुण्येन साकमात्मनोऽन्यथाख्यातिप्रख्यापनार्थं सर्वैः कल्पसूत्रकारैः एकविंशतिसंस्कारा उक्ताः। तत्र तमोगुणापवर्जनाय अष्टका, पार्वणः, श्राद्धं चेत्यादि-सप्तपाकसंस्थाः। रजोगुणापवर्जनाय अग्न्याधेयमग्निहोत्रं दर्शपूर्णमासौ चेत्यादि सप्तहविर्यज्ञसंस्थाः। सत्त्वगुणापवर्जनाय अग्निष्टोमोऽत्यग्निष्टोम उक्थ्यः इत्यादिसप्तसोमसंस्थाः। एवमत्र एकविंशतिसंस्कारैः विज्ञानमयकोशात् आऽऽनन्दमयकोशम् आर्त उपसङ्क्रामति।

आत्मज्ञानेन साकमेव अन्तर्यामित्वेनावस्थितस्य चोदनालक्षणस्य परमात्मनो ज्ञानमनुमानेन भवतीति आर्तोऽपि परमात्मानं भजते। महायज्ञैश्च यज्ञैश्च परमात्मानं सन्तर्पयति। तथा चोक्तं मनुना—

स्वाध्यायेन व्रतैर्होमैस्त्रैविद्येनेज्यया सुतैः।
महायज्ञैश्च यज्ञैश्च ब्राह्मीयं क्रियते तनुः॥ **(मनु० २.२८)**

गुणातीतानामेव अन्तर्यामित्वेन परमात्मदर्शनं सम्पद्यत इति दर्शनानन्तरमेव तस्य लक्षणं सामान्यधर्मान् विशेषधर्मांश्च ज्ञातुं साधकः प्रवर्तते इत्यत्रैव ब्रह्मजिज्ञासोदय इति जिज्ञासुरयम्। तथा च श्रुतिः —

आत्मा वा अरे द्रष्टव्यः श्रोतव्यो मन्तव्यो निदिध्यासितव्यः। (बृ० २.४.५)

इति आत्मदर्शनानन्तरमेव तस्य तत्त्वज्ञानार्थं श्रवणं मननं निदिध्यासनं च श्रुतिर्विदधाति। धर्मिज्ञानात् प्राक् तस्य धर्मजिज्ञासाऽशक्यप्रायैव।

अस्य जिज्ञासोरन्तर्यामिणः चोदनानुसरणमेव धर्मः। कामचाराभावाद् ईश्वरेच्छानुसारमेव क्रियासु प्रवृत्तिरित्यत्र कर्मसंन्यासः। स्वेच्छया क्रियाप्रवृत्तेरभावान् **करिष्ये वचनं तव** (गी० १८.७३) इत्येवात्र भूमिका। अयमेव भक्तियोगः सप्तमाध्यायमारभ्य द्वादशाध्यायपर्यन्तमुक्तः। सर्वभावेनात्र शरणं गच्छति योगी। तथा हि—

तमेव शरणं गच्छ सर्वभावेन भारत।
तत्प्रसादात् परां शान्तिं स्थानं प्राप्स्यसि शाश्वतम्॥ **(गी० १७.६२)**

एवञ्च आर्तो विज्ञानमयः, जिज्ञासुः पुनश्चिन्मयः।

जिज्ञासोर्जिज्ञासाविषय एवार्थो भवतीति ब्रह्मैवार्थः। तस्मादर्थार्थी ब्रह्मार्थी भवति। सगुणेन ब्रह्मणा साकमेकत्वं गच्छति। आनन्दमयः सम्पद्यते। अस्यां भूमिकायां धर्मस्थापनमेव धर्मः। अयमेव कर्मयोगः षष्ठाध्यायपर्यन्तमुक्तः। स च योगी **सर्वभूतानि चात्मनि** (गी० ६.२९) पश्यति, विश्वरूप ईश्वरो भवति।

एकत्वं गतो योगेश्वरः समाधौ निरुपाधिकेन ब्रह्मणा एकत्वं गच्छति तदाऽद्वितीयत्वं प्राप्नोति, ब्रह्ममयः सम्पद्यते। व्युत्थाने पुनरेकत्वमाप्नोति। अयमेव ज्ञानी सर्वज्ञः सम्पद्यते। अस्यैव समाधौ ज्ञानयोगो नैष्कर्म्यं धर्मः। व्युत्थाने च कर्मयोगः।

चिदात्मज्ञाने कृतान्तः सम्पद्यते अशरीरत्वात्। अत्रैव सांख्यशास्त्रस्य योगशास्त्रस्य च समाप्तिः। अत एवोक्तम्—

साङ्ख्ये कृतान्ते प्रोक्तानि। (गी० १८.१३)

अधिकारी च वेदं चितिशक्तिं वेत्तीति वैदिको भवति। यदा चितिशक्तेः निरुपाधिकेन ब्रह्मणा मीलनं सम्पद्यते, तदा वेदान्तो भवति। वेदस्य चितिशक्तेरन्तो भवति। अद्वितीयत्वं सम्पद्यते—

वेदा अवेदा भवन्ति। (बृ० ४.३.२२)।

एत एव चत्वारस्तपस्वी, ज्ञानी, कर्मी, योगी चेति धर्मान्तरेणोक्ताः। तथा हि—

तपस्विभ्योऽधिको योगी ज्ञानिभ्योऽपि मतोऽधिकः।
कर्मिभ्यश्चाधिको योगी तस्माद् योगी भवाऽर्जुन॥

तपस्वी आर्तो विज्ञानमयकोशस्थो यज्ञक्रियारतः। ज्ञानी जिज्ञासुर्भगवदाज्ञानुसरणं कुर्वाणो भक्तः। अर्थार्थी कर्मी एकत्वं गतः। धर्मस्थापनमेव कुर्वाणः कर्मयोगी। योगी समाधौ अद्वितीयत्वं गतो महायोगेश्वर इति।

(१०)

वैदिकानां साम्यवादः एकत्वं च

ब्रह्मवादिनामद्वितीयं ब्रह्म धर्मी, तस्य अद्वितीयत्वं धर्मः। ब्रह्मव्यतिरिक्ताः सर्वे पदार्था विनाशिनोऽनित्याश्चेति अधर्मिण एव। अत एव द्वितीयस्य धर्मिणोऽभावाद् द्वैताश्रितस्य भोगवादस्य अपवर्गवादस्य भोगापवर्गवादस्य पुरुषार्थवादस्य वा स्थानमेव नास्ति वैदिकदर्शने। धर्मधर्मिणोरेव विद्यमानत्वात् **अथातो धर्मजिज्ञासा** (पू. मी. १.१.१), **अथातो ब्रह्मजिज्ञासा** (उ० मी० १.१.१) चेति धर्म-धर्मिजिज्ञासा केवलं प्रस्तुता मीमांसकैः। पूर्वमीमांसायां धर्मः, उत्तरमीमांसायां च धर्मी क्रमेण मीमांसितः।

अद्वितीयस्य ब्रह्मणः पादत्रयं विकारावर्ति, एकपादश्च विकारवर्ती। तत्र विकारावर्तिना पादत्रयेण विकारवतिनः पादस्य एकत्वम्। प्रतिविकारं चात्मभेदो नास्ति, विकाराणामाद्यन्तवत्त्वादिति विकारवर्ति-ब्रह्मणोऽपि एकत्वम्। विकाराणां भेदादानन्त्याच्च प्रतिविकारमात्मभेदः प्रतीयेत, भेदप्रतीत्या च भोगवादः, भोगानां दुःखयोनित्वाद् अपवर्गवादः पुरुषार्थवादो वा समुज्जृम्भेतेति तन्निराकरणाय **एकमेवाद्वितीयम्** (छा० ६.२.१) इत्यत्र एवकारः। आत्मैकत्वमेव वैदिकः सिद्धान्तः। अत एव भगवत्पूज्यपादाचार्यैरुक्तम्— **आत्मैकत्वविद्याप्रतिपत्तये सर्वे वेदान्ता आरभ्यन्ते** (ब्रह्म० शां० भा० १.१.१) इति। अत एकत्वस्थापनमेव वैदिकानां धर्मः संवृत्तः। त्यागेनैव एकत्वमिदं स्थाप्यत इति एकत्वे त्यागो धर्मः। आत्मैकत्वे देहदृष्ट्या विविधेषु विशिष्टेषु विषमेषु विपरीतेष्वपि भूतेषु साम्यदृष्टिर्योगिनो भवति। तथा चोक्तं गीतायाम् (५.१८-१९)—

विद्याविनयसम्पन्ने ब्राह्मणे गवि हस्तिनि।
शुनि चैव श्वपाके च पण्डिताः समदर्शिनः॥

इहैव तैर्जितः सर्गो येषां साम्ये स्थितं मनः।
निर्दोषं हि समं ब्रह्म तस्माद् ब्रह्मणि ते स्थिताः॥

साम्यदृष्ट्यैव वैदिकैः पञ्चमहायज्ञा अहरहरनुष्ठीयन्ते। बुभुक्षा-पिपासायाश्चेतनाधर्मत्वात् तद्रूपाधर्माभ्युत्थान-विनाशार्थम् अन्नोदकेन धर्मसंस्थापनार्थं च सर्वेषां भूतानामन्नोदकप्राप्तिः अत्यावश्यकी। तदर्थमेव सर्वेषां भूतानां प्रयत्नः। कृतेऽपि प्रयत्ने येषामन्नोदकप्राप्तिर्न भवति, तेषां कृते आवश्यकस्त्यागः। अत एव वैदिकैः पञ्चमहायज्ञानामनुष्ठानमहरहः क्रियते। तत्र च आब्रह्मस्तम्बपर्यन्तं भूतानामन्नेन तृप्तिर्विधीयते। तर्पणे च जलेन। पञ्चमहायज्ञैः साम्यदृष्ट्या एकत्वं स्थाप्यते। तच्च आत्मन एव, न शरीरस्य, तस्य प्रतिभूतं भिद्यमानत्वात्। अन्नोदकस्य प्रतिभूतं शरीरधर्मस्थापनार्थमावश्यकत्वाद् वृत्त्यभावे अन्नाभावे च योगसूत्रोक्तम् **अस्तेयप्रतिष्ठायां सर्वरसोपस्थानम्** (२.३७) इति सार्वभौमम् अस्तेयव्रतं प्रत्याख्यातुमिव स्तेयमपि धर्मत्वेन विहितं धर्मशास्त्रकारैः। तथा चोक्तं मनुना (११.१६-१७)—

तथैव सप्तमे भक्ते भक्तानि षडनश्नता।
अश्वस्तनविधानेन हर्तव्यं हीनकर्मणः॥

खलात् क्षेत्रादगाराद्वा यतो वाऽप्युपलभ्यते।
आख्यातव्यं तु तत्तस्मै पृच्छते यदि पृच्छति॥

अस्य ब्रह्मधर्मस्य एकत्वस्य प्राप्त्यर्थं मीमांसकैः सोपानपङ्क्तिर्विरचिता। तथा हि—दम्पत्योरेकत्वम्। कुटुम्बस्य एकत्वम्। त्रिपुरुष-सपिण्डानामेकत्वम्। सप्तगोत्राणामेकत्वम्। सप्तगोत्राणि तु—

पिता माता च भार्या च भगिनी दुहिता तथा।
पितृमातृष्वसा चैव सप्त गोत्राणि वै विदुः॥

तत्त्वानि विंशति नृपा द्वादशैकादशा दश।
अष्टाविति च गोत्राणां कुलमेकोत्तरं शतम्॥

तत्त्वानि च चतुर्विंशतिः। ते च द्वादश पूर्वाः, द्वादश पराः।

शमीपत्रप्रमाणेन पिण्डं दद्याद् गयाशिरे।
उद्धरेत् सप्तगोत्राणि कुलमेकोत्तरं शतम्॥

—त्रिस्थलीसेतौ वायवीये। निर्णयसिन्धुः, पृ० २६७

शमीपत्रप्रमाणं वा पिण्डं दद्याद् गयाशिरे।
उद्धरेत् सप्तगोत्राणि कुलानि शतमुद्धरेत्॥

पितुर्मातुः स्वभार्याया भगिन्या दुहितुस्तथा।
पितृष्वसुर्मातृष्वसुः सप्त गोत्राः प्रकीर्तिताः॥

चतुर्विंशतिर्विंशश्च षोडश द्वादशैव हि।
रुद्रादि वसवश्चैव कुलान्येकोत्तरं शतम्॥ (वायुपुराणे ११०.२५-२७)

एतेषां सप्तगोत्राणामेकत्वस्थापनार्थमेव नित्यतर्पणमहालय-तीर्थश्राद्धादिविधिः।

साप्तपौरुषं सापिण्ड्यमिति सप्तपुरुषपर्यन्तानां सपिण्डानामेकत्वम्। तत्र दशाहाशौचमुक्तम्। चतुर्दशपुरुषपर्यन्तं सोदकत्वम्। तत्र त्रिरात्रमात्रमाशौचमुक्तम्। एकविंशतिपुरुषपर्यन्तं सगोत्रत्वम्। तत्र स्नानमुक्तम्। इत्थमेकविंशतिपुरुषपर्यन्तं कुलमुच्यते। तत्र त्यागेन एकत्वस्थापनं कुलधर्मस्थापनमुच्यते। त्यागेन आपदुन्मूलनं रक्षणं च। सम्पत्तौ विपत्तौ च विवाहादिषु माङ्गलिकेषु अमाङ्गलिकेषु च सर्वेषामेकीभावः। एकत्वेन कुलस्य अविनाशः। कुलधर्मोऽयमिदानीं नष्टप्राय एव। भ्रातॄणामपि एकत्वं नास्ति। भ्राता भ्रातुः कृते परित्यागं कर्तुं तस्य चापदं निर्मूलयितुं न मनागपि सन्नद्धो भवति, भोगैकपरायणत्वात्।

जातेरेकत्वम्। देहधर्मो जातिः, नात्मधर्मः। देहो हि जायते, नात्मा। शरीरस्य प्रकृतिभेदात् जातिभेदः। प्रकृतिभेदानामानन्त्यात् जातीनामप्यानन्त्यम्। क्रिया शरीरधर्म इन्द्रियाणां वा धर्म इति प्रकृत्यनुसारेणैव क्रिया भवन्ति। तथा हि—

प्रकृतेः क्रियमाणानि गुणैः कर्माणि सर्वशः।
अहङ्कारविमूढात्मा कर्ताऽहमिति मन्यते॥
सदृशं चेष्टते स्वस्याः प्रकृतेर्ज्ञानवानपि।
प्रकृतिं यान्ति भूतानि निग्रहः किं करिष्यति॥ (गी. ३.२७,३३)

न कर्तृत्वं न कर्माणि लोकस्य सृजति प्रभुः।
न कर्मफलसंयोगं स्वभावस्तु प्रवर्तते॥ (५.१४)

कार्यकारणकर्तृत्वे हेतुः प्रकृतिरुच्यते।
पुरुषः सुखदुःखानां भोक्तृत्वे हेतुरुच्यते॥
प्रकृत्यैव च कर्माणि क्रियमाणानि सर्वशः।
यः पश्यति तथाऽऽत्मानमकर्तारं स पश्यति॥ (१३.२०,२९)

नान्यं गुणेभ्यः कर्तारं यदा द्रष्टाऽनुपश्यति।
गुणेभ्यश्च परं वेत्ति मद्भावं सोऽधिगच्छति॥ (१४.१९)

प्रकृतिभेदानुसारेण क्रियाभेदो नियम्यते। स च देहधर्मो भवति। अत एव धर्मवादिभिः जातित्वं जन्मनैव स्वीकृतम्। मातृ-पितृबीजसंयोगेनैव शरीरमुत्पद्यत इति बीजप्रकृत्यनुसारेणैव शरीरप्रकृतिर्भवतीति जात्यनुसारेणैव क्रिया निर्णीयते। जन्मनैव जातित्वम्, जन्मनैव च क्रियानिर्णयः। स्वकर्मणैव सर्वभूतस्थितस्य भगवतः परिचर्या। अत एवोक्तं भगवद्गीतासु अपवर्गवादखण्डनपरे देहधर्मव्यवस्थापनपरे चाष्टादशाध्याये (श्लो. ४५-४८, ५९-६०)

स्वे स्वे कर्मण्यभिरतः संसिद्धिं लभते नरः।
स्वकर्मनिरतः सिद्धिं यथा विन्दति तच्छृणु ॥

यतः प्रवृत्तिर्भूतानां येन सर्वमिदं ततम्।
स्वकर्मणा तमभ्यर्च्य सिद्धिं विन्दति मानवः ॥

श्रेयान् स्वधर्मो विगुणः परधर्मात् स्वनुष्ठितात्।
स्वभावनियतं कर्म कुर्वन्नाप्नोति किल्बिषम् ॥

सहजं कर्म कौन्तेय सदोषमपि न त्यजेत्।
सर्वारम्भा हि दोषेण धूमेनाग्निरिवावृताः ॥

यदहङ्कारमाश्रित्य न योत्स्य इति मन्यसे।
मिथ्यैष व्यवसायस्ते प्रकृतिस्त्वां नियोक्ष्यति ॥

स्वभावजेन कौन्तेय निबद्धः स्वेन कर्मणा।
कर्तुं नेच्छसि यन्मोहात् करिष्यस्यवशोऽपि तत् ॥

इत्थं स्वकर्मणा सर्वभूतस्थितस्य भगवतोऽभ्यर्चने कामचारस्य अवकाश एव नोत्पद्यते। कामचाराभावात् धर्मचर्यया क्रमेण बुद्धिपर्यन्तं कामो नश्यति। कामनाशात् साधको रागद्वेषमोहैः विमुक्तो भवति। राग-द्वेष-मोहाक्रान्तान् दोषत्रयग्रस्तान् अन्नमय-प्राणमय-मनोमय-कोशान् विहाय विज्ञानमयकोशमुपसंक्रामति। तत्र च त्रैगुण्ययुक्तो भवति। तत्रापि कामस्याभावात् रजोगुणस्तमोगुणश्च शान्तस्तिष्ठति। सत्त्वगुणस्य च उदयो भवति। सत्त्वगुणस्योदयात् **विशोका वा ज्योतिष्मती** (यो० सू० १.३६) प्रवृत्तिरनायासेन भवति। प्रयत्नान्तराणां योगशास्त्रप्रोक्तानामावश्यकतैव नोत्पद्यते। अत एव आसुरीसम्पत्तिमतां विषयिणां समुद्धाराय भगवता—

तस्माच्छास्त्रं प्रमाणं ते कार्याकार्यव्यवस्थितौ।
ज्ञात्वा शास्त्रविधानोक्तं कर्म कर्तुमिहार्हसि ॥

इति शास्त्रप्रामाण्येनैव कार्याऽकार्य-व्यवस्थापनमुक्तम्, न स्वेच्छया। शास्त्रेण च जन्मनैव जात्यनुसारेण कार्याऽकार्यव्यवस्था व्यवस्थापिता। व्यवस्थामेतामवलम्ब्य सर्वेषां वृत्तिविधानं विहितम्। वृत्तिशून्यता धर्मवादे नास्ति।

भोगवादिनः अपवर्गवादिनो भोगापवर्गवादिनश्च जन्मना जातित्वं नाङ्गीकुर्वन्ति इति कार्याकार्यव्यवस्थापनं जन्मना जात्या वा न नियम्यते तैः, तेषां कामचारस्य स्वैराचारस्य वा प्रतिबन्धकत्वात्। ते हि धर्मवादिभिः प्रस्थापितं मनुष्येषु जातित्वं खण्डयन्ति। प्रकृतिसिद्धं जातित्वं जातिधर्मांश्च खण्डयित्वा कामचारं प्रवर्तयन्ति। इत्थं खण्डितेऽपि मानवजातित्वे मनुष्येतरेषु तृणपर्यन्तेषु चेतनपदार्थेषु मृत्तिकापर्यन्तेषु अचेतनेषु पदार्थेषु च विद्यमानमानुवंशिकं जातित्वं विद्यमानान् जातिधर्मांश्च खण्डयितुमसमर्थाः संवृत्ता उत्कृष्टभोगसिद्ध्यर्थं भोग्यानां

चेतनाचेतनानां च पदार्थानां जातित्वमङ्गीकुर्वन्ति, भोगोत्कर्षार्थमुत्कृष्टजातिपदार्थं परिगृह्णन्ति, हीनजातिपदार्थमपवर्जयन्ति इति महदाश्चर्यम्, महती प्रतारणा च। अनङ्गीकृते भोग्यपदार्थानां जातित्वे अनङ्गीकृतेषु भोग्यपदार्थानां जातिधर्मेषु प्राचीनानि अर्वाचीनानि दृश्यपदार्थ-धर्मत्वव्यवस्थापकानि शास्त्राणि व्याहन्येरन्, भोगोत्कर्षश्च नैव सिद्ध्येत्, सर्वलोकव्यवहारोच्छेदश्च प्रसज्येत। इत्थं मनुष्येषु जातित्वं जातिधर्माश्च विद्यन्त एवेति सिद्धान्तः। अत्र धर्मशब्देन अधर्माणामपि ग्रहणं भवति, अनित्येषु पदार्थेषु धर्माऽधर्मयोः द्वन्द्वस्य विद्यमानत्वात्।

भोगवादे कामचारात् सर्वेषां वृत्तिव्यवस्था नियन्तुं नैव शक्यत इति केचित् श्रीमन्तो भोगनिरता विलसन्ति। इतरे पुनर्वृत्तिशून्या बुभुक्षाक्षामा निवासरहिता इतस्ततः भ्रमन्ति। धर्मवादे आत्मैकत्ववादे वा सर्वेषां वृत्तिलाभार्थं जन्मनैव वृत्तिर्नियमिता, सर्वेषां वृत्तिव्यवस्था च कृता। सा च परम्परया प्रचलिताऽपि भोगवादप्रादुर्भावात् सर्वत्रोत्सन्ना। जातित्वं नाममात्रेण तिष्ठति। का वार्ता तत्रैकत्वस्य? द्वैते परस्य चिन्तैव नोत्पद्यते। त्यागोऽपि नैव सम्भवति द्वैतत्वादेव। इत्थं जातिधर्मो जातेरेकत्वं वा उत्सन्नप्रायमेव। गीताशास्त्रप्रोक्तैव (१.४३) स्थितिर्विद्यते। तथा हि—

उत्साद्यन्ते जातिधर्माः कुलधर्माश्च शाश्वताः।

अनेनैव प्रकारेण वर्णैकत्वम्, भूतानामेकत्वम्, ग्रामैकत्वम्, देशैकत्वम्, राष्ट्रैकत्वम्, विश्वैकत्वमिति आत्मैकत्वस्थापनप्रकारः क्रमेण विधीयते। अत्र अन्तरङ्गन्यायमाश्रित्य दम्पत्योः एकत्वमारभ्य आत्मैकत्वं प्रस्थापितं मीमांसकैः। अन्तरङ्गन्यायमाश्रित्यैव विवाह-व्यवस्था, संस्काराधिकारव्यवस्था, श्राद्धाधिकार-व्यवस्था, दायभाग-व्यवस्था चेत्यादि विधीयते धर्मवादे। व्यवस्थायामस्यां स्वैराचारस्य अवकाश एव नास्ति। अन्तरङ्गन्यायश्च लोकसिद्धः **असिद्धं बहिरङ्गमन्तरङ्गे** इति परिभाषायां सविस्तरं व्याख्यातो व्याकरणमहाभाष्ये परिभाषेन्दुशेखरे च (परि, ५०)। अन्तरङ्गन्यायमाश्रित्य क्रमेण एकत्वस्थापनमतीव सुकरं भवति। अक्रमेण आत्मैकत्वस्थापनाभ्यासो विफलो भवति। नहि शब्दोच्चारणमात्रेण एकत्वं प्रस्थापयितुं शक्यते। विश्वैकत्वं क्रमेणैव अभ्यासवैराग्याभ्यां सम्पद्यते। साधकश्च महात्मा विश्वात्मको वा भवति। तथा च मन्त्रवर्णः—

वेनस्तत् पश्यन् निहितं गुहा सत्
यत्र विश्वं भवत्येकनीडम्।
तस्मिन्निदं सं च वि चैति सर्वं
स ओतःप्रोतश्च विभूः प्रजासु॥

(मा० सं० ३२.८; म. ना० २.३)

एवं धर्मस्थापनेन विश्वस्य जगतः प्रतिष्ठा सम्पद्यते।

इदं सर्वं परिदृश्यमानं जगत् प्रमाणीकुर्वाणानामवैदिकानां वेदबाह्यानां च धर्मवादो नास्ति, धर्मिणोऽभावात्। त्रैकालिकसत्ताविहीनमाद्यन्तवत् जगत् सत्यमिति वक्तुं नैव शक्यते।

परिच्छिन्नकाले परिदृश्यमानत्वात् असत्यमिति निश्चेतुं नैव शक्यते। अत एव सदसद्विलक्षणमिदं जगत् मिथ्येति व्यपदिश्यते धर्मवादिभिः। एवमन्तवत्त्वात् जगद् धर्मीति व्यपदेष्टुं नैव शक्यते। तथापि—

अधर्मं धर्ममिति या मन्यते तमसावृता।

(गी. १८.३२) इति तमसावृतैरधर्मो धर्म इति, अधर्मी च पदार्थो धर्मीति परिगृह्यते। अधर्मवादो द्वैताश्रित एव। स च त्रिविधः— १. भोगवादः, २. अपवर्गवादः, ३. भोगापवर्गवादश्च। वादत्रयस्य स्वार्थमूलकत्वात् तज्जगतो विनाशायैव सम्पद्यते।

(११)

विविधा निःश्रेयसभेदाः

भोगवादिनां त्रिविधाया धर्माऽर्थकामरूपाया भोगकल्पनायाः प्रकृतितन्त्रत्वात् प्रकृतेश्च प्रतिभूतं भिद्यमानत्वाद् धर्मार्थकामानां प्रकृत्यनुसारेण भेदाः सम्पद्यन्ते। भोगसाधनान्यपि देशकालादि-सापेक्षतया भिद्यन्ते परिवर्त्यन्ते च। एवमपवर्गवादिनां मोक्षकल्पना मोक्षसाधनानि च पौरुषेयत्वात् प्रतितन्त्रं भिद्यन्ते। भोगवादिनां मोक्षवादिनां च ऐकमत्यं नास्तीति भोगवादो मोक्षवादश्च अप्रमाणं भवति, अनवस्थितत्वात्।

अवैदिकानां परमपुरुषार्थरूपस्य मोक्षवादस्य अप्रमाणत्वम्, अनवस्थितत्वं च प्रदर्शयितुं मोक्षवादिनां दार्शनिकानां निःश्रेयसभेदाः प्रदर्श्यन्ते विदुषां प्रमोदाय।

१. स्वातन्त्र्यं मृत्युर्वा मोक्ष इति **चार्वाका आहुः**।

२. आत्मोच्छेदो मोक्ष इति **माध्यमिकाः**।

३. धर्मिनिवृत्तौ निर्मलज्ञानोदयो महोदय इति **विज्ञानवादिनः**।

४. आवरणमुक्तिः मुक्तिरिति **आर्हताः**।

५. जीवस्य लिङ्गशरीरापगमो मोक्ष इति **भास्करीयाः**।

६. सर्वकर्तृत्वमेकं विहाय वासुदेवस्य सर्वज्ञत्वादीनां कल्याणगुणानामाप्तिमत्त्वे सति भगवद्याथात्म्यानुभवो मोक्ष इति **विशिष्टाद्वैतवादिनो रामानुजीयाः**।

७. जगत्कर्तृत्व-लक्ष्मीपतित्व-श्रीवत्सवर्जं भगवज्ज्ञानायत्त-निर्दुःखपूर्णसुखं मोक्ष इति द्वैतवादिनो **माध्वाः**। स च मोक्षस्तन्मते सालोक्य-सारूप्यसामीप्य-सायुज्यभेदात् चतुर्विधः।

८. द्विभुजकृष्णेन सह स्वांशभूतानां जीवानां गोलोके लीलानुभव इति **शुद्धाद्वैतवादिनो वल्लभीयाः**।

९. पारमैश्वर्यप्राप्तिः इति पाशुपतशास्त्रज्ञा नकुलीशाचार्यादयो **माहेश्वराः**।

१०. चन्द्रचूडवपुषः सतः पार्वत्यालिङ्गनमिति **कापालिकाः**।

११. पूर्णात्मतालाभ इति प्रत्यभिज्ञावादिनोऽ**भिनवगुप्तपादाचार्याः**।

१२. पारदरस-पानेन देहस्थैर्ये जीवन्मुक्तिरेव मोक्ष इति **रसेश्वरवादिनः**।

१३. आत्यन्तिकी दुःखनिवृत्तिरिति **गौतमीया नैयायिकाः** ।

१४. आत्यन्तिकी दुरितनिवृत्तिरिति **न्यायैकदेशिनः** ।

१५. दुःखात्यन्ताभाव एव मुक्तिरिति **प्राञ्चः** ।

१६. दुःखनिवृत्तिः (दुःखानुत्पादः) इति **काणादादयो वैशेषिकाः** ।

१७. परा पश्यन्ती मध्यमा वैखरीति वाणीचतुष्टये प्रथमायाः पराख्याया ब्रह्मरूपाया वाण्या दर्शनमिति **पाणिनीयाः** ।

१८. प्रकृत्युपरमे (प्रकृति-तद्विकारोपधानाद् विलये) पुरुषस्य स्वरूपेणावस्थानम् अहङ्कारनिवृत्तौ औदासीन्यम् आत्यन्तिक-दुःखत्रय-विगमो वा मुक्तिरिति **साङ्ख्याः** ।

१९. पुरुषस्य निर्लेपस्य कैवल्येनावस्थानं कैवल्यम् । पुरुषार्थशून्यानां गुणानां प्रतिप्रसवः कैवल्यम् । 'स्वरूपप्रतिष्ठा वा चितिशक्तिः' (यो० सू० ४.३४) मोक्ष इति **पातञ्जलाः** ।

२०. ऊर्ध्वगतिरिति **केचित्** ।

२१. निरुपप्लवा चित्तसन्ततिरिति **परे** ।

२२. अग्रिम-चित्तानुत्पादे पूर्वचित्तनिवृत्तिरिति **अपरे** ।

२३. आत्महानिरिति **एके** ।

२४. चित्तानुत्पादनं निरोधो वा अपवर्ग इति **अन्ये** ।

२५. स्वर्गादिरिति **मीमांसकाः** ।

२६. तत्र दुःखसाधनशरीरनाशे नित्य-निरतिशयसुखाभिव्यक्तिर्मुक्तिरिति तदेकदेशिनो **भट्टसर्वज्ञादयस्तौतातिकाः** ।

२७. तत्रापि नित्यसुखसाक्षात्कार इति **भाट्टाः** ।

२८. आत्यन्तिकदुःखप्रागभाव-परिपालनं मोक्ष इति **प्राभाकराः** ।

२९. आनन्दमये परमात्मनि जीवात्मलयो मुक्तिरिति **त्रिदण्डिनः** ।

३०. ब्रह्मांशिकजीवस्य अविद्याप्रभव-मिथ्याज्ञाननिवृत्तौ स्वस्वरूपाधिगम इति अद्वैतिनः **शङ्कराचार्यमतानुयायिनः** । (न्यायकोशे, पृ० ४१२)

इत्थमवैदिकैर्दार्शनिकैः परमपुरुषार्थत्वेन अभिमतो मोक्षः पौरुषेय-परस्परविरुद्ध-कल्पनयाऽप्रमाणमेव भवति। अत एव उत्तरमीमांसायां द्वितीयेऽध्याये द्वितीयपादे धर्मवादप्रतिपक्षीभूतानि द्वैतिनां दर्शनानि खण्डितानि। सर्वेषां दार्शनिकानां खण्डनेन तैः प्रवर्तितास्त्रयो वादा भोगवादोऽपवर्गवादो भोगापवर्गवादश्च खण्डितो धर्मवादश्च प्रतिष्ठापितः।

सर्वेषां दार्शनिकानां मध्ये प्रधानमल्ला हि साङ्ख्याः। ते च स्वपक्षस्थापनाय वेदान्तवाक्यान्यपि उदाहृत्य स्वपक्षानुगुण्येनैव योजयन्तो व्याचक्षते। तेषां यद् व्याख्यानं तद् व्याख्यानाभासम्, न सम्यग् व्याख्यानमिति सविस्तरं प्रदर्श्य तर्कपादे स्वतन्त्रस्तद्युक्तिप्रतिषेधः कृतः। सांख्यानां पुरुषार्थवादो वैदिकैः शिष्टैः स्मृतिषु महाभारतादिषु च स्वीकृतः। पुरुषार्थवादस्य शिष्टपरिगृहीतत्वात् स एव वैदिको वाद इति परतन्त्रप्रज्ञानां भ्रमो भवेदिति तद्वारणार्थमेव महान् प्रयत्नो भगवतः सूत्रकारस्य।

इत्थं सर्वाऽपि उत्तरमीमांसाप्रवृत्तिः धर्मिस्थापनार्थमेव। धर्मिस्थापनं द्वेधा भवति—स्वपक्षस्थापनेन परपक्षनिराकरणेन च। अत एव एकमेवाद्वितीयं ब्रह्म धर्मीति प्रतिष्ठाप्य परपक्षनिराकरणार्थं परैः स्वकीयेषु दर्शनेषु ये धर्मिणो नित्या वा पदार्थाः स्वीकृतास्तेषामनित्यत्वमधर्मित्वं वा तदीयैरेव प्रमाणैस्तर्कपादे प्रस्थापितम्। धर्मिणोऽद्वितीयत्वात् वैदिके सिद्धान्ते केवलं धर्मवाद एव। द्वैताश्रितानां त्रयाणामधर्मवादानामवकाश एव नास्ति।

द्वैतिभिराचार्यैः परिगृहीतस्य परमपुरुषार्थस्य मोक्षस्य कृतकत्वमनित्यत्वं चोपपादितं भगवत्पूज्यपादाचार्यैः। तथा हि—

अवस्थितेरिति काशकृत्स्नः।

इति सूत्रे (ब्र० सू० १.४.२२) भाष्ये।

स्थिते च क्षेत्रज्ञ-परमात्मैकत्वविषये सम्यग्दर्शने क्षेत्रज्ञः परमात्मेति नाममात्रभेदात् क्षेत्रज्ञोऽयं परमात्मनो भिन्नः, परमात्माऽयं क्षेत्रज्ञात् भिन्न इत्येवंजातीयक आत्मभेदविषयो **निर्बन्धो निरर्थकः**। एको ह्ययमात्मा नाममात्रभेदेन बहुधाऽभिधीयत इति।

नहि **सत्यं ज्ञानमनन्तं ब्रह्म, यो वेद निहितं गुहायाम्** (तै, उ. २.६) इति काञ्चिदेवैकां गुहामधिकृत्य एतदुक्तम्। न च ब्रह्मणोऽन्यो गुहायां निहितोऽस्ति। **तत्सृष्ट्वा तदेवाऽनुप्राविशत्** (तै० उ. २.६) इति स्रष्टुरेव प्रवेशश्रवणात्। ये तु निर्बन्धं कुर्वन्ति, ते वेदान्तार्थं बाधमानाः श्रेयोद्वारं सम्यग्दर्शनमेव बाधन्ते, कृतकमनित्यं च मोक्षं कल्पयन्ति। न्यायेन च न सङ्गच्छन्त इति। (शां० भा० १.४.२२)

इत्थं मीमांसादर्शनमेव धर्म-धर्मि-प्रतिपादनपरम्। दर्शनान्तराणि भोगवादपराणि मोक्षवादपराणि वा। वैदिकैरेव मीमांसितो धर्मः प्रतिष्ठापितश्च। प्रतिष्ठापिते धर्मे धर्मी प्रतिष्ठापितो भवति। अत एव जगद्गुरूणां शङ्कराचार्याणां पीठानि धर्मपीठानीत्येवाऽऽद्रियन्ते शिष्टैः। नहि मोक्षस्थापनार्थं पीठान्येतानि प्रतिष्ठापितानि भगवत्पूज्यपादैरिति।

(१२)

अकामहतानां वैदिकानामात्मैकत्ववादे ब्रह्मवादे वा क्रियाफलं कर्मगामि, न कर्तृगामि। 'व्यापाराश्रयः कर्ता, फलाश्रयं कर्मे'ति वैयाकरणानां सिद्धान्तः। स च सनातनः। तथा हि—'पचती'त्यत्र अंशद्वयमस्ति, व्यापारांशः फलांशश्च। तत्र पचतीत्यस्य 'पाकं करोती'ति व्याख्याने 'करोति' इत्यनेन वाच्यमानो व्यापारः कर्त्रा सम्बद्ध्यते। स च सम्बन्धः समवायस्तादात्म्योऽभेदो वा। अत एव व्यापारः कर्तुर्देवदत्तस्य इन्द्रियधर्मः शरीरधर्मो वा भवति, धर्मधर्मिणोः अभेद-सम्बन्धाभ्युपगमात्। 'पाकमि'त्यनेन वाच्यमानं फलं कर्मणा तण्डुलादिभिः साकं सम्बद्ध्यते। अयमपि सम्बन्धः समवायोऽभेदस्तादात्म्यो वा। अत एव फलं पाकरूपं कर्मणस्तण्डुलादेर्धर्मो भवति। धर्मधर्मिणोरभेदसम्बन्धात् कर्मणा तण्डुलादिभिः पाकादिरूपं

फलं परित्यक्तुं नैव शक्यते, इति कर्मफलत्यागस्य कल्पनाया अपि अत्रावकाशो नास्ति। पाको देवदत्तस्य कर्तुः कदापि न सम्भवतीति क्रियाफलं कर्तृगामि कदाचिदपि नैव सम्भवति। क्रियाफलं कर्मगामीत्येव अपौरुषेयः सिद्धान्तः, कर्मणः फलवत्त्वनियमात्।

फलयुक्तानि कर्माणि। **(का० श्रौ० सू० १.१.२)**

इत्यादिसूत्राणां कर्मगामिफलयुक्तानि इत्येवार्थः। अत एवाऽस्मिन् पक्षे फलाभिसन्धेः फलत्यागस्य अवकाश एव नास्ति।

सनातनमिदं सिद्धान्तमाश्रित्यैव भगवता गीताशास्त्रे उक्तम्—

कर्मण्येवाधिकारस्ते मा फलेषु कदाचन।
मा कर्मफलहेतुर्भूर्मा ते सङ्गोऽस्त्वकर्मणि॥ **(२.४)**

हे अर्जुन! ते तव कर्मण्येवाधिकारः। क्रियाया व्यापारस्य वा शरीरधर्मत्वात् कर्तुः क्रियायामेव केवलायामधिकारः। कर्ता व्यापार एव कर्मण्येव वा अधिक्रियते। एवकारेण फलांशयोगस्य व्यवच्छेदः क्रियते। फले अधिकारो नास्तीत्यर्थः। फले कर्मणोऽधिकारात्। कर्मैव फले अधिक्रियते, 'फलाश्रयं कर्मे'ति सिद्धान्तात्। कर्मण्येवेत्यत्र एवकारेण ध्वनितः फलभोगव्यवच्छेदः स्पष्टीक्रियते—'मा फलेषु कदाचन' इति। फलेन साकं कर्तुः सम्बन्ध एव नास्ति। कर्मैव तत्राधिक्रियते इति पचतीत्यत्र पाकस्तण्डुलानामेव भवति, न कर्तुः पाचकस्य।

एवं तर्हि कर्ता क्रियाफलहेतुर्भवतीति चेन्न। कर्तुर्निमित्तकारणत्वात्, निमित्तकारणस्य च अन्यथासिद्धत्वात् कर्ता निमित्तकारणमेव, न समवायिकारणम्। कुलालो घटं प्रति निमित्तकारणमित्यन्यथासिद्धः। अन्यथासिद्धत्वात् घटं प्रति तस्य हेतुत्वं नास्ति। एवं कर्ता केवलं कर्मफलहेतुरपि भवितुं नार्हति। कारणसामग्रीसत्त्वे कार्यसत्त्वमिति नैयायिकसिद्धान्तात्। समवाय्यसमवायि-निमित्त-कारणानामेकत्वमेव हेतुरित्येकत्वस्य हेतुत्वम्।

अयमेव सिद्धान्तो गीताशास्त्रे स्पष्टीकृतः। तथा हि—

मयैवैते निहताः पूर्वमेव निमित्तमात्रं भव सव्यसाचिन्। **(११.३३)**

मया परमेश्वरेण सर्वभूतस्थितात्मैकत्वेन पूर्वमेवैते निहताः, त्वं निमित्तमात्रं भव इति कर्तुरर्जुनस्य निमित्तकारणत्वमेवोक्तम्। निमित्तकारणस्य फलं प्रति अन्यथासिद्धत्वात् एकत्वधर्मस्यैव ब्रह्मणः फलं प्रति हेतुत्वमुक्तम्। निमित्तकारणस्य कर्तुरन्यथासिद्धत्वं चाऽपि स्पष्टीकृतं तत्रैव—

ऋतेऽपि त्वां न भविष्यन्ति सर्वे
येऽवस्थिताः प्रत्यनीकेषु योधाः। **(गी० ११.३२)**

'ऋतेऽपि विनाऽपि त्वां न भविष्यन्ति सर्वे योधाः। यदि त्वया युद्धाद्विरम्यते तर्हि केनाप्यन्येन अहमेतान् घातयिष्यामि। घातकोऽहमेव।' आत्मैकत्वस्वरूपेण ईश्वरणैवेते हताः, त्वं केवलं निमित्तमित्यर्थः। अत एवोक्तम्—

मया हतांस्त्वं जहि मा व्यथिष्ठा
युध्यस्व जेतासि रणे सपत्नान्। (गी० ११.३४)

एवं कर्मफलहेतुत्वं कर्तुर्नास्तीत्युपदिष्टम्—'**मा कर्मफलहेतुर्भूः**' इति। इत्थं कर्तुः अन्यथासिद्धत्वाद् गौणत्वम्। अत एव—

ज्ञानं कर्म च कर्ता च (गी० १८.१९)

इत्यत्र ज्ञानस्य कर्मणो वा प्राधान्यं कर्तुर्गौणत्वमुक्तम्।

आत्मैकत्वविद्याप्रतिपत्तौ क्रिया त्यागरूपा कर्मगामिफलरूपा वा भवति। द्वैते क्रिया भोगफला अपवर्गफला वा कर्तृगामिफलरूपा भवति। ज्ञानानुसारेणैव क्रियाफलं भिद्यत इति ज्ञानप्राधान्यम्। अत्र ज्ञानशब्देन आत्मैकत्वज्ञानमेवोक्तम्। तथा हि—

क्षेत्रज्ञं चापि मां विद्धि सर्वक्षेत्रेषु भारत। (गी० १३.२)
सर्वभूतेषु येनैकं भावमव्ययमीक्षते॥

अविभक्तं विभक्तेषु तज्ज्ञानं विद्धि सत्त्विकम्। (गी० १८.२०) इति।

अस्यैव प्रपञ्चः **अमानित्वमदम्भित्वम्** (गी० १३.७) इत्यारभ्य **एतज्ज्ञानमिति प्रोक्तमज्ञानं यदतोऽन्यथा** (गी० १३.११) इत्यत्र कृतः। कर्मशब्देन अत्र कर्मगामिफलं कर्मैव उक्तम्। कर्ता गौण इत्यन्ते उक्तः।

कर्म क्रिया कर्ता चेति धर्मवादे क्रमः। कर्ता कर्म क्रिया चेति अधर्मवादक्रमः। धर्मवादे कर्ताऽन्यथासिद्ध इति कर्तुर्निर्देशोऽपिकर्त्राऽन्येन वा न क्रियते, तत्कीर्तनेन धर्मस्य क्षरणात्। अतः केवलं क्रियाफलमेव गोचरं भवति। कामहतानाम् अधर्मवादे कर्तृगामिफलस्य अपेक्षितत्वात् कर्तुरुद्घोषेण निर्देशः क्रियते। कर्ताऽपि अस्मितापूर्वकं वारं वारं स्वकर्म श्लाघते इति विशेषः। अस्मिन्नेव पक्षे इतिहासो लिख्यते, लेख्यते च। धर्मवादे इतिहासो नास्ति।

यदि फले अधिकारो निराक्रियते, अथ च कर्मफलहेतुत्वमपि कर्तुर्नास्तीति स्थाप्यते, तर्हि किमर्थं कर्त्रा क्रिया कर्तव्या ? कर्माभाव एवास्तु ? पक्षस्यास्य प्रत्याख्यानार्थमेव उपदिष्टो धर्मः—'**मा ते सङ्गोऽस्त्वकर्मणि**' इति। ते तव '**अकर्मणि**' क्रियाभावे क्रियोपरमे प्रवृत्त्यपाये वा सङ्गः सक्तिर्माऽस्तु। कामहतानाम् अपवर्गवादिनां **दुःखजन्मेति...**(न्या० सू० १.१.२) इति सूत्रोक्तःसिद्धान्तस्त्वया नाश्रयणीय इत्यर्थः। क्रियायाःशरीरधर्मत्वात् यावत् शरीरं विद्यते, तावत् क्रियायोगः कर्मयोगो वा आवश्यक एव। न हि धर्मिणा धर्मः परित्यक्तुं शक्यते। क्रिया च शरीरधर्म इति यावत् शरीरं तावत् कर्मयोगो धर्मः। क्रियापरित्यागोऽधर्मः, तस्य अयोगत्वात्। अतियोगोऽयोगो मिथ्यायोगश्च अधर्मः। योगो धर्मः। काममन्तरेण धर्मत्यागो न सम्भवतीति अकर्मणि सङ्गोऽधर्मः काम एव वा। क्रियायाः शरीरधर्मत्वात् यावच्छरीरं विद्यते, तावत्

कर्मरूपस्य शरीरधर्मस्य परित्यागे मानाभावात् ब्रह्मनिष्ठैरपि धर्मवादिभिर्व्युत्थाने स्वकर्म नैव परित्याज्यमिति धर्मवादिनः सिद्धान्तः। स एवेत्थं विशदीकृतो भगवता—

कर्मणैव हि संसिद्धिमास्थिता जनकादयः।
लोकसङ्ग्रहमेवापि सम्पश्यन् कर्तुमर्हसि॥

यद्यदाचरति श्रेष्ठतत्तदेवेतरो जनः।
स यत् प्रमाणं कुरुते लोकस्तदनुवर्तते॥

न मे पार्थाऽस्ति कर्तव्यं त्रिषु लोकेषु किञ्चन।
नानवाप्तमवाप्तव्यं वर्त एव च कर्मणि॥

यदि ह्ययं न वर्तेयं जातु कर्मण्यतन्द्रितः।
मम वर्त्मानुवर्तन्ते मनुष्याः पार्थ सर्वशः॥

उत्सीदेयुरिमे लोका न कुर्यां कर्म चेदहम्।
सङ्करस्य च कर्ता स्यामुपहन्यामिमाः प्रजाः॥

सक्ताः कर्मण्यविद्वांसो यथा कुर्वन्ति भारत।
कुर्याद्विद्वांस्तथाऽसक्त-श्चिकीर्षुर्लोकसङ्ग्रहम्॥ **(गी. ३.२०-२५)**

इत्थं नित्यानि नैमित्तिकानि च कर्माणि यावज्जीवमनुष्ठेयानीति वैदिकानां मीमांसकानां सिद्धान्त एव प्रस्थापितो भगवता।

अपवर्गवादिभिस्तु क्रियाया रागद्वेषमोहात्मकत्वात् मोक्षविरोधित्वात् क्रियोपरम एवोपदिश्यते। शरीरस्य अधर्म एव विद्यमानेऽपि शरीर उपदिश्यत इति विशेषः। अपवर्गवादिनां सर्वेषां सिद्धान्तोऽयं धर्मविरुद्धत्वाद् अप्रमाणमेव भवति। अत एवोक्तं भगवद्गीतासु—

त्याज्यं दोषवदित्येके कर्म प्राहुर्मनीषिणः।
यज्ञ-दान-तपः-कर्म न त्याज्यमिति चापरे॥

निश्चयं शृणु मे तत्र त्यागे भरतसत्तम।
त्यागो हि पुरुषव्याघ्र त्रिविधः सम्प्रकीर्तितः॥

यज्ञ-दान-तपः-कर्म न त्याज्यं कार्यमेव तत्।
यज्ञो दानं तपश्चैव पावनानि मनीषिणाम्॥

एतान्यपि तु कर्माणि सङ्गं त्यक्त्वा फलानि च।
कर्तव्यानीति मे पार्थ निश्चितं मतमुत्तमम्॥

नियतस्य तु संन्यासः कर्मणो नोपपद्यते।
मोहात्तस्य परित्यागस्तामसः परिकीर्तितः॥ **(गी. १८.३-७)**

मीमांसकमतमेवात्र अनूदितं भगवता। नित्यानि नैमित्तिकानि च कर्माणि

यावज्जीवमनुष्ठेयानि। तत्र तु न फलसाधनत्वेन विधिः, किन्तु जीवननिमित्तसंयोगेन। अत एवात्र कर्तृगामिफलं नास्ति। फलाभावात् फलं दातुम् अपूर्वस्यावश्यकता नास्ति इत्यपूर्वाभावः। अपूर्वाभावादितिकर्तव्यता नास्ति। इतिकर्तव्याताया अभावाद् विकलाङ्गान्यपि नित्यानि नैमित्तिकानि चानुष्ठेयानीति निर्णीतं—

सर्वशक्तौ प्रवृत्तिः स्यात् तथा भूतोपदेशात् (पू० मी० ६.३.१)
इत्यारभ्य **प्रायश्चित्तविधानाच्च** (६.३.७)

इत्यन्तं पूर्वमीमांसायाम्। नित्यानां नैमित्तिकानां च कर्मणां यावज्जीवमकरणे प्रत्यवायः प्रायश्चित्तं च श्रूयते, न तथा काम्यानाम्।

नित्यानां नैमित्तिकानां च कर्मणां फलाभावादपूर्वं नास्ति। तथैव अपूर्वस्य अचेतनत्वात् फलप्रदानार्थं परमेश्वरस्यापि आवश्यकता नास्ति। अत एव **फलमत उपपत्तेः** (ब्र० सू० ३.२.३८) इति सूत्रेण समारब्धं फलाधिकरणं (३.२.३८-४१) अविद्यायुक्तैः प्राकृतैः विज्ञानमयकोशस्थैः त्रैगुण्ययुक्तैर्वैकृतैश्च दोषत्रययुक्तैः मनोमय-प्राणमया-ऽन्नमयकोशस्थितै अनुष्ठितानां काम्यानां निषिद्धानां च कर्मणां फलमीमांसार्थमेवेति सिद्धान्तः। कामहतानां कर्तृगामिक्रियाफलवादस्य पौरुषेयत्वाद् अशास्त्रीयत्वाच्च कर्मफलदातृत्वेन परिकल्प्यमानस्य अपूर्वस्य ईश्वरस्यापि पौरुषेयत्वमेव। संसारानादित्वकल्पनाऽपि अविद्याविलास एव। अत एव भगवत्पूज्यपादैः स्थानद्वये प्रत्याख्यातोऽयं पक्ष इति पूर्वं संक्षेपेण उपपादितम्।

अयं **सर्वकर्मफलत्यागं प्राहुस्त्यागं विचक्षणाः** (१८.२) इति गीताशास्त्रोपदिष्टः सर्वकर्मफलत्यागो वैदिकैः आत्मैकत्ववादिभिः अष्टाचत्वारिंशत्संस्कारैः संस्कृतैः आनन्दमयकोशस्थैः निस्त्रैगुण्यैः अशरीरैरेव कर्तुं शक्यते, न तु प्राकृतैः विज्ञानमयकोषस्थैः, न वा वैकृतैः मनोमय-प्राणमया-ऽन्नमयकोशस्थैः।

एते एव महात्मानः कुशला इत्याख्यायन्ते। तथा चोक्तं **तस्य सप्तधा प्रान्तभूमिः प्रज्ञा** (२.२७) इति योगसूत्रभाष्ये—

> "एतस्यामवस्थायां गुणसम्बन्धातीतः स्वरूपमात्रज्योतिरमलः केवली पुरुषः कुशल इत्याख्यायते। प्रतिप्रसवेऽपि चित्तस्य युक्तः कुशल इत्येव भवति, गुणातीतत्वात्" इति।

निस्त्रैगुण्यानां कुशलानामेव कर्मसु कौशलं गुणातीतत्वं च सम्भवतीति **योगः कर्मसु कौशलम्**(२.५०) इति गीताशास्त्रे उक्तम्। निस्त्रैगुण्या गुणातीता वा कुशलशब्देन व्यपदिश्यन्ते वेदान्तेष्वपि। तथा हि—

आश्चर्यो वक्ता कुशलोऽस्य लब्धा
आश्चर्यो ज्ञाता कुशलानुशिष्टः। (कठ० २.७)

अष्टाचत्वारिंशत्संस्कारैः संस्कृतानां ब्राह्मणानां धर्मप्रतिष्ठापनार्थमावश्यकं

निस्त्रैगुण्यमिति **ब्राह्मणं कुशलं पृच्छेत्** (२.१२७) इति मनुवचनं सङ्गच्छते। 'कच्चित् निस्त्रैगुण्योऽसि, न प्राकृतवत् त्रैगुण्यविषयो न वा वैकृतवत् त्रिदोषग्रस्तोऽसि?' इति प्रश्नतात्पर्यम्। निस्त्रैगुण्यैरेव धर्मः स्थापयितुं शक्यते, न त्रैगुण्यविषयैः, न वा त्रिदोषग्रस्तैः। एवं नित्यानि नैमित्तिकानि च कर्माणि संस्कारार्थमवश्यं कर्तव्यानि. ...ने हि तेषां परिगणनमष्टाचत्वारिंशत्संस्कारेषु। अत एवोक्तं मनुना—

महायज्ञैश्च यज्ञैश्च ब्राह्मीयं क्रियते तनुः। (२.२८) इति। ये च संस्कृताः संस्कारैश्चैकत्वं गतास्तैरपि लोकसङ्ग्रहार्थं धर्मस्थापनार्थं चावश्यं कर्तव्यानि नित्यानि नैमित्तिकानि च कर्माणि इति वैदिकः सिद्धान्तः।

इत्थं धर्मवादे क्रियाफलं कर्मगामीति सनातनः सिद्धान्तः। यज्ञो हि वैदिकानां धर्मः। यज्ञश्च—**द्रव्यं देवतात्यागः** (का० श्रौ० सू० २.२.२) इति त्यागरूपः। यथा पचतीति क्रियायाः फलं पाकः, एवं यजतीति क्रियायाः फलं यज्ञो यागो वा। त्यागेनैवात्मैकत्वं सम्पाद्यते, द्वैतभावश्च विनाश्यत इत्येकत्वप्रतिष्ठापको यज्ञो भवति। एकत्वं च ब्रह्मधर्मः। आत्मैकत्वप्रतिपत्तावेव आनन्दांशस्य प्रादुर्भावो न ततः प्राक्। अत एव **स्वरूपप्रतिष्ठा वा चितिशक्तिः**' (यो० सू० ४.३४) इति पुरुषबहुत्ववादे योगशास्त्रसमाप्तिः सङ्गच्छते। द्वैतिनो हि सांख्या योगाश्च नात्मैकत्ववादिनः। एवं यजतीति व्यापारस्य फलं यज्ञः। आत्मैकत्वं ब्रह्म, स्वर्ग आनन्दो वा। यजति-क्रिययैवात्मनः स्वधर्मे प्रतिष्ठापनं कर्तुं शक्यते। 'स्वर्गकामो यजेते'-त्यत्रापि यजतीति क्रियायाः फलं स्वर्गः श्रूयते। स च आनन्दपर्याय एव। आनन्दश्च ब्रह्मधर्म आत्मैकत्वे सिद्धे समुदेति। अत एव आनन्दकामो ब्रह्मधर्मप्राप्तिकामः अहंशब्दवाच्यस्य स्वधर्मप्राप्तिकामो वा यजेतेति वाक्यार्थः सम्पद्यते। यज्ञैः आत्मधर्मप्रतिष्ठा भवति। कामहतैर्भोगवादिभिः स्वर्गशब्दो भोगप्रद-देशविशेषपरतया व्याख्यातः। यज्ञाश्च भोगफलदा इत्येव सिद्धान्तितम्। अत एव मोक्षवादिभिर्यज्ञानां निन्दैव विधीयते। धर्मप्रतिष्ठापकः समग्रो वेदभाग एव निन्द्यते। धर्मवादिभिस्तु स्वर्गशब्द आनन्दापरपर्याय एव स्वीकृतः। तथा हि पूर्वमीमांसायां स्वर्गकामाधिकरणे—

द्रव्याणां कर्मसंयोगे गुणत्वेनाभिसम्बन्धः।

(मी० सू० ६.१.१) इति सूत्रे भाष्ये—

"तथेदमपरं सन्दिग्धम्। किं प्रीतिः स्वर्ग उत द्रव्यमिति। यदि द्रव्यं स्वर्गस्ततः प्रधानं कर्म द्रव्यं गुणभूतम्। अथ प्रीतिः स्वर्गस्ततो यागो गुणभूतः, स्वर्गश्च प्रधानमिति। कुतः संशयः? नास्त्यत्र कामस्य गुणत्वेन प्राधान्येव वा श्रुतिः। सम्बन्धमात्रं त्वस्य योगेन गम्यते। द्रव्यस्य तु कर्मार्थता स्वभावतः। पुरुषप्रयत्नस्य च फलार्थता। किं तावत् प्राप्तम्? स्वर्गो गुणतः कर्म प्रधानत इति। तत्रैवं तावद् वर्णयन्ति। द्रव्यं स्वर्ग इति। कथमवगम्यते? सर्वेषामेव शब्दानामर्थज्ञाने लौकिकः प्रयोगोऽभ्युपायः। तस्मिंश्च लौकिके प्रयोगे द्रव्यवचनः स्वर्गशब्दो लक्ष्यते। कौशेयानि सूक्ष्माणि वासांसि स्वर्गः। चन्दनानि स्वर्गः। द्व्यष्टवर्षाः स्त्रियः स्वर्ग इति।

यद्यत् प्रीतिमद् द्रव्यं तत्तत् स्वर्गशब्देनोच्यते। तेन सामानाधिकरण्यात् प्रीतिमद् द्रव्यं स्वर्ग इति मन्यामहे। उपमानाच्छब्दप्रवृत्तिरिति चेत्? न हि कस्मिंश्चिदनुपमिते लोके प्रसिद्धः यस्यैतदुपमानं स्यात्। तस्मान्नोपमानम्। अतो द्रव्यं स्वर्ग इति।

नेत्याह। प्रीतिः स्वर्ग इति। न द्रव्यं व्यभिचारात्। तदेव हि द्रव्यं कस्यांचिदवस्थायां न स्वर्गशब्दोऽभिदधाति। प्रीतिं तु न कस्यांचिदवस्थायां नाभिदधाति। तस्माद् अन्वयव्यतिरेकाभ्यामेतदवगम्यते प्रीतौ स्वर्गशब्दो वर्तत इति। नैतदस्ति प्रीतेरभिधायकः स्वर्गशब्द इति। कुतः? विशेषणत्वात् प्रीतेः। यद्विशेषणं न तच्छब्देनोच्यते। तद्यथा दण्डीति दण्डनिमित्तः पुरुषवचनः। दण्डोऽस्य निमित्तं नाभिधेयः। एवमेष न प्रीतिवचनः। प्रीतिसाधनवचनस्त्वेष स्वर्गशब्द इति। ननु स्वर्गशब्दो लोके प्रसिद्धो विशिष्टो देशे, यस्मिन्नोष्णं न शीतं न क्षुद् न तृष्णा नारतिः न ग्लानिः। पुण्यकृत एव प्रेत्य तत्र गच्छन्ति, नान्ये।

अत्रोच्यते—यदि तत्र केचिदमृत्वा न गच्छन्ति तत आगच्छन्ति अजनित्वा वा, न तर्हि स प्रत्यक्षो देश एवंजातीयकः। नाप्यनुमानाद् गम्यते। नान्येन। ननु चान्ये सिद्धाः केचित् दृष्टवन्तः, ते चाख्यातवन्तः इति चेत्? न तत्र प्रमाणमस्ति सिद्धा एवं जातीयकाः सन्ति ते च दृष्ट्वाऽऽचक्षीरन्निति। तस्मादेवंजातीयको देश एव नास्ति।

ननु च लोकादाख्यानेभ्यो वेदाच्चावगम्यते देश एवंजातीयकः स्वर्ग इति। तन्न; पुरुषाणामेवंविधेन देशेन असम्बन्धाद् अप्रमाणं वचः। आख्यानमपि पुरुषप्रणीतत्वाद् अनादरणीयम्। वैदिकमपि स्वर्गाख्यानं विधिपरं नास्त्येव। भवति तु विध्यन्तरेणैकवाक्यभूतं स्तुतिपरम्। यद्यपि केवलसुखश्रवणार्थापत्त्या तादृशो देशःस्यात्। तथापि अस्मत्पक्षस्याविरोधः प्रीतिसाधने स्वर्गशब्द इति। तेन देशेन व्यवहाराभावात् कुतस्तस्याभिधायकः स्वर्गशब्दो भविष्यति" इति।

भाष्येणैतेन स्वर्गशब्दः प्रीतिसाधने इति निर्णीतम्। अकामहतानां वैदिकानां मीमांसकानामात्मैकत्वमेव यागे यजति-क्रियायां त्यागे वा प्रीतिं साधयतीति आत्मैकत्वमेव स्वर्गः। आनन्दश्चात्मैकत्वधर्म एव। धर्मधर्मिणोरभेदाद् आत्मैकत्वमानन्दमयत्वमेव। तच्च स्वर्गः। अत एव आनन्दः स्वर्गः। इत्थं "आनन्दकामो यजेत, ब्रह्मधर्मप्राप्तिकामो यजेत, अथवा स्वीकृतं भयावहं परधर्मं परित्यज्य 'अहमः' स्वधर्मप्राप्तिकामो स्वधर्मप्रतिष्ठाकामो वा यजते"-ति वाक्यार्थः सम्पद्यते। कामहतानां द्वैतिनां तु त्यागे यागे वा श्रूयमाणं भोगफलमेव प्रीतिं साधयतीति भोगफलसाधको देशः स्वर्गो भवति। कामहतानां व्याख्यानमिदं भाष्ये प्रत्याख्यातमेव। काम्यकर्मप्रतिषेधात् मीमांसकानां भोगवादो नास्ति। नित्यनैमित्तिकानां यावज्जीवमपरित्यागाद् अपवर्गवादो नास्ति। एवं पुरुषार्थवादः सांख्यानां मीमांसकैः प्रत्याख्यात एव।

एवं यजतिफलं स्वर्ग एव। स च—

यन्न दुःखेन सम्भिन्नं न च ग्रस्तमनन्तरम्।
अभिलाषोपनीतं च तत्सुखं स्वःपदास्पदम्॥

इति श्रुतेः सुखपर्यायः आनन्दपर्यायो वा। दुःखासम्भिन्नं सुखमानन्द एव। स चात्मैकत्वधर्मः। तच्चात्मैकत्वं त्यागो यज्ञो वा यजतिक्रियया स्थाप्यत इति ब्रह्मधर्मप्रतिष्ठापको यज्ञो भवति। एकत्वस्थापनं भवति। सर्वत्राऽऽनन्दमयत्वं सम्पद्यत इति।

कामहतानामात्मबहुत्ववादे देहात्मवादे च "इदं सर्वं" दृश्यं प्रमाणीकुर्वाणानां भोगापवर्गवादिनां द्वैतिनां क्रियाफलं कर्तुगाम्येवेति सिद्धान्तः। क्रियाफलं कर्मगाम्येवेति सनातनः सिद्धान्तस्तैरनादृतः। फलं कर्तृगामि कदापि नैव भवतीति दृष्ट्वा तैः पौरुषेयं पारिभाषिकं फललक्षणं सूत्रितम्। तथा हि—

प्रवृत्तिदोषजनितोऽर्थः फलम् (न्या० सू० १.१.२०)

इति। यत्र मिथ्याज्ञानं तत्र रागद्वेषौ। रागादय एव ज्ञातारं पुण्ये पापे वा भोगे अपवर्गे वा प्रवर्तयन्तीति प्रवृत्तिहेतुत्वं रागादीनाम्। प्रवृत्तिहेतवो ये दोषा रागद्वेषमोहास्तैर्जनितोऽर्थः फलम्।

इन्द्रियाणि दशैकं च पञ्च चेन्द्रियगोचराः। (गी० १३.५)

इति। एकादशेन्द्रियाणि पञ्च महाभूतानि चेति षोडश विकाराः। विकाराश्रया एव रागद्वेषमोहाख्यास्त्रयो दोषा विकारा वा भवन्ति। मनः, पञ्च ज्ञानेन्द्रियाणि, पञ्च कर्मेन्द्रियाणि, पञ्च महाभूतानि चेति षोडश पदार्थाः केवलविकृतयः। अत एव मनोमयकोशमारभ्य अन्नमयकोशपर्यन्तं दोषत्रयावस्थानम्। आत्मा यदा विज्ञानमयकोशमुपसंक्रामति तदा दोषत्रयमुक्तो विकारमुक्तो वा भवति, गुणत्रययुक्तः प्राकृतो वा सम्पद्यते। यदा च आनन्दमयकोशमुपसंक्रामति तदा संस्कृतो भवति। एकत्वमद्वितीयत्वं चेत्यादिब्रह्मधर्माः उदिता भवन्ति। स्वयं ब्रह्मीभवति। आनन्दमयकोशमारभ्य विज्ञानमयकोशपर्यन्तं गीताशास्त्रोक्तं धर्मक्षेत्रम्। धर्मक्षेत्रे धर्मवादः। मनोमयकोशमारभ्य अन्नमयकोशपर्यन्तं कुरुक्षेत्रम्। कुरुक्षेत्रे अधर्मवादाः।

सर्वा प्रवृत्तिः प्रकृष्टं वा वृत्तिसारूप्यं स्वार्थमूलकम्, अत एव सदोषम्। दोषत्रयग्रस्तत्वात् फलाभिसन्धिपूर्विका क्रिया दुष्टैव भवति। अत एव मनोमये प्राणमये अन्नमये च कोशे अथवा कुरुक्षेत्रे स्थिता दुष्कृतिन इति गीतायां स्पष्टमुक्तम्।

न मां दुष्कृतिनो मूढाः प्रपद्यन्ते नराधमाः।
माययाऽपहृतज्ञाना आसुरं भावमाश्रिताः॥ (गी० ७.१५)

पक्षेऽस्मिन् क्रियाकर्त्रा यदर्थ्यते तदेव क्रियायाः फलं भवति। शास्त्रीयदृष्ट्या तु क्रियाकर्त्रा यस्माद् यदर्थ्यते तदेव तेन दीयत इति कर्त्रन्तरस्य क्रियायाः फलभागित्वं भवति, न तु स्वक्रियायाः। तथापि मोहग्रस्तत्वात् तत् स्वक्रियाया एव फलं गण्यत इति मोहग्रस्तानां

व्यवहारमनुसृत्यैतल्लक्षणं प्रवृत्तमाचार्यैश्च प्रवर्तितम्। अर्थ्यमानस्य फलत्वात् विद्यमाने च कामे अर्थित्वसंभवात् कामस्यैवैतत् फलं न क्रियायाः। अत एव मन्त्रवर्णः—

कोऽदात् कस्मा अदात् कामोऽदात् कामायाऽदात्।
कामो दाता कामः प्रतिग्रहीता कामैतत् ते॥ (मा० सं० ७.४८)

इति। कामस्यैव फलमिति प्रकृत्यनुसारेण कामभेदात् एकस्या एव क्रियायाः कामभेदेन फलभेदः। कामाभावे तु फलाभावः। कामस्यैवं परित्यक्तुं शक्यत्वात् कर्तृगामिक्रियाफलस्य अशास्त्रीयस्य शास्त्रीयत्वेन अभिमन्यमानस्य परित्यागो गीताशास्त्रे उपदिष्टः। कर्तृगामिक्रियाफलत्यागेनैव रागद्वेषमोहाख्येभ्यो मनोमय-प्राणमया-ऽन्नमयकोशस्थेभ्यः कुरुक्षेत्रस्थेभ्यो दोषेभ्यः साधकोऽनायासेनेव मुक्तो भवति, धर्मक्षेत्रं विज्ञानमयकोशं वा उपसंक्रामति। तस्य काम्येषु कर्मसु प्रवृत्तिरेव न भवति। तथा हि—

काम्यानां कर्मणां न्यासं संन्यासं कवयो विदुः।
सर्वकर्मफलत्यागं प्राहुस्त्यागं विचक्षणाः॥

(गी० १८.२) इति **फले सक्तो निबद्ध्यते** (गी० ५.१२) इति कर्तृगामिनि क्रियाफले पुरुषबुद्धिपरिकल्पिते अशास्त्रीये आसक्तिरेव बन्धः। फलत्योगेनैव मुक्तिरिति बन्धमोक्षकल्पनापि द्वैतिनामशास्त्रीया पौरुषेया च। अत एव गीताशास्त्रे—

कर्मबन्धं प्रहास्यसि। (२.३९)
मा फलेषु कदाचन। मा कर्मफलहेतुर्भूः। (२.४७)
बुद्धियुक्तो जहातीह उभे सुकृतदुष्कृते॥ (२.५०)
कर्मजं बुद्धियुक्ता हि फलं त्यक्त्वा मनीषिणः॥
जन्मबन्धविनिर्मुक्ताः पदं गच्छन्त्यनामयम्॥ (२.५१)
त्यक्त्वा कर्मफलासङ्गम्। (४.२०)
युक्तः कर्मफलं त्यक्त्वा शान्तिमाप्नोति नैष्ठिकीम्।
अयुक्तः कामकारेण फले सक्तो निबद्ध्यते॥ (५.१२)
अनाश्रितः कर्मफलं कार्यं कर्म करोति यः॥
स संन्यासी च योगी च न निरग्निर्न चाक्रियः॥ (६.१)
सर्वकर्मफलत्यागं ततः कुरु यतात्मवान्॥ (१२.११)
अफलाकाङ्क्षिभिर्यज्ञो विधिदृष्टो च इज्यते॥
यष्टव्यमेवेति मनः समाधाय स सात्त्विकः॥ (१७.११)
अभिसन्धाय तु फलं दम्भार्थमपि चैव यत्॥
इज्यते भरतश्रेष्ठ तं यज्ञं विद्धि राजसम्॥ (१७.१२)
श्रद्धया परया तप्तं तपस्तत् त्रिविधं नरैः।
अफलाकाङ्क्षिभिर्युक्तैः सात्त्विकं परिचक्षते॥ (१७.१७)

यत्तु प्रत्युपकारार्थं फलमुद्दिश्य वा पुनः ॥
दीयते च परिक्लिष्टं तद्दानं राजसं स्मृतम् ॥ (१७.२०)

सर्वकर्मफलत्यागं प्राहुस्त्यागं विचक्षणाः ॥ (१८.२)

एतान्यपि तु कर्माणि सङ्गं त्यक्त्वा फलानि च ॥
कर्तव्यानीति मे पार्थ निश्चितं मतमुत्तमम् ॥ (१८.६)

कार्यमित्येव यत् कर्म नियतं क्रियतेऽर्जुन ॥
सङ्गं त्यक्त्वा फलं चैव स त्यागः सात्त्विको मतः ॥ (१८.९)

यस्तु कर्मफलत्यागी स त्यागीत्यभिधीयते ॥ (१८.११)

अनिष्टमिष्टं मिश्रं च त्रिविधं कर्मणः फलम् ॥
भवत्यत्यागिनां प्रेत्य न तु संन्यासिनां क्वचित् ॥ (१८.१२)

नियतं सङ्गरहितमरागद्वेषतः कृतम् ।
अफलप्रेप्सुना कर्म यत् तत् सात्त्विकमुच्यते ॥ (गी० १८.२३)

रागी कर्मफलप्रेप्सुर्लुब्धो हिंसात्मकोऽशुचिः ॥
हर्षशोकान्वितः कर्ता राजसः परिकीर्तितः ॥ (१८.२७)

यया तु धर्मकामार्थान् धृत्या धारयतेऽर्जुन ॥
प्रसङ्गेन फलाकाङ्क्षी धृतिः सा पार्थ राजसी ॥ (१८.३४)

इत्यादिभिर्वचनैः कामहतैः परिकल्पितस्य कर्तृगामिक्रियाफलस्यैव स्थाने स्थाने परित्याग उक्तः, न पुनः कर्मगामि-क्रियाफलस्य। तस्य धर्मरूपत्वात्, अत एव परित्यक्तुमशक्यत्वात् ।

येषां कर्मणामैहिकं भोगफलं नास्ति, तेषां स्वर्गः फलं कल्प्यते । अस्मिन् पक्षे स्वर्गशब्द आनन्दापरपर्यायो नास्ति। अपि तु देशविशेषपरः। स चार्थः प्रत्याख्यातः शाबरभाष्ये। कामहतानां कर्तृगामिक्रियाफलवादिनां मतं प्रत्याख्यातुमेव देशविशेषपरः स्वर्गशब्दो गीताशास्त्रे उपन्यस्तः। तथा हि—

सङ्करो नरकायैव कुलघ्नानां कुलस्य च। (गी० १.४२)

उत्सन्नकुलधर्माणां मनुष्याणां जनार्दन।
नरके नियतं वासो भवतीत्यनुशुश्रुम ॥ (१.४४)

यदृच्छया चोपपन्नं स्वर्गद्वारमपावृतम् ।
सुखिनः क्षत्रियाः पार्थ लभन्ते युद्धमीदृशम् । (२.३२)

हतो वा प्राप्स्यसि स्वर्गं जित्वा वा भोक्ष्यसे महीम् । (२.३७)

यामिमां पुष्पितां वाचं प्रवदन्त्यविपश्चितः ।
वेदवादरताः पार्थ नान्यदस्तीति वादिनः ॥ (२.४२)

कामात्मानः स्वर्गपरा जन्मकर्मफलप्रदाम्।
क्रिया-विशेष-बहुलां भोगैश्वर्यगतिं प्रति ॥ (२.४३)

भोगैश्वर्य-प्रसक्तानां तयाऽपहृतचेतसाम्।
व्यवसायात्मिका बुद्धिः समाधौ न विधीयते ॥ (२.४४)

प्राप्य पुण्यकृताँल्लोकानुषित्वा शाश्वतीः समाः।
शुचीनां श्रीमतां गेहे योगभ्रष्टोऽभिजायते ॥ (६.४१)

आब्रह्मभुवनाल्लोकाः पुनरावर्तिनोऽर्जुन।
मामुपेत्य तु कौन्तेय पुनर्जन्म न विद्यते ॥ (८.१६)

त्रैविद्या मां सोमपाः पूतपापा
यज्ञैरिष्ट्वा स्वर्गतिं प्रार्थयन्ते।
ते पुण्यमासाद्य सुरेन्द्रलोक-
मश्नन्ति दिव्यान् दिवि देवभोगान् ॥ (९.२०)

ते तं भुक्त्वा स्वर्गलोकं विशालं
क्षीणे पुण्ये मर्त्यलोकं विशन्ति।
एवं त्रयीधर्ममनुप्रपन्ना
गतागतं कामकामा लभन्ते ॥ (९.२१)

कामहतानामविपश्चितामेव इयं देशविशेषस्य स्वर्गस्य कल्पना, न अकामहतानां विपश्चिताम्। वेदा भोगापवर्गपरा इति भोगापवर्गवादिनां मतमत्र 'अविपश्चितः', 'कामकामाः', 'कामात्मानः' इत्यादिभिर्विशेषणैःदूषितमेव भगवता। अत्र मीमांसकमतं दूषणार्थमुपन्यस्तमिति नैव भ्रमितव्यम्। मीमांसकैः काम्यस्य कर्मणो धर्मत्वेन नैव स्वीकारात्।

इह भोगाय अमुत्र भोगाय वा श्रूयते काम्यं कर्म। अत एव काम्यस्य कर्मणः फलमिह भोगोऽमुत्र भोगो वा। सा च फलप्राप्तिःकाम्ये कर्मणि साङ्गे अनुष्ठिते एव भवति। अङ्गवैकल्ये काम्यं कर्म निष्फलमेव भवतीति निर्णीतं पूर्वमीमांसायाम्। तथा हि—

काम्येषु चैवमर्थित्वात्।
असंयोगात्तु नैवं स्याद्विधेः शब्दप्रमाणत्वात्।
अकर्मणि चाप्रत्यवायात्। (६.३.८-१०)

अत एव विकलाङ्गं काम्यं कर्म नैव विधीयते। यदा सर्वाङ्गोपेतं कर्तुं शक्यते काम्यं कर्म, तदैव कर्तव्यम्। अन्यथा नैव कार्यम्।

काम्यकर्म-परित्यागे न प्रत्यवायः प्रायश्चित्तं वा श्रूयते। फलार्थिभिरेव आरभ्यन्ते काम्यानि कर्माणि, नाफलार्थिभिः। तथा हि—**फलयुक्तानामारम्भे यथाकामी फलार्थित्वात्** (का० श्रौ० सू० १.२.१०)। **न नियमनिमित्ताऽग्निहोत्र-दर्शपौर्णमासदाक्षायणाश्रयणपशुषु प्रवृत्तेः** (का० श्रौ० सू० १.२.११)। **सोमे चैके** (का० श्रौ० सू० १.२.१२) इति।

कर्तृगामि-क्रियाफलमाश्रित्यैव काम्यानि कर्माणि विहितानीति फलप्रदानार्थमपूर्ववादो मीमांसकानाम्। तथा हि—

ततो धात्वर्थातिरिक्तं कालान्तरभाव्यकाम्यफलसाधनमपूर्वमिति।

(जै० न्या० मा० पृ० ६३, पू० मी० सू० २.१.५)

अत एवात्र इतिकर्तव्यताया आवश्यकत्वम्। नित्यानां नैमित्तिकानां च कर्मणामितिकर्तव्यता नास्ति। तथा चोक्तम्—

नास्ति इतिकर्तव्यताऽपूर्वाभावात्।
कथमपूर्वाभावः? फलाभावात्। इति। (पू० मी० ६.३.२, टुप्टीका)

अपूर्वस्य अचेतनत्वात् **फलमत उपपत्ते** (ब्र० सू० ३.२.१८) इत्यत्र ईश्वरस्य फलदातृत्वं प्रस्थापितमुत्तरमीमांसायाम्। तदपि काम्यानां कर्मणां कर्तृगामिक्रियाफलवादं तार्किकपरिकल्पितं पौरुषेयमाश्रित्यैवेति स्थानद्वये प्रत्याख्यातं भगवत्पूज्यपादैः ब्रह्मसूत्रभाष्ये इति पूर्वं स्पष्टीकृतम्। कर्तृगामिक्रियाफलवादसिद्ध्यर्थमेव संसारानादित्वकल्पना **उपपद्यते चाप्युपलभ्यते च** (ब्र० सू० २.१.३६) इत्यत्र उपपादिताऽपि प्रत्याख्याता अन्यत्र भाष्यकारैरित्यपि पूर्वं विशदीकृतम्।

कर्तृगामि-क्रियाफलवादोऽविद्यामूलक एवेति सिद्धान्तितं योगसूत्रे। तथा हि—

अविद्या-ऽस्मिता-राग-द्वेषा-ऽभिनिवेशाः पञ्च क्लेशाः।

अविद्याक्षेत्रमुत्तरेषां प्रसुप्ततनुविच्छिन्नोदाराणाम्। क्लेशमूलः कर्माशयो दृष्टादृष्टजन्म-वेदनीयः।

सति मूले तद्विपाको जात्यायुर्भोगाः।
ते ह्लादपरितापफलाः पुण्यापुण्यहेतुत्वात्।
परिणाम-ताप-संस्कार-दुःखैर्गुणवृत्तिविरोधाच्च दुःखमेव सर्वं विवेकिनः।

(यो० सू० २.३-४; २.१२-१४)

आत्मैकत्वविद्याप्रतिपत्तौ अविद्यानाशे क्लेशमूलः कर्माशयो नास्ति। तद्विपाको दुःखं च नास्ति। जात्यायुर्भोगा ह्लादपरितापफला शरीरधर्मा नात्मधर्मा इति अविद्यानाशे जीवतोऽपि विदुषोऽमृतत्वम्। भोगेनाऽपर्गेण वा साकमात्मनः सम्बन्ध एव नास्ति। तथा चोक्तं योगभाष्ये (२.१८)—

'तावेतौ भोगापवर्गौ बुद्धिकृतौ बुद्धावेव वर्तमानौ कथं पुरुषे व्यपदिश्येते इति। यथा जयः पराजयो वा योद्धृषु वर्तमानः स्वामिनि व्यपदिश्यते, स हि तत्फलस्य भोक्तेति। बुद्धेरेव पुरुषार्थपरिसमाप्तिर्बन्धस्तदर्थावसायो मोक्ष इति।

एतेन ग्रहण-धारणोहापोहन-तत्त्वज्ञानाभिनिवेशा बुद्धौ वर्तमाना पुरुषेऽध्या-रोपितसद्भावाः। स हि तत्फलस्य भोक्तेति।'

कर्तृगामि-क्रियाफलवादमाश्रित्यैव उत्तरमीमांसायां तृतीयाध्याये प्रथमपादे विहितं कर्मानुरूपं स्वर्गनरकगत्यागतिचिन्तनमविद्यानिबन्धनमेव। तथा चोक्तं भगवत्पूज्य-पादाचार्यैः—

"तत्र प्रथमे तावत् पादे पञ्चाग्निविद्यामाश्रित्य संसारगतिप्रभेदः प्रदर्श्यते वैराग्यहेतोः, 'तस्माज्जुगुप्सेत्' इति चान्ते श्रवणात्। जीवो मुख्यः प्राणसचिवः सेन्द्रियः समनस्कोऽविद्या-कर्म-पूर्वप्रज्ञापरिग्रहः पूर्वदेहं विहाय देहान्तरं प्रतिपद्यत इत्येतदवगतम्। 'अथैनमेने प्राणा अभिसमायन्ति' इत्येवमादेः 'अन्यन्नवतरं कल्याणतरं रूपं कुरुते' (बृ० ४.४.१-४) इत्येवमन्तात् संसारप्रकरणस्थात् शब्दात् धर्माधर्म-फलोपभोग-सम्भवाच्च"

(ब्र० सू० भा० ३.१.१) इति।

अकामहतानां कामहतानां च कर्मगामि-क्रियाफलवादं कर्तृगामिक्रियाफलवादं चाश्रित्य **स्वरितञितः कर्त्रभिप्राये क्रियाफले** (पा० सू० १.३.७२) इति सूत्रितं भगवता पाणिनिना।

तस्मात् कामहतैः परिकल्पितः कर्तृगामिक्रियाफलवादः पौरुषेयोऽशास्त्रीयश्च। अकामहतैः धर्मवादिभिः सर्वथा परिहर्तव्यः। कर्मगामिक्रियाफलवादः सनातनः शास्त्रीयो धर्मरूपश्च। अत एव समग्रेऽपि गीताशास्त्रे कर्तृगामिक्रियाफलस्य अशास्त्रीयस्य अधर्मरूपस्य भूयोभूयः परित्याग एव उपदिष्टः, सनातनश्च धर्मः प्रस्थापित इति।

(१३)

स्वाध्यायाध्ययनस्य-नित्यत्वम्

अकामहतानां धर्मवादिनामेकत्विनां वैदिकानां जिज्ञास्यो धर्मी। स च एकमेवाद्वितीयं ब्रह्म। द्वितीयस्य धर्मिणोऽभावात्।

यतो वा इमानि भूतानि जायन्ते।
येन जातानि जीवन्ति॥

यत् प्रयन्त्यभि सं विशन्ति।
तद् विजिज्ञासस्व तद् ब्रह्मेति॥ (तै० उ० ३.१०)

इति तैत्तिरीयोपनिषद्वचने **ज्ञेयं यत्तत् प्रवक्ष्यामि** इत्यारभ्य **हृदि सर्वस्य विष्ठितम्** (गीता १३.१२-१७) इत्यादिगीतावचनेषु च ब्रह्मण एव केवलस्य जिज्ञासाकर्मत्वं दर्शितम्। अत एव **अथातो ब्रह्मजिज्ञासा** (ब्र० सू० १.१.१) इति सूत्रे जिज्ञास्यान्तरानिर्देशः। धर्मिणः सर्वधर्मज्ञानेनैव तस्य तत्त्वज्ञानं सम्पद्यत इति **अथातो धर्मजिज्ञासा** (पू० मी० १.१.१) इति धर्मविचारेणैव आरब्धं मीमांसाशास्त्रम्।

ब्रह्मधर्मो हि ब्रह्मणश्चतुर्थः पादः, भगवती परब्रह्मणो महाविद्या चितिशक्तिः, ईश्वरः, सगुणं

ब्रह्म, सर्वभूतस्थितमात्मैकत्वं वा। इदमेव सर्वभूतस्थितमात्मैकत्वं धर्मशब्देन वेदशब्देन वा व्यपदिश्यते निरुपाधिकस्य परब्रह्मणो धर्मरूपत्वाद् चिद्रूपत्वाच्च। धर्मधर्मिणोरभेदःसम्बन्ध इति अखण्डमेकमद्वितीयं ब्रह्म।

अस्यैव सगुणब्रह्मणो धर्मस्य वेदस्य वा लक्षणं चोदना। चोदनैव तस्यास्तित्वं प्रतिष्ठापयति। वैदिकानां क्रियाः सनातनस्य धर्मस्य, वेदस्य, सर्वभूतस्थितात्मैकत्वस्य, सगुणब्रह्मणः ईश्वरस्य वा चोदनानुसारमेव भवन्ति। सा च चोदना सर्वैः श्रूयते। तथापि आनन्दमयकोशस्थैः भक्तियोगनिष्ठैः संस्कृतैः विज्ञानमयकोशस्थैः प्राकृतैः श्रुतिमनुसृत्यैव व्यवह्रियते। मनोमय-प्राणमयाऽन्नमयकोशस्थैः वैकृतैः सा श्रुतिः अवज्ञायते। प्रकृतितन्त्रः अर्थकामतन्त्रो वा तेषां व्यवहारः। प्रकृतिर्हि अर्थः कामश्च पुरुषस्य।

इदमेव सगुणं ब्रह्म वैदिकानामर्थो भवति। **आत्मा वा अरे द्रष्टव्यः श्रोतव्यो मन्तव्यो निदिध्यासितव्यः** (मा० बृ० २.४-५;४.३.६) ।इति श्रुतेः। अत एव—

चतुर्विधा भजन्ते मां नराः सुकृतिनोऽर्जुन।
आर्तो जिज्ञासुरर्थार्थी ज्ञानी च भरतर्षभ॥

इत्यत्रोक्तेषु चतुर्षु भक्तेषु अर्थार्थिनः पूर्वमीमांसकाः ज्ञानिनो वेदान्तिनः।

उत्तरमीमांसायाः प्रथमसूत्र-प्रतिज्ञासिद्ध्यर्थमेव द्वैतिभिरभ्युपगतानां ब्रह्मातिरिक्तानां नित्यपदार्थानां नित्यत्वस्य द्वैतिनामेव प्रक्रियया प्रत्याख्यानं तर्कपादे। ब्रह्मातिरिक्तानां नित्यपदार्थानां प्रत्याख्यानेनैव ब्रह्मणो धर्मित्वेन अद्वितीयत्वं प्रतितिष्ठति।

जिज्ञास्यस्य धर्मिणो ब्रह्मणः एकत्वात् अद्वितीयत्वाच्च तस्य प्रतिपादकं प्रतिष्ठापकं च शास्त्रमपि एकमेवाद्वितीयम्। तच्च अभेदोपचारात् ब्रह्मेति वेद इति वा व्यपदिश्यते। वेदाध्ययनं ब्रह्मयज्ञ इत्येव श्रूयते। तथा हि—

अथ ब्रह्मयज्ञः। स्वाध्यायो वै ब्रह्मयज्ञः। तस्य वा एतस्य ब्रह्मयज्ञस्य वागेव जुहूर्मन उपभृच् चक्षुर्ध्रुवा मेधा स्रुवः सत्यमवभृथः स्वर्गो लोक उदगयनं यावन्तं ह वा इमां पृथिवीं वित्तेन पूर्णां ददन् लोकं जयति त्रिस्तावन्तं जयति भूयासं चाक्षय्यं य एवं विद्वानहरहः स्वाध्यायमधीते तस्मात् स्वाध्यायोऽध्येतव्यः।

(मा० शत० ११.५.६.३)

कृत्स्न आम्नायो भेदप्रपञ्चविलयमुखेन ब्रह्मप्रतिपादनपरः। तत्र वेदबाह्यानां वेदविरुद्धानां आत्मबाह्यानामात्मातिरिक्तानां वा—

महाभूतान्यहङ्कारो बुद्धिरव्यक्तमेव च।
इन्द्रियाणि दशैकं च पञ्च चेन्द्रियगोचराः॥

(गी० १३.५) इत्यत्रोक्तानां चतुर्विंशतिपदार्थानां संसर्गेण अविद्योत्पत्तौ आत्मैकत्वग्लानौ द्वैताभ्युत्थाने आत्मबहुत्वाभ्युत्थाने वा अष्टाचत्वारिंशत्- संस्कारैरात्मैकत्व-विद्योदयपरः। सनातनस्य धर्मस्य प्रतिष्ठापनपरत्वात् वेदोऽपि सनातन एव। वेदोक्तैः संस्कारैरात्मैकत्वविद्योदये ब्राह्मी स्थितिः प्राप्यते।

अस्यैव एकस्याद्वितीयस्य शास्त्रस्य तात्पर्यनिर्णयार्थं मीमांसाशास्त्रं प्रवृत्तम्। तथा चोक्तं भगवत्पूज्यपादैः—

१. तथा हि शास्त्रतात्पर्यविद आहुः। दृष्टो हि तस्यार्थः कर्मावबोधनम् इति। चोदनेति क्रियायाः प्रवर्तकं वचनम्। (शाब० भा० १.१.२) तस्य ज्ञानमुपदेशः। (जै० सू० १.१.५) तद्भूतानां क्रियार्थेन समाम्नायः (जै० सू० १.१.२५)। आम्नायस्य क्रियार्थत्वात् आनर्थक्यमतदर्थानाम् (जै० सू० १.२.१) इति च। (शां० भा० १.१.४)

२. यदपि शास्त्रतात्पर्यविदामनुक्रमणम्। दृष्टो हि तस्यार्थः कर्मावबोधनम्। (शाब० भा० १.१.१) इत्येवमादि। (शां० भा० १.१.४)

३. यद्यपीदं वेदान्तवाक्यानामैदम्पर्यं निरूपयितुं शास्त्रं प्रवृत्तं न तर्कशास्त्रवत् केवलाभिर्युक्तिभिः कञ्चित् सिद्धान्तं साधयितुं दूषयितुं वा प्रवृत्तम्। इति। (ब्र० सू० शां० भा० २.२.१)

तात्पर्यार्थो हि शास्त्रस्य श्रवणमनननिदिध्यासानन्तरमध्यवसीयते। न पुनर्वाच्यार्थ-लक्ष्यार्थ-व्यङ्ग्यार्थवत् सकृत् श्रवणमात्रेण। मीमांसकैश्च वेदानामद्वितीये ब्रह्मणि तात्पर्यं मीमांसितम्। धर्मविचारश्चारब्धः। ब्रह्मणो नित्यत्वात् अनुच्छित्तिधर्मत्वात् तस्मिन् अधर्मो नास्ति। अत एव अनित्यपदार्थवत् धर्माधर्मयोर्विचारो नास्ति। इति अथातो धर्माधर्मयोर्जिज्ञासा इति मीमांसाशास्त्रं नोपक्रान्तम्।

वैदिकानां धर्मी ब्रह्म एकमेवाद्वितीयं अखण्डमात्मतत्त्वं आत्मैकत्वं वा। तच्च अप्रमेयम्। तथा चोक्तं भगवद्गीतासु (२.१८) आत्मैकत्ववादसमाप्तिसूचके श्लोके—

अन्तवन्त इमे देहाः नित्यस्योक्ताः शरीरिणः।
अनाशिनोऽप्रमेयस्य तस्माद् युध्यस्व भारत॥

अत्र शरीरिण एकत्वाद् देहानां च अनेकत्वात् आत्मैकत्ववादः। आत्मैकत्वस्य अप्रमेयत्वात् अप्रमेयस्येति विशेषणं सङ्गच्छते। अत एव पुरुषसूक्ते **सहस्रशीर्षा पुरुषः** (मा० सं० ३१.१) ईश्वरगीतासु च—

प्रकृतिं पुरुषं चापि विद्ध्यनादी उभावपि।
(गी० १३.१९) इति पुरुषस्य एकत्वमेव धर्म उक्तः।

आत्मबहुत्ववादिनां तार्किकाणां प्रमेय आत्मा प्रतिशरीरं भिन्नः। वैदिकानां पुनरेकः अप्रमेयो वेदैकवेद्यःचिदेकवेद्यो वा। यदा **चितिशक्तिः स्वरूपप्रतिष्ठा** (यो० सू० ४.३४) सम्पद्यते तदैव आत्मैकत्वविद्यायाः प्रतीतिर्भवति।

इदमात्मैकत्वमेकत्वं वा आत्मधर्मः अविद्यास्तमये सांख्यानामप्यभिमत इति स्पष्टं प्रतीयते। तथा हि—

हेतुमदनित्यमव्यापि सक्रियमनेकमाश्रितं लिङ्गम्।
सावयवं परतन्त्रं व्यक्तं विपरीतमव्यक्तम्॥

त्रिगुणमविवेकि विषयः सामान्यमचेतनं प्रसवधर्मि।
व्यक्तं तथा प्रधानं तद्विपरीतस्तथा च पुमान्॥ (सां० का० १०-११)

इदानीं **तद्विपरीतस्तथा च पुमानि**त्येतद् व्याख्यायते-तद्विपरीतस्ताभ्यां व्यक्ताव्यक्ताभ्यां विपरीतः पुमान्। तद्यथा—त्रिगुणं व्यक्तमव्यक्तं च। अगुणः पुरुषः। अविवेकि व्यक्तमव्यक्तं च। विवेकी पुरुषः। तथा विषयो व्यक्तमव्यक्तं च। अविषयः पुरुषः। तथा सामान्यं व्यक्तमव्यक्तं च, असामान्यः पुरुषः। अचेतनं व्यक्तमव्यक्तं च, चेतनः पुरुषः। सुखदुःखमोहान् चेतयति संजानीते, तस्मात् चेतनः पुरुष इति। प्रसवधर्मि व्यक्तं प्रधानं च, अप्रसवधर्मी पुरुषः। न हि किञ्चित् पुरुषात् प्रसूयते। तस्मादुक्तं तद्विपरीतः पुमानिति।

तदुक्तम्-**तथा च पुमानि**ति। तत्पूर्वस्यामार्यायां प्रधानमहेतुमद् यथा व्याख्यातं तथा च पुमान्। तद्यथा—हेतुमदनित्यमित्यादि व्यक्तं तद्विपरीतमव्यक्तम्। तत्र हेतुमद् व्यक्तम्। अहेतुमत् प्रधानम्। तथा च पुमान् अहेतुमान्, अनुत्पाद्यत्वात्। अनित्यं व्यक्तम्। नित्यं प्रधानम्। तथा च नित्यः पुमान्। अव्यापि व्यक्तम्। व्यापि प्रधानम्। तथा च व्यापी पुमान्, सर्वगतत्वात्। सक्रियम् व्यक्तम्। अक्रियं प्रधानम्। तथा च पुमानक्रियः, सर्वगतत्वादेव। अनेकं व्यक्तम्। एकमव्यक्तम्।

तथा च पुमानप्येकः। आश्रितं व्यक्तम्। अनाश्रितमव्यक्तम्। तथा च पुमाननाश्रितः। लिङ्गं व्यक्तम्। अलिङ्गं प्रधानम्। तथा च पुमानप्यलिङ्गः। न क्वचिल्लीयत इति। सावयवं व्यक्तम्। निरवयमव्यक्तम्। तथा च पुमान् निरवयवः। न हि पुरुषे शब्दादयोऽवयवाः सन्ति। किं च परतन्त्रं व्यक्तम्। स्वतन्त्रमव्यक्तम्। तथा च पुमानपि स्वतन्त्रः। आत्मनः प्रभवतीत्यर्थः।—गौडपादाचार्यभाष्यम्।

सांख्यैर्व्यवहारावस्थायां

जनन-मरण-करणानां प्रतिनियमाद् अयुगपत्-प्रवृत्तेश्च।
पुरुषबहुत्वं सिद्धं त्रैगुण्यविपर्ययाच्चैव॥ (सां० का०, १८)

इति पुरुषबहुत्वं सप्रमाणं प्रस्थापितमिति ते स्वार्थिनः पुरुषार्थिनो भोगापवर्गवादिनो वा व्यवहारे संवृत्ताः। आत्मैकत्ववादिनस्तु वैदिकाः। तेषां व्यवहारावस्थायामपि एकत्वमिति ते धर्मवादिनः त्यागिनश्च संवृत्ताः। तेषां त्यागो द्विविधः। कर्मफलत्यागः, कर्तृत्वत्यागश्च। कर्तृगामिक्रियाफलस्य पौरुषेयत्वात् अधर्मरूपत्वाच्च। कर्तृत्वस्य आत्मधर्मत्वाभावात् कर्मत्यागो नास्ति। क्रियाया शरीरधर्मत्वात्। यावत् शरीरं विद्यते तावत् प्रकृतिधर्मानुसारेण वर्णधर्मानुसारेण वा क्रिया धर्मः।

अस्य आत्मैकत्वस्य ब्रह्मणो वा अप्रमेयत्वात्। आत्मैकत्वविद्याप्रतिपत्त्यर्थमेव उपनयनं द्वादशवर्षपर्यन्तं ब्रह्मचर्यव्रतं गुरुकुलवासश्च सर्वैरेव वैदिकैः कल्पसूत्रकारैः समाम्नातः। गुरोः सकाशात् आत्मैकत्वविद्याप्रतिपत्त्यनन्तरं तस्याः द्रढीकरणार्थं वेदाध्ययनं स्वाध्यायो ब्रह्मयज्ञो

वा। अयं प्रथम उपायो ब्रह्मचारिणाम्। उपायद्वयमवशिष्यते। विद्याया द्रढीकरणार्थमुपायत्रयमुपदिष्टं शास्त्रकारैः। तथा चोक्तं चरके विमानस्थाने—

तत्र उपायाननुव्याख्यास्यामः।

अध्ययनं अध्यापनं तद्विद्यसंभाषा चेत्युपायाः। (अ० ८.६)

अत एव समावर्तनानन्तरं गृहस्थानामध्यापनं तद्विद्यसंभाषा चेति उपायद्वयमाम्नातम्।

ब्रह्मणः सार्वदेशिकी सार्वकालिकी च सत्ता। अत एव ब्रह्म सदिति सत्यमिति वा व्यपदिश्यते। ब्रह्म धर्मप्रतिपादकं शास्त्रमपि सार्वदेशिकं सार्वकालिकं च सत्यं सनातनं वेति सच्छास्त्रमित्यभिधीयते। ब्रह्मातिरिक्तानामनित्यपदार्थानां प्रतिपादकानि शास्त्राणि असच्छास्त्राणीति व्यपदिश्यन्ते। अनित्यपदार्थानामानन्त्यात् शास्त्राण्यनन्तानि भवन्ति। तेषामध्ययनमेकेन कर्तुं न पार्यते।

समग्रो वेदराशिः आत्मैकत्वप्रतिष्ठापनपर एव। एकत्वमात्मधर्मः संस्कारैः समुदेति। संस्कारैरेव आत्मा परधर्मान् शरीरधर्मान् चतुर्विंशतिपदार्थधर्मान् वा अविद्यया स्वधर्मत्वेन अभिमन्यमानः परित्यजति स्वधर्मे ब्रह्मधर्मे वा प्रतिष्ठितो भवति। अत एवोक्तं मनुना—

महायज्ञैश्च यज्ञैश्च ब्राह्मीयं क्रियते तनुः। (२.२८)

भगवत्पूज्यपादैरपि उक्तम्—

यस्यैते अष्टाचत्वारिंशत् संस्काराः। (शां० भा० ३.४.३४)

ते च आनन्दगिरिणा प्रोक्ताः। तथा हि—गर्भाधानादयः सहधर्मचारिणी—संयोगान्ताश्चतुर्दश। पञ्च महायज्ञाः, सप्त सोमसंस्थाः, सप्त हविःसंस्थाः, सप्त पाकसंस्था इति चत्वारिंशत् संस्काराः। अनश्रत्संहिताध्ययनं प्रायणं कर्म, जप उत्क्रमणं दैहिकं भस्मसमूहनमस्थिसंचयनं श्राद्धानीत्येवमष्टाचत्वारिंशत् संस्काराः।

गौतमेन तु धर्मसूत्रे (१८.२५) चत्वारिंशत् संस्कारा अष्टौ आत्मगुणाश्च परिगणिताः; तथापि

निषेकादिश्मशानान्तो मन्त्रैर्यस्योदितो विधिः।
तस्य शास्त्रेऽधिकारोऽस्मिन् ज्ञेयो नान्यस्य कस्यचित्॥

इति मनुस्मरणात् (मनु २.१६) श्मशानान्तानामेव संस्कारत्वम्।

वेदोक्तैः कल्पसूत्रकारैः सूत्रितैरष्टाचत्वारिंशत्संस्कारैः क्रमेणानुष्ठितैः आत्मा क्रमेण प्रथमं मनः, पञ्चज्ञानेन्द्रियाणि, पञ्च कर्मेन्द्रियाणि, पञ्च महाभूतानि चेति षोडशविकृतिभिः सह सम्बन्धेन अविद्यया प्राप्तं वैकृतं जहाति। इहामुत्रार्थभोगराग एवात्र वैकृतम्। इहामुत्रार्थभोगविरागे सिद्धे विज्ञानमयकोशमुपसंक्रामति। तत्र च प्राकृतः सम्पद्यते। तत्र सप्तप्रकृतिभिः सह सम्बन्धेन प्राप्तं प्राकृतत्वं स्मार्तैः श्रौतैश्च संस्कारैर्विजहाति। कर्तृत्वत्यागेन अहङ्कारत्यागेन वा संस्कृतः सम्पद्यते। आनन्दमयकोशमुपसंक्रामति। तस्मिन् सर्वेषामात्मधर्माणामुदयो भवति। भक्तियोगेन एकः, ज्ञानयोगेन अद्वितीयश्च सम्पद्यते। योगद्वयेऽपि व्युत्थाने कर्मयोगः अशुक्लाकृष्णं कर्म वा फलत्यागात् कर्तृत्वत्यागाच्च। इयमेव ब्राह्मी स्थितिः।

संस्करणक्रिया हि नित्येषु अनित्येषु च पदार्थेषु दोषापनयनार्थं गुणाधानार्थं च विधीयते। संस्करणक्रियाया दोषा अधर्मा वा शान्ता भवन्ति, गुणानां धर्माणां वा प्रतिष्ठा भवति। तस्मात् संस्करणक्रियायाः फलं धर्मप्रतिष्ठा। सैव 'संस्कृति'शब्देन व्यपदिश्यते। संस्कृतिर्नाम संस्करणक्रियायाः फलम्। संस्करोति नाम संस्कारं संस्कृतिं वा करोति। तत्र करोति-शब्देन व्यापार उच्यते। स च कर्तृधर्मः, कर्त्रा सह तादात्म्यसम्बन्धेन सम्बद्धत्वात्। संस्कृतिशब्देन फलमुच्यते। तस्य कर्मणा सह समवायः सम्बन्धः। अत एव यत्र संस्करणक्रिया भवति, तस्य धर्मः सम्पद्यते। 'फलव्यापारयोर्धातुरि'ति वैयाकरणानां सिद्धान्तः। एतदेवांशद्वयं सिद्धावस्थापन्नो धात्वर्थः, साध्यावस्थापन्नो धात्वर्थश्चेति शब्दान्तरेण प्रतिपाद्यते। तत्र सिद्धावस्थापन्नो धात्वर्थो भाव उच्यते। तस्मिन् भावे स्त्रियां क्तिन् (३.३.९४) इति क्तिन्-प्रत्ययो भवति। संस्कृतिशब्दश्च निष्पद्यते।

संस्करणक्रियया धर्मप्रतिष्ठा भवति। धर्मप्रतिष्ठायां च धर्मिप्रतिष्ठा भवति। अत एव संस्कृतिर्नाम धर्मः। स च सनातनपदार्थनिष्ठः सनातनो भवति। अनित्यपदार्थनिष्ठोऽनित्यो भवति। देहादिषु अनित्येषु पदार्थेषु अधर्माभ्युत्थाने धर्मग्लानौ च संस्कारणक्रियया धर्मस्थापनार्थं आयुर्वेदादीनि शास्त्राणि प्रवृत्तानि। संस्करणक्रियया प्रतिष्ठापितेष्वपि अनित्यपदार्थेषु अधर्मबाहुल्यात् कालप्रभावेण च तेषां विनाशो भवति। संस्करणक्रिया मोघा भवति। संस्कर्तारश्च मोघकर्माणो भवन्ति। अत एव वैदिकैः कल्पसूत्रकारैः अनित्येषु पदार्थेषु संस्करणक्रिया नोक्ता। चितिशक्तेर्वेदस्य आत्मनो वा संस्कारार्थमेव अष्टाचत्वारिंशत् संस्कारा वेदे उक्ताः, कल्पसूत्रकारैश्च सूत्रिताः। संस्कारैरेतैः परधर्मान् क्षेत्रधर्मान् वा अविद्यया आत्मधर्मत्वेन स्वधर्मत्वेन वा अभिमन्यमान आत्मा सर्वान् परधर्मान् क्रमेण परित्यज्य एकत्वं गच्छति। स्वधर्मे ब्रह्मधर्मे वा प्रतिष्ठितो भवति। अत एवादिष्टं भगवता गीतासु—

सर्वधर्मान् परित्यज्य मामेकं शरणं व्रज। (१८.६६)

इयमेव वैदिकी सनातनी संस्कृतिः सनातनो वा धर्मः। अस्याः संस्कृतेः संरक्षणार्थं वैदिकैः शरीरमोहं परित्यज्य प्रयतितं प्रयत्यते च।

(१५)

निस्त्रैगुणत्रैगुण्यविषयाः वेदाः

अयं ब्रह्मापरपर्यायो वेदः स्वरूपप्रतिष्ठायां चितिशक्तौ स्वतः प्रादुर्भवतीति स्वतःप्रमाणं निस्त्रैगुण्यविषयश्च।

अनुभूतविषयासम्प्रमोषः स्मृतिः (यो० सू० १.११) इति सूत्रानुसारेण सर्वाः स्मृतयो वेदमूलका एव। तत्रायं ब्रह्मापरपर्यायो वेदो निस्त्रैगुण्यविषय इति वेदमूलकाः स्मृतयोऽपि निस्त्रैगुण्यविषयाः।

ब्रह्मातिरिक्तानामनित्यपदार्थानां वेदो ज्ञानं वा विज्ञानमिति व्यपदिश्यते। प्रतिपदार्थज्ञाने वैशिष्ट्यस्य वैविध्यस्य वैपरीत्यस्य च विद्यमानत्वात्। इदं विज्ञानं ब्रह्मबाह्यविषयं वेदबाह्यविषयं त्रैगुण्यविषयं चेति बाह्यपदार्थनिष्ठम्। अत एव तद्'आगम'शब्देन'तन्त्र'शब्देन वा व्यपदिश्यते। विज्ञानमूलकाः स्मृतयश्च वेदबाह्या उच्यन्ते।

कामहतानां भोगवादिनामपवर्गवादिनां भोगापवर्गवादिनां च तान्त्रिकाणां भोगार्थमपवर्गार्थं च जिज्ञास्यं 'इदं सर्वम्' प्रमेयं परिदृश्यमानं भोग्यमपवर्जनीयं च दुःखसंभिन्नत्वात् दुःखमनित्यं च जगत्। तस्यापि तत्त्वज्ञानं तस्य सर्वधर्मज्ञानमन्तरा न सम्भवतीति तैरपि धर्मविचार आरब्धः। तथा हि—

दृष्टवदानुश्रविकः स ह्यविशुद्धिक्षयातिशययुक्तः।
तद्विपरीतः श्रेयान् व्यक्ता-ऽव्यक्त-ज्ञ-विज्ञानात्॥ **(सां० का०, २)**

इति सांख्यैः आरोहक्रमेण, आदानक्रमेण, संहारक्रमेण, प्रलयक्रमेण वा व्यक्तधर्मान् अव्यक्तधर्मान् पुरुषधर्मांश्च विज्ञापयितुं धर्मविचार आरब्धः।

योगशास्त्रेऽपि—द्रष्टृ-दृश्य-संयोगे अविद्यया द्रष्टृ-धर्माणां दृश्यधर्माणां च इतरेतराध्यासात् सङ्करः। तत्रविभागसंयमात् दृश्यदर्शनार्थं दृश्यापवर्जनेन च द्रष्टुः स्वरूपावस्थापनार्थं दृश्यधर्मविचारः।

वैशेषिकैरपि—

अथातो धर्मं व्याख्यास्यामः।

यतोऽभ्युदयनिःश्रेयससिद्धिः स धर्मः।

तद्वचनादाम्नायस्य प्रामाण्यम्।

धर्मविशेषप्रसूताद् द्रव्यगुणकर्मसामान्यविशेषसमवायानां पदार्थानां साधर्म्य-वैधर्म्याभ्यां तत्त्वज्ञानान् निःश्रेयसम्। **(वै० सू० १.१.१-४)**

इति प्रमेयाणां पदार्थानां तत्त्वज्ञानार्थं धर्मविचारः स्वीये दर्शने आरब्धः।

नैयायिकैरपि—**प्रमाण-प्रमेय-संशय-प्रयोजन-दृष्टान्त-सिद्धान्ता-ऽवयव-तर्क-निर्णय-वाद-जल्प-वितण्डा- हेत्वाभास-च्छल-जाति-निग्रहस्थानानां तत्त्वज्ञानान् निःश्रेयसाधिगमः**। (न्या० सू० १.१.१) इति षोडशपदार्थानां तत्त्वज्ञानार्थं धर्मविचार आरब्धः। तत्र **आत्म-शरीरे-न्द्रिया-ऽर्थ-बुद्धि-मनः-प्रवृत्ति-दोषप्रेत्यभाव-फल-दुःखा-ऽपवर्गास्तु प्रमेयम्**। (न्या. सू. १-१-९) इति प्रमेयं सूत्रितम्।

भोगापवर्गवादिनां द्वैतिनां पक्षे जिज्ञास्यानां प्रमेयाणां पदार्थानामानन्त्यात् शास्त्राण्यपि अनन्तानि भवति। तेषां सर्वेषामध्ययनमशक्यप्रायम्। प्रतिपदार्थं विशेषधर्माणां भिद्यमानत्वात् सर्वपदार्थानां तत्त्वज्ञानं नैव सम्पद्यते। सामान्यज्ञानेनैव निर्वाहो भवति।

प्रमाणैरेव बाह्यानां प्रमेयाणां पदार्थानां दर्शनं ज्ञानं वेदो वा भवतीति एते वेदास्त्रैगुण्यविषया भवन्ति। बाह्यत आगच्छन्तीति 'आगम'शब्देन व्यपदिश्यन्ते। आगममूलाः स्मृतयः

'तन्त्र'शब्देन व्यपदिश्यन्ते। अनित्यपदार्थानां धर्माणां प्रतिपादनपरत्वादेतानि शास्त्राण्यसत्-शास्त्राणि इति व्यपदिश्यन्ते।

भोग्यानां प्रकृतिपर्यन्तानां सर्वपदार्थानां दुःखयोनित्वाद् दुःखपरिहारय अपवर्गवादिभिः सर्वं प्रमेयं जगत् संन्यस्तव्यमित्येव सिद्धान्तितम्। अत एव अपवर्गवादिपक्षे दुःखयोनीनां पदार्थानामपवर्जनात् तत्प्रतिपादकानि शास्त्राण्यपि उपेक्ष्यन्ते प्रयोजनाभावात्। अपवर्गवादिनां दार्शनिकानां प्राचुर्यात् भारते महती शास्त्रसम्पत्तिरुपेक्षया विनष्टा।

एवं भोगवादपक्षे अनित्यानां प्रमेयाणां पदार्थानां भोगार्थं जिज्ञासा आवश्यकी। धर्मवादपक्षे आद्यन्तवतामपि पदार्थानां धर्मरक्षणेन विनाशदूरीकरणार्थं जिज्ञासा आवश्यकी। अत एव अनित्यानामसत्पदार्थानां धर्मप्रतिपादकानामनन्तानामसच्छास्त्राणाम् अध्ययनमध्यापनं तद्विद्यसम्भाषा च भोगवादपक्षे धर्मवादपक्षे च सङ्गच्छते। एतेषामनन्तानामसच्छास्त्राणामध्ययनार्थमुपनयनसंस्कारो नास्ति। भोजनात् प्राक् अध्ययनविधानमध्ययनाचारश्च नास्ति, स्वाध्यायाभावात्।

इत्थं वादिविप्रतिपत्तेः संशयः—किं जिज्ञास्यं ब्रह्म ? प्रतिपदार्थं वैशिष्ट्येन त्रैविध्येन वैपरीत्येन च संभिन्नं 'इदं सर्वम्' परिदृश्यमानं जगत्, उभयं वेति ? किं सच्छास्त्राध्ययनं कर्तव्यम्, असच्छ्रास्त्राध्ययनं वा कर्तव्यम्, आहोस्विद् उभयम् ? इति।

तत्र जिज्ञासा नाम ज्ञातुमिच्छा। सा च जिज्ञासुना साकं समवायेन तादात्म्येन अभेदेन वा सम्बन्धेन विद्यत इति न स्वतन्त्रः पदार्थः। सा च पदार्थद्वयमाक्षिपति—कर्ता कर्म च, जिज्ञासुः जिज्ञास्यं चेति। इदमेव पदार्थद्वयं द्रष्टा दृश्यं च, प्रमाता प्रमेयं च, विषयी विषयश्च, नित्यः अनित्यश्च, धर्मी अधर्मी च, अस्मत्प्रत्ययगोचरः युष्मत्प्रत्ययगोचरश्च इति दार्शनिकैर्व्यपदिश्यते।

इत्थं पदार्थद्वयमेव जिज्ञासाविषयम्। तत्र प्रथमं जिज्ञासोर्जिज्ञासा, अनन्तरं जिज्ञास्यस्य जिज्ञासेति शास्त्रीयः क्रमः। क्रमोऽयं अवरोहक्रमः, सृष्टिक्रमः, विसर्गक्रम इति व्यपदिश्यते। तत्र जिज्ञासोर्जिज्ञासाकर्तृत्वात् सोऽपि जिज्ञास्यो भवतीति शास्त्रीयज्ञानमन्तरा भानमेव न भवति। विषया एव प्रकृतिपर्यन्ता जिज्ञास्या इत्येव प्रायोवादः। जिज्ञास्यानां विषयाणां जिज्ञासाफलं भोगः। स च दुःखयोनिरिति त्रिविधतापानन्तरं जिज्ञास्यं क्रमेणापवृज्यते। प्रकृतिपर्यन्तमपवर्गानन्तरं जिज्ञासुरात्मैव अवशिष्यत इति जिज्ञासोरात्मनः स्वाभाविकं भानं भवति। तस्य तत्त्वज्ञानं नैव सम्पद्यते, धर्मजिज्ञासोदयाभावात्। अत एव वैदिका ब्रह्मवादिनः आत्मैकत्ववादिनः एकत्विनो वा न दार्शनिकाः। व्युत्क्रमेण दार्शनिकानां जिज्ञासोर्भानं भवतीत्ययं क्रमो व्युत्क्रमः, आरोहक्रमः, आदानक्रमः, संहारक्रमः, संन्यासक्रम इति व्यपदिश्यते। आरोहक्रमो दार्शनिकैरास्थीयते। अवरोहक्रमो वैदिकैः। अत एव वैदिके भगवद्गीताशास्त्रे पदार्थानामवरोहक्रम एवास्थितः। निर्गुणं ब्रह्म सगुणं ब्रह्म आत्मा शरीरं च। अवरोहक्रमेण शास्त्रं प्रतिपादितम्। तथा हि— **ज्ञानयोगः**—सर्वभूतास्थितायाः परब्रह्मणः पादरूपायाश्चितिशक्तेः निरुपाधिकेन परब्रह्मणा योगः अद्वितीयत्वं वा। **कर्मयोगः**—

सर्वभूतस्थितायाश्चितिशक्तेःप्रकृत्या योगः। क्रियायाः शरीरधर्मत्वात् धर्मधर्मिणोरभेदसम्बन्धात् कर्मयोगः, एकत्वं वा। आत्मैकत्वे कर्मफलत्यागः, कर्तृत्वत्यागश्च। अत्र ब्रह्मधर्मसमाप्तिः, सनातनधर्मसमाप्तिः, चतुर्थाध्याये ज्ञानिनामुपनिषदः समाप्तिः।

चतुर्थाध्यायानन्तरं सनातनधर्मस्थापना आत्मैकत्वस्थापना वा। विभक्तस्य चिदात्मनो ब्रह्मणा साकमनन्यत्वं **भक्तियोगः**। विभक्तस्य प्रकृतिभोगे भगवतो वेदरूपस्य चोदनानुसारेण क्रिया। द्वादशाध्यायपर्यन्तं भक्तियोगः। गुह्यामृतशास्त्रसमाप्तिः। अर्थार्थिनामुपनिषदः समाप्तिः।

त्रयोदशाध्यायमारभ्य शास्त्रं ज्योतेस्तमसं सतोऽसतम् अमृतात् मृत्युञ्च गच्छति। त्रयोदशाध्याये क्षेत्र-क्षेत्रज्ञविभागो नित्याऽनित्यवस्तुविवेको वा। चतुर्दशाध्याये गुणातीतत्वं परं वैराग्यं वा। पञ्चदशाध्याये इहामुत्रार्थफलभोगविरागो वशीकारसंज्ञावैराग्यं वा। जिज्ञासोरुपनिषदः समाप्तिः, गुह्यतमशास्त्रसमाप्तिर्वा। षोडशाध्याये रागिणां भोगवादः स्वधर्मोपदेशश्च। सप्तदशाध्याये त्रिदोषस्वरूपम्। अष्टादशाध्याये अपवर्गवादखण्डनं शास्त्रसमाप्तिश्च। अन्तिममध्यायत्रयम् आर्तानामुपनिषत्। एवम् आर्तो जिज्ञासुः अर्थार्थी ज्ञानी चेति चतुर्णां भगवद्भक्तानां कृते चतस्त्र उपनिषदः। अत एव 'भगवद्गीतासु उपनिषत्सु' इत्यत्र बहुवचनं सङ्गच्छते।

यद्यपि गीताशास्त्रे शास्त्रप्रतिपादनं पदार्थानामवरोहक्रमेण कृतम्। अवरोहक्रमेण च पदार्थाःप्रथमाध्यायस्य प्रथमे श्लोके ध्वनिताः;तथापि नित्यानित्यवस्तुविवेकपरे त्रयोदशाध्याये प्रदार्थानामारोहक्रम एव समाश्रितः। क्षेत्राध्याये आरोहक्रमस्यैव परत्वम्। तथा हि—

इति क्षेत्रं तथा ज्ञानं ज्ञेयं चोक्तं समासतः।
मद्भक्त एवद्विज्ञाय मद्भावायोपजायते ॥ **(गी. १३.१८)**

अत्र क्षेत्रं ज्ञानं ज्ञेयं चेति पदार्थत्रयमुक्तम्। अत एव वेदमूलेयं स्मृतिरिति,वेदवादिभिः प्रस्थानत्वेन स्वीकृता। अत्र 'क्षेत्र"शब्देन—

महाभूतान्यहङ्कारो बुद्धिरव्यक्तमेव च।
इन्द्रियाणि दशैकं च पञ्च चेन्द्रियगोचराः ॥

(१३.५) इति चतुर्विंशतिपदार्था उक्ताः। एते किल साङ्ख्य-सिद्धान्तोक्तैः पदार्थैः संवदन्ति, तथाप्यस्ति विशेषः। प्रथमार्धे अष्टौ प्रकृतय आरोहक्रमेणोक्ताः। उत्तरार्धे च षोडश विकृतयोऽवरोहक्रमेण। तत्र च इन्द्रियाणामनन्तरं मनसः परिगणनमिति विशेषः। अव्यक्ताद् व्यक्तपदार्था न भेदिताः। क्षेत्रे एव अव्यक्तस्य व्यक्तानां पदार्थानां च समावेशः।

विज्ञानमयकोशस्थित आत्मा प्राकृतस्त्रैगुण्ययुक्तः सुकृती वा भवति। विज्ञानमयकोशस्थिते आत्मनि कार्यार्थं विकृतिभिः साकं सङ्गतेऽपि विकृतिस्त्रिदोषोद्भवा वा नास्ति। अत एव केवला प्रकृतिरेका, प्रकृतिविकृतयः सप्तेति विभागो नोक्तः। विज्ञानमयकोशस्थितस्य प्राकृतस्याऽऽत्मनोऽवरोहो नैव संभवति। स तु उदगेव अयने आरोहति, उच्छ्रियते वेत्यारोहक्रमः। अयमेव गीताशास्त्रोक्तः उदगयनभागो धर्मक्षेत्रं च।

मनोमयकोशपरित्यागेन साकं विषयाणां परित्यागो भवति। इहामुत्रार्थफलभोगविरागः सम्पन्नो भवति। कर्तृत्वमहङ्कारो वाऽवशिष्यते। अस्मिन्नेव कोशे सम्प्राप्त आत्मा पुरुषार्थान् स्वार्थान् वा जहाति स्वधर्मं च निषेवते। तस्य विषयभक्तिरपैति। ईश्वरभक्तिश्च उदेतीति ईश्वरस्तमुद्धरति। तथा चोक्तं भगवता—

तेषामहं समुद्धर्ता मृत्युसंसारसागरात्।
भवामि न चिरात् पार्थ मय्यावेशितचेतसाम्॥ (१२.७)

षोडशविकृतिभिः साकं सङ्गत आत्मा विकृतस्त्रिदोषग्रस्तो दुष्कृती वा सम्पद्यते। स दक्षिणायने च विषयी भवति। अयं गीताशास्त्रप्रोक्तो दक्षिणायनभागः कुरुक्षेत्रं वा। अत्रात्मनः अवरोह एव भवतीति अवरोहक्रमो विकृतीनाम्।

अपगतेषु इन्द्रियगोचरेषु पदार्थेषु इन्द्रियाणि शान्तानि भवन्ति। मनस्तु तानेवाऽनुगच्छतीति मनस इन्द्रियगोचराणां पदार्थनामन्तरङ्गः सम्बन्धः, इन्द्रियाणां च बहिरङ्ग इति दशेन्द्रियानन्तरं मनस एकस्य परिगणनं सङ्गच्छते।

एवं **व्यक्ताव्यक्तज्ञविज्ञानात्** (सां० का० २) इत्यत्रोक्ते पदार्थत्रये पदार्थद्वयस्य क्षेत्रे अन्तर्भावः। ज्ञानशब्देन तृतीयपदार्थस्य ज्ञशब्देन व्यपदिष्टस्य चिदात्मनः सङ्ग्रहः। तस्य चितिरूपस्य स्वधर्मेण पञ्चकोशेष्ववस्थितस्य व्यापिनः परिज्ञानार्थम्— **अमानित्वमदम्भित्वम्** (गी. १३.७) इत्यादिभिः, **एतज्ज्ञानमिति प्रोक्तमज्ञानं यदतोऽन्यथा** (१३.११) इत्यन्तैः पञ्चभिः श्लोकैः लक्षणान्युक्तानि। साङ्ख्यैरनुक्तः पदार्थो ज्ञेयशब्देनोक्तः—ज्ञेयपदार्थश्च **ज्ञेयं यत्तत्प्रवक्ष्यामि** (१३.१२) इत्यत्रोक्तः। तत्र **अनादिमत् परं ब्रह्म न सत् तन्नासदुच्यते** (१३.१२) इति श्लोकार्धेन निर्गुणं निरुपाधिकं विकारावर्ति वा परं ब्रह्मोक्तम्। **सर्वतः पाणिपादं तत्** (१३.१३) इत्यादिभिः **हृदि सर्वस्य विष्टितम्** (१३.१७) इत्यन्तैः पञ्चभिः श्लोकैः पञ्चकोशेष्ववस्थितेन चिदात्मना प्रतीयमानं सगुणस्य सोपाधिकस्य विकारवर्तिनो वा ब्रह्मणः स्वरूपमुक्तम्। ज्ञानेन चितिशक्त्या ज्ञेयं ब्रह्मेति ज्ञापनार्थं चितिशक्तिर्ज्ञानशब्देन ब्रह्म च ज्ञेयशब्देन निर्दिष्टम्। ज्ञानेनैव ज्ञेयत्वाद् ब्रह्म अप्रमेयमिति प्रतिष्ठापितम्। प्रमाणतो ब्रह्मप्रतिपत्तिर्न भवतीति चिदात्मा ज्ञानशब्देन ब्रह्म च ज्ञेयशब्देन उक्तम्।

(१५)

प्रामाण्यवादः

जिज्ञास्यस्य दृश्यस्य प्रमेयस्य वा प्रतिपत्तिः प्रमाणत एव भवति। प्रमाणमन्तरेण प्रतिपत्तेरसंभव एव। इन्द्रियार्थसन्निकर्षेण पदार्थोपलब्धिर्भवति। दृश्यानां पदार्थानां मोहापादकत्वात् पदार्थदर्शनेन इन्द्रियाणि विमूढानि भवन्ति। इन्द्रियचैतन्ये ज्ञातरि प्रमातरि वा जिज्ञासा समुदेति। पदार्थोऽयं सुखप्रदो दुःखप्रदो वा भोग्यः परित्याज्यो वा ईप्सितव्यो जिज्ञासितव्यो वेति।

इयं जिज्ञासा धर्मिजिज्ञासेति व्यपदिश्यते भोगवादिभिः। धर्माधर्मरूप - शक्तिद्वयेन युक्ताः सर्वेऽप्यनित्याः पदार्था इति शक्तिरेव धर्म इति धर्मलक्षणं विधाय अधर्ममपि धर्ममभिमन्यन्ते अनित्यं च पदार्थं धर्मीति व्यपदिशन्ति तार्किकाः। अत एवोक्तं भगवता गीतायाम् (१२.३२)—

अधर्मं धर्ममिति या मन्यते तमसावृता।
सर्वार्थान् विपरीतांश्च बुद्धिः सा पार्थ तामसी ॥

अधर्मिजिज्ञासेति धर्मवादिभिः। अनित्यपदार्थेषु धर्माधर्मयोर्द्वन्द्वस्य विद्यमानत्वाद् अधर्मसंपृक्तो धर्मोऽप्यधर्मो भवति। अधर्मस्याभ्युत्थानेन धर्मस्य ग्लानिर्भवति, पदार्थश्च विनश्यति।

पदार्थस्य तत्त्वज्ञानं प्रमितिर्वा ईप्सितव्यो जिहासितव्यो वा भोग्यः अपवर्जनीयो वेति निर्णयः पदार्थस्य सर्वधर्मज्ञानानन्तरं भवतीति धर्मिजिज्ञासा धर्मजिज्ञासामपेक्षते। धर्मजिज्ञासया प्रेरितो जिज्ञासुः पदार्थदर्शनानन्तरं तस्य नामधेयं संज्ञां वा तस्य असाधारणधर्मं सामान्यधर्मान् विशेषधर्मांश्च पदार्थाभिज्ञातारं यथोपदेष्टारं श्रद्धेयं गुरुं परिपृच्छति। अत एवोक्तं गीतासु (४.३९-४०)

श्रद्धावान् लभते ज्ञानं तत्परः संयतेन्द्रियः।
ज्ञानं लब्ध्वा परां शान्तिमचिरेणाऽधिगच्छति ॥

अज्ञश्चाश्रद्धधानश्च संशयात्मा विनश्यति।
नायं लोकोऽस्ति न परो न सुखं संशयात्मनः ॥

श्रद्धा सत्ये प्रतिष्ठिता, अश्रद्धा च असत्ये। तथा च मन्त्रवर्णः (मा० सं० १९.७७)—

दृष्ट्वा रूपे व्याकरोत् सत्यानृते प्रजापतिः।
अश्रद्धामनृतेऽदधात् श्रद्धां सत्ये प्रजापतिः ॥

आप्तवाक्यात् शब्दप्रामाण्यात् श्रुत्या वा पदार्थस्य सर्वधर्मज्ञानं तत्त्वज्ञानं वा सम्पद्यते। पदार्थो भोग्यो वा अपवर्जनीयो वेति निर्णीयते। गुरोः सकाशात् श्रुतानां भोग्यपदार्थधर्माणां मननं निदिध्यासनं च विधाय तेषां शान्तोदिताव्यपदेश्यानां सर्वधर्माणामस्तित्वं क्रमेण तस्मिन् पदार्थे साक्षात्क्रियते। सर्वधर्मसाक्षात्कारानन्तरमेव धर्मजिज्ञासा धर्मिजिज्ञासा च परिसमाप्यते। अपवर्जनीयत्वेन श्रुतानां पदार्थानां धर्मसाक्षात्कारार्थं न कश्चित् प्रयतते। शब्दप्रामाण्येन श्रद्धयैव ते संन्यस्यन्ते। नहि विषस्य मारकत्वधर्मसाक्षात्कारार्थं कश्चिद् व्याप्रियते। इयमेव रीतिराबाल्यात् सर्वैः सर्वत्राऽऽस्थीयते।

अनेन अविच्छिन्नेन लोकव्यवहारेण शब्दप्रामाण्यस्य प्राबल्यं प्रस्थाप्यते। कामं द्वैतिनः प्रामाणिकास्तार्किकाः प्रत्यक्षमनुमानं शब्दश्चेति क्रमेण प्रामाण्यवादं व्यवस्थापयन्तु। तेषां व्यवस्था प्रत्यक्षसिद्धेन लोकव्यवहारेण बाध्यत एव। शब्दनिरपेक्षेण केवलेन प्रत्यक्षेण अनुमानेन वा जीवनव्यवहार एवाऽशक्यप्रायः, दूरे पुनर्ब्रह्मज्ञानम्। अनेन लोकव्यवहारेण गुरोरावश्यकता गुरुपरम्पराया अविच्छिन्नत्वं च प्रतिष्ठाप्यते।

गुरुपरम्पराया आरम्भस्तु ईश्वरात् परब्रह्मणो वा भवति। तथा च श्रुतिः—

प्रजापतिर्ब्रह्मणो ब्रह्म स्वयम्भुर्ब्रह्मणे नमः।
(शत. १०.५.५.९; १४.५.५.२२; १४.७.३.२८)

यो ब्रह्माणं विदधाति पूर्वं
यो वै वेदांश्च प्रहिणोति तस्मै।
तं देवमात्मबुद्धिप्रकाशं
मुमुक्षुर्वै शरणमहं प्रपद्ये॥

(श्वे० ६.१८) । स्मृतिरपि—

इमं विवस्वते योगं प्रोक्तवानहमव्ययम्।
विवस्वान् मनवे प्राह मनुरिक्ष्वाकवेऽब्रवीत्॥ (गी. ४.१)

पूर्वेषामपि गुरुः कालेनानवच्छेदात्। (यो.सू. १.२६)

एवं परिदृश्यमानस्य जगतो विषयाणां जिज्ञास्यस्य वा जिज्ञासायाः फलं स्वार्थः आत्मार्थः पुरुषार्थो वा। स द्विविधः—१. भोगः, २. अपवर्गश्च। अत एवोक्तं योगशास्त्रे (यो० सू० २.१८)—

प्रकाशस्थितिक्रियाशीलं भूतेन्द्रियात्मकं भोगापवर्गार्थं दृश्यम्।

अत्र 'दृश्य'-शब्देन आत्मातिरिक्ताः साङ्ख्यसिद्धान्तोक्ताश्चतुर्विंशतिपदार्थाः सङ्गृह्यन्ते। सुखप्रदः पदार्थो भोगार्थमुपादीयते, दुःखप्रदश्च संन्यस्यते। भोग्यस्य प्रकृतेस्त्रैगुण्यानुरोधेन भोगस्य त्रैविध्यं सम्पद्यते—१. सात्त्विकः, २. राजसः, ३. तामसश्चेति। स एव क्रमेण धर्मः, अर्थः, कामश्चेति व्यपदिश्यते स्वार्थवादिभिः आत्मार्थवादिभिः पुरुषर्थवादिभिर्वा द्वैताचार्यैः। इत्थं स्वार्थस्य आत्मार्थस्य पुरुषार्थस्य वा चत्वारो भेदा भवन्ति—१. धर्मः, २. अर्थः, ३. कामः, ४. मोक्षश्चेति।

कामस्यैवेदं चतुर्विधं स्वरूपम्। तत्र निर्ज्ञातप्राप्येष्टार्थप्रार्थना अर्थः। अनिर्ज्ञातप्राप्येष्टार्थप्रार्थना च कामः, इत्यर्थकामयोर्भेदः। तत्र निर्ज्ञातप्राप्येष्टार्थस्य प्राप्तिर्दृष्टसाधनैरनायासेन भवति। अनिर्ज्ञातप्राप्येष्टार्थप्राप्तिस्तु सर्वैरपि दृष्टप्रयत्नैः कदाचिन्नैव भवति। तेन विषयिणो विषण्णा इष्टप्राप्त्यर्थमार्ता भवन्ति। लौकिकानामुपायानामभावात् अलौकिकानुपायान् ज्ञातुं कामहता एते द्वैतिनो नेतॄनुपगच्छन्ति। द्वैतिनो नेतारोऽप्येतान् काममोहितान् अर्थवादैर्विमोह्य अधिकारानुसारेण वैदिकान् तान्त्रिकान् पुराणोक्तान् उपायान् विधीन् वा बोधयन्ति। विधयश्चैते कामहतैर्निष्ठापूर्वकमितिकर्तव्यतानुसारं साङ्गा अनुष्ठीयन्ते। एते विधयो भोगवादिभिः इहामुत्रार्थभोगार्थमनुष्ठीयन्ते। ते च धर्मशब्देन व्यपदिश्यन्ते।

धर्मोऽयं सात्त्विकः स्वार्थः पुरुषार्थो वा। अत्र भोगप्राप्त्यर्थं त्यागः कर्तव्यो भवति। अस्यैव धर्मस्य भोगरूपफलप्रदानार्थम् अपूर्ववादो मीमांसकानाम्। ईश्वरस्य च फलदातृत्वमुत्तरमीमांसायाम्। कर्तृगामिक्रियाफलवादस्य स्वार्थमूलकत्वात् अविद्यानिबन्धनत्वात् अशास्त्रीयत्वात् अन्यथासिद्धत्वाच्च क्रियाफलं कदाचिद् भवति, अङ्गवैकल्ये कदाचिन्नैव

भवति। एवं क्रियाफलस्य अनिश्चितत्वेऽपि भोगवादिनस्त्यागे प्रवर्त्यन्ते अनेन प्रकारेण। प्रकारोऽयं नीतिरिति व्यपदिश्यते धर्मवादिभिः। अयमेव शास्त्रीयो भोगवादः। स च लौकिकाद् भोगवादादभिन्नः। अयमेव दूषणार्थमुपपादितो गीताशास्त्रे सप्तदशाध्याये (श्लोकः १)—

ये शास्त्रविधिमुत्सृज्य यजन्ते श्रद्धयान्विताः।

तेषां निष्ठा तु का कृष्ण सत्त्वमाहो रजस्तमः॥

कामहतेभ्यः कामस्य क्षेत्रधर्मत्वात् देहात्मवादिभ्यो लोकायतमतानुसारिभ्यः इहामुत्रार्थभोगार्थमलौकिकमुपायमुपदिशतां द्वैतिनामाचार्याणामेव निन्दा विधीयते लोकायतिकैः —

त्रयो वेदस्य कर्तारो भण्डधूर्तनिशाचराः।

(बृहस्पतिः, स० द० सं.) इति। निन्देयं समग्रो वेदराशिरिहामुत्रार्थभोगार्थमिति येषामभिप्रायस्तेषां द्वैतिनामेव। एकत्विनां तु भोगापवर्गवादो नास्त्येवेति भोगार्थम् अपवर्गार्थं वा धर्मानुष्ठानं नास्ति। समग्रो वेदराशिरात्मधर्मप्रतिष्ठापनपर एवेति एकत्विनां मीमांसकानां सिद्धान्तः। अत एव कर्तृत्वं कर्मफलं च संन्यस्यतामेकत्विनां कर्मयोगिनां धर्मवादिनामियं निन्दा नास्ति।

ये हि संस्पर्शजा भोगा दुःखयोनय एव ते।

आद्यन्तवन्तः कौन्तेय न तेषु रमते बुधः॥ (गी. ५.२२) इति लौकिकानामलौकिकानां भोगानां दुःखयोनित्वाद् धर्मवादिभिः अपवर्गवादिभिश्च भोगवादः परित्यज्यते।

परिणामतापसंस्कारैर्गुणवृत्तिविरोधाच्च दुःखमेव सर्वं विवेकिनः (यो० सू० २.१५) इति योगसूत्रानुसारेण प्रकृतिपर्यन्तस्य सर्वस्य दुःखरूपत्वाद् दुःखनिवृत्त्यर्थं प्रकृतिपर्यन्तं सर्वं क्रमेण अपवर्गवादिभिरपवृज्यते। प्रकृतिपर्यन्तं संन्यासानन्तरं स्वरूपप्रतिष्ठायां न पुनः परिगृह्यते। धर्मवादिभिः कर्मयोगिभिः शरीरस्य विद्यमानत्वात् क्रियायाः शरीरधर्मत्वाच्च क्रियार्थं शरीरं परिगृह्यते। क्रियासमाप्तौ संन्यस्यते। ज्ञानयोगस्य कर्मयोगस्य च सनातनस्य ब्रह्मणो धर्मरूपत्वात्। भक्तियोगस्य कर्मयोगस्य च आत्मनो धर्मरूपत्वात्।

अयमपवर्गक्रमः, संन्यासक्रमः, आरोहक्रमः, संहारक्रमः, प्रलयक्रमः, प्राकृतक्रमो वा योगशास्त्रे उपदिष्टः। स एव सर्वैर्मोक्षवादिभिः स्वसम्प्रदायानुसारं परिष्कृत्य उपयुज्यते। शास्त्रीयोऽयमपवर्गवादो लौकिकाद्अपवर्गवादाद् भिद्यते।

एवमपवर्गक्रमेण आत्मबोधो नैकजन्मसाध्यः। अत एवास्मिन् पक्षे जिज्ञासोस्तत्त्वज्ञानस्य आशैव नास्ति। जिज्ञास्यस्य जिज्ञासायाःफलं भोगोऽपवर्गश्च। उभयमपि जगतो विनाशायैव भवति, सर्वस्य पदार्थजातस्य स्वधर्मे प्रतिष्ठितत्वात्। अत एवायमारोहक्रमः, संहारक्रमः, आदानक्रमः, प्रलयक्रमः, प्राकृतः क्रमो व्युत्क्रमो वा सर्वथा परित्याज्यः। शास्त्रीयो जिज्ञासाया अवरोहक्रमः, सृष्टिक्रमः, विसर्गक्रमः, संस्कृतक्रमो वा स्वीकार्यः। संस्कृतक्रमानुसारेण प्रथमं सच्छास्त्राध्ययनम्, अनन्तरमसच्छास्त्राध्ययनं कर्तव्यमिति सिद्धान्तः। अत एवोक्तं मनुना—(१.१६८)

योऽनधीत्य द्विजो वेदमन्यत्र कुरुते श्रमम्।
स जीवन्नेव शूद्रत्वमाशु गच्छति सान्वयः॥

ब्रह्मातिरिक्तानामनित्यपदार्थानां धर्मप्रतिपादकानि शास्त्राणि असच्छास्त्राणि। सच्छास्त्राध्ययनं विहाय केवलमसच्छास्त्राध्ययनं वैदिकैर्धर्मवादिभिरुपपातकेषु परिगणितम्। तथा हि—

अनाहिताग्निता स्तेयमृणानामनपक्रिया।
असच्छास्त्राधिगमनं कौशलव्यस्य च क्रिया॥ (मनु० ११.६५)

असच्छास्त्राधिगमन - माकरेष्वधिकारिता।
भार्याया विक्रयश्चैषामेकैकमुपपातकम्॥ (याज्ञ० ३.२४२)

असच्छास्त्राध्ययनेन सच्छास्त्राध्ययनविधुरेण भोगेषु प्रवृत्तिर्भवति। भोगिभिश्च तेषां ज्ञानं स्वार्थायैवोपयुज्यते, न पुनः स्वधर्माय सर्वभूतहिताय वा। सच्छास्त्राध्ययनाभावे मानवः कामहतः स्वार्थान्धो विकृतश्च संपद्यते। तस्य सर्वभूतहिते रतिर्नोत्पद्यते, प्रत्युत भूतोपरोधो भवति। आत्मसंस्काराभावात् असच्छास्त्राभ्यासेन संस्कृतिर्नोत्पद्यते। स्वार्थवादिभिः पुरुषार्थवादिभिः जगतः प्रतिष्ठा कर्तुं न शक्यते, विनाश एव साध्यते। अत एव असच्छास्त्राध्ययनमुपपातकम्।

भोगानां दुःखयोनित्वात् त्रिविधतापतप्तो मानवः क्रमेण सर्वं परित्यजति। अपवर्गवादाश्रयणेन प्राकृतः सम्पद्यते। भोगापवर्गवादे संस्कृतेः स्थानं नास्ति। अत एव केवलमसच्छास्त्राध्ययनं सर्वैः सर्वथा परित्याज्यमेवेति सिद्धान्तः।

सच्छास्त्राध्ययनेन तत्रोक्तैरात्मसंस्कारैश्च संस्कृतिरुत्पद्यते। संस्कृतो भवत्यात्मा। तस्मिन् सर्वे ब्रह्मधर्मा उदिता भवन्ति। स स्वयं ब्रह्म संपद्यते। इयं संस्कृतिः सनातनपदार्थनिष्ठत्वात् सनातनी प्रतितिष्ठति। धर्मेणैव सर्वं प्रतिष्ठापयितुं शक्यते। अत एव अनुग्रहेण सनातनधर्मस्थापनार्थं ब्राह्मणानां सच्छास्त्राध्यनमावश्यकम्। निग्रहेण सनातनधर्मस्थापनार्थं क्षत्रियाणाम्, धर्माचरणार्थं च वैश्यानां सच्छास्त्राध्ययनमावश्यकम्। वैश्यानां रजःप्रधानत्वात् तैः कामं सच्छास्त्राध्ययनानन्तरं असच्छास्त्राण्यध्येतव्यानि। शूद्राणां सङ्कराणां च तमःप्रधानत्वात् सर्वभूतहिताय असच्छास्त्राध्ययने अधिकरः। तस्मात् जगतः प्रतिष्ठासिद्ध्यर्थं सच्छास्त्राध्ययनं सर्वेषामतीव आवश्यकमिति सिद्धान्तः।

(१६)

रक्षार्थं वेदानामध्येयं व्याकरणम् (म० भा० १.१.१)

अथ ब्रह्मयज्ञः —**स्वाध्यायोऽध्येतव्यः** (शत. ११.५.७.२), **स्वाध्यायो वै ब्रह्मयज्ञः** (शत. ११.५.६.३)इत्यादिश्रुतिभ्यःस्वाध्यायस्य ब्रह्मयज्ञस्य वेदाध्ययनस्य वा नित्यत्वं प्रतिष्ठापितम्।

सनातनस्य परब्रह्मणो धर्मस्य प्रतिष्ठापकत्वात् अनेकशाखाप्रभेदभिन्नो मन्त्रब्राह्मणात्मको वेदराशिः सनातनः। धर्मधर्मिणोस्तादात्म्यसम्बन्धस्य विद्यमानत्वाद् ब्रह्मधर्मप्रतिपादकः सनातनो वेदराशिः सनातने ब्रह्मण्येव तादात्म्यसम्बन्धेन प्रतितिष्ठति। अत एव **सैषा त्रय्येव विद्या तपति** (शत० १०.५.२.२) इत्यादिश्रुतिभ्यः परं ब्रह्म त्रयीमयं वेदमयं ज्ञानघनं चिन्मयमिति श्रूयते। ब्रह्मणस्त्रयीमयत्वात् अध्येतृपरम्पराया अभावात् उत्सन्ना अपि वेदशाखा ब्रह्मणि प्रतिष्ठन्ते। ताश्च महर्षयः पुनः सम्पादयन्ति। तथा चोक्तं वेदव्यासेन—

युगान्तेऽन्तर्हितान् वेदान् सेतिहासान् महर्षयः।
लेभिरे तपसा पूर्वमनुज्ञाताः स्वयम्भुवा॥ (शां० भा० १.३.२९) इति।

वार्तिककारैरपि—**आदित्यादिमानि शुक्लानि यजूंषि वाजसनेयेन याज्ञवल्क्येनाख्यायन्ते।** (शत० १४.९.४.३३; बृ० ६.४.२३)

बृहदारण्यकोपनिषद्भाष्यवार्तिके (६.५.१७-१९)—

वेदात्मनो रवेरेवं सम्प्रदायोऽयमागतः॥
परमेष्ठ्यादिकान् सर्वान् पारम्पर्येण मानुषान्॥
असंसृष्टं परं ब्रह्म सर्वदोषविवर्जितम्॥

एतदादित्यगं भाति तद्वेदानां परं वपुः॥
उत्सन्नमपि यद्ब्रह्म तदादित्ये न नश्यति॥
तदार्षेणैव विन्दन्ति तपस्तप्त्वा महर्षयः॥

अत एव वेदानां नित्यत्वम्। तच्च **अत एव च नित्यत्वम्** (ब्र० सू० १.३.२९) इति सूत्रे उत्तरमीमांसायां प्रतिष्ठापितम्। भगवत्पूज्यपादैश्चात्र प्रमाणत्वेन मन्त्रोऽप्युपन्यस्तः। तथा च मन्त्रवर्णः—**यज्ञेन वाचः पदवीयमायन् तामन्वविन्दन् ऋषिषु प्रविष्टाम्।** (ऋ० १०.७१.३) इति स्थितामेव वाचमनुविन्नां दर्शयति (शां० भा० १.३.२९)

अनेकशाखाप्रभेदभिन्नस्य मन्त्रब्राह्मणात्मकस्य सनातनस्य वेदराशेः नित्यत्वात् तस्य संरक्षणार्थं सर्ववेदपारिषदस्य नित्यस्य व्याकरणशास्त्रस्य आवश्यकत्वमिति महर्षयो व्याकरणशास्त्रं सूत्रयामासुः। तत्र भगवतो महर्षेः पाणिनेरद्वितीयेन शास्त्रेण सर्वाणि प्राचीनानि व्याकरणानि नामशेषाणि संवृत्तानि। भगवतः पाणिनेः शास्त्रमेवेदानीं वेदाङ्गत्वेन सर्वैरेव वैदिकैः शिष्टैः समादृत्य अधीयते अध्याप्यते च।

तदिदं भगवतः पाणिनेर्व्याकरणशास्त्रं अनेकशाखाप्रभेदभिन्नस्य मन्त्रब्राह्मणात्मकस्य समस्तस्य वेदराशेः संरक्षणार्थं न पुनः कस्याश्चिद् वेदशाखायाः प्रातिशाख्यवत् परिरक्षणार्थम्। अत एव वेदशाखासु यत्र यत्र प्रयोगभेदो दृष्टस्तत्र तत्र भगवता पाणिनिना बहुलम्, अन्यतरस्याम्, उभयथा, वा, एकेषाम् इत्यादिग्रहणेन प्रयोगद्वयस्यापि शाखाभेदेन साधुत्वं व्यवस्थापितम्।

एतदेव प्रयोजनं भगवता भाष्यकारेण स्थाने स्थाने प्रदर्शितम्। तथा हि—

अवश्यं खल्वस्माभिरिदं वक्तव्यं बहुलम् अन्यतरस्याम् उभयथा वा एकेषामिति।

सर्ववेदपारिषदं हीदं शास्त्रम् । तत्र नैकः पन्थाः शक्य आस्थातुम् । (महा० भा० २.१.५८;६.३.१४)

अनया भाष्यकारोक्त्या सर्वेऽपि विकल्पाः शाखाभेदेन व्यवस्थापनीयाः। वैदिकैर्वैयाकरणैरेतादृशः प्रयत्नोऽवश्यं कर्तव्यः। अद्यापि न केनापि कृतः।

वैयाकरणानां प्रबोधनार्थं वैयाकरणानामवैयाकरणानां च यथा अनायासेन बोधो भवेत् तथैव दिङ्मात्रमत्रोदाह्रियते—

अनुस्वारस्य ययि परसवर्णः (पा. सू. ८.४.५८) **वा पदान्तस्य** (८.४.५९) इति सूत्रद्वयं वर्तते। तत्र '**वा पदान्तस्ये**'ति सूत्रं रक्षार्थं वेदानामावश्यकम्। बह्वृचाः पदान्तस्य अनुस्वारस्य ययि परतः परसवर्णं न कुर्वन्ति। याजुषास्तु कुर्वन्ति। इत्थं शाखाभेदेन परसवर्णस्य व्यवस्थितत्वात् वा पदान्तस्येति सूत्रं रक्षार्थं वेदानाम्।

याजुषास्तु शलि परतः श-ष-स-हेषु वा परतः अनुस्वारस्य **ꣳ** इत्यादेशं कुर्वन्ति। अनुस्वारं न उच्चारयन्ति। यथा—हंसः शुचिषद् (ऋ० ४.४०.५) इति बह्वृचाः। ह**ꣳ** सः शुचिषत् (मा० सं० १०.२४; १२.१४) इति याजुषाः।

अत एव यासु शाखासु पदान्तस्य अनुस्वारस्य परसवर्णो नित्यस्तासां शाखानां संहिता-ब्राह्मणानां परसवर्णरहितं मुद्रणमशुद्धमेवेति वैदिकै-र्वैयाकरणैर्विभावनीयम्।

रक्षार्थं वेदानां व्याकरणशास्त्रस्य अनावश्यकत्वे तु 'न पदान्तस्य' इत्येव सूत्रयितुं युक्तम्। मुद्रितेषु लौकिकग्रन्थेषु पदान्तस्यानुस्वारस्य परसवर्णो नैव विधीयत इति। तस्मात् लोकभाषासंरक्षणार्थं पाणिनीयं व्याकरणं नास्तीति।

शुक्लयजुर्वेदस्य माध्यन्दिनशाखायां द्वित्वं नित्यमिति सर्वाणि द्वित्वविधायकानि सूत्राणि माध्यन्दिनशाखासंरक्षणार्थमावश्यकानि। माध्यन्दिनशाखासदृशीषु लुप्तशाखासु भगवता पाणिनिना द्वित्वं नित्यं दृष्टं शाखान्तरेषु न दृष्टमिति द्वित्वविकल्पः शिष्टः। लोकभाषायाः कृते नावश्यकानि सूत्राणि, लौकिकग्रन्थेषु शिष्टैर्द्वित्वस्य परित्यक्तत्वात्। अत एव माध्यन्दिनसंहितायाः शतपथब्राह्मणस्य **छन्दोवत् सूत्राणि भवन्ति** (कात्यायनप्रतिज्ञासूत्रम्) इति वचनात् कात्यायनश्रौतसूत्रस्य गृह्यसूत्रस्य च द्वित्वरहितं परसवर्णरहितं च मुद्रणमशुद्धमेव।

वा शरि (८.३.३६) शरि परे विसर्जनीयस्य विसर्जनीय एव वा स्यात्। विकल्पोऽयं शाखाभेदेन व्यवस्थितः। तथा हि पुरुषसूक्ते—

सहस्रशीर्षा पुरुषस्सहस्राक्षस्सहस्रपात्।

इति ऋग्वेदपाठः।

सहस्रशीर्षा पुरुषः सहस्राक्षः सहस्रपात्।

इति माध्यन्दिनपाठः।

सर्ववेदपारिषदं हीदं शास्त्रमिति 'वा शरीति' सूत्रितं भगवता। अत एव मुद्रितेषु ऋग्वेदग्रन्थेषु मुद्रितः सविसर्गपाठः प्रामादिकः। बह्वृचाः सकारमधीयते। माध्यन्दिना

विसर्गम्।

कुप्वोः ≍क≍पौ च (८.३.३७) कवर्गे पवर्गे च परे विसर्जनीयस्य क्रमात् जिह्वामूलीयोपध्मानीयौ स्तः। चाद्विसर्गः।

त्रिपादूर्ध्व उदैत् पुरुषः पादः (पुरुषसूक्तम्) इत्यत्र सविसर्गं माध्यन्दिना अधीयते। सोपध्मानीयं बह्वृचाः इति शाखाभेदेन व्यवस्था। माध्यन्दिनानां जिह्वामूलीयोपध्मानीयौ न स्तः। तथा हि कात्यायन-प्रातिशाख्यसूत्रम्—

तस्मिन् ळ्ळह जिह्वामूलीयोपध्मानीयनासिक्या न सन्ति माध्यन्दिनानाम्। लृकारो दीर्घः। प्लुतश्चोक्तवर्जम्। (८.३५)

खर्परे शरि वा विसर्गलोपो वक्तव्यः　　　　**(वा० कौमुदी १५१)**

माध्यन्दिना विसर्गलोपमेव कुर्वन्ति। तथा हि कात्यायनप्रातिशाख्यसूत्रम्—**लुङ् मुदि जित्परे** (३.१३)। यथा—अन्धः स्थ। अन्धस्थान्धो वो भक्षीय। (मा० सं० ३.२०)। स्थालीभिः स्थालीः। स्थालीभिस्थालीराप्नोति। (मा० सं० ९.२७)

एवमेव सर्वाणि बहुलम्, अन्यतरस्याम्, उभयथा, एकेषामित्यादीनि ग्रहणानि व्यवस्थापनीयानि। एतेन सर्ववेदपारिषदं हीदं शास्त्रमिति भाष्यकारस्य सिद्धान्तः प्रतिष्ठापितो भवति।

अत्रैके प्रत्यवतिष्ठन्ते। यथा वेदानां रक्षार्थं तथा लोकभाषारक्षार्थमपीदं व्याकरणम्।

(१) **विभाषा भाषायाम्** (६.६.१८), **भाषायां सदवसश्रुवः**। (३.२.१०८) इत्यादिसूत्रेषु भाषाशब्दग्रहणात्।

(२) **अथ शब्दानुशासनम्।... केषां शब्दानाम्? लौकिकानां वैदिकानां च** (महा० भा० १.१.१) इत्यत्र महाभाष्ये लौकिकशब्दग्रहणात्।

(३) प्रक्रियाग्रन्थेषु लोकभाषायाः कृते स्वररहितायाः प्रक्रियायाः प्रतिपादनाच्च।

तत्र ब्रूमः—परिवर्तनशीला हि लोकभाषा भवति। देशतः कालतश्चावश्यं परिवर्तते। तस्याः संरक्षणार्थं प्रयत्नो मोघः। प्रयत्नकर्तारश्च मोघकर्माणः। नहि महर्षीणां मोघे कर्मणि प्रवृत्तिः कल्पयितुं शक्यते। इदानीं वैदिकी भाषा लोकभाषा नास्ति। तस्या एव प्राकृतं वैकृतं वा स्वरूपं प्राप्ता इदानीन्तनाः सर्वा लोकभाषाः। ताश्च परिवर्तनशीला एव। तासां व्याकरणशास्त्रेण निबन्धनमशक्यप्रायम्।

विभाषा भाषायाम् (६.६.१८१), **भाषायां सदवसश्रुवः** (३.२.१०८) इत्यादिसूत्रेषु प्रयुक्तो भाषाशब्दो लोकभाषापर इति प्रौढिवादः। सूत्रेषु ज्ञापकं नास्ति। महर्षिणा जैमिनिना भाषाशब्दो ब्राह्मणपर्यायः प्रयुक्तः। तथा हि—**भाषास्वरोपदेशादैरवत् प्रावचनप्रतिषेधः** (पू० मी० १२.३.२०)। **मन्त्रोपदेशो वा न भाषिकस्य। प्रायापत्तेर्भाषिकश्रुतिः** (पू० मी० १२.३.२१)। क्रतौ संहितास्वरेण मन्त्रः प्रयोक्तव्यो ब्राह्मणस्वरेण वेति मीमांसितमस्मिन्नधिकरणे।

ब्राह्मणस्वरादिविधायकानि प्रातिशाख्यपरिशिष्टभूतानि सूत्राणि भाषिकसूत्राणीति व्यपदिश्यन्ते। अत एव सूत्रकारैर्महर्षिभिः भाषाशब्दो ब्राह्मणपर्यायवाची प्रयुक्तः।

शब्दानुशासनस्य प्रयोजनानि प्रतिपादयता भाष्यकारेण यथा रक्षार्थं वेदानामध्येयं व्याकरणमिति प्रयोजनमुक्तं न तथा कुत्रापि लोकभाषारक्षार्थं व्याकरणमध्येयमिति।

'यर्वाणस्तर्वाणो नामर्षयो बभूवुः प्रत्यक्षधर्माणः परापरज्ञा विदितवेदितव्या अधिगतयाथातथ्याः। ते तत्रभवन्तो यद्वानस्तद्वान इति प्रयोक्तव्ये यर्वाणस्तर्वाण इति प्रयुञ्जते। याज्ञे पुनः कर्मणि नापभाषन्ते। तैः पुनरसुरैर्याज्ञे कर्मण्यपभाषितं ततस्ते पराभूताः' (महा० भा० १.१.१) इति महाभाष्यमेव ज्ञापयति लोकभाषारक्षणार्थं व्याकरणस्य प्रयोजनं नास्तीति।

लौकिकानां वैदिकानां च (महा० भा० १.१.१) इत्यत्र प्रयुक्तो लौकिकशब्दो न लोकभाषापरः। याज्ञे कर्मणि ऊहादिषु प्रयुज्यमानाः शब्दा लौकिका इत्युच्यन्ते, मन्त्रब्राह्मणात्मके वेदे पाठाभावात्। शब्दानुशासनप्रयोजनेषु परिगणितः ऊहः। **रक्षोहागमलघ्वसन्देहाः प्रयोजनम्** (महा० भा० १,१.१) इति। आदिपदेन विभक्तिं कुर्वन्ति—'सारस्वतीम्' इत्यादीनां प्रयोजनानां ग्रहणम्।

प्रक्रियाग्रन्थेषु स्वररहितं प्रक्रियाप्रतिपादनं पाणिनीयमपाणिनीयं वेति वैयाकरणैरवश्यं विचारणीयम्। **प्रत्ययः। परश्च। आद्युदात्तश्च। अनुदात्तौ सुप्पितौ** (३.१.१-४) इत्यादिसूत्रैः पाणिनिना सस्वरं शब्दा अनुशिष्टाः। भवति। भवतः। भवन्ति इत्यादि रूपाणां सस्वरं पठनं पाठनं च पाणिनीयं भवति। उदात्तस्वरः शतपथब्राह्मणवद् अधोरेखया प्रदर्शनीयः। ऊर्ध्वरेखया स्वरितः। यथा स्व॑। उच्चारणं च उदात्तं निहत्य कर्तव्यम्। तिङ्ङतिङः (अ० ८.१.२८) इत्यनेन पाणिनिना उदात्तनिघात एव प्रदर्शितः।

व्याकरणशास्त्रनिष्पन्नानां सस्वराणां शब्दानामेकः कोशो वैयाकरणैरवश्यं निर्मातव्यः। सम्भूय प्रयत्नोऽयं कार्यः। वैयाकरणानां परम्परा वर्तत इति सफलः प्रयत्नो भविष्यति इति।

(१७)

यज्ञो वै श्रेष्ठतमं कर्म

वेदाध्ययनस्य नित्यत्वं रक्षार्थं वेदानां च व्याकरण-शास्त्रस्य आवश्यकत्वं प्रतिष्ठापितम्। वेदानामैदम्पर्यं निरूपयितुं प्रवृत्तैर्मीमांसकैः द्विविधो हि वेदार्थो मीमांसितः—धर्मो धर्मी च। यजतिः यज्ञश्च। ब्रह्मचर्यं ब्रह्म च। तत्र पूर्वभागे धर्मो मीमांसितः। उत्तरभागे च धर्मी। धर्मी च अद्वितीयं ब्रह्मेति सिद्धान्तितम्। अत एव ब्रह्मचर्यं धर्मः संवृत्तः। ब्रह्मचर्यं नाम ब्रह्मधर्मेण चरणं चर्या वा। कर्तृत्वस्य भोक्तृत्वस्य च ब्रह्मधर्मत्वाभावाद् आत्मधर्मत्वाभावाच्च कर्तृत्वं भोक्तृत्वं च संन्यस्य अहङ्कारं ममत्वं वा परित्यज्य या चर्या सा ब्रह्मचर्यमिति वैदिकैर्व्यपदिश्यते।

इयमेव चर्या कर्मयोगशब्देन गीताशास्त्रे व्यपदिष्टा। कर्मयोगो नाम कर्मणा साकमात्मनो योगः। नहि क्रिया क्रियावन्तमन्तरेण स्वातन्त्र्येण अवतिष्ठत इति कर्मणा साकं योगो नाम क्रियावतां बुद्ध्यादि-महाभूतान्तानां त्रयोविंशतिपदार्थानां साकमात्मनो योगः। योगशब्देन वियोगोऽपि लक्ष्यते। क्रियासमाप्तौ त्रयोविंशतिपदार्थानां संन्यासः। कर्तृत्वाभावात् भोक्तृत्वाभावात् नैष्कर्म्यं च। आत्मनःसंयोगेन शरीरं सक्रियं भवति। सक्रियत्वं त्रयोविंशतिपदार्थानां धर्म इति शरीरं स्वधर्मे तिष्ठति। अक्रियत्वमात्मनो धर्म इति कर्तृत्वत्यागात् भोक्तृत्वत्यागाच्च आत्मा स्वधर्मे तिष्ठति। स च क्रियासमाप्तौ निष्कर्मा सम्पद्यते। तस्य नैष्कर्म्यमनायासेन सिद्ध्यति। नैष्कर्म्ये कर्मयोगस्य पूर्वभावित्वं कर्मयोगे च नैष्कर्म्यस्य उत्तरभावित्वं विद्यते। नैष्कर्म्य-कर्मयोगयोरविनाभावः सम्बन्धः।

अस्यां चर्यायां कर्मफलत्यागात् कर्तृत्वत्यागाच्च समग्रं कर्म प्रविलीयते (गी० ४.२३)। कर्म ब्रह्मार्पणमेव भवति (गी० ४.२४)। आत्मनश्च द्वेधा अवस्थितिर्भवति—समाधौ संन्यासेन, व्युत्थाने च योगेन। अत एवोक्तं गीतासु—

यत् करोषि यदश्नासि यज्जुहोषि ददासि यत्।
यत् तपस्यसि कौन्तेय तत् कुरुष्व मदर्पणम्॥

शुभाशुभफलैरेवं मोक्ष्यसे कर्मबन्धनैः।
संन्यासयोगयुक्तात्मा विमुक्तो मामुपेष्यसि॥ **(९.२७.२८)**

संन्यासो योगश्च ब्रह्मधर्मौ आत्मधर्मौ च। इयमेव चर्या 'यज्ञ' शब्देन व्यपदिश्यते वेदेषु। अत एव श्रूयते—**अथ यद् यज्ञ इत्याचक्षते ब्रह्मचर्यमेव तत्** (छा, ९.५.१)। सर्वेष्वेव वैदिकेषु यज्ञेषु द्विविधस्त्यागो भवति। न ममेति त्यागेनैव यज्ञः प्रतिष्ठते। अत एवोक्तं महाभारते (१०.१३.३)—

ममेति च भवेन् मृत्युर्न ममेति च शाश्वतम्।

कर्तृत्वत्यागात् कर्मफलत्यागाच्च यज्ञस्य कर्तृगामिफलं नास्ति। कर्तृगामिफलाभावात् सुखदुःखान्यतर-साक्षात्काररूपं भोगफलं नास्ति। पुण्यफलं सुखं पापफलं दुःखमिति पुण्यपापयोरधर्मेऽन्तर्भावः। भोगेन साकं शरीरस्य सम्बन्धो नात्मनः। अत एव भोगो नात्मधर्मः। यज्ञश्च धर्म एव। कर्तृत्वत्यागात् कर्माशयोऽपि बुद्धौ नावतिष्ठते। नैष्कर्म्यसिद्धिः स्वाभाविकी सम्पद्यते।

अत एव यज्ञस्य (गी. १८.१२)—

अनिष्टमिष्टं मिश्रं च त्रिविधं कर्मणः फलम्।
भवत्यत्यागिनां प्रेत्य न तु संन्यासिनां क्वचित्॥

इति त्रिविधः फलाभाव उक्तः। त्रिविधस्य फलस्याभावात् 'इदं कर्म शुक्लं कृष्णं मिश्रं वा' इति वक्तुं न शक्यते। अपि तु अशुक्लाकृष्णमेवैतत् कर्म। अत एवोक्तं योगसूत्रे (४.७)—

कर्माऽशुक्लाकृष्णं योगिनस्त्रिविधमितरेषाम् ।

योगिनां संन्यासयोगयुक्तानाम् अशुक्लाकृष्णं कर्म । विकर्मिणां साहङ्कारं साभिलाषं च कर्म कुर्वतां त्रिविधं कर्म फलं च । त्रिविधेषु कर्मसु इष्टफलदत्वात् शुक्लं कर्म **वरं श्रेष्ठं** वेति व्यपदिश्यते । **मिश्रमवरम्** । **कृष्णं कनिष्ठमि**ति । अशुक्लाकृष्णं कर्म च **श्रेष्ठतममिति** व्यपदिश्यते वैदिकैः ।

अस्य वैदिकस्य शब्दस्य संग्रहः—**अतिशायने तमविष्ठनौ** (पा. सू. ५.३.५५) इति सूत्रे, **तदन्ताच्च स्वार्थे छन्दसि दर्शनं श्रेष्ठतमायेति** (३) इति वार्तिके भगवता कात्यायनेन कृतः । प्रयोगोऽयं—**देवो वः सविता प्रार्पयतु श्रेष्ठतमाय कर्मणे** (मा० सं० १.१ तै० सं० १.१.१) इति यजुर्वेदस्य प्रथमे मन्त्रे श्रूयते । तस्य व्याख्याने भाषायां वा **यज्ञो वै श्रेष्ठतमं कर्म** (शत० १.७.१.५) **यज्ञो हि श्रेष्ठतमं कर्म** (तै० ब्रा० ३.२.१) इति श्रूयते ।

अनया चर्यया अन्नमय आत्मा क्रमेण ब्रह्ममयो भवति । आत्मसंस्कारार्थमियं चर्या वेदे उपदिष्टा । सा च कल्पसूत्रकारैर्महर्षिभिः सूत्रिता । तैश्च सूत्रिता अष्टाचत्वारिंशत्-संस्कारा आत्मसंस्कारार्थम् । परधर्मं क्षेत्रधर्मं वा गतस्य तस्य स्वधर्मे ब्रह्मधर्मे वा अवस्थापनार्थम्, न पुनरिहामुत्रार्थभोगार्थम् । अष्टाचत्वारिंशत्संस्कारैः सनातन आत्मा संस्क्रियते इति वैदिको धर्मः सनातन इति व्यपदिश्यते ।

अत एव ब्रह्मसिद्धौ, मण्डनमिश्रैः संस्कारपक्ष एव सिद्धान्तितः । तथा हि—'संस्कारपक्षो वा स्मृतेः, संस्कृतस्य हि विद्योत्पत्तेः । तदुक्तम् ।

विहितत्वाच्चाश्रमकर्मापि । (ब्र० सू० ३.४.३२) इति । ब्रह्मसिद्धिः, ब्रह्मकाण्डः (पृ० ३६) ।

उत्तरमीमांसायामपि—**सर्वापेक्षा च यज्ञादिश्रुतेरश्ववत्** (ब्र० सू० ३.४.२६) इति सर्वापेक्षाधिकरणे **विहितत्वाच्चाश्रमकर्मापि** इति आश्रमकर्माधिकरणे च यज्ञादीनां संस्कारपक्षः प्रतिष्ठापितः ।

अत एव यज्ञानां स्तुतिः स्थाने स्थाने श्रूयते स्मर्यते च । तथा हि—**यज्ञेन यज्ञमयजन्त देवास्तानि धर्माणि प्रथमान्यासन्** । (ऋ० १०.९०.१६; मा० सं० ३१.१६) । **यज्ञं प्रतिष्ठन्तं यजमानोऽनु प्रतिष्ठति** । (छा० ४.१६.४) । **यज्ञे सर्वं प्रतिष्ठितं तस्माद् यज्ञं परमं वदन्ति** । (म० ना० १७.१०) ।

यज्ञार्थात् कर्मणोऽन्यत्र लोकोऽयं कर्मबन्धनः ॥
तदर्थं कर्म कौन्तेय मुक्तसङ्गः समाचर ॥ (गी० ३.९)
यज्ञशिष्टाशिनः सन्तो मुच्यन्ते सर्वकिल्बिषैः ॥ (३.१३)
यज्ञायाचरतः कर्म समग्रं प्रविलीयते । (४.२३)
यज्ञक्षपितकल्मषाः । (४.३०)
यज्ञशिष्टामृतभुजो यान्ति ब्रह्म सनातनम् । (४.३१)

यज्ञदानतपःकर्म न त्याज्यमिति चापरे। (१८.३)

अपरे स्वीयाः।

यज्ञो दानं तपः कर्म न त्याज्यं कार्यमेव तत्॥

यज्ञो दानं तपश्चैव पावनानि मनीषिणाम्॥ (१८.५)

एतान्यपि तु कर्माणि सङ्गं त्यक्त्वा फलानि च।

कर्तव्यानीति मे पार्थ निश्चितं मतमुत्तमम्॥ (१८.६)

इत्थं संन्यासयोगयुक्तानां अकामहतानां आत्मैकत्ववादिनां ब्रह्मवादिनां वा एकत्विनां पक्षे यज्ञो वै श्रेष्ठतमं कर्म सम्पद्यते।

कामहतानां भोगापवर्गवादिनां द्वैतिनां पक्षे तु यज्ञः अवरं कर्म सम्पद्यते। इहामुत्रार्थभोगार्थं द्वैतिभिर्यज्ञा अनुष्ठीयन्ते नात्मनः संस्कारार्थम्। अत एव यज्ञानां फलमिहामुत्रार्थभोगः। भोगवादे आत्मा कर्ता भोक्ता च भवति। अकर्तृत्वमभोक्तृत्वं च स्वधर्मं वा परित्यज्य कर्तृत्वं भोक्तृत्वं चेत्यधर्मान् परधर्मान् क्षेत्रधर्मान् वा अविद्यया स्वीकरोति। अत एव भोगवादोऽधर्मवादः। इहामुत्रार्थभोगार्थं क्रियमाणं कर्म विकर्मेति गीताशास्त्रे व्यपदिष्टम्। क्षेत्रज्ञसंयोगेन चेतनाभिः षोडशविकृतिभिः क्रियमाणं कर्म विकर्मैव भवति।

अविशुद्धि-क्षयातिशययुक्तत्वात् यज्ञियं कर्म शुक्लं श्रेष्ठमिति वा वक्तुं न शक्यते। इहामुत्रार्थभोगप्रदत्वात्, कृष्णं कनिष्ठमिति वा वक्तुं न शक्यते। अत एव परिशेषात् मिश्रमवरमिति वा व्यपदिश्यते। अत एव सर्वैरपवर्गवादिभिर्यज्ञानां निन्दा कृता, कर्मणां परित्यागश्चोक्तः। तथा हि—

दृष्टवदानुश्रविका स ह्यविशुद्धिक्षयातिशययुक्तः। (सां० का० २)

इच्छाद्वेषपूर्विका धर्माधर्मप्रवृत्तिः। (वै० सू० ६.२.१४)

प्रवृत्तिर्वाग्बुद्धिशरीरारम्भः। (न्या० सू० १.१.१७)

प्रवर्तनालक्षणा दोषाः। (न्या० सू० १.१.१८)

दोषाश्च राग-द्वेष-मोहा इति धर्माधर्मप्रवृत्तिस्त्रिदोषदुष्टा वर्तते अत एव अपवर्गार्थं तस्यास्त्याग एवोक्तः। तथा हि—

दुःखजन्मप्रवृत्तिदोषमिथ्याज्ञानानामुत्तरोत्तरापाये तदनन्तरापायादपवर्गः।

(न्या० सू० १.१.२)

प्रशस्तपादैरप्युक्तम्—'अविदुषो रागद्वेषवतः प्रवर्तकाद् धर्मान् प्रकृष्टात् स्वल्पाधर्मसहितात् ब्रह्मेन्द्रप्रजापतिपितृमनुष्यलोकेषु आशयानुरूपैरिष्टशरीरेन्द्रियविषय- सुखादिभिर्योगो भवति। तथा प्रकृष्टादधर्मात् स्वल्पधर्मसहितात् प्रेततिर्यग्योनिस्थानेषु अनिष्टशरीरेन्द्रियविषय-दुःखाभियोगो भवति। एवं प्रवृत्तिलक्षणाद्धर्मादधर्मसहिताद् देवमनुष्यतिर्यङ्नारकेषु पुनः पुनः संसारबन्धो भवति। ज्ञानपूर्वकात् तु कृतात् असङ्कल्पितफलात् विशुद्धकुले जातस्य दुःख-

विगमोपायजिज्ञासोः आचार्यमुपसंगम्य उत्पन्नषट्पदार्थतत्त्वज्ञानस्य अज्ञाननिवृत्तौ विरक्तस्य रागद्वेषाद्यभावात् तज्जयोर्धर्माधर्मयोरनुत्पत्तौ पूर्वसञ्चितयोश्च उपभोगान्निरोधे सन्तोषसुखं शरीरपरिच्छेदं चोत्पाद्य रागादिनिवृत्तिलक्षणः केवलो धर्मः परमार्थदर्शनजं सुखं कृत्वा निवर्तते। तदा निरोधात् निर्बीजस्यात्मनः शरीरादिनिवृत्तिः पुनः शरीराद्यनुत्पत्तौ दग्धेन्धनानलवत् उपशमो मोक्ष इति।' (पृ० ३५५)

एष एव सिद्धान्तः गीताशास्त्रे खण्डनार्थमुपन्यस्तः। तथा हि—

त्याज्यं दोषवदित्येके कर्म प्राहुर्मनीषिणः।

एके मनीषिणः मनश्चैतन्यवादिनो वैशेषिका इत्यर्थः।

एतेषामेव इहामुत्रार्थभोगार्थं क्रियमाणानां यज्ञानां निन्दैव श्रूयते, स्मर्यते च। तथा हि—

प्लवा एते अदृढा यज्ञरूपा
अष्टादशोक्तमवरं येषु कर्म।
एतच्छ्रेयो येऽभिनन्दन्ति मूढा
जरामृत्युं ते पुनरेवापि यन्ति॥ (मुण्ड० १.२.७)

कामात्मानः स्वर्गपरा जन्मकर्मफलप्रदाम्।
क्रियाविशेषबहुलां भोगैश्वर्यगतिं प्रति॥

दूरेण ह्यवरं कर्म बुद्धियोगाद् धनञ्जय।
बुद्धौ शरणमन्विच्छ कृपणाः फलहेतवः॥ (गी० १.४२-४९)

त्रैविद्या मां सोमपाः पूतपापा
यज्ञैरिष्ट्वा स्वर्गतिं प्रार्थयन्ते।
ते पुण्यमासाद्य सुरेन्द्रलोक-
मश्नन्ति दिव्यान् दिवि देवभोगान्॥
ते तं भुक्त्वा स्वर्गलोकं विशालं
क्षीणे पुण्ये मर्त्यलोकं विशन्ति।
एवं त्रयीधर्ममनुप्रपन्ना
गतागतं कामकामा लभन्ते॥ (गी० ९.२०-२१)

एवं 'यज्ञो वै श्रेष्ठतमं कर्म' इति धर्मवादिनामकामहतानां एकत्विनां पक्षः। 'अवरं कर्म इति भोगापवर्गवादिनां कामहतानां द्वैतिनां पक्ष इति सिद्धान्तः।

(१८)

वैदिकावैदिक-दर्शनमीमांसाया उपसंहारः

अवसितः प्रासङ्गिको विचारः। उपसंह्रियते इदानीमियं वैदिकावैदिक-दर्शनमीमांसा। विस्तरेण इयमुपपादिता समग्रे गीताशास्त्रे। तत्र वैदिकः सिद्धान्तः प्रतिष्ठापितः। अवैदिको

दार्शनिकस्तान्त्रिको लौकिको वा पक्षः प्रत्याख्यातः। अथवा ब्रह्मवादो ब्रह्मचर्यं च प्रतिष्ठापितम्। प्रधानवादो भोगापर्गवादः पुरुषार्थवादः कामचर्या च निराकृता। तथा हि—

व्यवसायात्मिका बुद्धिरेकेह कुरुनन्दन। (गी० २.४७) इति वैदिकः पक्षः।

बहुशाखा ह्यनन्ताश्च बुद्धयोऽव्यवसायिनाम्॥

इत्यवैदिको दार्शनिकस्तान्त्रिको लौकिको वा पक्षः। एवमेव सर्वत्र ज्ञेयम्। समग्रं च गीताशास्त्रं प्रथमे श्लोके ध्वनितम्। प्रथमः श्लोकः समस्तस्य सारसङ्ग्रहभूतः। अत एव तमेव श्लोकं सविस्तरं व्याख्याय वैदिकावैदिक-दर्शनमीमांसेयमुपसंह्रियते।

धृतराष्ट्र उवाच

धर्मक्षेत्रे कुरुक्षेत्रे समवेता युयुत्सवः।
मामकाः पाण्डवाश्चैव किमकुर्वत सञ्जय॥ (गी० १.१)

धृतराष्ट्रो नाम पञ्चविंशतितत्त्वात्मकः पदार्थः। तत्र चतुर्विंशतितत्त्वात्मकं क्षेत्रं शरीरं वा, पञ्चविंश आत्मा। तत्रात्मा सर्वान् स्वधर्मान्—अद्वितीयत्वम्, एकत्वं, ब्रह्ममयत्वं वा आनन्दमयत्वं, चिन्मयत्वं, ज्ञानमयत्वं च परित्यज्य अव्यक्तधर्मान् व्यक्तधर्मांश्च प्रकृतिधर्मान् विकृतिधर्मान् क्षेत्रधर्मान् वा स्वधर्मत्वेन अविद्यया अभिमन्यमानः पूर्वरूपं ब्रह्मधर्मान् वा विहाय पररूपं परधर्मान् क्षेत्रधर्मान् प्राकृतत्वं वैकृतत्वं वा प्राप्तः, व्यापिन्या प्रकृत्या विकृतिरूपेण परिणतया धृत्या धृतो बद्धो व्याप्तश्चायं व्यापको विवेकी चात्मा अव्यापी अविवेकी च भूत्वा चतुर्विंशतितत्त्वात्मकस्य शरीरस्य धर्मी सन्नपि धर्मः संवृत्तः। तथा चोक्तं गीताशास्त्रे—

भूतानामस्मि चेतना। (गी० १०.२२)

संघातश्चेतना धृतिः। (गी० १३.६)

अस्यामवस्थायां क्षेत्रसङ्गी आत्मा चतुर्धा अवतिष्ठते—(१) विज्ञानमयकोशे विज्ञानमयः। (२) मनोमयकोशे मनोमयः। (३) प्राणमयकोशे प्राणमयः (४) अन्नमयकोशे चान्नमयः। धृतराष्ट्रस्य अन्धत्वात् दर्शनाभाव इति तस्यात्मा प्राणमयकोशेऽपि नास्ति, अपि तु अन्नमयकोशे वर्तते। एतादृशेन अन्नमयकोशस्थितेन काममयेन कामहतेन वा धृतराष्ट्रेन गीताशास्त्रमुपक्रान्तमिति प्रथमे श्लोके वैदिकस्य दर्शनस्य समस्तस्य गीताशास्त्रस्य वा वाच्यार्थेन अवरोहक्रमेण सारसंग्रहः अशक्यप्रायः, अशास्त्रीयश्चेति समग्रं गीताशास्त्रं ध्वनितं प्रथमे श्लोके।

ध्वनिकाव्यस्योदाहरणं प्रथमः श्लोकः। वाच्यार्थस्य निरोधनमेवात्र सम्पद्यते। श्लोकेऽस्मिन् वाच्यार्थो न्यग्भावितः, उपसर्जनीकृतः, अप्रधानीकृत इति यावत्। समग्रं च गीताशास्त्रं वैदिकं दर्शनं वा अस्मिन् प्रथमे श्लोके ध्वनितमिति श्लोकोऽयं विस्तरेण व्याख्यायते वैदिका-ऽवैदिकदर्शनमीमांसा-प्रबोधाय।

द्वया ह प्राजापत्या देवाश्चासुराश्च। (मा० बृ० १.१.१)

द्वौ भूतसर्गौ लोकेऽस्मिन् दैव आसुर एव च। (गी० १६.६)

सृज्यते इति सर्गः। भूतानां सर्गौ भूतसर्गौ। द्वौ द्विसंख्याकौ। भूतानि पञ्चविंशतितत्त्वात्मकानि। तत्रात्मा अजः अव्ययश्चेते उत्पत्तिविनाशरहितः। अवशिष्टानि चतुर्विंशतितत्त्वानि अनित्यानि। अत एव चतुर्विंशतितत्त्वात्मकं क्षेत्रमुत्पद्यते विनश्यति च। तदेवेह 'भूत'शब्देन गृह्यते। तस्य क्षेत्रस्य शरीरस्य वा उत्पद्यमानस्य प्रकारद्वयम्—दैवं आसुरं च। संस्कृतं प्राकृतं च। गुणमयं दोषमयं च। आनन्दमयं दुःखमयं च। अक्लिष्टं क्लिष्टं च। तदेवोपन्यस्तं प्रथमे श्लोके धर्मक्षेत्रं कुरुक्षेत्रं च।

धर्मक्षेत्रम्

धर्मक्षेत्रं नाम धर्मस्य क्षेत्रम्। तथा चोक्तं गीतासु **इदं शरीरं कौन्तेय क्षेत्रमित्यभिधीयते।** (१३.१) क्षेत्रं नाम शरीरम्। 'शीर्यत इति शरीरम्'। अत एव तत् सादि सान्तं च। तच्च चतुर्विंशतितत्त्वात्मकम्। तथा चोक्तं भगवद्गीतासु (१३.५)

महाभूतान्यहङ्कारो बुद्धिरव्यक्तमेव च।
इन्द्रियाणि दशैकं च पञ्च चेन्द्रियगोचराः।

अवशिष्टः पञ्चविंशः पदार्थः पुरुषः क्षेत्रज्ञः, आत्मा वा। स एवात्र 'धर्म' शब्देन निर्दिष्टः। अत एवाऽत्र धर्मशब्देन 'आत्मा' गृह्यते प्रकरणात्।

ननु आत्मनः आत्मशब्देनात्र निर्देशः कर्तुं शक्यते—आत्मक्षेत्रे इति ? बाढमेवम्। तथापि तथानिर्देशे कृते आत्मनः क्षेत्रेण ब्रह्मणा च साकं सम्बन्धो ज्ञातुं न शक्यते। स च अवश्यं ज्ञापनीय इति वैदिकस्य दर्शनस्य प्रबोधनार्थं धर्मशब्देन आत्मनो निर्देशः। धर्मशब्देन आत्मनो निर्देशात् अनुक्तोऽपि धर्मी आक्षिप्यते इति अवरोहक्रमेण पदार्थत्रयं वैदिके दर्शने सम्पद्यते—धर्मी, धर्मः क्षेत्रं च। ब्रह्म, आत्मा शरीरं च। एतदेव पदार्थत्रयं गीताशास्त्रे आरोहक्रमेणोक्तम्। तथा हि (गी० १३.१८)—

इति क्षेत्रं तथा ज्ञानं ज्ञेयं चोक्तं समासतः।
मद्भक्त एतद्विज्ञाय मद्भावायोपपद्यते॥

अत्र क्षेत्रशब्देन शरीरम्, ज्ञानशब्देन धर्मवाचकेन धर्मी आत्मा ज्ञेयशब्देन च ब्रह्म प्रतिपादितम्। क्षेत्राध्याये क्षेत्रस्य प्राधान्यात् आरोहक्रमः पदार्थानाम्।

धर्मशब्देन आत्मनो निर्देशात् धर्मिणा ब्रह्मणा क्षेत्रेण च साकमात्मनः स्वधर्मेण सम्बन्धः सिद्धो भवति। आत्मनः स्वधर्माः परधर्माश्च सांख्यकारिकायामुक्ताः। तथा हि—

हेतुमदनित्यमव्यापि सक्रियमनेकमाश्रितं लिङ्गम्।
सावयवं परतन्त्रं व्यक्तं तद्विपरीतमव्यक्तम्॥

त्रिगुणमविवेकि विषयः सामान्यमचेतनं प्रसवधर्मि।
व्यक्तं तथा प्रधानं तद्विपरीतस्तथा च पुमान्॥ (सां. का. १०-११)

'तद्विपरीतः पुमान्' इत्यनेन विद्यावस्थायामात्मनः क्षेत्रयोगे प्रकृतिविकृतियोगे वा स्वधर्मा

उक्ताः। 'तथा च पुमान्' इत्यनेन आत्मनः अविद्यावस्थायां क्षेत्रसङ्गे प्रकृतिविकृतिसङ्गे वा परधर्मा उक्ताः। स्वधर्म-परधर्मविभागोऽयं प्रदर्शितो गीताशास्त्रे (३.३५)। तथा हि—

श्रेयान् स्वधर्मो विगुणः परधर्मात् स्वनुष्ठितात्।
स्वधर्मे निधनं श्रेयः परधर्मो भयावहः ॥

'तद्विपरीतः पुमान्' इत्यनेनोक्ता आत्मनः स्वधर्मा यथा—१. अहेतुमत्त्वं कारणशून्यत्वं वा, २. नित्यत्वम्, ३. व्यापकत्वम्, ४. निष्क्रियत्वम्, ५. एकत्वम्, ६. अनाश्रितत्वम्, ७. अलिङ्गत्वम्, ८. निरवयवत्वम्, ९. स्वतन्त्रत्वम्, १०. अत्रिगुणत्वं निस्त्रैगुण्यं वा, ११. विवेकित्वम्, १२. अविषयत्वम्, १३. असामान्यत्वम्, १४. चेतनत्वम्, १५. अप्रसवधर्मित्वम्, १६. साक्षित्वम्, १७. केवलत्वम्, १८. मध्यस्थत्वम्, १९. द्रष्टृत्वम्, २०. अकर्तृत्वं चेति विंशतिरात्मधर्माः।

एते धर्मा द्विविधाः—भावरूपा अभावरूपाश्च। धर्मस्य भावरूपत्वाद् अभावरूपा धर्माः क्षेत्रवैधर्म्यप्रतिपादनार्थाः। आत्मा एकः अद्वितीयश्च इति साधर्म्याभावः। तत्राऽऽत्मनो भावरूपा धर्मा यथा—१. नित्यत्वम्, २. चेतनत्वम्, ३. व्यापकत्वम्, ४. एकत्वम्, ५. विवेकित्वं च।

तत्र नित्यत्वेन सत्यत्वं ज्ञानमयत्वं वा, चेतनत्वेन चिन्मयत्वं, व्यापकत्वेन अनन्तत्वम् आनन्दमयत्वं, वा एकत्वेन ब्रह्ममयत्वं अद्वितीयत्वं प्रधानत्वं वा। अत्र अद्वितीयो नाम न द्वितीयः। विवेकित्वेन अद्वितीयत्वम्-न विद्यते द्वितीयं यत्र तदद्वितीयं ब्रह्म प्रतिपाद्यते।

तत्राऽऽत्मनः क्षेत्रेण साकं विवेकित्वे सति व्यापित्वेन सम्बन्धः। विवेकित्वेन असङ्गत्वं बोद्ध्यते। क्षेत्रेण साकमात्मनः व्याप्य-व्यापकभावसम्बन्धमन्तरा सम्बन्धान्तरं प्रस्थापयितुं न शक्यते। अत एव यत्र यत्र क्षेत्रं तत्र तत्र आत्मा इति अन्वयव्याप्तिः। आत्मव्यतिरेकेण क्षेत्रस्य जगतो वा अभावः। अत एवोक्तं भगवत्-पूज्यपादैः शारीरकमीमांसाभाष्ये—

एवमस्य भोग्यभोक्त्रादिप्रपञ्चजातस्य ब्रह्मव्यतिरेकेण अभाव इति द्रष्टव्यम्।
(शां० भा० २.१.१४)

"तथा च सशरीरत्वस्य मिथ्याज्ञाननिमित्तत्वात्। नह्यात्मनः शरीरात्माभिमानलक्षणं मिथ्याज्ञानं मुक्त्वा अन्यतः सशरीरत्वं शक्यं कल्पयितुम्। नित्यमशरीरत्वमकर्मनिमित्तत्वादित्यवोचाम। तत्कृतधर्माधर्म-निमित्तं सशरीरत्वमिति चेन्न। शरीरसम्बन्धस्यासिद्धत्वात् धर्माधर्मयोरात्म-कृतत्वासिद्धेः। शरीरसंबन्धस्य धर्माधर्मयोस्तत्कृतत्वस्य चेतरेतराश्रयत्वप्रसङ्गाद् अन्धपरम्परैषाऽनादित्वकल्पना। क्रियासमवायाभावाच्च आत्मनः कर्तृत्वानुपपत्तेः। सन्निधानमात्रेण राजप्रभृतीनां दृष्टं कर्तृत्वमिति चेन्न। धनदानाद्युपार्जित-भृत्यसम्बन्धत्वात् तेषां कर्तृत्वोपपत्तेः, न त्वात्मनो धनदानादिवच्छरीरादिभिः स्वस्वामिसम्बन्धनिमित्तं किञ्चिच्छक्यं कल्पयितुम्।

मिथ्याभिमानस्तु प्रत्यक्षः सम्बन्धहेतुः। एतेन यजमानत्वमात्मनो व्याख्यातम्।" (शां० भा० १.१.४)

धर्मधर्मिणोरनन्यः सम्बन्ध इति धर्मिणा ब्रह्मणा साकं धर्मस्य आत्मनः अनन्यः सम्बन्धः। क्षेत्रेण साकं व्याप्यव्यापकभावः सम्बन्धः। तेन ब्रह्मणा साकमनन्यत्वे सति क्षेत्रेण साकं विवेकित्वे असङ्गत्वे अन्यत्वे वा सति व्यापित्वेन अवस्थानमात्मधर्मः। अत एव ब्रह्मणा साकमनन्यत्वे सति क्षेत्रेण साकं विवेकित्वेन व्यापित्वेन अवस्थितस्य आत्मनःपरब्रह्मणो धर्मस्य वा क्षेत्रं धर्मक्षेत्रम्।

कुरुक्षेत्रम्

कुरुक्षेत्रं नाम कुरोः कुरूणां वा क्षेत्रम्। 'क्षेत्र'शब्देन चतुर्विंशतितत्त्वात्मकं शरीरमुच्यते। अवशिष्टः पदार्थ आत्मा। स एवात्र 'कुरु'शब्देन निर्दिष्टः। आत्मशब्देन निर्देशे तस्य ब्रह्मणा क्षेत्रेण च साकं सम्बन्धो ज्ञातुं न शक्यते। तस्य ज्ञापनार्थम् आत्मनःकुरुशब्देन निर्देशः। कुत्सितं रौतीति कुरुः। दुःखत्रयाभिघातात् क्षेत्रस्थ आत्मा कुत्सितं रौतीति कुरुशब्देन व्यपदिष्टः। दुःखं च क्षेत्रधर्मो नात्मधर्मः। तथा चोक्तं गीताशास्त्रे (१३.६)—

इच्छा द्वेषः सुखं दुःखं सङ्घातश्चेतना धृतिः।
एतत् क्षेत्रं समासेन सविकारमुदाहृतम्॥

अत एव क्षेत्रेऽस्मिन्नात्मा क्षेत्रधर्मे वा वर्तते, स्वधर्मे नास्ति।

द्रष्टा आत्मा ब्रह्मदर्शनं परित्यज्य दृश्यं विषयं क्षेत्रं वा पश्यति, विषयी च भवति। विषय-विषयिणोः युष्मदस्मत्प्रत्ययगोचरयोः क्षेत्र-क्षेत्रज्ञयोः अविद्यया अविवेकेन वा मिथ्याभिमाननिबन्धनःतादात्म्यसम्बन्धो भवति। विषयाः चतुर्विंशतितत्त्वानि क्षेत्रं वा विषयिणः आत्मनो धर्मो भवति। इत्थं धर्म-धर्मिसम्बन्धे सम्पन्ने सर्वान् विषयधर्मान् क्षेत्रधर्मान् प्रकृति-विकृतिधर्मान् व्यक्ताव्यक्तधर्मान् वा अत्यन्तविरुद्धान् अविद्यया स्वधर्मत्वेनाभिमन्यते आत्मा इति दुःखत्रयाभिहतो भवति, कुत्सितं च रौति।

अस्यामवस्थायामात्मा प्रकृतिसरूपो विकृतिसरूपश्च सम्पद्यते। पूर्वरूपं ब्रह्मधर्मान् ब्रह्मचर्यं वा परित्यजति। पररूपं परधर्मान् क्षेत्रधर्मान् कामचारं वा प्राप्नोति। तांश्च धर्मान् अविद्यया स्वधर्मत्वेन अभिमन्यते। तथा च स्मृतिः—

अधर्मं धर्ममिति या मन्यते तमसावृता।
सर्वार्थान् विपरीतांश्च बुद्धिः सा पार्थ तामसी॥ **(गी० १८.३२)**

परधर्माश्च 'तथा च पुमान्' (सां० का० १०-११) इत्यनेन सांख्यकारिकायामुक्ताः। ते च यथा—

१. हेतुमत्त्वम्, २. अनित्यत्वम्, ३. अव्यापित्वम्, ४. अनेकत्वं नानात्वं वा, ६. आश्रितत्वम्, ७. लिङ्गत्वम्, ८. सावयवत्वम्, ९. परतन्त्रत्वं चेति नव व्यक्तधर्माः। १. त्रिगुणत्वम्, २.

अविवेकित्वम्, ३. विषयत्वम्, ४. सामान्यत्वम्, ५. अचेतनत्वम्, ६. प्रसवधर्मित्वमिति षट् व्यक्ताव्यक्तयोः साधारणधर्माः।

धर्मस्य भावरूपत्वात् अभावरूपा धर्मा क्षेत्रस्य आत्मनो वैधर्म्यं प्रतिपादयन्ति। भावरूपा धर्मा यथा—१. हेतुमत्त्वम्, २. क्रियावत्त्वम्, ३. आश्रितत्वम्, ४. लिङ्गत्वम्, ५. सावयवत्वम्, ६. परतन्त्रत्वम्, ७. त्रिगुणत्वम्, ८. विषयत्वम्, ९. सामान्यत्वम्, १०. प्रसवधर्मित्वं चेति।

अत एवात्र क्षेत्रेण साकमात्मनः अविवेकित्वेन अनन्यत्वेन वा अव्यापित्वेन च सम्बन्धः। आत्मनः अविवेकित्वात् अव्यापित्वाच्च व्यापिन्या प्रकृत्या व्याप्यतेऽयमात्मा। प्रकृत्या समावृतत्वात्, ब्रह्मणा साकमस्य सम्बन्धो विच्छिद्यते, अन्यत्वं च सम्पद्यते, ब्रह्मणोऽदर्शनं च भवति। एतेन ब्रह्मणा साकमन्यत्वे सति क्षेत्रेण साकं अविवेकित्वेन अनन्यत्वेन वा अव्यापित्वेन च अवस्थितस्य आत्मनः दुःखत्रयाभिहतस्य, अत एव कुरोः क्षेत्रं कुरुक्षेत्रम्।

APPENDIX I

ENGLISH ARTICLES

(1) AYURVEDIC USES OF IRON*

(Iron is a valuable remedy in all systems of medicine. It is curative in a wide range of diseases. But its forms are different in different systems; the principle of application is also different in various systems. The true action of iron in human system cannot be diffeerent, and intensive research can determine its true action. Its Ayurvedic use and principles are given here by the learned scholar Mr. J.S. Pade. The usefulness of this kind of research can scarcely be overrated.)

There are three different schools of treatment of diseases in Ayurveda, namely, 1. The Divine, 2. The Human and 3. the Demoniac. Treatment of diseases by mercury and other metals is called the Divine; by herbs and vegetable drugs is called the Human; and by surgical instruments is called the Demoniac treatment.

Mercury and metals have an immediate and unfailing effect on all sorts of diseases, while the herbs and vegetable drugs have comparatively a slow effect. Different drugs are prescribed for different diseases, while mercury or any one of the metals is sufficient to cure very speedily all sorts of diseases. Thus the divine treatment by its speedy and unfailing results has rendered the human and the demoniac treatments almost useless and superfluous. Even boils and carbuncles are cured by the divine treatment more speedily and effectively than they are by surgical operations. Thus the divine treatment is superior to the other two treatments which were neglected in course of time. Charaka and Sushruta, the authoritative works of the human and demoniac schools respectively are useful only for the theoretical side of Ayurveda, while the practical purpose is served by the Rasashastra. Metals are

---

* Baroda Homoeopathic Bulletin, II 3, April, 1947.

effective only if the knowledge of *dosha* or the element at fault is accurate.

In Rasashastra, the use of iron is very common and all sorts of diseases are cured by it. Hence the properties of Iron, the diseases on which it is specially used, the wholesome and prohibited diets while the treatment of iron is taken are briefly stated below.

Iron is sweet, astringent, and bitter in taste. It is cold, laxative, heavy, and coarse. It prevents senile decay, improves eyesight, reduces fat, and increases a little of *Vat* in the system. It pacifies an excess of *Kaf, Pitt* and *Vat* and cures toxin, colic, swelling of the body, piles, spleen, anaemia, obesity, and worms. It increases strength and longevity, cures diseases and is aphrosidiac. It is one of the best remedies for senility.

Iron can cure all diseases if used with suitable accompaniments. Still however it is found more effective on the following diseases: 1. Colic 2. Chronic fever, 3. Rheumatism, Paralysis and other diseases due to the excess of *Vat*. 4, Asthama, 5. Cold, 6. Spermetorrhoea. 7. Diseases due to excess of three doshas. 8. Fever due to the excess of *Vat-Pitt,* and *Pitt-Kaf.* 9. Shivering due to the excess of *Vat*. 10. Diseases affecting bone joints. 11. Senile decay. 12. Leprosy. 13. Anaemia. 14. 20 different kinds of Gonorrhoea. 15. Gleet and Stricture. 16. All sorts of diseases. 17. For increasing the power of digestion, nutrition and physical beauty.

The following articles of vegetarian and non-vegetarian food are wholesome for people under iron treatment. 1. Lavaka (a migratory bird, a sort of a Quail). 2. Tittiri. 3. Godha. 4. Peacock. 5. Hare. 6. Vataka. (a bird) 7. Kalavinka (sparrow). 8. Varti (a bird). 9. Haritala (green partridge). 10. Hawk. 11. Big Lava. 12. All sorts of deer. 13. Fresh and wholesome fish such as Madgura, Rohita, and Shakula. 14. Vegetables like Papita, Patola, and Dindisi. 15. Eatable sprouts arising inside a palm fruit. 16. Shatavari. 17. Soft blossoms of a Vetra plant. 18. The soft portion inside from the uppermost part of a palm tree. 19. Tanduliyaka. 20. Vastuka. 21. Leaves of Dhanya plant. 22. Siramaluka. 23. Punarnava. 24. Cocoanut. 25. Date fruit. 26. Pomegranates. 27. Lavali fruit. 28. Shringataka. 29. Ripe and sweet mango. 30. Grapes. 31. Jatiphala. 32. Lavanga. 33. Betel- nut. and 34. Betel-leaves.

One who takes Iron should avoid the following : 1. Lakucha. 2. Kola, 3. Karkandhu, 4. Badara. 5. Lemon. 6. Bijapur. 7. Karamarda. 8. Tintrini. 9. Meat of animals other than those prescribed before. 10. Krakara. 11. Pimaraka. 12. Goose. 13. Swan. 14. Water-crow. 15. Madgu. 16. Crow. 17. Crane. 18. Masha gram. 19. Tubers of all kinds (such as potato, etc.). 20. Karira shoot of a bamboo and a thorny plant of that name. 21. Chanka gram. 22. Kadamba fruit. 23. Kuśmanda (a kind of pumpkin ground). 24. Karkoti. 25. Kevuka. 26. Banana fruit. 27. Kalashaka. 28. Kasheru. 29. Karkati. 30. All sorts of pulses. 31. Tila oil. 32. Rasona. 33. Rajika. 34. Wine. 35. Sour things. 36. Bad fish. 37. Jeera. 38. Vartaka. 39. Masa graṁ. 40. Karavella. 41. Physical exercise. 42. All sorts of fermented things. 43. Asava. 44. Sitting for a long time. 45. Physical exertion. 46. Excess of talking. 47. Excess of bathing, drinking, eating and exposure to coldness and wind. 48. Eating at unusual times. 49. Eating articles of food- stuff which is taken with the same meal produce injurious effects (such as milk with fish, meat or sours) 50. Sleeping in day time. 51. Keep late at night. 52. All things having the property of increasing *Vat* and *Pitt*. 53. Things which are pungent, sour, bitter, and astringent. 54. Sexual indulgence. 55. Anger. 56. Physical exertion. 57. and all things calculated to antidote mercury and all metals.

Thus it will seem that all sorts of diseases can be cured by one metal, Iron. But it requires the mastery over the pulse and a thorough knowledge of the theory of Tridosha. Metals are not very effective these days because the theory of Tridosha and the study of pulse are neglected by the followers of Ayurveda, and they are imitating doctors by giving medicines against the diseases and not against the doshas or elements at fault. According to Ayurveda the medicine should be used against the *dosha* and not against the disease. If the followers of Ayurveda only care to revive their study of pulse and if they direct their treatment against the dosha, Ayurveda again will shine with its full lustre.

Thanks to Dr. Bhattacharya belonging to the family of renowned Pandits of Bengal, a deep scholar of both Ayurveda and homoeopathy and who is keeping the torch of his ancestral erudition burning with great pride, who has upheld the theory of Tridosha and who, by his accurate knowledge of pulse and his effective homoeopathic medicines used, not against the disease like doctors but against the dosha, is rendering all other treatments fruitless. Dr. Bhattacharya is teaching a lesson to the followers of Ayurvada not to imitate false modern theories, but to study and assimilate the theory of Tridosha very deeply. With great admiration towards the respected scholar the present article is written to show his readers how the ancient sages with their accurate knowledge of *Vat*, *Pitt*, and *Kaf* could cure all sorts of diseases very speedily and effectively with the help of one metal, Iron.

(2) AYURVEDIC USES OF SILVER*

(Our worthy colleague Mr. J.S. Pade, M.A. has given another article, this time on silver. Diseases that are cured by silver in Ayurveda can also be cured by homoeopathic silver like Argentum Metallicum and Argentum Nitricum. That goes without saying, and it is worth attempting.)

Silver is of three different kinds, viz., 1. Natural. 2. Mineral and 3. Artificial. Natural silver is found in Kailasa and cures diseases by mere touch. Mineral silver is found in the peaks of the Himalayas and in other places. It cures diseases and prevents senility. Tin, copper, or lead

* Baroda Homoeopathic Bulletin, II 4, July, 1947.

transformed into silver by mercury is called artificial silver. It cures all sorts of diseases if administered properly.

The best silver is heavy, white, smooth and glassy. Silver which becomes red, yellow or black when heated and that which is coarse, brittle, light and rough is not used for medical purposes.

Silver is astringent and sour in taste and turns sweet when digested. It is cool, laxative and soothing. It increases appetite, enhances beauty, pacifics Vat and Pitt, increases the digestive heat in the stomach, strengthens the body and retains youth and memory.

Silver is found effective on the following diseases. 1. Phthisis. 2. Anaemia. 3. *Udara*. 4. Piles, 5. Asthama. 6. Cough. 7. Loss of sight. 8. Inflammation. 9. Gonorrhea. 10. Gulma. 11. Consumption. 12. Thinness. 13. Enlargement. 14. Dropsy. 15. Senile decay. 16. Excess of Vat and Pitt. 17. Diseases due to the excess of Pitt.

Silver, like other metals, is *yogavāhī* and hence it is made effective on all diseases by administering it with accompaniments according to the Doshas or elements at fault. Without taking into consideration the *yogavāhic* property of metals let us examine the properties of silver given above and see on which Doshas it will have its effect.

Silver by its astringent taste, pacifies Pitt and Kaf but increases Vat and by its sour taste pacifies Vat but increases Pitt and Kaf. Due to the combination of astringent and sour taste, silver restores the equillibrium of the three Doshas into their normal position and thereby cures all diseases, strengthens the body and retains youth. Silver being harmless, no diet is prescribed or prohibited for persons under its treatment. Silver being cool, soothing and sweet when digested goes against Kaf and Vat both being cold, but completely pacifies Pitt and Vat-Pitt where Vat being *Yogavāhī* becomes hot when associated with Pitt. This is the reason why ancient writers have prescribed it on diseases due to the excess of Pitt and Vat-Pitt.

From the above discussion it will be clear that Silver is an enemy of Pitt and Vat-Pitt, and while using it against the diseases given above every care must be taken to see that the element of Kaf or Vat-Kaf is not at fault.

(3) AYURVEDIC USES OF GOLD*

(Our worthy colleague Mr. J.S. Pade contributes this third article on the Ayurvedic uses of metals for the inquisitive readers of this Bulletin. According to the author's learned observations, Ayurvedic gold is used in 24 different diseases listed by him in their crude Ayurvedic form. There is no reason why potentiazed gold of homoeopathy cannot be used successfully in all these 24 diseases, and in fact, homoeopathic gold in potencies is being used in these very diseases with great success. Gold is a curative medicine for asthama. Ayurveda uses crude gold for curing asthama. Homoeopathy uses potentized gold for curing the self-same disease asthama. I would ask homoeopaths all over the world to tell me whether gold cures asthama because it produces asthama in crude form, or because it is a cure for asthama both in its crude as well as in its potentized form. Gold surely destroys Kaf or the element of water, and by creating heat saves life. Mr. Pade deserves our thanks for salvaging valuable facts from obscure Ayurvedic lore containing eternal wisdom of the ancient Rishis.)

The principal metals according to Indian chemistry or Rasashastra are seven, namely gold, silver, copper, iron, zinc, tin and lead. They are called Dhatus as they prevent senility, cure diseases and thus sustain the system. (Dhatu from Dha to sustain). Among the seven metals gold is the most important.

Gold and its uses were known from the Vedic times. Its properties that it cures all diseases, increases strength and longevity and wards off the evil influences of supernatural beings are described by the Vedic seers. References to gold are numerous in Vedic literature.

---

* Baroda Homoeopathic Bulletin, III 1, Octo., 1947.

The properties of gold are mentioned in Charaka and Sushruta, the earliest works on Ayurveda. But there we do not meet with the frequent use of mercury and metals on different diseases. The reason is obvious. The object of the two works is to deal thoroughly with the theoretical and the surgical portions of the Ayurveda respectively. Both the authors are not particular about medicines. According to them if the principles of Ayurveda are clearly understood any substance can be utilized as medicine. Secondly, herbs are available everywhere while metals require purification etc. which is not possible for all. Hence they have shown the simplest possible medicines.

Chemistry or Rasashastra is a separate branch of Ayurveda. It has its origin in Shaivism which as we know belongs to the pre-Vedic period. The School of Shaivism that deals with chemistry and alchemy is called the Raseshvara School. The Buddhists and the Jains have dealt with this subject in their Tantras and thus we find chemistry and alchemy in both the Brahmanic and Buddhistic Tantras.

Disease was the first obstacle in the path of an ascetic who aspired for liberation in this life. It became his duty therefore to make himself a glorified body, and in as much as mercury and metals possessed the properties of removing diseases and imparting youth and longevity, the attention of the ascetics was attracted towards them.

Although chemistry and alchemy can be traced to the pre-Vedic period, still however, the earliest works written on the subject are now lost and the authors are known by names only. The earliest work now available on the subject belongs to the 11th century A.D. The progress and speedy spread of chemistry gave a deadly blow to surgery which never revived afterwards with the result that we find only a few very old works on surgery and the subject neglected altogether.

The treatment of herbs given in Charaka was successfully replaced by mercury and metals and from the 12th century we find a new school of writers on Ayurveda which combined the theoretical portion of Charaka with the treatment of metals in Chemistry. The combination has become so effective that it is followed throughout India by all Ayurvedic scholars till today. The following information on gold is available in ancient works on the subject.

Gold is of two knds, namely, that which is transformed from base metals through the agency of mercury specially prepared and that which is obtained from mines. The first variety is the purest, best and prevents and cures senility while the second variety cures all diseases only when duly purified and incinerated and taken with suitable accompaniments.

According to the theory of Ayurveda all substances are composed of five elements namely the earth, water, fire, air and ether. One of these elements predominates in every substance which is classified under the category of that element. The classification becomes useful in administering the substance on the element at fault in the body. Among the five elements, only three air, fire and water are important so far as the treatment of diseases is concerned. Among the three elements, again fire or Agni or Sun and water or Moon play an important part; air or Vat being Yogavahi becomes hot or cold according as it is combined with fire-Pitt or water-Kaf. Hence the ultimate principle of Ayurveda is that the whole world is composed of two elements only, namely fire or Agni-Sun and water or Soma-Moon; and they conclude with the Vedic words, "*Agniṣomātmakaṁ jagat*". Gold according to Ayurveda is a fiery substance, the element of fire being predominant in it. The Nyaya philosophers also have established the luminosity of gold by spending much argument to prove it and they have classified it under light or fire. Some take it as an earthy substance. Apart from the logical discussions of different schools of philosophy we can accept for our Ayurvedic purpose that the element of fire is predominant in gold. Fiery substances generally are luminous, they increase heat, the power of digestion and beauty. Gold is not an exception to this general principle. Gold is effective on diseases when the element of Kaf, Vat or Vat-Kaf is at fault. It should not be administered on diseases where the element of Pitt or Vat-Pitt is at fault. On diseases where the element of Pitt-Kaf is at fault, gold is given along with a watery substance. According to Ayurveda, there are 80 Vat and 20 Kaf derangements. Gold can safely be given on them.

The properties of gold are as follows: gold is bitter and astringent in taste and turns sweet when digested. It creates a soothing effect in the system. It is pure and nutritive, strengthens the body, cures poison, insanity and senility, sharpens intelligence and retentive faculties, increases appetite, power of digestion, beauty, vitality, longevity, sexual power and the flow of menses in women, is beneficial to eye-sight and heart stabilises the purity of speech; purifies the evil influence exerted by ghosts on human beings.

Gold is found very effective on the following diseases : 1. Fever, 2. Chronic diarrhea, 3. Dysentery, 4. Piles, 5. Loss of appetite, 6. Jaundice, 7. Phthisis, 8. Asthama, 9. Nausea, 10. Insanity, 11. Hysteria, 12. Acute gout, 13. Kidney diseases, 14. Inflammation, 15. Scrofula, 16. Syphilis, 17. Diseases of eyes, 18. Amenorrhoea, 19. Habitual abortion, 20. Sterility, 21. Poison, 22. Impotence, 23. Senility, 24. Skin diseases.

This is the third article on metals which will be useful to the readers of the Bulletin. During the last two centuries Ayurveda was neglected by the literary men of this country with the result that the surgery has again acquired its supreme position in India. The followers of Ayurveda will be glad to see that the principles of Ayurveda are again upheld by Dr. B. Bhattacharyya, who combines in him eminence both in scholarship and homoeopathy. He is the pioneer of a third school where the principles of Ayurveda are combined with the potentized medicines of homoeopathy. His efforts will be fruitful if the attention of the allopaths and homoeopaths is drawn to the principles of Tridosha and we may expect history to repeat and the future generation to see surgery losing importance.

(4) AYURVEDIC USES OF COPPER*

(Copper, the metal of Mars releases high curative forces when potentized, or its powers are given a momentum by any other process. Highly destructive diseases are the field of copper and chronic diseases like-leprosy, pthisis, rheumatism, dropsy, and the like come within the benefic influence of copper. Copper is mixed in temperament and is akin to the elements of fire and water. Joined with Kaf, Pitt becomes chronic and in this condition copper becomes invaluable. The learned author Mr. Pade makes this new but very useful contribution to our study of metals.)

Copper is of two kinds, namely, that which is found in Nepal and that which is found elsewhere. The second variety is known as Mlecchha copper. Nepal copper is very soft, smooth, malleable, red and heavy. It does not lose its properties by the application of heat. Mlecchha copper is red with white or black tints, hard, assumes black appearance when washed off and causes vomiting.

Copper which is red like Japa flower, soothing, soft, malleable and free from iron or lead is used for medical purposes. Copper which is pale, blackish, full of cracks, light, coarse, and consists of layers is not used for medical purposes.

The property of copper is as follows:- Copper is astringent, sweet and bitter and turns sour and pungent when digested in the stomach. It is purgative, cool, light,

---

* Baroda Homoeopathic Bulletin, III 2, Jan., 1948.

heals boils and carbuncles, etc, cures all sorts of *udars* and obesity and increases semen, nutrition, beauty and eye-sight.

The properties and uses of copper are known from the earliest time. It is recommended in Charaka, the earliest work on Ayurveda on all sorts of eye-diseases, cough, asthama, hiccough and for vomiting in poisoning.

The writers on Rasashastra have recommended it on the following diseases:- 1. Fever, 2. Anaemia, 3 Anasarca, Piles, 5. Leprosy, 6. Cough, 7. Asthama, 8. Pthisis, 9. Ozoena, 10. Dyspepsia, 11. Dropsy, 12. Worms, 13. Colic, 14. Obesity. 15. Poison, 16. Eye- disease, 17. Cholera. 18. Diarrhoea, 19. Gonorrhoea, 20. Hysteria, 21. Heart-diseases, 22. Epilepsy, 23. Gout, 24. and Rheumatism. Externally copper is used for local application in piles, leprosy, skin-diseases and ozoena. Sour and pungent things should be avoided while taking copper.

So far we have seen the properties of copper and the different diseases on which it is recommended. Ayurveda is based on the theory of Tridosha; and unless the elements predominant in copper and the effect of copper on the elements at fault in the body are known, copper cannot be administered successfully on the diseases mentioned above.

The elements predominant in a substance are determined from its properties and tastes and *vice versa*. Sweet substances are dominated by the element of water; sour by earth and fire, saline by fire and water, pungent by air and fire; bitter by air and ether and astringent by air and earth.

Astringent, sweet and bitter tastes of copper show the predominance of the elements of air and water in it in the proportion of 2:1. Copper becomes sour and pungent when digested in stomach. So after digestion the elements of fire and air in the proportion of 2:1 predominate in it.

Thus in the initial stage and after assimilation the element of air is predominant in copper. It therefore, cannot be used on diseases where the element of air is at fault. Similarly, the element of fire predominates after vipaka and the element of water in the initial stage in the proportion of 2:1 showing the prominence of the element of fire in copper. Thus it can be successfully used on diseases where the element of Kaf is at fault and cannot be used when the element of Pitt is at fault.

The later writers on Ayurveda have vaguely mentioned that copper pacifies Kaf and Pitt both without giving reasons. This may be due to the presence of the element of water in it. But they have not mentioned the stage of Pitt in which copper can be successfully given. According to Ayurveda, there are four stages of every element in the body, namely 1. decrease, 2. normality, 3. increase and 4. excitement. The element remains in its own place in an increasing stage, but leaves its own place and enters the places of other elements when excited and creates diseases. Copper is fiery after vipaka or digestion and hence cannot be used on Pitt when it is in an excited condition. But due to the presence of the element of water in copper in the initial stage if it can be used on Pitt then it can be used only when Pitt is in the increasing stage while Kaf in the excited condition. With these principles in view copper should be administered on diseases mentioned above.

(5) AYURVEDIC USES OF TIN*

There are two kinds of tin, namely Khuraka and Misraka. Khuraka is white, soft, soothing, heavy and capable of being melted quickly. Misraka is blackish, white in colour and is not used for medical purposes.

Tin is bitter and saline. The bitter taste aggravates Vat

* Baroda Homoeopathic Bulletin, III 3, April, 1948.

and mitigates Pitt and Kaf as it is dominated by the elements of air and ether. The salt taste aggravates Pitt and Kaf and mitigates Vat as it is dominated by the elements of earth and fire. The combination of the two tastes in Tin makes it very effective on all the three doshas or the elements at fault.

The writers on Ayurveda say that Tin slightly increases Pitt. This may be due to the combination of the elements of air and fire in it. Vayu or the element of air is cold according to Ayurveda, as it is aggravated by cold substances and mitigated by hot ones. The distinction between the coldness of Vayu and that of Kaf is that Vayu is cold in action only, while Kaf is cold in action and touch. In cases where Pitt-Kaf is aggravated the action of both Pitt and Kaf is experienced; while in cases where Vat-Pitt is aggravated the action of Pitt alone is experienced, since the coldness of Vat disappears completely due to the heat of of Pitt. Similarly, the combination of the elements of air and fire in Tin gives rise to a slight increase of Pitt. With these principles in view Tin should be administered on different diseases.

The properties of Tin are as follows :- Tin is bitter, saline, warm, coarse, laxative, light, nutritious and reducer of fat. It improves eye-sight, increases strength, power of digestion, appetite, intelligence and beauty. It produces a cooling effect on the system. It cures spermatorhoea, phlegm, obesity, worms, anaemia and asthma. It makes all the Dhatus stable, cures all sorts of Pramehas and prevents nocturnal discharges.

The writers on Rasashastra have recommended Tin on the following diseases:-1. Anaemia, 2. Gulma, 3. Amlapitta (sour dyspepsia), 4. Indigestion, 5. Asthama, 6. Bad smell coming out of the mouth and body, 7. Inflammation of the body, 8. Skin-diseases, 9. Decay of bones, 10. Leprosy, 11. Impotency, 12. Head-diseases, 13. Hunch-backedness, 14. Enlargement of spleen, 15.

Hysteria, 17. Dropsy, 17. Sciatica, 18. For conceiving a male child, 19. Semen- diseases, 20. Senility, 21. Worms and 22. all sorts of Pramehas (gonorrhoeal complaints).

(6) JAMBĪRA*

The word Jambīra is often met in Sanskrit literature. It is variously interpreted by scholars and consequently it has become extremely difficult to determine the exact meaning of the word. The standard Ayurvedic works with their commentaries even do not help much, and the problem remains unsolved. The exact meaning of the word can only be decided after a critical examination of all the important references to this word from the Sanskrit literature. It is not possible, however, to discuss all of them in this small article. I have, therefore, attempted here to examine critically the most important references only from the four standard Ayurvedic works namely *Suśruta*, *Caraka*, *Aṣṭāṅga-saṁgraha* and *Aṣṭāṅgahṛdaya*.

Suśruta-Saṁhitā

Jambīra is mentioned by *Suśruta* in the *Phalavarga* of *Sūtrasthāna* chapter 46 in the following lines:-

अत ऊर्ध्वं फलान्युपदेक्ष्यामः । तद्यथा दाडिमामलकबदरकोलकर्कन्धु.....
नारङ्गजम्बीरलकुचभव्यपारावत....................कोशाम्राम्लीकाप्रभृतीनि ।
१३९ सु. सू. स्था. अ. ४६

नारङ्गजम्बीरलकुचानि प्रसिद्धानि । टीका । डल्हणः ।
अम्लानि रसतः पाके गुरूण्युष्णानि वीर्यतः ॥
पित्तलान्यनिलघ्नानि कफोत्क्लेशकराणि च ॥
१४० सु. सू. स्था. अ. ४६

तेषां सामान्यगुणमाह । अम्लानीत्यादि । अम्लानि अम्लरसोत्कटानि ।
टीका डल्हणः ।

* Prof. P.K. Gode Commemoration Volume, 1960, p. 133.

Jambīra is here included in the list of fruits which are all sour. This reference clearly shows that *Jambīra* is a fruit of sour taste. Whether *Jambīra* remains sour even when it is ripe or becomes somewhat sweet is not clear. According to the commentator Dalhaṇa, *Jambīra* is too well-known to require any explanation.

The properties of *Jambīra* are further described by *Suśruta* in the following verse:-

तृष्णाशूलकफोत्क्लेशच्छर्दिश्वासनिवारणम्।
वातश्लेष्मविबन्धघ्नं जम्बीरं गुरु पित्तकृत्॥
ऐरावतं दन्तशठमम्लं शोणितपित्तकृत्॥ १६२ सु.सू.स्था.अ. ४६

तृष्णेत्यादि। इमं जम्बीरगुणपाठं पञ्जिकाकारो न मन्यते। ऐरावतं दन्तशठमम्लं शोणितपित्तकृत्। इति दन्तशठशब्देन जम्बीरस्य वक्ष्यमाणत्वात्। जम्बीरनानाविधत्वाद्युक्तोऽयं पाठ इत्यन्ये। टीका। डल्हणः।

This verse contains three lines. The first two lines describe the properties of *Jambīra*. According to *Āyurveda*, substances having sweet taste pacify *Pitta* or the element of fire and increase *Kapha* or the element of water. Had there been any tinge of sweetness in *Jambīra* even in the ripened stage, *Suśruta* would not have described it as aggravating *Pitta* and pacifying *Vāta* and *Kapha* and would have added a line like : पक्वं तु मधुरं किञ्चिद्वातपित्तापहं मतम्॥ Hence the description given above shows that *Jambīra* is absolutely sour.

Jambīra as a fruit is mentioned and described in the *Phalavarga* only by *Suśruta*. Neither *Caraka* nor *Vāgbhaṭa* in his *Aṣṭāṅgasaṁgraha* and *Aṣṭāṅgahṛdaya* has mentioned it in *Phalavarga*. Hence it is doubtful whether this verse is genuine or an interpolation. The commentator Dalhaṇa has recorded two contradictory views on this point. Pāñjikākāra does not accept the reading of the verse describing the properties of *Jambīra*. According to him *Jambīra* and *Dantaśaṭha* are indentical and *Jambīra* is described by the word *Dantaśaṭha* in the line ऐरावतं दन्तशठमम्लं which forms the second half of the verse No. 191. According to others this description of *Jambīra* is genuine, because there are many varieties of *Jambīra* and *Dantaśaṭha* is one of them. Hence *Jambīra* and *Dantaśaṭha* cannot be taken as identical.

The third line ऐरावतं दन्तशठमम्लं is again repeated in *Suśruta* quoted below with the commentary of Dalhaṇa:

ऐरावतं दन्तशठमम्लं शोणितपित्तकृत्॥ १९१/२ सु. सू. स्था. अ. ४६

ऐरावतदन्तशठयोर्गुणमाह। ऐरावतमिति। ऐरावतमैरावणिका कृष्णलोहिताम्लफला। दन्तशठं जम्बीरफलम्। अन्ये जम्बीरभेदमाहुः। डल्हणः।

The learned editors of the Nirnayasagar and Chowkhamba editions have failed to notice this repetition. There is no propriety in repeating the same line again; and it must be removed either from verse 162 or from verse 191. Dalhaṇa's commentary is available on the line in verse 191. Hence the reading of the line in verse 191 is genuine. Dalhaṇa refers to the first two lines describing the properties of *Jambīra* in his commentary on verse 162. The reading of third line in the verse seems to be unknown to him as he is not making any reference to it, in his commentary on verse 162. The term वक्ष्यमाणत्वात् in the commentary used for the line shows that *Dantaśaṭha* is described later on in verse 191. Hence the third line in verse 162 is definitely an interpolation and must be removed from the text. The term वक्ष्यमाणत्वात् in the commentary seems to have misled the editors who have maintained the line in the text.

Thus out of the three lines of the verse 162, the third line is decidedly an interpolation. The reading of the first two lines is accepted by some but rejected by Pañjikākāra.

Dalhaṇa is silent. He seems to have been confused and hence could not decide the problem. His confusion becomes clear when his commentary is put to a critical examination :

1. The reading of the word *Jambīra* in the list of fruits beginning with *Dāḍima* is accepted by him as genuine, because he has commented upon it.
2. When the word *Jambīra* is accepted as genuine in the list, it naturally follows that the description of the properties of *Jambīra* also must be accepted as genuine. But Dalhaṇa is silent and does not express his opinion.
3. If the description of *Jambīra* is accepted as genuine *Jambīra* and *Dantaśaṭha* cannot be indentical and *Dantaśaṭha* must be taken as a variety of *Jambīra*. But Dalhaṇa while commenting on verse 191 identifies *Dantaśaṭha* with *Jambīra* and remarks that according to some it is taken as a variety of *Jambīra*.

Thus it will be seen that Dalhaṇa is not clear on this point. But as he has identified *Dantaśaṭha* with *Jambīra* it can be said that he is not in favour of accepting the reading of the verse 162 and the mention of the word *Jambīra* in the list also, as authentic.

There is another way of interpreting the commentary of Dalhaṇa. Dalhaṇa is expressing his own opinion here by the word 'अन्ये'. If this interpretation is accepted, which I think would be more probable, there remains no difficulty in understanding Dalhaṇa's opinion. According to him the verse describing *Jambīra* is genuine and *Dantaśaṭha* is a variety of *Jambīra*, different from it.

Jambīra is not mentioned in the *Phalavarga* of *Caraka*, *Aṣṭāṅgasaṁgraha* and *Aṣṭāṅgahṛdaya*. *Saśruta* is followed by

Vāgbhaṭa and naturally *Vāgbhaṭa* would not fail to mention and describe such a well-known fruit like *Jambīra,* as Dalhaṇa calls it, in his two well-known standard works. But the word *Jambīra* and the verse describing it must be absent in the text of *Suśruta* in *Vāgbhaṭa's* times, and hence the term could not come in *Vāgbhaṭa's* works. The word *Jambīra* and the verse describing it must have been interpolated after *Vāgbhaṭa* and before Dalhaṇa.

Pañjikākāra and Dalhaṇa identify *Dantaśaṭha* with *Jambīra*. *Dantaśaṭha* is absolutely sour according to *Suśruta*:

Jambīra is again mentioned by *Suśruta* in the *Śākavarga* of *Sūtrasthāna* - chapter 46 in the following lines:-

पिप्पलीमरिच................कुस्तुम्बुरुजम्बीरसुमुख ....

पलाण्डुकलायप्रभृतीनि। २२१ सु.सू. स्था.अ. ४६

कटून्युष्णानि रुच्यानि वातश्लेष्महराणि च॥

कृतान्नेषूपयुज्यन्ते संस्कारार्थमनेकधा॥ २२२ सु.सू.स्था.अ. ४६

जम्बीरः हरितशाकमुत्तरापथे जम्बीरगन्धि किञ्चिदम्लम्। टीका। डल्हणः।

जम्बीरः पाचनस्तीक्ष्णः कृमिवातकफापहः॥ २३२

सुरभिर्दीपनो रुच्यो मुखवैशद्यकारकः॥

कफानिलविषश्वासकासदौर्गन्ध्यनाशनः॥ २३३ सु.सू.स्था.अ. ४६

The taste of this *Jambīra* is pungent according to *Suśruta*. Dalhaṇa observes that it is known in North, it possesses the odour of *Jambīra* and it is somewhat sour. Dalhaṇa's explanation does not throw any light on the identification of this pungent *Jambīra*.

Caraka-Saṁhitā

Caraka mentions *Dantaśaṭha* in the *Phalavarga* of *Sūtrasthāna* chapter 27 in the following verse:-

अम्रातकं दन्तशठमम्लं सकरमर्दकम्॥

रक्तपित्तकरं विद्यादैरावतकमेव च॥ १६१

दन्तशठः जम्बीरः। केचिदम्लोटं वदन्ति। —टीका। चक्रपाणिदत्तः।

Dantaśaṭha is here identified with *Jambīra* by the commentator. *Dantaśaṭha* is, of course, sour. *Jambīra* is not at all mentioned by *Caraka* in *Phalavarga*. According to the commentator some identify *Dantaśaṭha* with *Amloṭa*.

Jambīra is mentioned in the *Haritavarga*— *Sūtrasthāna* chapter 27 in the following verse:—

रोचनो दीपनस्तीक्ष्णः सुगन्धिर्मुखशोधनः ॥
जम्बीरः कफवातघ्नः क्रिमिघ्नो भक्तपाचनः ॥ १६७
जम्बीरः पर्णासभेदः । जम्बीरफलं सुगन्धि ।–टीका । चक्रपाणिदत्तः ।

Here the meaning of the word *Jambīra* is doubtful. *Caraka* is silent on the point of taste. According to Amara, *Parṇāsa* is different from *Jambīra*. Amara has mentioned the synonyms of *Jambīra* in the following verse :—

समीरणो मरुबकः प्रस्थपुष्पः फणिज्जकः ॥
जम्बीरोऽप्यथ पर्णासे कठिञ्जरकुठेरकौ ॥ ८०६

अमरः काण्ड-२ वनौ.व.

Instead of mentioning any one of the four synonyms given by Amara, the reason why the commentator is using the term पर्णासभेदः is not clear. The explanation पर्णासभेदः also does not make the meaning clear. Can the term connote anything definite? *Vāgbhaṭa* distinguishes between *Phaṇijja* and *Jambīra* in his two works, while Amara identifies them. Whom are we to believe ?

The reasons that led the commentator to explain the word as पर्णासभेदः may be as follows :-

1. *Jambīra* is mentioned in *Haritavarga*.
2. *Suśruta*, *Aṣṭāṅgasaṁgraha* and *Aṣṭāṅgahṛdaya* mention pungent *Jambīra* in *Haritavarga*.
3. Hence the commentator thinks that pungent *Jambīra* is implied here and not being able to identify it clearly explains it as *Parṇāsabhedaḥ*.

Pandit Shankar Shastri Pade in his सार्थचरकसंहिता translates *Jambīra* by the Marathi word लिंबू. The reasons may be as follows :-

1. The proximity of *Ārdraka* or Ginger and the usual association of Ginger and *Nimbū,*
2. *Nimbūka* is *Amlajambīra,*
3. The attributes show that it can be taken as sour also.

Aṣṭāṅgasaṁgrahaḥ

Jambīra is mentioned in the *Haritavarga* of *Sūtrasthāna,* chapter 7, in the following verse:—

फणिज्जर्जिकजम्बीरखराह्वकालमालिकाः ॥
दीप्यकः क्षवकद्वीपिवस्त्रगन्धादिबद्धविट् ॥ १४४

जम्बीरः खरपत्रः । टीका । इन्दुः ।

रसे पाके च कटुकं दोषोत्क्लेशकरं लघु ॥
विदाहि रूक्षतीक्ष्णोष्णं दृक्शुक्रक्रिमिनाशनम् ॥ १५५

The taste of this *Jambīra* is pungent. The commentator explains it by mentioning its synonym खरपत्र given in the *Rājanighaṇṭu.* (Anandashram, ed. Poona 1896 p. 144.)

The word *Dantaśaṭha* is mentioned in the following verse:—

तथाम्लं कोलकर्कन्धुलिकुचाम्रातकारुकम् ॥ २००
ऐरावतं दन्तशठं सन्तुदं मृगलिण्डिकम् ॥

अ.सं.सू. स्था.अ. ७

दन्तशठं जम्बीरम् । टीका । इन्दुः ।

Here also *Dantaśaṭha* is identified with *Jambīra* by the commentator.

Aṣṭāṅgahṛdayam

Jambīra is mentioned in the following verse of

Śākavarga, Sūtrasthāna chapter 6 :-

कुठेरशिग्रुसुरससुमुखासुरिभूस्तृणम् ॥
फणिज्जार्जकजम्बीरप्रभृति ग्राहि शालनम् ॥१०६
विदाहि कटु रूक्षोष्णं हृद्यं दीपनरोचनम् ॥
दृक्शुक्रकृमिहृत्तीक्ष्णं दोषोत्क्लेशकरं लघु ॥१०७
अर्जकः खरपत्रकः । जम्बीरः करपत्रकः ।

टीका । अरुणदत्तः ।

The taste of this *Jambīra* is pungent. The commentator identified it with करपत्रकः. In the *Aṣṭāṅgasaṁgraha* the commentator Indu indentifies *Jambīra* with खरपत्र while here Aruṇadatta identifies अर्जकः with खरपत्रकः and *Jambīra* with करपत्रकः. The distinction between खरपत्रकः and करपत्रकः is not known. Dr. Garde in his *Marāṭhī* translation of *Aṣṭāṅgahṛdaya* equates *Jambīra* with गवती चहा. He understands गवती चहा by खरपत्रः. Hemādri's comment जम्बीरः जम्बीरसदृशः किञ्चित्तीक्ष्णः does not convey any sense.

Dantaśaṭha is mentioned in the following verse of *Phalavarga* of the *Aṣṭāṅgahṛdaya—Sūtrasthāna* Chapter 6:

तथाम्लं कोलकर्कन्धुलकुचाम्रातकारुकम् ॥ १३७
ऐरावतं दन्तशठं सतूदं मृगलिण्डिकम् ॥

दन्तशठं जम्बीरम् । टीका । अरुणदत्तः ।

The taste of *Dantaśaṭha* is sour and according to Aruṇadatta it is identical with *Jambīra*. Dr. Garde translates it by the *Marāīhī* word *Nimbū*. The commentator Hemādri identifies दन्तशठ with *Jambīra*.

Thus from the above critical examination of the references it will be seen that.

1. The word *Jambīra* is mentioned in *Haritavarga* or *Śākavarga* in all the four works.
2. The taste of this *Jambīra* is pungent.
3. The word is variously interpreted as mentioned below:

जम्बीरः — हरितशाखमुत्तरापथे जम्बीरगन्धि किञ्चिदम्लम्। डल्हणः।

" — जम्बीरः पर्णासमेदः। जम्बीरफलं सुगन्धि। चक्रपाणिदत्तः।

" — खरपत्रः। इन्दुः।

" — करपत्रकः। अरुणदत्तः।

" — जम्बीरसदृशः किञ्चित्तीक्ष्णः। हेमाद्रिः।

" — लिंबू (मराठी) आ. म. शङ्करशास्त्री पदे।

" — गवतीचहा (मराठी) । डॉ. गर्दे.

" — पुदिना. चरक-हिन्दी भाषान्तर.

4. All these various interpretations show that *Jambīra* is not clearly identified, and the exact meaning of the word is doubtful.

5. The word *Jambīra* is not mentioned in the *Phalavarga* by *Caraka* and *Vāgbhaṭa*. In *Suśruta* only, the word is mentioned and the properties of the fruit are also described but the verse is definitely an interpolation and cannot be taken as authentic. Hence it can be said that a fruit identified by the word *Jambīra* is unknown to *Caraka, Suśruta* and *Vāgbhaṭa*.

6. The word *Dantaśaṭha* is mentioned in all the four works. All the commentators identify *Dantaśaṭha* with *Jambīra,* while some take it to be a variety of *Jambīra*. The word *Dantaśatha* is mentioned among the synonyms of *Jambīra* by Amara. But the word *Dantaśaṭha* is not very common in later literature while the word *Jambīra* is commonly used. The meaning of the word *Jambīra* is not clear because there are many varieties of *Jambīra*. Similarly the meaning of the word *Dantaśaṭha* is also not clearly understood, as it is explained by all the commentators by the word *Jambīra*. If *Dantaśaṭha* is really identical with *Jambīra* or a variety of *Jambīra* its properties show that it is absolutely sour.

Among all the varieties of *Jambīra, Nimbūka* or *Citrus medica* is the only variety which remains absolutely sour even when it is ripe. Later writers idenfify *Nimbūka* with *Amla Jambīra* and mention *Amla Jambīra* as the synonym of *Nimbūka*. I am, therefore, inclined to identify *Dantaśaṭha* with *Citrus medica* or *Nimbūka*.

APPENDIX II

(१) रुक्मिणीस्वयंवरम्*

कविः—ज.श्री.पदे

(१)

वर्षानीलाभ्रमालारुचिभरनिवहोत्सेकसंहारयित्री
वीणामाधुर्यभिन्नस्वरमुखमुरलीमूर्च्छनामुन्नयन्ती ।
वृत्तालङ्कारत्नद्युतिनिकरपरिद्योतमाना समन्ता-
देषा श्रीकृष्णमूर्तिः क्षणमपि मनसः स्रग्धरा नापयायात् ।।

(२)

पुरन्दर इव श्रिया परिवृतो मृगाङ्कच्छविः
कुशेशयनिभाननो नयविदां मतीनां पतिः ।
सदार्थिसुरपादपः पितृसमः प्रजावत्सलो
बभूव पृथिवीपतिः प्रथितविक्रमो भीष्मकः ।

(३)

स कुण्डिनं कुण्डिनतुल्यशोभमुपेन्द्रवज्रायुधभीमवीर्यः ।
श्रिया च धीवत् परिदीप्यमानो धिया च श्रीवच्चिरमध्युवास ।।

(४)

एतस्य राज्ञः किल रुक्मिणीति नाम्ना प्रसिद्धा तनया बभूव ।
पञ्चाभवन्नुग्रतरा सुताश्च देवेन्द्रवज्राधिकदेहसाराः ।।

(५)

कृष्णरिपू रुक्मी बहुगर्वो रुक्मरथो रुक्माधिकबाहुः ।
रुक्मकचो रुक्माधिकमाली रुक्मवती कन्या किल धन्या ।।

(६)

आबाल्यादनवरतं प्रहर्षिणी सा
रूपेणाप्रतिमगुणैर्विरोचमाना ।

---

* Baroda College Magazine-1933-37.

यत्पादोपमविभवं सहस्रपत्रं
खिन्ना यद्गतिमवलोक्य राजहंसाः ॥

(७)

वृत्ते जङ्घे श्रीजितेभेन्द्रशुण्डादण्डोत्सेकं शोभनं चोरुयुग्मम्।
काञ्चीस्थानं सर्वलोकैकरम्यं धत्ते लीलाशालिनी भूपबाला ॥

(८)

मध्यक्षतमा पृथुकुचयुगभारानम्रा
बाहुद्वन्द्वं सुभगमृदुलपुष्पश्रीकम्।
पीवग्रीवां जलजसहजकम्बुच्छायां
रम्यं बभ्रे जितसरसिजगर्वं वक्त्रम् ॥

(९)

स्मितकौमुदीकिरणहृष्टबान्धवा
श्रुतिवल्लकीनिनदमञ्जुभाषिणी।
मदिरेक्षणा नृपतिभीष्मकात्मजा
नयनाम्बुजेन मधुरेण वीक्षते ॥

(१०)

अधररुचिसरस्वतीसङ्गता हरितमणिनवप्रभामूर्च्छिता।
सुतनुदशनकान्तिमन्दाकिनी जनयति वदनं प्रयागद्युतिम् ॥

(११)

चिकुरसमूहसमूढमालतीकुसुमसमाहृतषट्पदावलिः।
पतति विभिन्नसरोजविभ्रमात् स्मितमहिते ननु रुक्मिणीमुखे ॥

(१२)

गजगतिर्नृपसुता गुणवती समुदिता।
उपचिता सुललिता सुमहिता किमु लता ॥

(१३)

फुल्ला वसन्ततिलका नववल्लरीव
सा रुक्मिणीगुणगणैरुपचीयमाना।

देया कथं गुणवते नृपसत्तमाये-
त्याप प्रजाहितपरो नृपतिः स चिन्ताम् ॥

(१४)

निशम्य तां धरणिसुरास्तपस्विनो
वदान्यतामतिरुचिरां प्रजावितुः ।
विभास्वरं सुरपतिमन्दिरश्रिया
दिने दिने नृपसदनं ययुर्मुदा ॥

(१५)

श्रुतिस्मृतिप्रमाणिकां विधाय भूसुरार्हणाम् ।
प्रपूर्य तन्मनोरथान् मुदा जगाद भीष्मकः ॥

(१६)

रामः शस्त्रधरैर्यमो रिपुगणैः शार्दूलविक्रीडितैः
कन्दर्पो वरवर्णिनीभिरचलाकल्पद्रुमो याचकैः ।
ब्रह्मण्यो विबुधैः स्वधर्मनिरतः पौरैश्च यो वीक्ष्यते
कः पृथ्वीपतिरीदृशो विजयते भूमण्डलेऽस्मिन् द्विजाः ॥

(१७)

प्रश्न एष उचितस्तव राजन् कन्यकावत इति द्रुतमुक्त्वा ।
स्वागतामुदितमानसविप्रा भीष्मकं सपदि चोत्तरमूचुः ॥

(१८)

दैत्येन्द्रवंशाग्निरहो विराजते श्रीकृष्ण एकः खलु मेदिनीतले ।
नूनं तदीयार्णवगा विलोकिता द्वारावती चेत् किममर्त्यराट् पुरा ॥

(१९)

सिन्धुना पुरी विभाति सागरस्तया विभाति ।
श्रीः समानिकाऽनया न कुत्रचिन् महीतलेऽस्ति ॥

(२०)

अन्या कान्तिर्लक्ष्मीरन्या कीर्तिश्चान्याऽन्यत् सामर्थ्यम् ।
अन्या विद्युन्मालादीप्तेः श्रीकृष्णस्य प्रज्ञा लोके ॥

(२१)

न भवेन्समाप्तिरनन्तः कथयेद्यदि देवकीसुतगुणान् नृपते।
इयमस्मदीयभणितिः सुतरां प्रमिताक्षरा ननु कथं प्रभवेत्॥

(२२)

इति वनमालिगुणान् कथयित्वा स्फुटमुखतामरसं नरपालम्।
अवनिसुराः प्रययुर्निजगेहं वियति ममौ न धरापतिमोदः॥

(२३)

मेने गोविन्दं रुक्मिणी योग्यकान्तं
तस्याः सम्पन्नाऽऽराधना वैश्वदेवी।
लक्ष्मीः सौन्दर्यं तस्य वीर्यं च लीला
तस्या हि स्वान्तं संचकर्षैव नूनम्॥

(२४)

राजा बहु मेने कृष्णं गुणराशिं कन्यामणिमालायोग्यं जलजाक्षम्।
रुक्मी प्रतिकूलश्चैद्यं नृपवर्यं नूनं गुरुकार्ये विघ्नप्रतिघातः॥

(२५)

रुक्मिणोत्पादितं विघ्नमाज्ञाय सा
दुःखिता रुक्मिणी श्रीर्ननु स्रग्विणी।
चिन्तयित्वा द्विजं पत्रयुक्तं मुदा
द्वारकां सत्वरं शार्ङ्गिणे प्राहिणोत्॥

(२६)

महीसुरोऽसौ समुपेत्य तां पुरीं
सुश्राव्यवंशस्तनितानुकर्षिणीम्।
ददर्श तूर्णं किल विस्मयावहं
मुकुन्दसौधं विधुमण्डलस्पृशम्॥

(२७)

तस्मिन् सौधे कृतपदपद्मन्यासः
क्षोणीदेवः स्मितमुख ईक्षाञ्चक्रे।
गाढं नीलां जलधरमालामन्या-
मध्यासीनां मणिमयपीठं रम्यम्॥

(२८)

अवनिसुरेक्षणमुदितो मुदिररुचिर्यदुकुलजः ।
त्वरितगतिः परिजगृहे दुरितहरौ द्विजचरणौ ॥

(२९)

तं मणिमध्यं पीठमधिष्ठाप्य मुरारिर्विप्रवरम् ।
स्नेहयुतः पूजां विदधे सज्जनमान्यो मेघरुचिः ॥

(३०)

भूसुरवर्यः पङ्क्तिपवित्रः ।
काममभूङ्क्त श्रीहरिगेहे ॥

(३१)

वीक्ष्य प्रीतिं कंसारातेः ।
सिद्धं मेने कन्याकार्यम् ॥

(३२)

द्विजं सोमराजीव्यपेताखिलाघम् ।
उपस्थातुकामो मुकुन्दोऽभ्युपेतः ॥

(३३)

अभिमृशन् द्विजपादसरोरुहं
सरज आशु रजस्ततिवारणम् ।
द्रुतविलम्बितमञ्जुपदोक्तिभिः
सविनयं तमपृच्छदधोक्षजः ॥

(३४)

विबुध मधुमतीसुकृतविलसितम् ।
तदपि जयति ते व्यपगतविपदम् ॥

(३५)

यत्रासौ मदलेखा किञ्चिन् नो बहुदोषा ।
सन्तुष्टिः परिपूर्णा तं वन्दे द्विजराजम् ॥

(३६)

कच्चित् क्षोणीपालाल्लोकत्राणासक्तेः ।
विद्युल्लेखादीप्ते धर्मात्मन् ते क्षेमम् ॥

(३७)

किमर्थमत्र सम्प्राप्तो निःशङ्कं ब्रूहि मेऽखिलम् ।
अनुष्टुभ्नामि विपदं कृतार्थो भव भूसुर ।

(३८)

एवं परिपृष्टो वृत्तं तनुमध्याम् ।
कन्यामधिकृत्य प्रोचे द्विजराजः ॥

(३९)

अथ मुरहन्त्रे प्रणयमनोज्ञम् ।
अददत पत्रं शशिवदनायाः ॥

(४०)

श्रुत्वा वृत्तं द्विजवरगीतं मत्तारातिद्विपमृगराजः ।
ईक्षाञ्चक्रे किल वनमाली सोत्कण्ठं तद्वरतनुपत्रम् ॥

(४१)

गुणानां वृन्दं ते हृदयपरितापप्रशमनं
नितान्तं सौन्दर्यं भुवनरमणीविस्मयकरम् ।
निशम्याजस्त्रं मे नृपशिखरिणीजातिसुलभां
विहायाशु व्रीडां त्वयि विशति चेतो मुररिपो ॥

(४२)

नलिननिलया दासीभूता त्वदीयपदाम्बुजं
त्यजति न मनाङ् मेघश्याम त्वयि प्रचुरादरा ।
जलजनयनः सौन्दर्येणाधरीकृतमन्मथो
हृदयनिलयः कस्या न स्याद् भवान् हरिणीदृशः ॥

(४३)

स्मारं स्मारं तव गुणनिवहं ध्यायन्त्यास्त्वां ननु मम कुरुते ।
पादाम्भोजे तव रसरुचिरे लीनं चेतो भ्रमरविलसितम् ॥

(४४)

योऽयं देवो विहितमतिभिर्दुर्लभो योगिवृन्दै-
राशाबन्धो गगननलिनीतुल्यतां याति तस्मिन्।
भूयो भूयो मधुरमधुरैः प्रार्थयन्तीं वचोभिर्
मन्दाक्रान्तां त्वयि गणय मां नाथ गाढं सतृष्णाम्॥

(४५)

परिचररक्षितां वद कथं भवतीमवरोधवर्तिनी-
मनिहतसोदरः परिणयामि बलादिति युक्तिरुच्यते।
कृतनवमङ्गला सह पुरन्ध्रिगणैः सरसीरुहेक्षण
व्रजति समर्चितुं नववधूर्वरदां तुहिनाद्रिकन्यकाम्॥

(४६)

सुनिभृतमपराजिताशु समेत्य तद्-
हिमनगतनयालयं हि ससैनिकः।
रिपुकुलमथनं विधाय निराश्रया-
मुपयमविधिनासुरेण वृणीष्व माम्॥

(४७)

व्रतनियमार्हणाभिरसकृत् सुसेविता देवता
विभवबलादमोघफलदा दृढव्रतिनां सदा।
अवसर एष पूर्वसुकृतैरुपस्थितः प्रार्थये
यदुकुलनन्दन कुरुत मे सरोजनेत्रं पतिम्॥

(४८)

इति रुक्मिणीप्रहितपत्रिकां मध्वरि-
र्मधुमञ्जरीमधुरवर्णविद्युत्वतीम्।
सदयः पठन् प्रणतरक्षणैकादरो
जयमङ्गले मुदितमानसः सम्बभौ॥

(४९)

लोकमोहनगुणैरथोद्धता रुक्मिणी त्वयि दृढादरा पुनः।
प्राह भूसुरवरस्तदा हरिं याहि कुण्डिनपुरं मया द्रुतम्॥

(५०)

चन्द्रवर्त्मगमनैः सुरनिवहैः पूजितोऽयमवनित्रिदशवरम् ।
प्राह विष्णुरमलं हतहृदयो रुक्मिणीपरिगतैः सुरसगुणैः ॥

(५१)

राजन्यपापापसदोपजातीरुन्मथ्य युद्धे तरलायताक्षीम् ।
तामानयाम्याशु निबद्धरागामपारसौन्दर्यविलासलक्ष्मीम् ॥

(५२)

कलहंसकण्ठनिनदो द्विजराजं
प्रतिसन्निगद्य सह तेन रथाग्र्यम् ।
जवनैस्तुरङ्गमवरैरनुयुक्तं
द्रुतमारुरोह सुदृढं यदुवर्यः ॥

(५३)

विचार्य निपुणं विवाहसुदिनं स राजदुहितुर्विलोक्य विपदम् ।
जलोद्धतगतिः सुरारिमथनो विवेश तरसा विदर्भविषयम् ॥

(५४)

तत्रापश्यन् मत्तमयूरीकृतलास्यं
मध्येमार्गं वैरिनिहन्ता जलजाक्षः ।
हित्वा सर्वं संशयजातं विजयाप्तौ
प्रीतः पौरैः कुण्डिनवासैः परिणूतः ॥

(५५)

पुत्रमते योग्यवरं चैद्यनृपं माणवकम् ।
वीक्ष्य नृपस्तद्दुहितुर्मङ्गलकं संविदधे ॥

(५६)

यदुपतिवरलाभः स्यादिति नृपवरपुत्री सा ।
भुजगशिशुभृतामस्तौत् सततमवहिता गौरीम् ॥

(५७)

तरला द्विजस्य वीक्षणे सरला भुजङ्गसङ्गता ।
पतिता विचारसागरे महिला मुकुन्दलालसा ॥

(५८)

श्रीहरिसङ्गमलास्यविभावा स्वेष्टमनोरथपूरणकामा।
अभवन् मङ्गलदोधकभावा भूपसुता शुभनेत्रविनामा॥

(५९)

नृपसङ्कुलिते गजराजगते दमघोषसुते नगरोपगते।
करपीडनतोटकवृत्तकराः परितो जनिता भयदाः शकुनाः॥

(६०)

हरेः कुण्डिने वाडवोक्त्याऽशृणोत् सा
भुजङ्गप्रयातानुकल्पं प्रवेशम्।
स्वलेखार्थसंवाहकाय प्रहृष्टा
द्विजेन्द्राय रत्नं ददौ राजबाला॥

(६१)

रिपुभयचकितो नीलवासास्तदा
मुररिपुमनुयातो बलैरन्वितः।
निजनगरमुपेतौ क्षमायाः पति-
र्विपुलकुशलपूर्णोऽर्चयामास तौ॥

(६२)

वीरेन्द्रैर्गुप्ता नरपतिदुहिता दुर्गां
गत्वा पद्भ्यां मङ्गलनिलयगतां देवीम्।
नत्वाऽसम्बाधा सुतपतिसहितामस्तौत्
कृष्णो भूयान्मम पतिरिति शुभाशंसा॥

(६३)

हिमनगदुहितानवमणिनिलयाद्
वलति सुवदना नरवरतनुजा।
व्यथयति च सुमप्रहरणकलिका
नरपतिहृदयं विकसितवदना॥

(६४)

वीरैर्गुप्तां राजदुहितरं निष्क्रामन्तीं
गौरीगेहान् मङ्गलवसनां मुक्ताहाराम्।

तूर्णं जित्वा रक्षकनिवहं कंसाराति-
वामामाहार्षीच्छ्रियमिव वासन्तीं वीरः ॥

(६५)

माधवेन सङ्गतां विलोक्य राजकन्यकां
सेनया रुरोध रोषितो नृपात्मजो बली।
तूणकाच्छरैर्विजित्य तं बबन्ध माधवः
पादयोर्निपत्य मोचयाम्बभूव रुक्मिणी ॥

(६६)

यदुपतिरथ देवी मालिनी रुक्मिणी सा
विकसितवदनौ स्वां जग्मतू राजधानीम्।
धृतपरिणयभूषौ रेजतू दम्पती तौ
परमसुखसमृद्धामक्षयां प्राप्य लक्ष्मीम् ॥

(२) गीर्वाणवाणीवैभवम्*

धरासुरसुधायिनी रुचिरबन्धविद्योतिनी
समुन्नतिविवर्धिनी धवलकीर्तिविस्तारिणी।
तमःपटलभेदिनी वृजिनसङ्घसंहारिणी
परामृतविधायिनी सुरसरस्वती सेव्यताम् ॥१॥

भगवतो विधातुः सृष्टिनिर्माणचातुरीसीमान्तलेखा हि मानुषी सृष्टिः। न हि राजतेऽस्य सर्गे मानवातिशायी कश्चिज्जन्तुः। न खल्वसाम्प्रतमिदं यत्परमेण प्रमोदेनैनामवलोक्य सृष्टिमेषा ह्यवसानभूमिरात्मनः कृतिपाटवस्येति निश्चित्य निरवधिं समाधिं विदधे भगवान् परमेष्ठी। एष हि विशेषः सर्वेभ्यश्चेतनेभ्यो मनुष्याणां यदेतान् बुद्धिविशेषेण योजयामास भगवान् पितामहः। बुद्धिविशेष एव प्रभवति मनुष्यपश्वादिभेदाय। तदभावे तु पश्वादिभिरविशेषः स्यात्।

तेषामभ्युदयनिःश्रेयससिद्धये चतुरेण चतुराननेन चतुर्भ्यो वक्त्रेभ्यश्चत्वारो वेदाः शास्त्राणि च नानाविधानि विसृष्टानि। यत्र नरीनर्ति सुरस्वरस्वती। यानि च प्रकल्पन्ते बुद्धिविशेष-विशिष्टानामभ्युदयनिःश्रेयससिद्धये। यथा यथा भवति दृढभूमिः शास्त्राभ्यासस्तथा तथा देदीप्यतेऽस्य बुद्धिविशेषो मणिरिव शाणोल्लीढः।

शास्त्रेष्ववगाहिष्यमाणेन पुरस्तात् कर्तव्यो भवति प्रकामं विबुधभारतीपरिचयः। न खलु सुलभान्येतान्यनभ्यस्तगीर्वाणभाषाणाम्। गीर्वाणभाषाभ्यासश्च शीलनाच्छब्दानुशासनस्य परिचयादितिहासपुराणानामास्वादात्काव्यमकरन्दस्य पर्यालोचनान्नाटकानां वाचनाच्च रसपरिप्लुतानां कथानाम्।

का प्रकृतिः कः प्रत्ययः कः प्रकृत्यर्थः कः प्रत्ययार्थ इति सम्यग् ज्ञात्वा शास्त्रेष्वप्रतिहतसञ्चारो भवत्यधीतशब्दानुशासनः। इतिहासपुराणपरिचयो हि कथमापत्सु वर्तितव्यमिति शिक्षयति धर्मं बोधयति नीतिमनुशास्ति दोषान् दूरीकरोति मनः प्रसादयति ज्ञानसोपानं चाधिरोहयति। नीत्युपदेशानामाकरो ज्ञानभाण्डागारं शतसहस्रश्लोकसङ्ख्याकं महाभारतमद्वितीयत्वेन भासते धरामण्डले। काव्यनाटकाभ्यासो व्यवहारं ज्ञापयति चेतो रञ्जयति भाषाभ्यासं च वर्धयति।

परमा समृद्धा खलु काव्यनाटककथाभिर्गीर्वाणवाणी। यत्र वीणानिनादमाधुरीमप्यधरीकुर्वती पण्डितराजकवितामाधुरी, पदलालित्यललिता श्रीहर्षवाणी, अर्थगौरवगंभीरा भारवेर्भारती, सर्वाङ्सुन्दरा माघकवेः कृतिः, उपमयानुपमं कालिदासकाव्यं, प्रतिपदरससिक्तं शाकुन्तलं, ग्रावाणमपि रोदयन्ति भवभूतेर्वचांसि, हृदयलग्ना सहृदयान् बाण इव घूर्णयन्ती बाणवाणी, कविदर्पदलनलोकोत्तरपदलालित्य-चातुरीधुरीणः सुबन्धोः प्रबन्धः। भर्तृहरिचाणक्यादीनां कृतीनभ्यस्य केन नाप्यते नीतिशास्त्रपाटवम्। गङ्गालहरी मयूरभाषितं

---

* Baroda College Magazine September, 1932.

सूर्यशतकं शङ्कराचार्याणां स्तोत्राणि चाकर्ण्य कस्य नाम सहृदयस्य भक्तिरसेन नाप्लाव्यते चेतः। द्वादशदर्शनपदार्थान् साहित्यसौहित्यस्य पराकाष्ठां चैकत्र द्रष्टुकामः को नाम साहित्यसम्राजां गङ्गाधरशास्त्रिणामलिविलासिसंलापं विलोक्य मोघाशो भवेत्। इत्थमर्थिमनोरथप्रपूरणाय धृतकङ्कण इव विभाति काव्यसंघातः।

एवमेतेषां परिशीलनेन संजाते भाषाभ्यासे भवति निःश्रेयसाभ्युदयसाधनेषु शास्त्रेषु बुद्धिप्रवेशः। अधीतिनस्तेषु पाखण्डिदिग्गजकुतर्कशुण्डादण्डैरुन्मूलिताञ् शास्त्रशाखिनो विलोक्य विमुह्यते चेतः। किमु पाखण्डिमतमाश्रयितव्यं किमु श्रद्धेयानि मुनिवचनानीति भ्राम्यति बुद्धिः। संशय्यते च न खलु वितथवादिनो मुनय इति। नन्वत्र शास्त्रेषु वर्तमानानामर्थानां परोक्षत्वमेव निदानम्। नो चेत्कथं संशयमापद्येत।

अतो हि प्रथमं तर्कोऽध्येतव्यः। स हि करतलामलकवत्प्रकाशयति सूक्ष्मातिसूक्ष्मान् पदार्थांश्छेदयति संशयग्रन्थिं निराकरोति मोहं यथार्थमवभासयति पदार्थान् प्रभवति च पाखण्डिमुखमुद्रणाय। को नाम तार्किकपञ्चाननमन्तरेण पाखण्डिदिग्गजाक्षेपगण्डस्थलानि विदारयेदिति तर्कमभ्यस्य कैवल्यप्राप्तये विधेयोऽष्टाङ्गयोगाभ्यासः।

तत्र महान् खल्वन्तरायो व्याध्यादीनाम्। असाध्या हि धर्मक्रिया व्याधिग्रस्तस्य। अतो हि तेषां प्रशमाय स्वस्थातुरहितमायुर्वेदाध्ययनं कर्तव्यम्। भाव्यशुभज्ञानार्थं च ज्यौतिषाभ्यासो विधेयः। स हि ग्रहाणामवगमय्य राशिस्थितिं ज्ञापयति शुभाशुभफलानि। तत्राशुभनिरासाय बहूपयुक्तस्तन्त्राभ्यासः। प्रत्यक्षा हि सिद्धिस्तन्त्राणाम्। मन्त्राश्चामोघफलदा इति नात्र विवदन्ते बालिशा अपि। नास्त्यापत्तिरेतादृशो यस्या नोपदिष्टोऽत्र प्रतीकारः।

एवं निरस्तेष्वन्तरायेषु सुप्रकाशो भवति निःश्रेयसाभ्युदयसिद्धिमार्गः। ततो साङ्ख्यशास्त्रात् तत्त्वज्ञानमधिगम्य वेदार्थज्ञानाय मीमांसाशास्त्रमधीत्य साङ्गानभ्यस्य वेदान् ब्रह्मज्ञानयोग्यतासिद्धये च वेदोपदिष्टान् क्रतून् कृत्वा संजातायां विरक्तौ संन्यस्यानवरतमुपनिषद्विचारेण स्वयं ब्रह्मैव सन् ब्रह्माप्येति।

भवानीश्रीकण्ठप्रबलपरिचर्यानवफला
महाकाव्याभ्यासाल्ललितपदविन्यासससुभगा।
स्मृतिश्रेयोवादाकलितपुरवाग्रम्यविभवा
कृतिर्जागन्नाथी जयति विबुधामोदजनका॥

(३) कुमारपरीक्षा*

नमस्कृत्य भवानीशं कालिदासकवेः कृतिः ।
कुमारसंभवं नाम महाकाव्यं परीक्ष्यते ॥

अथ विचारयामो भारतललामभूतस्य बधिरीकृतदिग्गजश्रुतियशोदुन्दुभेरनवरतधावद्रसिकालिमालास्वादितकाव्यारविन्दभकरन्दस्य कविकुलगुरोः कालिदासस्य काव्यानामन्यतममधिकृत्य कुमारसंभवम् । चित्रं खल्वेतद्यदत्र कालिदासेन केवलमनूदितमेव क्कचिच्छिवपुराणं क्वचिद्ब्रह्मपुराणं च । तथाहि ।

शिवपुराणे त्रयोदशाध्याये	**कुमारसंभवे प्रथमे सर्गे**
१. दिशः प्रसेदुः पवनः सुखं ववौ शङ्खं निदध्मुर्गगनेचरास्तथा । पपात मौलौ कुसुमाञ्जलिस्तदा बभूव तज्जन्मदिनं सुखप्रदम् ॥	प्रसन्नदिक् पांशुविविक्तवातं शङ्खस्वनानन्तरपुष्पवृष्टि । शरीरिणां स्थावरजङ्गमानां सुखाय तज्जन्मदिनं बभूव ॥२३ ॥
२. मेना तया पूर्णनिशेशवक्त्रया स्फुरत्प्रभामण्डलया रराज ह । यथा विदूराचलभूमिरञ्जसा घनोत्थया रत्नशलाकया मुने ॥	तया दुहित्रा सुतरां सवित्री स्फुरत्प्रभामण्डलया चकाशे । विदूरभूमिर्नवमेघशब्दा- दुद्भिन्नया रत्नशलाकयेव ॥२४ ॥
३. तां पार्वतीत्याभिजनाच्च नामतो जहाव तद्बन्धुजनः स्वभावतः । मात्रा निषिद्धा तपसे यदा तु सा ययावुमाख्यां भवभक्तिभाविनी ॥	तां पार्वतीत्यभिजनेन नाम्ना बन्धुप्रियां बन्धुजनो जुहाव । उमेति मात्रा तपसो निषिद्धा पश्चादुमाख्यां सुमुखी जगाम ॥२६ ॥
४. समाधेरनुमेने तां गिरिशः परिपन्थिनीम् । समाधिनिश्चलत्वं च सर्वेषां दर्शयन् मुने ॥	प्रत्यर्थिभूतामपि तां समाधेः शुश्रूषमाणां गिरिशोऽनुमेने ।
५. गिरिशमुपचचार प्रत्यहं सा सुकेशी ।	गिरिशमुपचचार प्रत्यहं सा सुकेशी । नियमितपरिखेदा तच्छिरश्चन्द्रपादैः ॥६० ॥
चतुर्दशाध्याये	**द्वितीयसर्गे**
६. एतस्मिन्नन्तरे काले तारकेण दिवौकसः । आजौ पराजिता आसन् शक्रदर्पविघातिना ॥	तस्मिन् विप्रकृताः काले तारकेण दिवौकसः ॥
तदा सर्वे तुरासाहं कृत्वाग्रे हतविक्रमाः । स्वायम्भुवं ययुर्धाम सत्यलोकमिति श्रुतम् ॥	तुरासाहं पुरोधाय धाम स्वायम्भुवं ययुः ॥९ ॥

* Baroda College Magazine February, 1933.

७. दृष्ट्वा तत्र जगन्नाथं विकसत्सुमुखश्रियः । बभूवुः पङ्कजानीव प्रातर्दृष्ट्वा दिवाकरम् ॥	तेषामाविरभूद्ब्रह्मा परिम्लानमुखश्रियाम् । सरसां सुप्तपद्मानां प्रातर्दीधितिमानिव ॥२ ॥
८. स्त्रीस्वरूपी भवानेव पुमानसि जगत्पते । तस्मात्सर्वेषु भूतेषु विख्यातो पितरौ भवान् ॥	स्त्रीपुंसावात्मभागौ ते भिन्नमूर्तेःसिसृक्षया । प्रसूतिभाजः सर्वस्य तावेव पितरौ स्मृतौ ॥७ ॥
९. त्वत्तो वेदाः समुद्भूता ऋग्यजुःसामसंज्ञिकाः । कर्मयज्ञाः स्वर्गफलाः साङ्गोपनिषदः शुभाः ॥	उद्घातःप्रणवो यासां न्यायैस्त्रिभिरुदीरणः । कर्मयज्ञाः फलं स्वर्गस्तासां त्वं प्रभवो गिराम् ॥१२ ॥
१०. धर्मार्थकाममोक्षाणामादिभूतां सनातनीम् । त्वामामनन्ति प्रकृतिं पुरुषार्थविदः प्रभो ॥	त्वामामनन्ति प्रकृतिं पुरुषार्थप्रवर्तिनीम् ॥१३ ॥
११. मरीच्यादिविधातॄणां विधातासि जगद्गुरो । परतोऽपि परोऽसि त्वं सर्वेन्द्रियविगोचरः ॥	परतोऽपि परश्चासि विधाता वेधसामपि ॥१४ ॥
१२. इदानीं तु कथं सर्वे नष्टभासोऽभवन् सुराः । तुषारच्छन्नतेजांसि ज्योतींषीव विहायसि ॥	किमिदं द्युतिमात्मीयां न बिभ्रति यथा पुरा । हिमक्लिष्टप्रकाशानि ज्योतींषीव मुखानिव ॥१४ ॥
१३. न एते द्वादशादित्या दृश्यन्ते गततेजसः । भित्तिभागे गृहाणां च चित्रिकैर्लिखिता इव ॥	अमी च कथमादित्याः प्रतापक्षतिशीतलाः । चित्रन्यस्ता इव गताः प्रकामालोकनीयताम् ॥ २४ ॥
१४. महासुरस्तारकाख्यस्त्वत्तः प्राप्तपराक्रमः । सर्वलोकविनाशाय केतुराजिरिवोत्थितः ॥	भवल्लब्धवरोदीर्णस्तारकाख्यो महासुरः । उपप्लवाय लोकानां धूमकेतुरिवोत्थितः ॥३२ ॥
१५. चन्द्रस्तु तं सदाकालं कलाभिः परिषेवते । चन्द्रशेखरमूर्धस्थां कलामेकां विहाय च ॥	सर्वाभिः सर्वदा चन्द्रस्तं कलाभिर्निषेवते । नादत्ते केवलां लेखां हरचूडामणीकृताम् ॥३४ ॥
१६. एवमाराधितश्चापि स क्लिश्नाति जगत्त्रयम् । शाम्येत्प्रत्यपकारेण नोपकारेण दुर्जनः ॥	इत्थमारध्यमानोऽपि क्लिश्नाति भुवनत्रयम् । शाम्येत्प्रत्यपकारेण नोपकारेण दुर्जनः ॥४० ॥
	तृतीयसर्गे
१७. असम्मतः कस्तवेन्द्र मुक्तिमार्गमपेक्षते । तं सुंदरीकटाक्षैस्तु बध्नाम्याज्ञापय प्रभो ॥	असम्मतः कस्तव मुक्तिमार्गं पुनर्भवक्लेशभयात्प्रपन्नः । बद्धश्चिरं तिष्ठतु सुन्दरीणा- मारेचितभ्रूचतुरैः कटाक्षैः ॥५ ॥
१८. धैर्यच्युतिं करिष्येऽहं भवस्यापि तवाज्ञया । अन्येषां चैव देवानामसुराणां च का कथा ॥	तव प्रसादात्कुसुमायुधोऽपि सहायमेकं मधुमेव लब्ध्वा । कुर्यां हरस्यापि पिनाकपाणे- र्धैर्यच्युतिं के मम धन्विनोऽन्ये ॥१० ॥
२१. तस्मिन्वने संयमिनां मुनीनामूर्ध्वरेतसाम् ।	तस्मिन्वने संयमिनां मुनीनां तपः समाधेः प्रतिकूलवर्ती ।

समाधेः प्रतिकूलस्तु कामो विजयते मुने ॥	सङ्कल्पयोनेरभिमानभूतप्रात्मानमाधाय मधुर्जजृम्भे ॥१४ ॥
२०. विवृद्धमन्योस्तस्याथ तृतीयनयनान्मुने । स्फुरन्नुदर्चिरग्निस्तु पपात मदनोपरि ॥	तपःपरामर्षविवृद्धमन्योर्भ्रूभङ्गदुष्प्रेक्ष्यमुखस्य तस्य । स्फुरन्नुदर्चिः सहसा तृतीयादक्ष्णः कृशानुः किल निष्पपात ॥
२१. क्रोधं संहर हे देव इति यावद्वदन्ति खे । इन्द्रादिसकला देवास्तावद्भस्मीचकार तम् ॥	क्रोधं प्रभो संहर संहरेति यावद्गिरः खे मरुतां चरन्ति । तावत्स वह्निर्भवनेत्रजन्मा भस्मावशेषं मदनं चकार ॥७२ ॥
षोडशाध्याये	**पञ्चमसर्गे**
२२. साकं सखीभ्यां सुमुखी सा गौरीशिखरं ययौ चकार वसतिं यस्माद्गौरीशिखरमुच्यते ॥	प्रजासु पश्चात्प्रथितं तदाख्यया । जगाम गौरी शिखर शिखण्डिमत् ॥७ ॥
२३. तपोविपाककाले तां जिज्ञासुर्भगवाञ् शिवः । ब्रह्मचर्यव्रतधरो विवेश तपसोऽचलम् ॥ अजिनाषाढधारी च प्रगल्भवचनो मुने । ज्वलन्निव जटाधारी ब्रह्मज्ञो ब्रह्मवर्चसा ॥	अथाजिनाषाढधरः प्रगल्भवाग् ज्वलन्निव ब्रह्ममयेन तेजसा ॥ विवेश कश्चिज्जटिलस्तपोवनं शरीरबद्धः प्रथमाश्रमो यथा ॥३० ॥
२४. चतुर्थे त्यक्तपर्णा च अपर्णाख्यामवाप सा ।	स्वयं विशीर्णद्रुमपर्णवृत्तिता परा हि काष्ठा तपसस्तया पुनः ॥ तदप्यपाकीर्णमतः प्रियंवदां वदन्त्यपर्णेति च तां पुराविदः ॥२८ ॥
२५. अपि क्रियार्थं सुलभं पुष्पवारिसमित्कुशम् । अपि देवि तपोमूर्ध्नि स्वशक्त्यापि प्रवर्तसे ॥	अपि क्रियार्थं सुलभं समित्कुशं जलान्यपि स्नानविधिक्षमाणि ते ॥ अपि स्वशक्त्या तपसि प्रवर्तसे शरीरमाद्यं खलु धर्मसाधनम् ॥३३ ॥
२६. तस्योद्वाहनकाले च हाहाकर्तुं भविष्यति । फणिकङ्कणसंयोगं यदा ते कंकणं भवेत् ॥	अवस्तुनिर्बन्धपरे कथं नु ते करोऽयमामुक्तविवाहकौतुकः । करेण शम्भोर्वलयीकृताहिना सहिष्यते तत्प्रथमावलम्बनम् ॥६६ ॥
२७. दुकूलं तव सुश्रोणि तद्वासस्तु गजाजिनम् ।	त्वमेव तावत्परिचिन्तय स्वयं कदाचिदेते यदि योगमर्हतः । वधूदुकूलं कलहंसलक्षणं गजाजिनं शोणितबिन्दुवर्षि च ॥६७ ॥
२८. यः करोति महादेवनिन्दामात्मविनाशिनीम् । स पापिष्ठतरस्तस्माद्यः शृणोति स पापभक् ॥	न केवलं यो महतोऽपभाषते शृणोति तस्मादपि यः स पापभाक् ॥

२९. क्रीतस्तवास्मि दासोऽहं घोरेण तपसाऽमुना। अद्यप्रभृत्यवनताङ्गि तवास्मि दासः
क्रीतस्तपोभिरिति वादिनि चन्द्रमौलौ ॥

एवं प्रतिसर्गं दृश्यते हि भूयिष्ठं सादृश्यम्। तथापि विस्तरभिया नोदाहृतानि पद्यान्तराणि। अत्र हि प्रतिपद्यं लक्ष्यते विशेषः कोऽपि। तथाहि। क्वचित्प्रतिबिम्बतया क्वचिदालेख्यप्रख्यतया क्वचिच्च तुल्यतया च्छायोपजीवनम्। क्वचिदुक्त्युपजीवनम्। क्वचित्समस्यापूरणं क्वचित्पदपरिवृत्तिः। क्वचिद्व्यस्तानां समासः समस्तानां व्यासश्च। न परोक्षं कृत्स्नमेतदुदाहृतेषु पद्येषु पण्डितप्रकाण्डानामिति कृतं प्रपञ्चितेन।

एवं प्रदर्शिते सादृश्ये प्रवर्तयामः कदानीं किल कालिदासेन काव्यमिदं विरचितमिति विचारमितुम्। काव्येऽस्मिन्नालोक्यते लेशतोऽपि कालिदासस्य प्रतिभा काव्यनिर्माणाभ्यासो वा। तस्मान्नासाम्प्रतमिदमभिधातुं यद्रचितमिदं कालिदासेनाभ्याससमय एवेति। न प्रभवतीदं तुलामप्यधिरोढुं श्रीहर्षविरचितस्य नैषधीयचरितस्य। क्व सा लोकात्तरा श्रीहर्षप्रतिभा क्व चाऽयमनुवादः पुराणानाम्। उपलभ्यते बहुषु पुराणेषु कुमारसंभवः। ततस्तत उद्धृत्य शब्दार्थजातं कालिदासेनात्र निबद्धमिति विस्तरशः प्रपञ्चयितुमुचितम्। तथाप्यवकाशाभावादत्र दिङ्मात्रमेव प्रदर्शितम्।

महागुरुवचःश्रेणीमकरन्दमधुव्रतः।
पर्यकार्षीज्जगन्नाथः कुमारस्य परीक्षणम्॥

(४) दण्डकौशलम्*

अध्यापक आह।

शिक्षा तथैव कर्तव्या यया सम्यक् प्रबुध्यते।

शिक्षितः प्राड्विवाकेन कुटीदाही धनी यथा ॥१॥ इति।

छात्रा ऊचुः। कथमेतत्। अध्यापकः प्रोवाच। श्रूयताम्।

मेदिन्याः कस्मिंश्चित्सुदूरे प्रदेशे सुरम्ये हर्म्ये कश्चिद्धनिको निवसति स्म। केवलमसौ पिबति खादति निद्राति क्रीडतीत्येतैः कर्मभिर्निजकालं यापयामास। तस्याज्ञासंपादकाः शुश्रूषमाणाः प्रीतिमन्तो बहवः परिचारका आसन्। नास्मै केनाप्युपदिष्टं सत्यम्। नावधारितमनेनापि। ततोऽनुपदिष्टसत्यो बहुकिङ्करत्वान्मदान्धतया चाहमेव जगदीश्वरो नान्यः कश्चन मत्तः प्रभुर्ममाराधनायैवैतेषामकिञ्चनानां जननमिति गुरुगर्वगुम्फितोऽभूत्।

श्रीमदान्धस्यैतस्य भवनान्नातिदूरे कश्चन निर्धनो वसति स्म। स द्रविणरहितोऽपि सत्यनिरत उद्योगनित्यश्चासीत्। तस्य गृहाङ्गणे शाद्वलभूमौ समुत्पन्नानि तृणविशेषाणि प्रच्छिद्यातपे शोषयित्वा तेषां करण्डान्नातिह्रस्वान्निर्माय स वृत्तिं कल्पयति स्म। अनवरतोद्योगमन्तरेण पर्याप्तां वृत्तिमलभमानः सूपौदनपोलिकान्नमन्तरा मिष्टान्नमखादमानः करण्डावशिष्टतृणशय्योऽपि सुखभाक् संतुष्टो मोदमानश्चासीत्। नित्योद्योगमूलाद्व्यायाम- बाहुल्यात्तत्कदन्नमप्येनं रुचिरमास्वादमुदपादयत्। स्वापे चापर्यङ्कायतभूमिः। तस्य सद्गुणैर्भूतेषु दयालुत्वाद्व्यवहारेषु प्रामाण्येन सत्यभाषणाभ्यासेन च प्रातिवेशिकास्तस्मिन् प्रीतिं कुर्वाणाः सादरा आसन्।

नित्योद्योगिनः करण्डकारस्य व्यायामो निद्रामुत्पादयति स्म। धनिकस्तु व्यायामाभावादालस्यातिशयेन च चन्द्रिकाधवलास्तरणयुक्तायामपि मृदुशय्यायां निद्रां नालभत। न चैव शशाकोच्चावचान् भक्ष्यभोज्यान् भोक्तुमध्यशनाद्व्यायामाभावादालस्येन वातभूयिष्ठे प्रदेशे विहरणाभावच्च। आलस्येनाध्यशनेन च सततमसौ रोगभूमिः। सर्वत्र दुष्कर्मणोऽस्य न कोऽपि मित्रम्। परोक्षमेनं भृत्या अपि निन्दन्ति स्म। अनेन पीडिताः प्रातिवेशिका अमुमद्विषन्। प्रमोदमानान् मानवानवलोक्यासौ तान् प्रद्वेष्टि स्म। बहुभिरेतैः कारणैरसौ पराङ्मुखसुखो बभूव।

धनिकस्तु शिबिकामास्थायानतिधनस्य करण्डानां निर्मातुरुटजासन्नेन मार्गेण चङ्क्रम्यमाण उटजद्वारि गायं गायं करण्डान् वयन्तं करण्डकारं विलोकयांबभूव। दर्शं दर्शं चैनं जातामर्षो विचारयामास। आश्चर्यमाश्चर्यम्।

हीने कुले समुत्पन्नो धनैर्विरहितः सदा॥

संतुष्टः सर्वदा भाति ग्राम्यो बुद्धिविवर्जितः ॥२॥

---

* Baroda College Magazine September, 1931.

कुले महति संजातः समृद्धो मतिमानहम् ॥
विषण्णो दीनवदनो विपरीता विधेः कृतिः ॥३ ॥

नक्तंदिवमस्मिन् विचारे निमग्नस्य तस्य करण्डानां कर्तरि समजनि सुमहान् द्वेषः। एवं करण्डकर्तुः सुखाधिक्यमसहमानोऽनिग्रहान्मनसस्तं परिपीडयितुमुपचक्रमे।

अथ निष्ठुरो धनिकः कस्यांचिद्रजन्यां दग्धव्या एते निर्धनगृहं परितो वर्तमानास्तृणविशेषाश्चेत्यादेशभंगभीरून् निदेशकारिण आदिदेश। तदनुरोधेन तैस्तृणविशेषान् परिसंदीपितो मरुत्सरवो जज्वाल। स हि सुतरामुष्णप्रदेशः। असौ च समयो निदाघस्य। सपद्येव तस्मात् समाक्रान्ता सा शाद्वलभूमिर्दहनेन। निःशेषं दग्धाश्च ते तृणविशेषाः। महता वेगेन प्रवर्धमानो विभावसुर्यावत्कुटीं दग्धुमाजगाम तावद्यदृच्छया प्रबुद्धः स करण्डकारः कुटीं परितो दंदह्यमानां विलोक्यानन्यगतिर्जीवितार्थी सर्वं परित्यज्य ससंभ्रमं पलायनं चकार।

ततो दरिद्रश्चिन्तयामास। अहो मयाऽस्य स्वप्नेऽपि नापकृतम्। किमर्थमकारणमनेन दग्धा मे वृत्तिः। अथवा नास्ति खलस्य परापकारे निमित्तापेक्षा। इत्येवं चिन्तयतस्तस्य धनरहितस्य कियन्महद्दुःखं कियदाश्चर्यं च संजातं तदवधार्यं सज्जनैः। अथवा साध्विदमुच्यते।

श्रीमद्दरिद्रयोर्लोके दुर्वृत्तः प्रायशो धनी ॥
निर्धनान् बाधते नित्यं दयाहीनः सुदुर्मतिः ॥४ ॥

कृतापराधं धनिकं दण्डयितुमसमर्थः सपदातिरेव स्वग्रामाधिकृतं प्राड्विवाकमुख्यं जगाम। तस्मै चाश्रुपूर्णाक्षोऽसौ कारुण्यमुत्पादयन्तं निखिलं वृत्तान्तं निवेदयामास। समनन्तरमेव तथ्यार्थवेदी सुशीलश्चाक्षदर्शकः सपद्येवापराधिनं धनिकं राजपुरुषैरानाययामास। तत आगत्य धनिकेन व्यवहाराणां द्रष्टुः समीपं स्वापराधः संप्रतिपन्नः। अथागतं धनिकं संप्रतिपन्नापराधं विलोक्य व्यवहारद्रष्टा दरिद्रमुवाच। श्रेष्ठमात्मानं मन्यमानो गर्वेणोद्धतो निर्धनान् सततं परिभावयन्नयं महान्तमेतमपराधं चक्रे। एतावती मे खलता तिरस्करणीयता लोकेष्वनुपयुक्तता चेति प्रत्यायनार्थमवश्यं शिक्षयितव्योऽयं मयेत्येतदर्थमुपायश्चिन्तितो भवताप्यनुमन्तव्यः। तथा हि।

दण्डस्तथैव कर्तव्यः स्वापराधं पुनर्यथा।
नैव कुर्यात् प्रबुध्येत सुवृत्तश्च सदा भवेत् ॥५ ॥

अतो यत्रोभयोर्गमनं मयाऽऽदिष्टं स्यात्तत्र स त्वयाऽनुगन्तव्य इति।

कारण्डकारः प्रत्युवाच। आर्य कदापि नासीन्मे पुष्कलं धनम्। यदप्यासीत्तृणविशेषभूतं जीविकासाधनं तदप्यधुना विनष्टम्। एवं सर्वस्वनाशात्समनन्तरसंजातक्षुधाप्रशमनोपायमन्विष्यन्नपि जगतीतलेऽस्मिन्नावलोकये। तस्मादुपस्थितमेव मेऽत्रभवद्भिराधिकरणिकचरणैरादिष्टे प्रदेशे गमनम्। तस्मिन्देशे कृतापराधेऽप्यस्मिन्न तथा भवामि यथामय्यसौ। अथ च सुखेनोपदेक्ष्याम्येनम्। कथं व्यवहर्तव्यं दीनेषु। किंच स्वरूपं भूतदयायाः। कियद्दुःखं च निर्धनानामेतादृशेनाकुलीकरणेनेति। ततो व्यवहारदर्शकस्तौ

नाव्यधिकृतान् नौकया विदेशं प्रापयितुमाज्ञापयामास। यत्र विनयहीना उटजवासिनो मत्स्यबन्धनेन वृत्तिं कुर्वाणा वनेचरा निवसन्ति स्म।

प्रधानेन साहसिकानां दण्डयित्रा यथाज्ञप्तास्ते कर्णधारास्तौ समुद्रस्य परं तीरं प्राप्य विदेशे व्यसृजन्। अथ च तस्मिन् देशे निवसद्भिराश्चर्येण विलोकयद्भिर्लोकैस्तौ परितः परिवेष्टितौ। धनिकस्तदा विचारयामास। हा धिक् कष्टम्। ग्राम्याः खल्वेते। नावगम्यते भाषाप्येतेषाम्। अथ नियंतारः। नात्र गोप्ता। न सहायः। किं कर्तव्यम्। इति हस्ताभ्यां भूमितलं ताडयन्नरोदीत्। आबाल्याल्परिचितसंकटस्तु करण्डकारश्चेष्टाभिस्तान् बोधयामास। मित्रं मामवगच्छथ। परिचरिष्यामि च भवतो यथाशक्तीति। एवंप्रतीत्य लोकैरपि संकेतैस्तौ परिज्ञापितौ। न भविष्यति युययोः पीडालेशोऽपि। काष्ठानयने मत्स्यानां च बंधने केवलं युवामुपयोक्ष्याम इति।

ततस्ते विपिनेचरास्तौ समीपवर्ति काननं नीत्वा दर्शयामासुः कानिचित्स्थूलकाष्ठानि। अज्ञाप्तौ च तैः। उटजं प्रति नेतव्यान्येतानीति। तदनु ताभ्यामारब्धं काष्ठवहनम्। बलवान् शीघ्रकारी दरिद्रो यावन्निजकार्यं समापितवान् तावदनभ्यस्तपरिश्रमो बलहीनो धनिको निजकार्यपादमपि नानुष्ठितवान्। प्रत्यक्षीकृत्यैतद्वनेचरैरभिहितम्। अहो बहूपयुक्तं करण्डकारेण। न धनिकेनेति। अतस्ते करण्डकाराय बहून् मत्स्यान् स्वादूनि च मूलानि प्रददुः। धनिकाय तु किंचित्प्रतिपादितम्। तथापि न तेन तस्य क्षुधा शशाम। बहुकालमनभ्यवहारात् संजातक्षुधोऽसौ तदपि भक्षयामास। गृहे निवसतोऽस्य नैतादृशी क्षुधा।

अपरस्मिन्नप्यहनि तौ पुनः काष्ठाहरणाय प्रस्थितौ। करण्डकारेणातीते दिवसे काष्ठनयनं यथा स्वल्पेन कालेन समीचीनतया समापितं तथाऽस्मिन्नपि दिवसे। आलस्यशीलो धनिकस्तु श्रमासहिष्णुत्वात् पूर्वस्मिन् दिन इव कार्यपादमपि कर्तुं न शशाक। इत्यालोच्य करण्डकारेण सह बहुमानपुरःसरं लोकानां व्यवहारः। धनिकस्तु लोकैरनेकप्रकारैः परिभूतः।

एवं जातपरिभवेन धनिकेनाहो लघिष्ठैव मे मतिर्मया मिथ्याभूतामीश्वरोऽहमिति कल्पनामुररीकृत्य तिरस्कृताः सर्वे बान्धवा परिजनाश्चेत्यवधारितम्। समनन्तरभाविना वृत्तेन च तद् दृढीकृतम्। अत्रान्तरे वनेचरेषु केनचित् पट्टिकासदृशं किंचिदुपलब्धम्। अलंकृतं च तेन स्वशिरः। ततश्चासा अहो कीदृशी मे शोभा संजातेति विस्मयाविष्टो जातः। करण्डकारस्त्वनलङ्कारमलङ्कारं मन्वानं तं विलोक्य तृणविशेषानुत्पाट्य रमणीयां मालां तैर्निर्माय समनन्तरमेव लोचनविषयं यातस्य जनस्य शिरो भूषयांचक्रे। तया मालया मुदितोऽसौ सहर्षं ननर्त। इतस्ततश्चोत्प्लुत्य लोकानुपगम्य दर्शयामास। रुचिरमभिनवं चैतद् भूषणमवलोक्य विस्मिताः सर्वे। तेष्वपरः कश्चिदल्पेन कालेन करण्डाकारमेत्य चेष्टाभिस्तं बोधयामास। वाञ्छामि यथा मे सखा शिरोभूषणेन भूषितस्तथाऽहमप्यनुग्राह्य इति। एवं सर्वे जानपदा मालास्वौत्सुक्यं प्रकटीकृत्य मोचयित्वा करण्डकारं काष्ठाहरणान् मालाग्रथने व्यापारयामासुः। यः समजनि संतोषो मालाभिर्जानपदानां तस्य कृतवेदितया दयालुतया च करण्डकाराय तत्रोत्पन्नानि नानाविधान्यन्नानि प्रतिपाद्य निवासाय कुटीं निर्माय विनिमयं चक्रुः। अथ च सर्वे लोका मालाकांक्षिणोऽभूवन्। तेषां सर्वेषां मालाकाक्षां समर्थयितुं निर्बलं बुद्धिहीनं च धनिकं

तृणविशेषोत्पाटनरूपां शिक्षां विधाय करण्डकारस्य दास्यत्वे नियोजयामासुः।

एवंवर्तमानयोस्तयोरतीताः केचिन्मासाः। तदनु प्रधानव्यवहारदर्शकाज्ञया तौ स्वदेशं प्राप्य रक्षिभिस्तत्पुरत आनीतौ। ततः प्राड्विवाको धनिकं सक्रोधमाह। ईदृशी ते दुर्जनता दुर्बलता मित्रहीनता त्वया पीडितादस्मात्करण्डकाराल्लघुता चेति त्वामवगमय्य त्वया पीडितायास्मै सुखं विधातुमुपक्रम इति। यस्मान्निर्धनस्यास्य सर्वस्वं त्वया विनाशितं तस्मात्तव सर्वस्याःसंपत्तेरादानं चेद्भविष्यत्तदैव दोषार्हो दण्डोऽभविष्यत्। तथाप्यतः साधुवृत्तिर्भविष्यसीत्याशास्यादिश्यते। त्वया पीडितायास्मै त्वदीयार्धसंपत्तिर्दातव्येति।

तदाकर्ण्य प्रशस्य चादेशं दण्डयितुरपराधानां करण्डकारः प्राह। आर्य समुत्पत्तिर्मे दरिद्राणां कुले। संवर्धितश्च दारिद्य्र एव। नित्यमभ्यासः परिश्रमस्य। किं मे धनेन। न हि जानामि तदुपयोगम्। केवलमभ्यर्थये यथापूर्वमसौ मे जीविकासाधनं दापयितव्यो भूतेष्वनुकम्पयितव्यश्चेति। विलोक्य वदान्यतामेतां करण्डकारस्य विस्मितो धनिकः। इतः परमपराधदण्डदुःखसंजातानुभवोऽसौ न केवलं करण्डकारमेव मित्रमिवामन्यत किन्तु सर्वानन्यान् निर्धनान् स्वजनांश्च सुखयितुं स्वधनमुपयोजयामास। अतोऽहं ब्रवीमि।

शिक्षा तथैव कर्तव्या यया सम्यक् प्रबुध्यते।
शिक्षितः प्राड्विवाकेन कुटीदाही धनी यथा॥ इति॥६॥

बोधाय द्रविणान्धानामुज्ज्वलं दण्डकौशलम्।
अवर्णयज्जगन्नाथः पदेशास्त्रिकुलोद्भवः॥७॥

APPENDIX-III
HINDI ARTICLE
फलज्योतिषका प्रामाण्यवाद*

आकाशीय ग्रहस्थिति से व्यक्ति और विश्व का इष्ट और अनिष्ट फल जिस शास्त्र के आधार पर बताया जाता है, उसे 'फलित ज्योतिषशास्त्र' कहते हैं। यह शास्त्र वैदिक-काल से प्रचलित है। यह अथर्ववेद के कालसूक्त (१९ ।५३-५४) और शुक्लयजुर्वेदीय माध्यन्दिन-संहिता के निम्नलिखित मन्त्रों से प्रमाणित होता है:

> **'प्रज्ञानाय नक्षत्रदर्शमाशिक्षायै प्रश्निनमुपशिक्षाया अभिप्रश्निनं मर्यादायै प्रश्नविवाकम्।' (शुक्लयजुः० ३० ।२०) 'ग्रामण्यं गणकमभिकोशकं तान् महसे।'**
>
> **(यजुः० ३० ।२०)**

इस शास्त्र का उत्तरोत्तर विकास होता गया और आज भी होता जा रहा है।

शास्त्रों का सिद्धान्त है कि ग्रह ही स्थावर, जंगमात्मक जगत् के इष्टानिष्ट फलों के कारण हैं। यही सिद्धान्त महर्षि याज्ञवल्क्य ने निम्नलिखित श्लोक (याज्ञ० १ ।३०८) से कहा है:

> **'ग्रहाधीना नरेन्द्राणामुच्छ्रायाः पतनानि च।**
> **भावाभावौ च जगतस्तस्मात् पूज्यतमा ग्रहाः।'**

धर्मसूत्र मे महर्षि गौतम ने भी यही माना है: **'यानि दैवोत्पातचिन्तकाः प्रब्रूयुस्तान्याद्रियेत, तदधीनमपि ह्येके योगक्षेमं प्रतिजानीते।'** कौटिल जैसे प्राचीन अर्थशास्त्रकार ने भी इस शास्त्र को मान्यता दी है।

फलितज्यौतिष शास्त्र है और शास्त्र होने से उसके प्रमेयों का सप्रमाण विचार किया गया हैं। यदि इस शास्त्र के सिद्धान्त अप्रमाण होते तो इसे शास्त्रत्व ही न प्राप्त होता। इसलिए इस शास्त्र के प्रति कथमपि अप्रमाण्यशंका को अवकाश नहीं है।

विश्व में अनुभूयमान इष्टानिष्ट फलों की कारणमीमांसा चिरकाल से दार्शनिक आचार्य करते आ रहे हैं। जिसे जैसा दीखा, उसने अपने दर्शन में उसकी वैसी ही मीमांसा की। अतएव दर्शन-भेद से सिद्धान्त-भेद खड़ा हुआ। न्यायसूत्र (१-१-२७) में सर्वतन्त्र सिद्धान्त, प्रतितन्त्र सिद्धान्त, अधिकरण सिद्धान्त और अभ्युपगम सिद्धान्त ये चार प्रकार के सिद्धान्त माने गये हैं। सभीतन्त्रों = शास्त्रों द्वारा मान्य सिद्धान्त सर्वतन्त्र सिद्धान्त कहा जाता है। 'इष्टानिष्टफलप्राप्ति के एकमात्र कारण ग्रह ही हैं, ज्योतिष का यह सिद्धान्त सभी तन्त्र मान लेते तो यह सर्वतन्त्र-सिद्धान्त बन जाता और उसके प्रामाण्य के लिए विचार का कारण ही

---

* सिद्धान्त, वाराणसी, वर्ष १७, अंक १२ पृष्ठ ४९३-४९६ और वर्ष १८, अंक १, १९६४, पृष्ठ १४-२०

शेष न रहता। किन्तु केवल ज्योतिषशास्त्र ने ही यह सिद्धान्त माना और अन्य दर्शनों ने इसे मान्यता नहीं दी, इसलिए यह प्रतितन्त्र सिद्धान्त बन गया है। इसी कारण यह सन्देह होता है। इस संशय के निराकारणार्थ ज्योतिष का यह सिद्धान्त प्रमाण है या अप्रमाण, इसका विचार करना आवश्यक है।

प्राचीन दर्शनशास्त्र में चार वाद प्रसिद्ध हैं : १. कर्मवाद, २. कालवाद, ३. दैववाद और ४. स्वभाववाद। मीमांसकों का कथन है कि इष्टानिष्ट-फलप्राप्ति का एकमात्र कारण ही कर्म है। काल ही कारण है, यह ज्योतिषियों का मत है। दैववादी उपासक मानते हैं कि देवताओं के निग्रहानुग्रहही इसके कारण है। और चार्वाकादि नास्तिक स्वभाव को ही कारण बतलाते हैं। किन्तु फलप्राप्ति में ये चारों ही कारण हैं। कोई एक ही नहीं। तथापि कर्म इनमें प्रधान कारण है, यह भगवत्पाद श्री शङ्कराचार्य का सिद्धान्त है। फलितज्योतिष के सिद्धान्त की प्रस्थापना करते समय विरोधी सिद्धान्तों की समीक्षा आवश्यक होने से उसी क्रम से विचार करते हुए प्रकृत विषय पर आयें, यही उचित होगा।

सुख-प्राप्ति और दुःखपरिहार के लिए प्राणी अहोरात्र व्यग्र रहता है। तदर्थ वह कर्म करता और उचित समय पर उसका फल पाता है, तो मानने लगता है कि एकमात्र कर्म ही फलप्राप्ति का हेतु है। संसार में कुछ लोग जन्मतः सुखी तो कुछ जन्मतः दुःखी दीख पड़ते हैं। इस जन्म का कोई भी कर्म उनके दिखने वाले इन सुख-दुःखों का कारण मालूम नहीं पड़ता। 'कर्म ही फलप्राप्ति का कारण है' इस सिद्धान्त की उपपत्ति यहाँ बिना कर्म माने बैठ नहीं सकती, एतदर्थ पुनर्जन्मवाद मानना पड़ता है और जन्मान्तरीय कर्मों से उन सुख-दुःखों की उपपत्ति लगायी जाती है। कर्म, फल और उनका सम्बन्ध सनातन नियमों से बद्ध है। यदि इनमें कोई नियम न होता तो चाहे जिस कर्म से चाहे जो फल मिलता। सत्कर्म का फल दुःख और असत्कर्म का फल सुख मिलता। किन्तु अमुक कर्म, का फल अमुक ही मिलता है, यह नियम होने से वैसी आपत्ति नहीं आती। जिन नियमों से ये कर्म, फल एवं कर्मफलसम्बन्ध बद्ध हैं, वे नित्य हैं और पौरुषेय यानी पुरुषप्रणीत नहीं हैं। इन सनातन नियमों का विचार कर जिस शास्त्र में कर्माकर्म का प्रतिपादन किया है, उन्हें भी नित्य और अपौरुषेय मानना पड़ता है। वेदों में कर्माकर्म का विचार कर विधिनिषेध बताये जाने से मीमांसक उन्हें अपौरुषेय मानते हैं। जो दार्शनिक विश्व को ईश्वरनिर्मित मानते हैं, उन्हें वे नियम ही ईश्वरप्रणीत मानने पड़ते हैं। उन नियमों के अनुसार कर्मप्रतिपादक वेदों को भी ईश्वरप्रणीत मानना पड़ता है। वेदों में

'पुण्यो वै पुण्येन कर्मणा भवति पापः पापेन'

जैसे अनेक श्रुतिवाक्य होने से मीमांसको का मत है कि कर्म फलप्राप्ति के कारण हैं।

कर्म ही फलप्राप्ति का कारण है और फल दिये बिना नहीं रहता — यह मीमांसकों का सिद्धान्त होने पर भी कर्मों का फल मिलने में कितना काल लगता है, इस सम्बन्ध में उन्होंने कोई विचार नहीं किया। फल की दृष्टि से कर्मों का विचार करने पर कुछ कर्म सद्यः फलप्रद

होते हैं, कुछ का फल कालान्तर से मिलता है, तो कुछ जन्मभर फल नहीं देते। कर्म का फल बिना मिले नहीं रहता। शेष कर्मों का फल जन्मान्तर में भी मिलता है। इसी तरह इस जन्म के किसी भी तरह के कर्म के बिना जन्मान्तरीय कर्मों से सुख-दुःख की प्राप्ति होती है। कर्मों के इन स्वभावों के आधार पर उनके तीन भेद किये जाते हैं। (१) जो कर्म फल दिये बगैर बैठा रहता है, उसे 'संचित' कहते हैं। (२) जो फलोन्मुख होकर फल देने लगता है, उसे 'प्रारब्ध', कहते हैं। और (३) जो कर्म किया जाता है, उसे 'क्रियमाण' कहते हैं।

कर्मों को फलोन्मुख होने के लिए कुछ काल लगता है। अनेक जन्मों के सञ्चित कर्मों में से कौन फलोन्मुख होते हैं और कौन जन्मान्तर में फलोन्मुख होने लिए पड़े रहते हैं, इस विषय में कर्मवादियों का सिद्धान्त है कि सञ्चित कर्मों में जितने कर्मों के पाकोन्मुख होने में जन्मकाल अनुकूल होता है, उतने ही कर्म पाकोन्मुख होते है, शेष जन्मान्तर में फल देने के लिए बधे रहते हैं। जन्मकाल के अनुरोध से जो कर्म फलोन्मुख हुए, उनका फल जन्मभर भोगना पड़ता है और इसीको 'प्रारब्ध' कहते हैं। सञ्चित के शेष कर्मों का फल नहीं मिलता वह जन्मान्तर में मिलता है। क्रियमाण कर्मों का फल भी कुछ समय से मिलता है। इस तरह प्रारब्ध का अर्थ है, पूर्वजन्म के फलोन्मुख कर्म।

कर्मवादियों के इस सिद्धान्त का थोड़ा सूक्ष्म परीक्षण करें। वे मानते हैं कि कर्म के फलोन्मुख होने में काल अपेक्षित होता है। प्रारब्ध का विचार करते समय वे यह सिद्धान्त बताते हैं कि सञ्चित में से जितने कर्मों के लिए जन्मकाल अनुकूल होता है, उतने ही पाकोन्मुख होते हैं। कर्मवादी 'काल' शब्द का प्रयोग कर मुक्त हो जाते हैं। काल-विचार उनकी कक्षा से बहिर्भूत होने से वे उसका विशेष विचार नहीं करते। किन्तु थोड़ा सूक्ष्म विचार करने पर स्पष्ट होगा कि आकाशीय ग्रहस्थिति के आधार पर ही काल-गणना होती है। यथा : रवि-चन्द्र के १२ अंश अन्तर से तिथि, चन्द्र से मास, रवि से सौर मास और सौर वर्ष की गणना होती है। इसलिए 'काल' शब्द का अर्थ 'आकाशीय ग्रहस्थिति' ही होता है। इस पर से जन्मकाल यानी जन्मकालीन ग्रहस्थिति यही सीधा अर्थ होता हैं । यानी सञ्चित में से जितने कर्मों का जन्मकाल (यानी जन्मकालीन ग्रहस्थिति) फलोन्मुख होने के अनुकूल रहता है, उतने ही कर्म फलोन्मुख होकर वह उनका प्रारब्ध बनता है। अर्थात् जन्मकालीन ग्रहस्थिति ही सञ्चित कर्मों के फलोन्मुख होने का मुख्य कारण है। मीमांसकों के सिद्धान्त से यही अभिप्राय निकलता है।

जन्मकालीन ग्रहस्थिति कर्म के फलोन्मुख होने का मुख्य कारण होने से उस ग्रहस्थिति का विचार किये बिना इस जन्म के प्रारब्ध कर्म और उससे प्राप्त होनेवाले सुख-दुःखादि फलों का बोध सम्भव नहीं। सुख या दुःख प्राप्त होने पर और उसे इस जन्म का कर्म कारण रूप में न मिले तो पूर्वजन्म का कर्म कारण है, ऐसा कर्मवादी कह सकता है। किन्तु वह इस जन्म के सुख-दुःखादि फलों की कल्पना जन्मकाल में कर नहीं सकेगा। ग्रहस्थिति उपर्युक्त प्रकार से प्रारब्ध का कारण होने से उस ग्रहस्थिति पर से ही प्रारब्ध की निश्चित क़ल्पना की जा

सकती है। इस तरह कर्मवाद में काल यानीं ग्रहस्थित कर्म को फलोन्मुख करने का कारण होने से परम्परया फल में भी वहीं कारण है, यह विवशतः मानना पड़ेगा। कर्मवाद का सूक्ष्म विचार करने पर फल कर्म का मिलता है, पर उसके मिलने का मुख्य कारण काल यानी ग्रह हैं, यही सिद्धान्त स्थिर होता है। योग्य काल के अभाव में कर्म फलोन्मुख न होने से काल ही फलप्राप्ति का मुख्य कारण है—कालवादियों का यह सिद्धान्त, कर्मवाद के आधार पर दृढ़ होता है।

जन्मकाल या जन्मकालीन ग्रहस्थिति के अनुरोध से निश्चित प्रारब्ध कर्म का इष्टानिष्ट फल सभी को निश्चित रूप से प्राप्त होता है या नहीं, इसका कर्मवाद के अनुसार विचार करना आवश्यक है।

'भोगेन त्वितरे क्षपयित्वा सम्पद्यन्ते।' **(ब्रह्मसूत्र ४-१.१९)**

इस सूत्र के अनुसार मुमुक्षु प्रारब्ध कर्मों का क्षय भोग से ही करते हैं। प्रारब्ध का भोग न करने पर पुनः जन्म लेना पड़ता है, इसलिए वे प्रारब्ध का प्रतीकार करने की तनिक चेष्टा नहीं करते। उन्हें सञ्चित या क्रियमाण का फल आगे भोगना नहीं पड़ता। मुक्तों के शेष भोग्य कर्मों का नाश भी नहीं होता। कर्म का फल बिना मिले नहीं रहता और मुक्तों के लिए उनका भोग सम्भव नहीं, इसलिए उनके सत्कर्मों का फल उनके दायादों को और असत्कर्मों का फल उनके शत्रुओं को भुगतना पड़ता है। प्रारब्ध मात्र स्वयं उन्हें ही भोगना पड़ता है। किन्तु साधारण जन प्रारब्धप्राप्त अनिष्टफलोंका प्रतीकार करने के लिए दैवी और मानुष उभय प्रकार के उपाय करते हैं, जिससे उनके अनिष्ट फलों का परिहार होता है। इससे यह निष्कर्ष निकलता है कि कर्मवाद के अनुसार जन्मकाल या जन्मकालीन ग्रहस्थिति से निश्चित प्रारब्ध कर्मों का सुख-दुःख रूप फल मुमुक्षुओं के विषय में ठीक-ठीक उतरता है और अन्य लोगों के विषय में उनके क्रियमाण से उसमें कुछ अन्तर पड़ सकता है। इसका विशेष विचार आगे किया जायगा।

ऊपर विवेचित कर्मवाद से निम्नलिखित निष्कर्ष निकलता है।

(१) इहजन्म में प्राप्त होनेवाला सुख-दुःख जन्मान्तरीय कर्मों का फल है।

(२) जन्मान्तर में कृत कर्म का सुख-दुःखादि फल इस जन्म में प्राप्त होने में जन्मकाल या जन्मकालीन ग्रहस्थिति ही कारण है।

(३) जन्मकालीन ग्रहस्थिति से प्रारब्ध कर्म कर्मफल या प्रारब्ध की निश्चित कल्पना की जा सकती है।

(४) ग्रहस्थिति से निश्चित फल, प्रारब्ध भोग के द्वारा निःशेष करनेवाले योगियों में अचूक सत्य ठहरता है।

(५) साधारण मानव के विषय में क्रियमाण कर्म से प्रतिबन्ध होने से प्रारब्ध बदलता जाता है और ग्रहस्थिति के आधार पर निर्धारित भविष्य पूरा-पूरा ठीक नहीं उतरता।

इससे यह अर्थ निकलता है कि फलित ज्यौतिष प्रमाणभूत शास्त्र है,उसकी निश्चित कल्पना ग्रहों के आधार पर की जा सकती है और प्रतिबन्ध न होने पर उसके द्वारा फल निश्चित ठीक उतरता है।

पूर्ववर्णित कर्मवाद की तरह 'दैववाद' भी एक बलवत्तर वाद है। किन्तु आज इस वाद के पुरस्कर्ता अधिक नहीं है। साधारणतः लोग दैववाद का अर्थ प्रारब्धवाद भी समझते हैं और ऐसा मानने में कुछ प्रमाण भी है। किन्तु दैव का अर्थ पूर्वजन्मीय कर्मों से प्राप्त होनेवाले सुख-दुःख मान लेने पर कर्मवाद और दैववाद में कुछ अन्तर ही नहीं रह जाता। शास्त्रों में वर्णित दैववाद कर्मवाद न होकर एक स्वतन्त्रवाद है।

मीमांसकों के कर्मवाद का कर्म अचेतन होने से वह फल नहीं दे सकता। उसके द्वारा स्वीकृत 'अपूर्व' भी अचेतन है। फलतः उससे भी फलप्राप्ति संभव नहीं। दोनों फल प्रदान में असमर्थ होने से वेदान्ती 'ईश्वर से फलप्राप्ति' का सिद्धान्त स्थापित करते हैं। यह सिद्धान्त ब्रह्मसूत्र के—

'फलमत उपपत्तेः' (३-२-३८), **'श्रुतत्वाच्च** (३-२-३९), **'धर्मं जैमिनिरत एव'** (३-२-४०), **'पूर्वं तु बादरायणो हेतुव्यपदेशात्'** (३-२-४१)

इन चार सूत्रों द्वारा प्रस्थापित किया गया है। इसी तरह आदित्य-मण्डलान्तर्वर्ती पुरुष ही ईश्वर है, यह बात—

'अन्तस्तद्धर्मोपदेशात्।'(१-१-२०)
भेदव्यपदेशाच्चान्यः।' (१-१-२१)

इन दो सूत्रों द्वारा तथा—

'स यश्चायं पुरुषे यश्चासावादित्ये' (तैत्तिउप० २।८) जैसे अनेक श्रुतिवाक्यों द्वारा बताया गया है।

ऋग्वेद के 'सर्वानुक्रमसूत्र' में आरम्भ में ही देवता का विचार करते समय सभी देवों का अन्तर्भाव अग्नि, वायु और सूर्य इन तीन देवों में किया गया है और अन्त में एक ही देव है और वही परमात्मा है, यह कहा गया है—'सूर्य आत्मा जगतस्तस्थुषश्च।' सभी देव इसीकी विभूतियाँ हैं, यह भी कहा गया है। इस परमात्मरूप सूर्यनारायण की उपासना 'शतपथ-ब्राह्मण' (१०।५।२) में विस्तार से बतायी गयी है। वहाँ २०वीं कण्डिका में—

'तमेतमग्निरित्यध्वर्यव उपासते, यजुरित्येष हीदं सर्वं युनक्ति,

सामेति च्छन्दोगा एतस्मिन् हीदं सर्वं समानम्।' कहा गया है। अर्थात् अध्वर्यु उसकी अग्निरूप से, और छन्दोग सामरूप से उपासना करते हैं तथा वह वैसा ही रूप धारण कर रक्षा करता है। भगवद्गीता के **'यो यो यां यां तनुं भक्तः'** इस श्लोक का भी यही आशय है।—'शतपथ' की इसी २०वीं कण्डिका में—

यातुरिति यातुविद एतेन हीदं सर्वं यतम्।' कहा गया है। 'यातुविदः' यानी अथर्ववेदी

लोग इस ईश्वर की 'यातु' रूप में उपासना करते हैं। कारण इस ईश्वर ने यह स्थावर जंगमात्मक समस्त जगत् नियमित किया है। ईश्वर सबका शास्ता है और वही सबका नियमन करता है। इसीलिए अथर्ववेदी उसके इसी स्वरूप की उपासना करते हैं और ईश्वर की इस नियन्तृत्वशक्ति के बल पर अपने मन्त्रों से चाहे जैसा निग्रहानुग्रह कर पाते है। यहाँ टीकाकारों ने—

'यातुर्नाम अथर्वणवेदप्रमेयं नानाविधप्रयोगलक्षणम्' यह 'यातु' शब्द का अर्थ किया है। 'यातु' शब्द का उच्चारण माध्यन्दिन 'जातु' करते हैं और उसी पर से 'जादू' शब्द बना है। ईश्वर में निग्रहानुग्रह की अचिन्त्य शक्ति हैं। इस शक्ति का उपयोग कर अथर्ववेत्ताओं के निग्रहानुग्रह-प्रयोग सिद्ध होते हैं। इन प्रयोगों से असाध्य बातें भी साध्य हो सकती हैं और मानव इष्ट-प्राप्ति और अनिष्ट परिहार कर लेता है।

इससे यह स्पष्ट होता है कि फल देना ईश्वर के अधीन होने से उसकी विभिन्न रूपों में उपासना करने पर उसके प्रसाद से इष्टफल प्राप्त किया जा सकता है। इसके लिए कर्मादि की अपेक्षा नहीं रहती। अथर्ववेद का उपयोग इष्ट-प्राप्ति और अनिष्ट-परिहार के लिए ही है। ईश्वर से फल मिलता है, यह दैववाद का सिद्धान्त है। इस वाद में अथर्ववेदीय उपासना का महत्त्व है और उसीसे फलप्राप्ति हो सकती है।

आज अथर्ववेद के प्रयोग पीछे पड़ गये हैं। उनका स्थान तन्त्रशास्त्रों ने ले लिया है। तान्त्रिक प्रयोग करनेवाले और उनके बल पर असाध्य फल साध्य कर दिखानेवाले तान्त्रिक आज भी हमारे बीच विद्यमान हैं। जिन्होंने उन प्रयोगों का अनुभव किया है, उन्हें देवता के प्रसाद से असाध्य बातें भी सिद्ध कर लेने के विषय में संदेह नहीं हो सकता। जब मानवीय प्रयत्न की पराकाष्ठा हो जाने पर भी कार्य नहीं होता, ज्योतिष से भी आपत्ति-निरास का अन्त समझ में नहीं आता, उस समय देवतानुग्रह का उपयोग होता और आपत्ति मिट जाती है। अलङ्कारशास्त्र के तर्करसिक अर्वाचीन ग्रन्थकार पण्डितराज जगन्नाथ के 'रस-गङ्गाधर' की निम्नलिखित पंक्ति से स्पष्ट दीख पड़ेगा कि उन दिनों तन्त्रशास्त्र का कितना प्रभाव और प्रचार था—

'तस्याश्च हेतुः क्वचिद्देवता-महापुरुषप्रसादादिजन्यमदृष्टम्।... प्रतिवादिना मन्त्रादिभिः कृते कतिपयदिवसव्यापिनि वाक्स्तम्भे विहितानेकप्रबन्धस्यापि कवेः काव्यानुदयस्य दर्शनात्।'

इस उल्लेख से स्पष्ट दीखता है कि पण्डितराज के समय से विलक्षण व्युत्पत्ति या काव्य-निर्माण करने के अभ्यास के अभाव में केवल देवताप्रसाद या महापुरुष-प्रसाद से छोटे-छोटे बालकों में भी प्रतिभा का उदय होता आ रहा है। मन्त्रों से वाणी का विरोध (वाक्स्तम्भ) करने का भी उन दिनों प्रचार था।

इससे स्पष्ट है कि फलप्राप्ति के लिए ईश्वर या उसकी विभूति देवताओं का प्रसाद कारण है। इसे ही 'दैववाद' करते है। दैववाद न मानने पर अथर्ववेद और तन्त्रशास्त्र निरर्थक हो

जायेंगे। जिन पर देवता का अनुग्रह होता है और जो उसके बल पर इष्टसाधन कर लेते हैं, उनकी फलप्राप्ति का कारण ईश्वर या देवता हैं, यही सिद्ध होता है।

दैववाद के पश्चात् 'स्वभाववाद' भी एक स्वतन्त्र वाद है। किन्तु उसे चार्वाकादि नास्तिकों ने माना है और अभ्युदय-निश्रेयस के लिए उससे कोई लाभ भी नहीं। अतएव यहाँ उसका विचार नहीं किया जाता। 'काल-वाद' ज्यौतिषशास्त्र का वाद है और आगे उसी पर विचार किया जायगा।

भगवान् शङ्कराचार्य ने बृहदारण्यक उपनिषद् के भाष्य में इन सभी वादों का विचारकर अपना ऐसा सिद्धान्त स्पष्ट किया है, जो सर्वसामान्य सा और सभी शास्त्रों के उपयोग में आनेवाला है। आचार्य का भाष्य, उस पर सुरेश्वराचार्य का वार्तिक और उस वार्तिक की आनन्दगिरि व्याख्या से यह विषय पूर्ण स्पष्ट हो जाता है। अतएव यहां उन्हें दिया जा रहा है :

"मैव कारकं नान्यत् फलप्राप्ताविति केचित्। दैवमेवेत्यपरे। काल इत्येके। द्रव्यादिस्वभाव इति केचित्। सर्वे एते संहता इत्यपरे। तत्र कर्मणः प्राधान्यमङ्गीकृत्य वेदस्मृतिवादाः, 'पुण्यो वै पुण्येन कर्मणा भवति पापः पापेन' इत्यादयः। यद्यपि एषां स्वविषये कस्यचित् प्राधान्योद्भवः, इतरेषां तत्कालीनप्राधान्यशक्तिस्तम्भः, तथापि न कर्मणः फलप्राप्तिं प्रति अनैकान्तिकत्वम्। शास्त्रन्यायनिर्धारितत्वात् कर्मप्राधान्यस्य।"

(बृहदारण्यकोपनिषद्-भाष्य, १.४-१०)

'कर्मैव कारणं केचित् फलप्राप्तौ प्रचक्षते।
दैवमेके परे कालं स्वभाव इति चापरे ॥१४८७

श्रुतयः स्मृतिवादश्च कर्मप्राधन्यमेव तु।
अङ्गीकृत्य प्रदृश्यन्ते प्रवृत्ताः सर्व एव हि ॥१४८८

पुण्यः पुण्येन भवति पापः पापेन कर्मणा।
वचांस्येवं सुबहुशो लक्ष्यन्ते शास्त्रभूमिषु ॥१४८९

य अप्येवं स्वविषये प्राधान्यं कस्यचित् क्वचित्।
अप्राधान्यं तदन्येषां तथापि तु न कर्मणाम्।
फलप्राप्तावहेतुत्वं शास्त्रन्यायावधारणात् ॥१४९०

(भाष्यवार्तिक, १-४)

'भ्रान्तिहेतुविप्रतिपत्तिमाह। कर्मेति एवकारो हेत्वन्तरनिरासार्थः। केचिदिति मीमांसकग्रहणम्। 'दैवमेव परं मन्ये पौरुषं तु निरर्थकम्' इति न्यायेन देवताकाण्डीयमतमुक्तं दैवमिति। ज्योतिःशास्त्रविदामङ्गीकारं दर्शयति अपर इति। स्वभाववादस्तु लोकायतादिभिरङ्गीकृतः।'

(आनन्दगिरि-व्याख्या, वार्तिक १४८७-९०)

उपर्युक्त भाष्य में आचार्य ने प्रथम चार वादों का निर्देश किया है। इन चारों वादों के सिद्धान्त लोक और शास्त्र में प्रसिद्ध हैं। कर्म फल देता है, यह आबाल-वृद्ध जानते हैं। ईश्वर की शक्ति अचिन्त्य होने से कर्मफल देने और विघ्न उत्पन्न करने का सामर्थ्य ईश्वर में है। इसी तरह काल, मन्त्र, औषध और तप का सामर्थ्य भी अचिन्त्य है। इस तरह अनेक पक्ष होते हुए भी फल कर्म का ही मिलता है। कर्म के बिना काल, दैव आदि कुछ नहीं कर सकते। इसी तरह काल और ईश्वर की शक्ति अचिन्त्य होने पर भी वे कर्मफल का विपर्यास नहीं कर सकते। यानी वे बुरे कर्मों का फल अच्छा और अच्छे कर्मों का फल बुरा नहीं दे सकते। अकेला कर्म भी फल नहीं दे पाता, उसे कालादि की अपेक्षा रहती ही है। इस तरह कर्म, काल, दैव और स्वभाव परस्पर सापेक्ष होने से कभी कर्म प्रधान होता है। तो कभी दैव। साधारण जनता को इनका गौण-प्राधान्यभाव ध्यान में नहीं आता; अतएव व्यामोह उत्पन्न होता है। फलतः तरह-तरह के वाद उत्पन्न होते हैं।वस्तुतः सभी कारण हैं और कर्म से ही फल मिलता है। अतः इनमें कर्म ही प्रधान है, यही सिद्धान्त है। आचार्य शङ्कर का यह सिद्धान्त मान लेने पर सभी शास्त्रों की निर्बाध उपपत्ति हो जाती है और कहीं कठिनाई नहीं पड़ती।

इसी तरह यहाँ कर्मवाद, दैववाद, स्वभाववाद का विचारकर आचार्य ने संक्षेप में श्रौत सिद्धान्त बता दिया। इस सिद्धान्त के आधार पर अब फलित ज्यौतिष के प्रामाण्य का विचार करें। फलित ज्यौतिष में काल ही फलप्राप्ति का मुख्य कारण माना जाता है। इस कालवाद में फल कर्म का ही मिलता है, इस विषय में कोई विवाद नहीं। किन्तु ऊपर कर्मवाद के विवेचनानुसार फलप्राप्ति होने में काल या ग्रहस्थिति ही कारण है। कर्म काल के बिना फल नहीं दे सकता, इसलिए काल प्रधान हो जाता है और कर्म गौण। जन्मकाल से निश्चित फल मुमुक्षुओं के विषय में ठीक-ठीक उतरता है, इसका कर्मवाद में विवेचन किया जा चुका है। मात्र कर्मवाद की तरह क्रियमाण कर्म से प्रारब्ध के परिवर्तन का अवसर आता है, उससे निश्चित फल में अन्तर पड़ जाता है। यह अन्तर होने से कर्ममार्गी सामान्य जनता के विषय में फलित ज्योतिष के अप्रामाण्य होने की आपत्ति आती है। इसलिए ज्यौतिष की दृष्टि से इसीका विशेष विचार कर्तव्य हो जाता है।

ज्यौतिषशास्त्र के आधार पर जीवन के इष्ट-अनिष्ट फलों की प्राप्ति का ज्ञान हो जाने पर मानवमात्र का झुकाव उस अनिष्ट के प्रतीकार की ओर स्वाभाविक है। वह उस प्रकार के प्रयत्न की पराकाष्ठा कर देता है। अनिष्ट-प्रतीकार के लिए शास्त्रों में जो अनेक उपाय बताये गये हैं, उनका भी सहारा लिया जाता है। इन उपायों से प्रारब्ध का प्रतीकार होता है, यह कर्मवाद का सिद्धान्त हुआ। किन्तु वास्तविकता वैसी नहीं है। कर्मवादी अपने शास्त्रानुसार विचारकर अलग हो जाते हैं। क्रियमाण कर्म प्रारब्ध बदल सकता है, यह सिद्धान्त ठीक है। परंतु क्रियमाण कर्म भी काल के बिना फल नहीं दे सकता। क्रियमाण का फल कब मिलेगा और प्रारब्ध कब बदलेगा, यह कर्मवादी बता नहीं सकता। वह कालवाद का

विषय है। जन्मकालीन ग्रहस्थितिसे ही उसका निर्णय होगा। क्रियमाण कर्म से प्रारब्ध में परिवर्तन संभव है या नहीं और संभव है तो कब यह काल पर से ही निश्चित हो सकता है। जन्मकाल में वैसा योग होने पर ही क्रियमाण कर्म का उपयोग होता है। अन्यथा सारा प्रयत्न व्यर्थ जाता है। बहुतों को इसका प्रत्यक्ष अनुभव आता है। क्रियमाण कर्म काल के अभाव में हाथ पर हाथ धरे बैठा रहता है और जन्मान्तर में उसका फल मिलता है। इससे यह सिद्ध होता है कि क्रियमाण कर्मों के पाकोन्मुख होने का अवसर (काल) जीवन में है या नहीं, इसका ज्ञान जन्मकालीन ग्रहस्थिति से ही होता है। अतः काल या ग्रहस्थिति ही फलप्राप्ति के मुख्य कारण हैं।

दैववाद में देवता का प्रसाद ही इष्टप्राप्ति और अनिष्ट-परिहार का मुख्य कारण माना जाता है। देवता के अनुग्रह से प्रारब्ध बदल जाता है। यह सब ईश्वर में रहनेवाली अचिन्त्य शक्ति का ही प्रभाव माना जाता है। साधारणतः समझा जाता है कि उसे कर्म या काल की अपेक्षा नहीं रहती। किन्तु यह ठीक नहीं, कारण यदि ईश्वर का प्रसाद कर्म-निरपेक्ष हो जाय तो लोगों की कर्म परसे श्रद्धा उठ जायगी और कर्ममार्ग ही उच्छिन्न हो जायगा। पापियों का उद्धार होगा और पुण्यात्माओं को दुःख भुगतना पड़ेगा। अतः ईश्वर का अनुग्रह कर्म-निरपेक्ष नहीं माना जा सकता।

'**वैषम्यनैर्घृण्ये न सापेक्षत्वात्, तथा हि दर्शयति**' इस ब्रह्मसूत्र (२-१-३४) के भाष्य में भगवत्पाद श्रीशङ्कराचार्य कहते हैं :

'**ईश्वरस्तु पर्जन्यवद् द्रष्टव्यः।**'

इसके अतिरिक्त ईश्वर-प्रसाद कोई सर्वसाधारण मनुष्य को सुलभ होनेवाली वस्तु नहीं। उसके लिए गुरु की आवश्यकता होती है, चित्तशुद्धि और मन्त्रसिद्धि अपेक्षित हुआ करती है। किसी भाग्यवान् को ही वे प्राप्त होती है। साधारण जनों को बहुत उपासना करने पर भी सिद्धियाँ हाथ नहीं लगती। फिर देवतोपासना भी एक प्रकार का कर्म ही है और उसके सम्पन्न होने का योग और उसके होने पर सिद्धिप्राप्ति का योग है या नहीं, इसका ज्ञान भी ज्यौतिष के बिना हो नहीं सकता। जन्मकाल में ही जिसके वैसे योग होते हैं, उसे ही मन्त्रसिद्धि प्राप्त होती है। दूसरों को सिद्धि के लिए पुनर्जन्म लेना पड़ता है। इस तरह दैववाद में भी काल ही प्रधान कारण है। जन्मकालीन ग्रहस्थिति से मन्त्रसिद्धि होकर प्रारब्ध-परिवर्तन का योग होने पर ही मन्त्रसिद्धि होती है। अन्यथा उपासना निरर्थक हो जाती है। इससे यह निश्चित होता है कि काल ही फल प्राप्ति का कारण है और जन्मकाल से ही जीवन के सुख-दुःखों का निश्चित ज्ञान होता है। ज्यौतिषशास्त्र प्रमाणभूत शास्त्र है, उसके आधार पर प्रारब्ध का निर्णय होता है और वह प्रारब्ध भोगना ही पड़ता है, यह निष्कर्ष निकलता है।

इस तरह शास्त्रीय पद्धति से फलित ज्यौतिष का प्रामाण्य सिद्ध करने पर भी प्रतिवादी की ओर से इस शास्त्र पर निम्नलिखित आक्षेप किये जा सकते हैं।

ग्रहों परसे जो फल बताया जाता है, वह सदैव एकरूप होना चाहिए। किन्तु अनुभव इससे भिन्न ही आता है। परिस्थिति के अनुसार फल बतलाये जाते हैं। जब वर्णाश्रम-धर्मानुसार समाज-व्यवस्था चलती थी,तब हरएक को अपना नियत व्यवसाय ही करना पड़ता और उसीसे अर्थप्राप्ति हुआ करती। उन दिनों उसका भविष्य भी उसी प्रकार बताया जाता था। आज प्रत्येक व्यक्ति मनचाहा व्यवसाय करता है। इसलिए परिस्थिति के अनुसार ज्योतिषी को भी उसी प्रकार भविष्य बतलाना पड़ता है। पहले बाल-विवाह हुआ करते थे। उन दिनों विवाह-काल बचपन में ही बताया जाता। किन्तु आज वैसा नहीं बताते। आजकल तो मिश्र-विवाह, पुनर्विवाह, तलाक आदि भी चल पड़े हैं, इसलिए कुण्डली में उनका भी योग देखना पड़ता है। पहले यह प्रसंग नहीं आता था। आज राजसत्ता नष्ट हो गयी है। स्त्रियों को भी अधिकार-योग प्राप्त होते हैं। परिस्थिति के अनुसार ज्योतिष को भी वैसा भविष्य बतलाना पड़ता है। बालविवाह जब रूढ़ था,तो स्त्रियों को बचपन में ही सन्तान-योग बताया जाता था। किन्तु आज केवल विद्यायोग ही देखना पड़ता है, आदि। सारांश, वे ही ग्रह और वही शास्त्र रहते फल बतलाने में यह परिवर्तन क्यों ? यदि वह प्रमाण होता तो आज भी उसी ग्रह का फल पहले की तरह ही मिलता। इससे तो यह मालूम पड़ता है कि शास्त्र अप्रमाण है और अज्ञजनों को ठगने के लिए इसकी प्रवृत्ति है।

इन आक्षेपों का समुचित उत्तर न मिल पाने से ज्योतिषशास्त्र के कतिपय अभिमानी यह समाधान देते हैं कि 'काल केवल दिग्दर्शक है। ग्रह दिग्दर्शक हैं। परिस्थिति के अनुसार फलप्राप्ति संभव होने पर ही वैसा फल बतलाना चाहिए, अन्यथा नहीं। परिस्थिति का विचार न कर यदि कोई फल बतलायें ,तो कभी वे ठीक नहीं बैठ सकते।' किन्तु इस समाधान से फलित ज्योतिष का प्रामाण्य सिद्ध नहीं हो सकता। प्रत्युत अप्रामाण्य ही सिद्ध होता है। इसलिए इस आक्षेप के शास्त्रीय समाधान पर भी अवश्य विचार करना होगा।

काल एक, विभु और नित्य है। वह सभी कर्मो की उत्पत्ति, स्थिति और प्रलय में तथा क्षण, लव, निमिष, काष्ठा, कला, मुहूर्त, याम, अहोरात्र, अर्धमास, मास, ऋतु, अयन, संवत्सर, युग, कल्प, मन्वन्तर, प्रलय, महाप्रलय—इन सभी व्यवहारों का कारण है। इस एक, विभु एवं नित्य काल को ही अनवच्छिन्न काल, उपाध्यविशिष्ट काल, अखण्ड काल या महाकाल कहा जाता है। यह महाकाल ईश्वर से भिन्न नहीं। इसीको पौराणिक लोग 'शिव' कहते हैं और तान्त्रिक भैरव-विशेष मानते हैं। इस काल के खण्डकाल और महाकाल ये दो भेद हैं। दोनों शब्द सापेक्ष हैं। युग और कल्प के बीच सर्वत्र 'कल्प' महाकाल और 'युग' खण्डकाल समझना चाहिए। महाकाल के साधारण फल के अनुरोध से खण्डकाल में फल मिलता रहता है। फलतःखण्डकाल के फल का विचार करते समय प्रथम महाकाल के फल का विचार करना पड़ता है। तदनुसार खण्डकाल का फलादेश बताना पड़ता है।

सर्वाधिक सुबोध दृष्टान्त बताना हो तो जन्मकुण्डली को लिया जा सकता है। जन्मकालीन ग्रहस्थिति महाकाल कहा जा सकता है। उस ग्रहस्थिति के आधार पर जीवन के सुख-दुःख

की कल्पना की जा सकती है। वे जितने परिमाणों में हो, उतने ही परिमाण में ग्रहों के गोचर भ्रमण से होनेवाले खण्डकालों में फलप्राप्ति होती है। जन्मकाल में किसी को अत्यन्त दरिद्रता का योग हो और उसके अपने पराक्रम से कितना ही उत्कृष्ट द्रव्यप्राप्ति का योग आये, तो भी वह श्रीमान् नहीं होगा। इसी पर से खण्डकाल का फल महाकाल के अनुरोध से देखने का शास्त्रीय सिद्धान्त बना है। इस सिद्धान्त के अनुसार फलादेश का विचार करने पर उपर्युक्त आक्षेप इस शास्त्र पर नहीं आ सकते। महाकाल के आधार पर जागतिक या देश की परिस्थिति का और उस कालखण्ड में होनेवाले परिवर्तनों का निश्चय करें तो उस कालखण्ड में उत्पन्न होनेवाले व्यक्ति का उसी प्रकार का फल मिलेगा, यह निश्चित है और यह भी निश्चित है कि उसका फलादेश उसी तरह बतलाना चाहिए। साधारण ज्योतिषी महाकाल में होनेवाले जागतिक परिवर्तनों का विचार ही नहीं करते। वे परिवर्तन कौन-सी ग्रहस्थिति से हुए, इसकी उन्हें कल्पना भी नहीं रहती। यदि उसका निश्चित ज्ञान हो जाय तो उपर्युक्त आक्षेपों को अवकाश ही नहीं रहता। इसी तरह जो ज्योतिषी यह समाधान करते हैं कि ग्रह दिग्दर्शक होते हैं और फल परिस्थिति देख बताना चाहिए, उसे भी अवकाश नहीं करता।

कालचक्र का जितना अध्ययन होना चाहिए, उतना अभी नहीं हुआ है। उपलब्ध ग्रहों के आधार पर इस कालचक्र का विचार करने पर अनेक कालखण्ड होते हैं। गुरु का १२ वर्षों का काल, राहु का १८ और शनि ३०-इन तीन ग्रहों के आवर्तनों का विचार करें तो गुरु-राहु का ३६ वर्षों का कालखण्ड, गुरु-शनि का ६० वर्षों का, राहु-शनि का ९० वर्षों का और गुरु, राहु तथा शनि का १८० वर्षों का कालखण्ड होता है। इसका अर्थ यह कि ये ग्रह एक बार जिस स्थिति में आते हैं, उस स्थिति में पुनः आने में इन्हें उपर्युक्त प्रकार से काल लगता है। आजकल उपलब्ध युरेनस्, नेपच्यून, प्लूटो का उपर्युक्त प्रकार से विचार करें तो गुरु-युरेनस् ८४ वर्ष, राहु-युरेनस् २५२ वर्ष, शनि-युरेनस् ४२० वर्ष, शनि-नेपच्यून ३३० वर्ष, गुरु-नेपच्यून ६६०, राहु-नेपच्यून ६९०, और यूरेनस्-नेपच्यून ४६२० वर्ष आदि कालखण्ड पड़ते हैं। इन सब ग्रहों का विचार करने पर स्थूल मान से ८५९३२० वर्ष लगते हैं। यानी आठ लाख वर्षों से अधिक समय लगता है। यह काल कलियुग की वर्षसंख्या से भी अधिक और द्वापर की वर्षसंख्या जितना है। इस पर से कहा जा सकता है कि सूर्य के घेरे में ये ग्रह एक बार जिस स्थिति में होते है, पुनः उस स्थिति में आने के लिए ६ लाख वर्षो से अधिक समय लगता है इस तरह कालचक्र का सतत आवर्तन होता रहता है। उसके जगत् पर इष्ट-अनिष्ट परिणाम हुआ करते हैं। कालचक्र के परिवर्तनानुसार जागतिक स्थिति का भी लगातार परिवर्तन होता रहता है। कालचक्र के इस आवर्तन से होनेवाले फलों का विचार करके उस-उस कालखण्ड में उत्पन्न होनेवाले व्यक्तियों का भविष्य देखा जाय तो उसमें किसी प्रकार की गलती नहीं होगी और शास्त्र पर जो अज्ञानमूलक आक्षेप किये जाते हैं, उन्हें भी स्थान नहीं रहेगा।

विद्वानों द्वारा फलित ज्यौतिष के इस भाग की अवहेलना हुई है और आज भी वह जारी है। ज्यौतिषी व्यक्ति का भविष्य देखने में ही स्वयं को कृतार्थ मानते हैं। व्यक्ति का भविष्य

देखना और उस पर श्रम करना अर्थप्राप्ति की दृष्टि से सद्यः फलदायी होने से ज्यौतिष के उपर्युक्त शास्त्रीय अंग की उपेक्षा हो रही है। ज्यौतिषशास्त्र का साङ्गोपाङ्ग अध्ययन होना और ऐसे अध्ययन को प्रोत्साहन प्राप्त होना अत्यावश्यक हे। विद्वान् ज्यौतिषियों को इस पर अवश्य विचार करना चाहिए।

सारांश काल ही फल-प्राप्ति का मुख्य कारण हैं। फलित-ज्यौतिषशास्त्र प्रमाणभूत शास्त्र है। उस पर से इष्ट-अनिष्ट का निश्चित ज्ञान होता है। महाकाल और खण्डकाल दोनों का विचार करने पर फलादेश में गलती नहीं होती और फल का असन्दिग्ध ज्ञान होता है। इस तरह योगीश्वर याज्ञवल्क्य के इस श्लोक का यह सिद्धान्त निर्बाध सिद्ध होता है।

'ग्रहाधीना नरेन्द्राणामुच्छ्रायाः पतनानि च।
भावाभावौ च जगतः तस्मात् पूज्यतमा ग्रहाः ॥'